WESTMAR COLLEGE LIBRARY

W9-BUD-735

PIONEERS AND PROFITS:

Land Speculation on the Iowa Frontier

PIONEERS AND PROFITS:

Land Speculation on the Iowa Frontier

ROBERT P. SWIERENGA

The Iowa State University Press, Ames

333.3309777
S976

HD
266
.I8
S9

ROBERT P. SWIERENGA is Associate Professor of History, Kent State University, Kent, Ohio. He was formerly Assistant Professor of History, Calvin College, Grand Rapids, Michigan. He holds the masters degree from Northwestern University and the doctor of philosophy degree from the State University of Iowa, Iowa City. His field of special interest has been research in Iowa land history of the nineteenth century, especially in state land grants and in delinquent tax lands.

FRONTISPIECE: Native Iowa prairie. *Courtesy of Frederick W. Kent.*

© 1968 The Iowa State University Press
Ames, Iowa, U.S.A. All rights reserved

Composed and printed by the Iowa State University Press

Stock #1262

First edition, 1968

Library of Congress Catalog Card Number: 68–11198

88853

To
ALLAN G. BOGUE
Teacher, Scholar, and Friend

PREFACE

Although historians have recognized that land speculation was a major factor in public land disposal, few have presented statistically supported evidence of the extent of speculation or its profitability on a significant area basis. Such information is needed, however, before we can measure the impact of frontier land investments on American economic development in the nineteenth century. Judging by the amount of investment capital channeled into frontier real estate, this impact must have been considerable.

Iowa was selected for this concentrated analysis not only for its location in the heartland of agricultural America but also because government land entry and resale records in 33 central counties—recently abstracted for an Indian Claims case—were made available to me. Tabulated in both alphabetical and chronological sequence, these compilations considerably eased the otherwise onerous task of identifying the large entrants and tracing their initial resales.

Many must share the credit for whatever merit this book may deserve. I benefited from the assistance of attorneys for the present Sac and Fox and Iowa Indian tribes, state and county officials, and local abstracting firms who allowed free access to their invaluable tract books. I am grateful to librarians who guided me into newspaper and manuscript collections in depositories in Virginia, Massachusetts, New Jersey, Michigan, Wisconsin, Illinois, Minnesota, and Washington, D.C., as well as the three major Iowa libraries—those of the University of Iowa and the State Historical Society at Iowa City and the State Department of History and Archives at Des Moines. I am indebted to Michael D. Green, Erling A. Erickson, George R. Nielsen, Charles L. Blank, and Lois Ackerman Raap for assistance in compiling data and constructing charts and tables. James Thoreson wrote the PROFIT program for the IBM 7044 digital computer at the University of Iowa's Computer Center which was used to calculate per acre sale prices and rates of return earned by speculators on their land investments. Gerard P. Weeg, Paul Wolfe, and James C. Hickman helped overcome practical and mathematical problems involved in the computer study. Conrad H. Hammar classified land entered by speculators according to soil type. Norman Sage assisted in the reproduction of the charts, maps, and tables. I am especially indebted to Frank Paluka, Head, Special Collections Department, Library, University of Iowa, for the use of the end-sheet map of early Iowa by Henn, Williams & Co. Mr. Paluka permitted me to use this rare map and arranged for its reproduction.

Robert R. Dykstra, Raleigh Barlowe, Malcolm J. Rohrbough, and L. John Van Til gave the draft a critical reading and made many valuable suggestions, for which I am grateful. To Merritt E. Bailey and the editorial staff at the Iowa State University Press I am thankful both for cordial cooperation and for many helpful comments. In addition to the dedicatory note, I wish to acknowledge a special debt to Allan G. Bogue who guided me through the early dissertation stage of this manuscript and continued to encourage me thereafter. Drawing on his own research experience and vast knowledge of midwestern agricultural and land history, Professor Bogue freely offered methodological advice and saved me from countless errors of fact and interpretation. For permission to reprint material that has appeared in their publications, I am indebted to the editors of *The Journal of Economic History* and *Business History Review*. Finally, I wish to thank my wife, Joan Boomker Swierenga, for her constant encouragement and willingness to spend many long hours at the typewriter despite the pressing demands of a busy household. Any shortcomings, of course, are mine alone.

ROBERT P. SWIERENGA

CONTENTS

TABLES

ILLUSTRATIONS

APPENDICES

INTRODUCTION

I NVESTORS ventured their capital on frontier real estate in the firm expectation of profits. Despite this fact, which can be taken as axiomatic, most historical studies of land speculation have stressed the social while ignoring the economic dimensions of such activity. Writing in the progressive tradition that dominated early economic history, scholars have been content to show how "mistaken" land policies encouraged "land jobbing," absentee ownership, the "rapid creation of a tenancy class," and "economic stultification." Land "profiteering," it is argued, thwarted the goal of a "democratic" land distribution system and retarded the development of the West—not to mention the poison it injected into the lifestream of American politics through bribery and influence peddling and the creation of vast wealth which would be used to resist social reform.[1]

Because of the distorted perspective, the story of frontier land investment, unlike studies of other types of business enterprises, has never broken out of the old polemical framework. Land investment is still "speculation"; other capitalist enterprise

---

[1] For a classic expression of this view see Paul W. Gates, "The Role of the Land Speculator in Western Development," *Pa. Mag. Hist.*, LXVI (July, 1942), 314–33. Writes Gates: "Only recently has the United States come to realize the monstrous errors it permitted to develop in this land use pattern. Likewise, only recently has it become apparent that this pattern is the product in part of mistaken land policies which were once thought to be establishing a democratic system of land ownership." See also Gates, "From Individualism to Collectivism in American Land Policy," in Chester McA. Destler (ed.), *Liberalism as a Force in American History* (New London, 1953), 14–35. William J. Stewart more recently expressed similar views in "Settler, Politician, and Speculator in the Sale of the Sioux Reserve," *Minn. Hist.*, XXXIX (Fall, 1964), 92; and "Speculation and Nebraska's Public Domain, 1863–1872," *Nebr. Hist.*, XLV (Sept., 1964), 271–72, as did Victor Westphall in *The Public Domain in New Mexico, 1854–1891* (Albuquerque, 1965), 120–21 and *passim.* "Given a sensible [land] system," Westphall declared, "sensible people would largely have followed it. Given an impossible system, even sensible people rebelled against it."

is now "business." While in no way an *a priori* rationalization for the possible social damage of large-scale land speculation it seems fair to say that the subject is long past due for a more dispassionate treatment on its own terms—that is, as economic history.

I

THIS IS NOT to deny a perennial interest by historians in frontier land investment. Dozens of published works on land disposal and land tenure from the seventeenth through the twentieth centuries treat the subject either centrally or peripherally.[2] We have excellent narratives of the activities of early land companies and individual colonial proprietors, but these studies give little attention to real estate as an investment.[3] The political and social views of Lord Baltimore and William Penn are well known, for example, but the economic development of their land holdings has been neglected. The famous land companies and individual (especially fraudulent) speculators of the eighteenth and early nineteenth centuries in the Old West have been the

---

[2] For bibliographical discussion see Bureau of Land Management, U.S. Department of the Interior, *Public Lands Bibliography* (Washington, 1962); Henrietta M. Larson, *Guide to Business History: Materials for the Study of American Business History and Suggestions for Their Use* (Cambridge, 1948); Ray A. Billington, *Westward Expansion: A History of the American Frontier* (3rd ed.; New York, 1967), 765 ff.; Paul W. Gates, *The Farmer's Age: Agriculture, 1815–1860* (New York, 1960), 430–33. A key article, largely bibliographical, is Paul W. Gates, "Research in the History of American Land Tenure, a Review Article," *Agr. Hist.*, XXVIII (July, 1954), 121–26.

[3] See Roy H. Akagi, *The Town Proprietors of the New England Colonies* (Philadelphia, 1924); Florence M. Woodard, *The Town Proprietors in Vermont: The New England Town Proprietorship in Decline* (New York, 1936); William Haller, *The Puritan Frontier: Town-Planting in New England Colonial Development, 1630–1660* (New York, 1951); Susie M. Ames, *Studies of the Virginia Eastern Shore in the Seventeenth Century* (Richmond, 1940), esp. chap. ii; Elizabeth K. Henderson, "The Northwestern Lands of Pennsylvania, 1790–1812," *Pa. Mag. Hist.*, LX (Apr., 1936), 131–60; Abbot E. Smith, "The Indentured Servant and Land Speculation in Seventeenth Century Maryland," *Am. Hist. Rev.*, XL (Apr., 1935), 467–72. More recent articles noteworthy for their revisionism and analytical approach are Charles S. Grant, "Land Speculation and the Settlement of Kent, 1738–1760," *New Eng. Quart.*, XXVIII (Mar., 1955), 51–71; Aubrey C. Land, "A Land Speculator in the Opening of Western Maryland," *Md. Hist. Mag.*, XLVIII (Sept., 1953), 191–203.

[4] The best are Paul D. Evans, *The Holland Land Company* (Buffalo, 1924); Helen I. Cowan, *Charles Williamson: Genessee Promoter* (Rochester, 1942); Edith M. Fox, *Land Speculation in the Mohawk Valley* (Ithaca, 1949); David M. Ellis, *Landlords and Farmers in the Hudson-Mohawk Region, 1790–1850* (Ithaca, 1946); Archer B. Hulbert, "The Methods and Operations of the Scioto Group of Speculators," *Miss. Vy. Hist. Rev.*, I (Mar., 1915), 502–15, and II (June, 1915), 56–73. Two excellent general surveys are Thomas P. Abernethy, *Western Lands and the American Revolution* (New York, 1937), and the newer, revisionist Jack M. Sosin, *Whitehall and the Wilderness: The Middle West in British Colonial Policy, 1760–1775* (Lincoln, 1961). See also Henry M. Dater, "Albert Gallatin—Land Speculator," *Miss. Vy. Hist. Rev.*, XXVI

subjects of narrative history.[4] Much emphasis, however, has been given to the merely episodic and colorful—as, for instance, in Aaron M. Sakolski's popular account, *The Great American Land Bubble: The Amazing Story of Land-Grabbing, Speculations, and Booms from Colonial Days to the Present Time* (New York, 1932).[5]

The great nineteenth century capitalists—John Jacob Astor, Stephen Girard, George Croghan, Erastus Corning, Jay Cooke, and Henry Morganthau, Sr., to name a few—all invested heavily in frontier real estate; but their biographers, except for Irene D. Neu in her study of Corning, seldom attempt to answer more than superficially such vital questions as the profitability of their ventures.[6] Similarly, general histories of public land disposal perfunctorily discuss land speculation but seldom give quantitative evidence to indicate its magnitude or success.[7]

(June, 1939), 21–38; Roy B. Cook, *Washington's Western Lands* (Strasburg, Va., 1930); William S. Lester, *The Transylvania Company* (Spencer, Ind., 1935); George E. Lewis, *The Indiana Company, 1768–1798: A Study in Eighteenth Century Frontier Land Speculation and Business Venture* (Glendale, Calif., 1941); and Kenneth P. Bailey, *The Ohio Company of Virginia and the Westward Movement, 1748–1792* (Glendale, Calif., 1939). A model of the new economic approach is Alfred P. James, *The Ohio Company: Its Inner History* (Pittsburgh, 1959).

[5] See also Sakolski's more recent *Land Tenure and Land Taxation in America* (New York, 1957); Gustavus Myers, *History of the Great American Fortunes* (New York, 1907); Shaw Livermore, Jr., *Early American Land Companies: Their Influence on Corporate Development* (New York, 1939).

[6] Biographers who fail to treat the subject are John B. McMaster, *The Life and Times of Stephen Girard, Mariner and Merchant* (Philadelphia, 1918); Albert T. Vowiler, *George Croghan and the Westward Movement: 1741–1782* (Cleveland, 1926); Henrietta M. Larson, *Jay Cooke, Private Banker* (Cambridge, 1936). The exceptions are Irene D. Neu and Kenneth W. Porter. Neu, *Erastus Corning: Merchant and Financier, 1794–1872* (Ithaca, 1960), devoted three entire chapters to Corning's western land investments but her treatment, of necessity, was largely narrative since Corning's accounts and ledgers are not extant. Porter, *John Jacob Astor: Business Man* (Cambridge, 1931), presented data in one paragraph of his concluding chapter on the total cost and net receipts of Astor's frontier land investments in western New York. Models which future land historians might emulate are Henrietta M. Larson, "A China Trader Turns Investor—A Biographical Chapter in American Business History," *Harvard Bus. Rev.,* XII (July, 1934), 345–57; Elva C. Tooker, "A Merchant Turns to Money-lending in Philadelphia," *Bus. Hist. Soc. Bul.,* XX (June, 1946), 71–85, and *Nathan Trotter, Philadelphia Merchant, 1787–1853* (Boston, 1955).

[7] See Benjamin H. Hibbard, *A History of the Public Land Policies* (New York, 1924), chap. xii; Roy M. Robbins, *Our Landed Heritage: The Public Domain, 1776–1936* (Princeton, 1942), chap. iv; Payson J. Treat, *The National Land System, 1785–1820* (New York, 1910), chap. iii and *passim;* Paul W. Gates, *The Farmer's Age,* chaps. ii–iv and *passim;* Addison E. Sheldon, *Land Systems and Land Policies in Nebraska* (Lincoln, 1936), 41–51 and *passim;* Roscoe L. Lokken, *Iowa Public Land Disposal* (Iowa City, 1942), chap. vi; Charles L. Green, *Administration of the Public Domain in South Dakota* (Pierre, S.D., 1940), chap. viii; and W. W. Robinson, *Land in California: The Story of Mission Lands, Ranchos, Squatters, Mining Claims, Railroad Grants, Land Scrip, Homesteads* (Berkeley, 1948), *passim.*

Studies of land speculation on the southern frontier are limited to the Texas borderlands and the Indian lands of the Old Southwest in the ante bellum period, the postwar boom in California, and the pine belt of the Gulf states in the 1880's.[8] On the northern frontier the accounts deal primarily with the exploitation of natural resources—timberland in the Sierras, iron lands in Minnesota, and the pineries of Wisconsin.[9]

Historians have shed more light on frontier land speculation in the Middle West and Plains states than in any other area of the country. Although Joseph Schafer sparked the first flames in several Wisconsin studies in the 1920's,[10] this illumination is due largely to the prolific research of Paul Wallace Gates. Gates published his first midwestern study in 1931, an account of speculation in the disposal of the public domain of Illinois.[11] In subsequent years, he analyzed large investments in Indiana, Iowa, Wisconsin, and Kansas.[12]

---

[8] Mattie Russell, "Land Speculation in Tippah County, 1836–1861" (M.A. thesis, University of Mississippi, 1940); Edwin W. Chapman, "Land Speculation in Tate County, 1836–1861" (M.A. thesis, University of Mississippi, 1942). The work of these two scholars was summarized by their graduate director, James W. Silver, in "Land Speculation Profits in the Chickasaw Cession," *J. So. Hist.*, X (Feb., 1944), 84–92. A model of the quantitative approach is Mary E. Young, *Redskins, Ruffleshirts, and Rednecks: Indian Allotments in Alabama and Mississippi, 1830–1860* (Norman, 1961). See also Leo Hershkowitz, " 'The Land of Promise': Samuel Swarthwout and Land Speculation in Texas, 1830–1838," *N.Y. Hist. Soc. Quart.*, XLVIII (Oct., 1964), 307–25; Elgin Williams, *Animating Pursuits of Speculation: Land Traffic in the Annexation of Texas* (New York, 1949); Gordon T. Chappell, "Some Patterns of Land Speculation in the Old Southwest," *J. So. Hist.*, XV (Nov., 1949), 463–77; Paul W. Gates, "Federal Land Policy in the South, 1866–1888," *J. So. Hist.*, VI (Aug., 1940), 303–30. For studies of speculation in California, see Gates, "California's Embattled Settlers," *Calif. Hist. Soc. Quart.*, XLI (June, 1962), 99–130, "California's Agricultural College Lands," *Pac. Hist. Rev.*, XXX (May, 1961), 103–22, and *California Ranchos and Farms, 1846–1862* (Madison, 1967); Glenn S. Dumke, *The Boom of the Eighties in Southern California* (San Marino, 1944); Gerald D. Nash, "Henry George Reexamined: William S. Chapman's Views on Land Speculation in Nineteenth Century California," *Agr. Hist.*, XXXIII (July, 1959), 133–37.

[9] Roy E. Appleman, "Timber Empire From the Public Domain," *Miss. Vy. Hist. Rev.*, XXVI (Sept., 1939), 193–208; Fremont P. Wirth, *The Discovery and Exploration of the Minnesota Iron Lands* (Cedar Rapids, Iowa, 1937), esp. chap. vi; John Ise, *The United States Forest Policy* (New Haven, 1920); Paul W. Gates, *The Wisconsin Pine Lands of Cornell University: A Study in Land Policy and Absentee Ownership* (Ithaca, 1943).

[10] Schafer, *Wisconsin Domesday Book: Town Studies*, I (Madison, 1924); *Wisconsin Lead Region: Wisconsin Domesday Book, General Studies*, III (Madison, 1932).

[11] "The Disposal of the Public Domain in Illinois, 1848–1856," *J. Econ. and Bus. Hist.*, III (Feb., 1931), 216–40.

[12] Although only a partial list, the monographs that bear mention are *The Illinois Central Railroad and Its Colonization Work* ("Harvard Economic Studies," Vol. XLII [Cambridge, 1934]); *Frontier Landlords and Pioneer Tenants* (Ithaca, 1945); *Fifty Million Acres: Conflicts Over Kansas Land Policy, 1854–1890* (Ithaca, 1954). Relevant articles are "Land Policy and Tenancy in

Soon other scholars joined the investigation of midwestern land disposal and real estate investments. There were four statistical studies of land disposal in individual Nebraska counties, most notably that of Robert Diller in 1941; and a more recent general study by William J. Stewart.[13] Theodore L. Carlson measured speculation in the Illinois Military Tract while Margaret B. Bogue did the same for the Grand Prairie of the east central part of the same state.[14] Homer E. Socolofsky plotted the Scully land holdings in Kansas and Paul Gates, Richard C. Overton, and Howard F. Bennett outlined the disposal of land grants by the Illinois Central, Burlington, and Hannibal and St. Joseph railroads, respectively.[15] Homer Hoyt charted a new approach in his time-trend analysis of real estate values in Chicago.[16]

The role of western land agents has not been entirely ignored. Larry Gara described the activity of the remarkable Cyrus Woodman of Wisconsin in a full-length biography and Kenneth Duckett published a study of another Wisconsinite, Moses Strong.[17] Robert R. Jost and Rodney C. Loehr have given us a clear portrait of Jason C. Easton, a leading territorial banker and land agent of Minnesota, while Curtis L. Johnson has done the

the Prairie States," *J. Econ. Hist.*, I (May, 1941), 60–82; "Southern Investments in Northern Lands before the Civil War," *J. So. Hist.*, V (May, 1939), 155–85; "The Homestead Law in Iowa," *Agr. Hist.* XXXVIII (Apr., 1964), 67–78; "Land and Credit Problems in Underdeveloped Kansas," *Kan. Hist. Quart.*, XXXI (Spring, 1965), 41–61.

[13] Diller, *Farm Ownership, Tenancy, and Land Use in a Nebraska Community* (Chicago, 1941); for articles by Stewart see n. 1; John A. Caylor, "The Disposition of the Public Domain in Pierce County, Nebraska" (Ph.D. dissertation, University of Nebraska, 1951); Evan E. Evans, "An Analytical Study of Land Transfer to Private Ownership in Johnson County, Nebraska" (M.A. thesis, University of Nebraska, 1950); James A. Stone, "Disposition of the Public Domain in Wayne County, Nebraska, 1868–1893" (M.A. thesis, University of Nebraska, 1952); Dallas Lee Jones, "Survey and Sale of the Public Land in Michigan, 1815–1862," (M.A. thesis, Cornell University, 1952).

[14] Carlson, *The Illinois Military Tract: A Study of Land Occupation, Utilization and Tenure* ("Illinois Studies in the Social Sciences," Vol. XXXII, No. 2 [Urbana, 1951]); Bogue, *Patterns from the Sod: Land Use and Tenure in the Grand Prairie, 1850–1900* ("Collections of the Illinois State Historical Library," Vol. XXXIV, Land Series, Vol. I [Springfield, Ill., 1959]).

[15] Socolofsky, "The Scully Land System in Marion County," *Kan. Hist. Quart.*, XVIII (Nov., 1950), 337–75; Gates, *Illinois Central Railroad;* Overton, *Burlington West: A Colonization History of the Burlington Railroad* (Cambridge, 1941); Bennett, "The Hannibal & St. Joseph Railroad and the Development of Northern Missouri, 1847–1870: A Study of Land and Colonization Policies" (Ph.D. dissertation, Harvard University, 1941).

[16] Hoyt, *One Hundred Years of Land Values in Chicago: 1830–1933* (Chicago, 1935). For an earlier unpublished time-trend analysis of Iowa land values, see Adrian H. Lindsey, "The Nature and Causes of the Growth of Iowa Land Values" (Ph.D. dissertation, Iowa State University, 1929).

[17] Gara, *Westernized Yankee: The Story of Cyrus Woodman* (Madison, 1956); Duckett, *Frontiersman of Fortune: A Biography of Moses Strong* (Madison, 1955). An earlier sketch of Strong is Joseph Schafer, "A Yankee Land Speculator in Wisconsin," *Wis. Mag. Hist.*, VIII (June, 1925), 377–92.

same for Eugene S. Ellsworth, an Iowa land baron of the post-Civil War period.[18]

II

IN THEIR APPROACHES, most of the studies noted above are narrative and descriptive, written from a traditional historical rather than an economic viewpoint. Few students of frontier land speculation have undertaken quantitative analyses and these have met with only scattered success.

In the early decades of the twentieth century, two University of Wisconsin historians, Joseph Schafer, whose name has already been mentioned, and Benjamin H. Hibbard, decided to chart the land entries and initial resales of leading speculators in Iowa and Wisconsin. Hibbard abstracted the entries of a few individuals but became discouraged by the uneven quality of information given in the deed registers. He finally concluded that it was "impossible" to trace resales.[19] A decade later, after compiling a list of 2,000 of the largest entrants in Iowa, Hibbard, still disillusioned by his previous experience, reported that he had not found it "feasible to follow what became of these big purchases or how well the purchasers fared." He did, however, examine one case and concluded that most raw land investments in Iowa were not profitable.[20]

Schafer, less easily discouraged, compiled cost and sale data on a number of Wisconsin speculators and attempted an extensive analysis of returns earned by several. But his technique for computing returns was so defective that later historians have largely discredited his findings.[21] Like Hibbard, Schafer concluded that speculators were often disappointed in their expectation of profits.

Paul Gates elected not to follow Schafer's method of searching the county conveyance books to determine if speculators were

---

[18] Jost, "An Entrepreneurial Study of a Frontier Financier, 1856–1863" (Ph.D. dissertation, University of Minnesota, 1957); Loehr, "Jason C. Easton, Territorial Banker," *Minn. Hist.*, XXIX (Sept., 1948), 223–30; Johnson, "E. S. Ellsworth in Iowa Falls, 1864–1907" (M.A. thesis, University of Iowa, 1952), and "E. S. Ellsworth: Iowa Land Baron," *Annals of Iowa, 3rd Ser.*, XXXV (July, 1959), 1–35. The postwar business activity of John Weare, pioneer Cedar Rapids realtor, is described in Allan G. Bogue, *Money at Interest: The Farm Mortgage on the Middle Border* (Ithaca, 1955).

[19] *The History of Agriculture in Dane County, Wisconsin* (Madison, 1904), 100, 192–202.

[20] *History of the Public Land Policies*, 224.

[21] *Wisconsin Domesday Book: Town Studies*, I, 10 and *passim; Wisconsin Lead Region*, 148–54. Scholars who attacked Schafer's technique were Gates, *Wisconsin Pine Lands*, 85, n. 48; and Allan G. Bogue and Margaret B. Bogue, " 'Profits' and the Frontier Land Speculator," *J. Econ. Hist.*, XVII (Mar., 1957), 3–4.

successful. Rather, he concentrated on abstracting from federal land entry records the names and total entries of the "influential land jobbers" in each state. Once identified, the careers of these "profiteers" were traced in manuscript collections, county histories, and biographical dictionaries to uncover questionable financial and political activity. Gates' ultimate aim was to demonstrate how a supposedly democratic land policy allowed for the concentration of the public domain in the hands of a few—a situation detrimental to the development of an equalitarian pattern of farm ownership.[22]

Only a very few scholars have attempted to quantify data on land speculation in the manner of Schafer and Hibbard. In his 1941 study, Diller plotted land ownership patterns in a 60,000 acre tract in eastern Nebraska. However, after compiling a list of the major speculative holdings, he failed to trace resales systematically or give more than an impressionistic picture of the major types of entrepreneurs involved.[23] More promising at first glance were two studies of individual counties in Mississippi which aimed specifically at measuring the extent of speculation and its profitability. But these authors, despite the best of intentions, were hampered by incomplete information in the deed records and, more seriously, by their own lack of precision in calculating profits.[24]

A decade after the Mississippi studies, three students at the University of Nebraska devoted their theses to the study of land disposal in individual counties in that state. Although the subject of land speculation was not their only concern, two of the authors isolated the entries of the large purchasers and abstracted subsequent resale data from the conveyance records. With the necessary raw information for a careful analysis at their fingertips, however, these scholars chose merely to determine whether the individual speculators generally held their land more or less than ten years, whether they sold it in unit sizes of more or less than 320 acres, and if the prices obtained were above or below "average" (a term never carefully explained).[25]

In his study of land disposal in the Illinois Military Tract,

---

[22] The best example is "Southern Investments in Northern Lands," 155–85.
[23] Farm Ownership, Tenancy, and Land Use, 17–26, 151–54.
[24] Russell, "Land Speculation in Tippah County," 72–73, and Chapman, "Land Speculation in Tate County," 65–66, merely subtracted the purchase from the sale price to find total "profit," divided this sum by the amount invested to obtain the percentage of "profit," and divided the percentage in turn by the number of years the investment was held to determine the "annual return." Although she had solved the methodological problems, Young, Redskins, Ruffleshirts, and Rednecks, 124, similarly was stymied by a lack of information in her desire to measure returns on speculative investments in Indian allotments in the Old Southwest.
[25] Caylor, "Disposition of the Public Domain in Pierce County," 48, 51, 54; Stone, "Disposition of the Public Domain in Wayne County," 59–60.

Theodore Carlson isolated the largest investors and determined average purchase and sale prices on some of their holdings.[26] But he too aborted his analysis with a few generalizations about the lack of profits realized by the speculators. Carlson, however, did adopt one of the methods that future investigators should follow—that is, to select for intensive study a geographic area of considerable size.

Allan G. Bogue in the early 1950's surmounted another hurdle in his study of moneylending and land speculation on the middle border.[27] Attempting to find a means to gauge the financial success of land investments similar to that used by economists to measure common stock and bond yields, he developed a more sophisticated concept, that of the rate of return, as distinct from the much abused and misunderstood term "profits." More important, Bogue illustrated the rewards awaiting the student who can break free of the old moralistic debate and treat western land investments as a legitimate form—and indeed one of the most significant forms—of business enterprise of the nineteenth century.

III

THIS REORIENTATION requires new tools, a more precise methodology, and a greater degree of accuracy in measuring the extent of speculation than has previously been the case. Totaling the acreage of the few dozen largest entrants and roughly estimating speculative activity by manipulating aggregate census figures will no longer suffice. Original land entry and resale registers must be abstracted either on a massive scale or by reliable statistical sampling techniques, and the resulting data adapted for mechanical manipulation. The records are so detailed and voluminous, in fact, that the student can only scratch the surface without the assistance of modern data processing equipment.

Methodological innovation is only one of several approaches to land history awaiting exploration. The collective biography technique has yielded significant new insights in the last two decades at the hands of business historians such as Thomas C. Cochran and William Miller.[28] By applying the same approach

---

[26] *Illinois Military Tract,* 40–64, esp. 57.

[27] Bogue first outlined the new technique in his study of "Farm Land Credit in Kansas and Nebraska, 1854–1890" (Ph.D. dissertation, Cornell University, 1951), 71–79, subsequently published as *Money At Interest.* Margaret B. Bogue applied the method with only a slight revision in the averaging process in her study, *Patterns from the Sod,* 271–72. Their technique is also explained in " 'Profits' and the Frontier Land Speculator," 8–10.

[28] Cochran, *Railroad Leaders, 1845–1890: The Business Mind in Action* (Cambridge, 1953); Miller, "American Historians and the Business Elite," *J.*

in a study of land speculation, hopefully, a picture will emerge of the types of entrepreneurs who invested in western real estate. The military bounty land warrant market still awaits investigation. Although every work in public land disposal during this period devotes some space to summary discussions of soldiers' warrants and their use by speculators, only one full-length study, concerned mainly with the origin of warrant legislation and its application in the Ohio Valley, has yet been completed on the subject. And this work, now long outdated, failed to plumb the operations of the land warrant market or demonstrate more than superficially how speculators used warrants.[29] As a result, little is known of the legal requirements governing their use, the function of the eastern brokerage houses, and the forces causing almost daily fluctuations in warrant price quotations on eastern and western markets throughout the mid-nineteenth century. The prices themselves remain largely a mystery, although some eastern newspapers quoted them regularly.

Scholars have investigated and debated the types of land in terms of soil, topography, and vegetation that settlers coveted, but none has attempted to map and classify speculator holdings by the smallest legal subdivision (40 acres) to determine what types of land appealed to the speculators and whether they were knowledgeable buyers. Here is an opportunity for interdisciplinary research in conjunction with agronomists, agricultural economists, and geographers.

Apart from Gara's biography of Cyrus Woodman, the role of the western realtor—absolutely essential though he was to the nonresident investor—has seldom been investigated thoroughly.[30] Even less well known is the role of speculators in the disposition of state lands. This is an outgrowth of the almost total disregard of state land records. In Iowa, for example, where such lands outnumbered homesteaded acres by nearly ten to one and comprised almost 25 per cent of the total acreage in the state, typewritten tract books compiled from original land patents by employees of

Econ. Hist., IX (June, 1949), 184–208; Frances W. Gregory and Irene D. Neu, "The American Industrial Elite in the 1870's; Their Social Origins," in William Miller (ed.), Men in Business (New York, 1954), 193–211.

   [29] William Thomas Hutchinson, "The Bounty Lands of the American Revolution in Ohio" (Ph.D. dissertation, University of Chicago, 1927). Writing in the Progressive tradition, Hutchinson's concern was to demonstrate that the national government erred in donating land warrants instead of cash to American soldiers.

   [30] Gara, Westernized Yankee, 239–41, did not present any quantitative data on the scope of Woodman's operations or the returns earned on his investments despite the availability of some business ledgers, particularly those of the Boston and Western Land Company. Gates in his study of the Wisconsin pine lands of Ezra Cornell compiled total net profit figures but elected not to calculate annual rates of return (Bogue and Bogue, " 'Profits' and the Frontier Land Speculator," 5). Porter, John Jacob Astor, 100, similarly did not compile annual figures.

the federal government in the 1930's have never been used by scholars.[31]

In the final analysis, the primary purpose of speculation and the economic criterion for judging its success or failure is profits. Yet, despite strong and continuing curiosity, few historians have ventured into the deed registers to trace resales and even fewer have attempted to compare earnings in land with alternative forms of investment. Business records of several major investors survive but have never been analyzed by accounting methods although they have been the subject of occasional monographs.

Despite all that has been written about it, therefore, the general problem of frontier land speculation remains an entity about which our knowledge is far from complete. In the pages that follow, aided by research techniques now made possible by digital computers, I have addressed myself to these persistent gaps in the record. Whether my results, however definitive for the pioneer era in central Iowa, are truly representative of frontier land speculation in other places and at other times is a question to which only subsequent scholars can provide an answer. Happily, the new breed of econometric historians led by Professor Robert W. Fogel have recently turned their attention to this problem of western land investments.[32] We are poised on the threshold of a new era in the study of American land history.

[31] The tract books are in the office of the Iowa secretary of state. Several studies that consider speculation in state-owned lands in some detail are Harry N. Scheiber, "State Policy and the Public Domain: The Ohio Canal Lands," *J. Econ. Hist.*, XXV (Mar., 1965), 86–113; Joseph Schafer, "Wisconsin's Farm Loan Law, 1849–1863," *Wisc. St. Hist. Soc. Publ.* (1920), 156–91; Gates, *Wisconsin Pine Lands* and "California's Agricultural College Lands"; W. H. Glover, "The Agricultural College Lands in Wisconsin," *Wisc. Mag. Hist.*, XXX (Mar., 1947), 261–72; Thomas LeDuc, "State Disposal of the Agricultural College Land Scrip," *Agr. Hist.*, XXVIII (July, 1954), 99–107; Margaret B. Bogue, "The Swamp Land Act and Wet Land Utilization in Illinois, 1850–1890," *ibid.*, XXV (Oct., 1951), 169–80; Neu, *Erastus Corning*, chap. ix; Daniel F. Clynch, "An Introduction to Swamp Land Disposal in Iowa: 1854–1880" (M.A. thesis, University of Iowa, 1957). Although students of Iowa history have not devoted their full attention to the subject, none has overlooked the significance of frontier land speculation in the state. See Lokken, *Iowa Public Land Disposal*, chap. vi; Allan G. Bogue, *From Prairie to Corn Belt: Farming on the Illinois and Iowa Prairies in the Nineteenth Century* (Chicago, 1963), chap. ii; William G. Murray, *An Economic Analysis of Farm Mortgages in Story County, Iowa, 1854–1931* (Iowa Agr. Exp. Sta., Res. Bul. No. 156 [Ames, 1933]), 378. Gates tabulated the entries of several large speculators and briefly described their activities in "Southern Investments in Northern Lands," "Land Policy and Tenancy in the Prairie States," and "The Homestead Law in Iowa."

[32] Fogel is presently engaged in a "pilot project" on land disposal and economic development in Illinois from 1840 to 1880 (*Agr. Hist.*, XL [July, 1966], 234). See also Lance E. Davis, "Monopolies, Speculators, Causal Models, Quantitative Evidence, and American Growth," paper delivered before the Association of American Historians, Chicago, Apr. 27, 1967.

PIONEERS AND PROFITS:

Land Speculation on the Iowa Frontier

Chapter One

THE LAND SPECULATION TRADITION

L AND SPECULATION in America is almost as old as the history of European settlement in the New World. Within a generation after the Puritans planted their ideal community on the Massachusetts coast, one of their divines was driven to exclaim: "Land! Land! hath been the Idol of many in New England." The first settlers had considered themselves rich with an acre per person and twenty acres per family, but Increase Mather declared in 1676, "How many Men since coveted after the earth, that many hundreds, nay thousands of Acres, have been engrossed by one man, and they that profess themselves Christians, have forsaken Churches, and Ordinances, and all for land and elbowroom enough in the World." Thus, concludes Puritan historian Perry Miller, "the real estate speculator makes his entrance into American literature, as the second and third generations grew longer and longer elbows."[1]

From the Puritan frontier of the seventeenth century to the closing of the public domain in the twentieth, frontier land speculation was endemic in American history.[2] Both the late Colonial and early National periods, historians have shown, were studded with speculation schemes—from Benjamin Franklin's Illinois-Wabash Company of the Revolutionary era to the "Yazoo Affair" and the North American and Connecticut land companies of the early National period.[3] Lest a mistaken impression be created, however, it should be noted that large eastern capitalists—the traditional villains—were not the only

---

[1] *The New England Mind: From Colony to Province* (Boston, 1953), 37.
[2] See for example Aaron M. Sakolski, *The Great American Land Bubble: The Amazing Story of the Land-Grabbing, Speculations, and Booms from Colonial Days to the Present Time* (New York, 1932).
[3] Thomas P. Abernethy, *Western Lands and the American Revolution* (New York, 1937); Arthur P. Whitaker, "The Muscle Shoals Speculation, 1783–1789," *Miss. Vy. Hist. Rev.*, XIII (Dec., 1926), 365–86, and "The South Carolina Yazoo Company," *ibid.*, XVI (Dec., 1929), 383–94.

speculators. Charles S. Grant, in a study of agricultural land
speculation on the Connecticut frontier in the mid-1700's, discovered that the residents ("sturdy farmer-speculators") rather
than seaboard aristocrats were the foremost speculators.[4] Most
frontier land speculation probably fits this generalization.

The first real craze of speculation in the National period
occurred immediately after the War of 1812 in the Old Southwest and the Ohio Valley. Sparked by a combination of forces—
business prosperity, easy credit, immigration, an emerging interest in "internal improvements," and the government's mar-
keting of great quantities of newly offered land—investors
throughout the country flocked to the land offices in hopes of
gaining windfalls. Pausing only briefly during the depression of
1819, speculators increased their activity in the next decade, operating mainly in Michigan, Illinois, Indiana, and Mississippi.
Reaching its peak in 1836, this second spree was halted abruptly
by the "specie circular" and panic of 1837. By the middle 1840's,
however, buyers in ever greater numbers again plunged into the
land market, creating by the 1850's one of the greatest speculative
flurries in American history.[5]

Although temporarily quenched by the crisis of 1857 and
supposedly crushed forever by the Homestead Act, land speculation increased rather than diminished as railroads opened new
sections of the country and prospectors uncovered mineral and
oil deposits. Thus, all along the frontier, from the Atlantic to the
Pacific coasts, speculation and settlement proceeded apace. Ray
A. Billington was correct in chiding Frederick Jackson Turner
for not including the land speculator among his list of frontier
types, for the speculator was an ever-present figure on the frontier.[6]

I

PRECISE DEFINITION of the term "speculator" is difficult because
of the many forms of speculation on the frontier.[7] Perhaps this

[4] "Land Speculation and the Settlement of Kent," 1738-1760," *New Eng. Quart.*, XXVIII (Mar., 1955), 57.

[5] Arthur C. Cole, "Cyclical and Sectional Variations in the Sale of Public Lands, 1816-60," *Rev. Econ. Stat.*, IX (Jan., 1927), 41-53; Paul W. Gates, "Charts of Public Land Sales and Entries," *J. Econ. Hist.*, XXIV (Mar., 1964), 22-28.

[6] Ray Allen Billington, "The Origin of the Land Speculator as a Frontier Type," *Agr. Hist.*, XIX (Oct., 1945), 204-12. Speculation has accompanied the opening to settlement of new agricultural areas not only in the United States, but in all parts of the modern world; from France to Canada, from Australia to Manchuria (Lewis Cecil Gray, "Land Speculation," *Ency. Soc. Sci.* [New York, 1933], IX, 64-70). See also Pearl Janet Davies, *Real Estate in American History* (Washington, 1958), 17-23.

[7] Richard T. Ely, Frederick Jackson Turner's colleague at the University

is best illustrated by a scribbled notation that an eastern investor jotted in his diary in 1855 after an extensive tour of Illinois and Iowa. Under the heading, "How to make profitable investments in the West," the prospective entrepreneur listed nine possible speculative ventures, and only the first was strictly agricultural:

I A stock farm. . . .

II Speculate in real estate—in improved or unimproved farms.

III Assume a land agency—buy & sell on commission. . . .

IV Loan money at 10 per cent, and for as much more as can be exacted from the necessity of borrowers, or drawn from speculators, who are often anxious to have opportunities given them of paying premiums for money—even 2 per ct. per month.

V Buy land, improve & rent on shares, relying on the rise of land in price to realize a heavy interest on the money invested.

VI Buy government land in Iowa, Minnesota or Wisconsin & wait for a rise to dispose.

VII Buy Pine timber land on the branches of the Upper Mississippi, viz. in Wisconsin or Minnesota. . . .

VIII Buy land near growing Towns in the country.

IX Buy lots in towns that are to become centres of business & commerce as Chicago, St. Louis, Cairo, Milwaukie, Burlington, Davenport, Muscatine, Lyons, Dubuque, St. Paul.[8]

The land investor might indeed deal in government or secondhand agricultural land, timberland, or town lots, operate a land agency, loan money, or rent farms on shares. In common parlance, frontiersmen indiscriminately labeled all such enterprise as speculation, particularly if it was by eastern capitalists. To Horace Greeley, editor of the New York *Tribune* and long-time land reformer, the term "speculator," on the other hand, included settlers who bought more land than they could personally use as well as western promoters and businessmen who purchased large quantities of wild land for resale after the inevitable price rise.[9]

of Wisconsin and a pioneer land economist, devoted an entire journal article to a study of the term and its various meanings at law and in common usage. See "Land Speculation," *J. Farm Econ.*, II (July, 1920), 121–35. For subsequent discussions of this problem see Paul W. Gates, "The Role of the Land Speculator in Western Development," *Pa. Mag. Hist.*, LXVI (July, 1942), 315–17; Billington, "Land Speculator as a Frontier Type," 205; Allan G. Bogue and Margaret B. Bogue, " 'Profits' and the Frontier Land Speculator," *J. Econ. Hist.*, XVII (Mar., 1957), 1.

[8] John Honeyman Journal, 1798–1874, Rutgers University Library, New Brunswick, N.J. The entry is undated but was likely written during Honeyman's extended western tour of 1855.

[9] Editor Greeley included most squatters in his definition of speculators. These were people, Greeley noted, "who call themselves settlers, and who would be farmers if they were anything. To see a man squatted on a quarter-section in a cabin which would make a fair hog-pen, but is unfit for human habitation, and there living from hand to mouth by a little of this and a little of that, with hardly an acre of prairie broken (sometimes without a fence up), with no garden, no fruit trees, 'no nothing'—waiting for someone to come

Many prominent present-day students of frontier land speculation have accepted Greeley's designation; namely, that a speculator was anyone who claimed or purchased raw land with no
intent to farm it or who acquired more land than he could expect to develop.[10] That definition, of course, is tied to a pre-
development stage of land use. Modern economists also recognize
speculation as a phenomenon that can be associated with any
level of land use. One economist recently defined land speculation as "the holding of land resources in their present uses (often
in lower uses than those justified by current market conditions)
while waiting for an expected increase in property sale values."[11]
In either case, however, the speculator's primary interest is returns from the sale of his property rather than from its operation
or management. While not in any sense a denial of the essential
importance of the settler-speculator, in this book the term will
be used to designate the large-scale investor in government land
as a distinct entrepreneural type.

II

OF ALL the public land states, speculators were most active in
Iowa. In fact, one scholar, after an investigation of land entry
records, asserted that in the 1850's "land buyers swarmed into
the State at a rate unparalleled elsewhere in the country, before
or since."[12] White settlement in Iowa, a district of Wisconsin
Territory until 1838, dates from 1833 when a 50-mile-wide strip
of land west of the Mississippi River was opened following the
signing of the Black Hawk Treaty of the previous year. In the
next two decades, through 1851, the national government extin-
guished Indian titles in the remainder of the state by negotiating
a series of cession treaties, as Figure 1.1 indicates.[13]

---

along and buy out his 'claim' and let him move on to repeat the operation
somewhere else—this is enough to give a cheerful man the horrors" (Charles
T. Duncan [ed.], *An Overland Journey from New York to San Francisco in
the Summer of 1859 by Horace Greeley* [New York, 1964], 52).

[10] See Gates, "Role of the Land Speculator," 316; Billington, "Land Spec-
ulator as a Frontier Type," 206; Thomas LeDuc, "History and Appraisal of
U.S. Land Policy to 1862," in Howard W. Ottoson (ed.), *Land Use Policy and
Problems in the United States* (Lincoln, 1963), 9–15.

[11] Raleigh Barlowe, *Land Resource Economics: The Political Economy of
Rural and Urban Land Resource Use* (Englewood Cliffs, 1958), 227.

[12] Paul W. Gates, "Land Policy and Tenancy in the Prairie States," *J.
Econ. Hist.*, I (July, 1941), 70–71.

[13] Map from Roscoe F. Lokken, *Iowa Public Land Disposal* (Iowa City,
1942), 15. For further information on the cession treaties see Charles C. Royce,
Indian Land Cessions in the United States ("Bureau of American Ethnology,
18th Annual Report, 1896–1897," 56th Cong. 1st Sess., H.R. Doc. 736, [Wash-
ington, 1899]); F. R. Aumann, "Dispossession of the Tribes," *Palimpsest*, IX
(Feb., 1928), 56–57, "The Acquisition of Iowa Lands from the Indians," *Annals of Iowa, 3rd Ser.*, VII (Jan., 1906), 283–90.

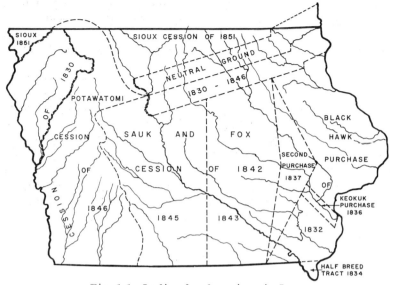

Fig. 1.1. Indian land cessions in Iowa.

As soon as federal border patrols opened each new cession area, eager whites swept in. Iowa's population increased at a rapid rate—far more rapid than any neighboring state except Wisconsin—reaching 40,000 persons within scarcely more than a decade and almost 200,000 by 1850, only 18 years after the first treaty.[14]

The population influx followed the major river systems—the Mississippi River and its tributaries: the Des Moines, Skunk, Iowa, Cedar, Wapsipinicon, Maquoketa, and Turkey. The settlement pattern was really a natural expansion of the frontier from neighboring states. People from northeastern Missouri and southwestern Illinois overflowed into southeastern Iowa following the Des Moines and Mississippi rivers. While the river towns of Keokuk, Fort Madison, and Burlington were platted in the south, Dubuque with the attraction of its lead mines became the "port of entry" for the northern third of the state. It, too, was the result of a natural population movement westward across northern

---

[14] Raleigh Barlowe and Conrad H. Hammar, "Valuation of Lands in Southcentral Iowa: 1839–1843; Royce Cession Area 262," presented before the Indian Claims Commission, Doc. 153, *Sac and Fox and Iowa Tribes v. the United States of America* (1965), 74, 98; Cardinal Goodwin, "The American Occupation of Iowa: 1833 to 1860," *Ia. J. Hist. and Pol.*, XVII (Jan., 1919), 83–102; Dan E. Clark, "The Westward Movement in the Upper Mississippi Valley During the Fifties," *Miss. Vy. Hist. Assn. Pro.*, XII (1913–14), 212–19. A series of maps taken from Barlowe and Hammar, "Valuation of Lands in Southcentral Iowa," 94, showing population trends in eastern and southcentral Iowa is in Appendix III.

Illinois.[15] By the late 1840's the fingers of settlement had likewise followed the Missouri River north into the Council Bluffs
area of southwestern Iowa. The spread of settlement over north-
western Iowa was delayed for the most part until after the Civil
War.

Migrants entered the area by steamboat and by wagon. The
main steamboat route was from the middle Atlantic states and
upper South via the Ohio and Mississippi rivers to Keokuk,
Fort Madison, and Burlington. The major overland route was a
trail across northern Illinois from Chicago to Dubuque, although
some chose to follow the Rock River from Rockford, entering by
way of Clinton and Davenport. By 1854, with the inauguration
of railroad service west to the Mississippi River, the early routes
were largely abandoned. Wagons continued to be used for most
internal migration, however, until long after the Civil War.

III

PATENT TITLES could not be obtained in Iowa until the completion of the surveys and the initial government land sales, which
commenced in November of 1838. For the next three decades, as
the government surveying outfits worked their way westward
across the state, Congress created new land districts, each with
its separate land office (Figure 1.2).[16] For the first five years,
1838–42, only the river towns of Burlington and Dubuque
boasted land offices. But in 1842, Congress opened new offices
further west at Fairfield and Marion, and after the acquisition of
the "New Purchase" (as the Southcentral area, Royce Cession 262,
was popularly known) in 1843, Iowa City became a key office
site. In 1852, with the surveys completed across the lower two-
thirds of the state, the lawmakers created the Chariton, Fort Des
Moines, and Council Bluffs land districts. Three years later
another trio of land offices was established in the northern and
northwestern portion of Iowa—Fort Dodge, Sioux City, and Decorah. The next year Congress authorized the twelfth and final
Hawkeye land office at Osage.

The new land offices of the 1840's and 1850's reflected the
growing interest in Iowa real estate by both settlers and nonresident speculators. The publication of immigrant guides,
maps and newspapers, the circulars of land companies and real
estate agencies, and the letters of residents to their friends and

---

[15] Ellen C. Semple and Clarence F. Jones, *American History and Its Geographic Conditions* (rev. ed., Boston, 1933), 168–70.
[16] Lokken, *Iowa Public Land Disposal,* chap. v. The map was adapted
from that on page 119.

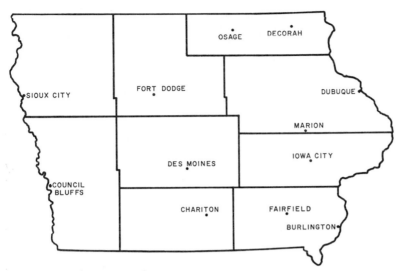

Fig. 1.2. Public land districts in Iowa, 1885.

relatives all served to publicize the advantages of the state as an
area for profitable investment.

Guides and handbooks written by Albert M. Lea, John
Plumb, J. H. Colton, Isaac Galland, Jesse Williams, John B.
Newhall, Willard Barrows, and others appeared in the two
decades preceding the Civil War. Typical was one produced by
George B. Sargent, a partner in Iowa's first major land agency.
The Sargent prospectus contained information concerning the
state, its counties and towns, its rivers, mineral deposits, and
plants, the Iowa Constitution of 1846, names of state officers,
hints to immigrants, "contemplated railroads," and the promise
of a "satisfactory profit" if nonresidents invested in Iowa land.[17]

Sargent and his partner, Ebenezer Cook, opened their agency
in Davenport in 1847 and were quickly emulated by dozens of
competitors. The realtors' advertisements dotted the local press,
and the larger firms distributed printed circulars widely through
the East. One of Cook & Sargent's early broadsides promised:

> Particular attention paid to Purchase and Sale of Lands, Pay-
> ment of Taxes, and Location of Bounty Land Warrants. . . .
> Having resided in this State for past fifteen years—one of us
> extensively engaged in the practice of law, and the other for

[17] *Notes on Iowa: With a New and Beautifully Engraved Map, Showing
the State, County, and Township Lines, Public Roads and Contemplated Railroads and Including the Most Recent Settlements and Improvements* (New
York, 1848). A microfilmed copy of the original was furnished by the New
York City Public Library.

many years as Government Surveyor, and having an extensive acquaintance with lands throughout the State, we feel confident that we can give full satisfaction to those who may engage our services.[18]

Settlers and prospective settlers also helped spread the word abroad about land profits to be had in Iowa. George Sheppard, leader of an English colony in Clinton County, for example, urged investors in the Old Country to buy all the vacant land in the vicinity, thus securing the profits "ordinarily clutched by mere speculators. They, above all beings," Sheppard continued, "are the most to be dreaded. It is known in Davenport that they had their eyes upon our proceedings. . . . What you do must be done quickly, unless you wish to hunt for honey after others have stripped the hive. I can lead you to thousands of acres as good as those we are purchasing, and at no great distance from them."[19]

One such speculator who wished to "strip the hive" was the Illinois store clerk who penned these lines to his cousin in New Hampshire:

> I wish to save money to purchase either Government land or improved land in Iowa Territory and let it lay and sweat until it is very valuable as it is bound to be in a few years, emigration is strong for that country at present. Many eastern folks are here now. . . . I am at present fast for entering land in Iowa and shall probably make a push for it this fall. . . . Come out here if you want to make a fortune.[20]

Samuel J. Bayard, receiver at the Fairfield Land Office, was another who urged an eastern friend to consider the possibilities of profitable real estate investment in the state. Referring to land between the Des Moines and Skunk rivers in central Iowa, he wrote in 1843 that "these 60 townships . . . comprehend a country of great beauty & fertility and will sell off rapidly. A little money judiciously invested here will be placed at good interest. . . . I am much pleased with the Country & all my savings I invest in the soil."[21]

---

[18] A copy of the circular, dated Oct. 15, 1850, is in the Corcoran & Riggs Papers, Library of Congress.

[19] Sheppard to Iowa Emigration Society (Hull, England), Aug. 15, 1850, in Grant Foreman, "English Emigrants in Iowa," *Ia. J. Hist. and Pol.*, XLIV (Oct., 1946), 415.

[20] G. R. Clark to Samuel S. Clark, June 6, 1844 or 1845, G. R. Clark Collection, Chicago Historical Society.

[21] Bayard to Lucius Lyon, Oct. 23, 1843, Lucius Lyon Papers, William L. Clements Library, University of Michigan, Ann Arbor. See also Charles Negus, "Early History of Iowa," *Annals of Iowa, 1st Ser.*, IX (Apr., 1871), 481–82. Of another investor it was said that "he had great faith in the future of the central part of the state, and invested every dollar he could obtain in

The land laws at this time provided that all of the public domain must be offered at public auction, excepting only that land subject to preemption claims, land in publicly platted townsites, and land reserved for special purposes such as the sixteenth (school) sections or the lead lands around Dubuque. Once offered, all tracts remaining unsold were subject to private entry at the minimum price of $1.25 per acre. Payment was demanded in cash—gold, silver, or authorized paper currency. No credit was given.

IV

UNTIL the government surveyed and sold the public domain in Iowa, legal titles were nonexistent. Claimants, however, often outran survey crews, and the initial public auctions in the various districts lagged up to six and seven years behind settlement.[22] Unwilling to wait for title deeds, these eager speculators traded "claims," which enjoyed a semi-legal status.[23] Bayard aptly described the situation when he declared in late 1844 that "population is vastly ahead of the public sales in this Territory. Several counties have been laid off of the unsurveyed land; & I suppose I speak within bounds when I say that a million & a half [acres] of the public lands in this Territory are overrun & occupied—converted into farms—bargained & sold under the Territorial Laws, over which the chain of no surveyor has yet been carried." All of these "adventurers," Bayard added, are willing to sell their claims at any time.[24] In actuality eleven counties in the New Purchase were established before it was legally possible for settlers to occupy and claim lands.[25]

Nonresident investors speculated in these claims in at least three ways. They entered land for claimants under credit arrangements at the public auctions; they purchased quitclaim deeds outright from owners and held the land for future resale; and they filed their own claims with local claim clubs. All three methods were popular and profitable. At the initial land sales in Burlington, for example, several leading moneylenders loaned over $100,000 apiece to buyers at rates of 40 per cent on one year's

land, with the fullest confidence that his money would be returned fourfold" (P. M. Casady, "Memoir of Madison Young," *ibid.*, XII [Jan., 1874], 16).
    [22] Barlowe and Hammar, "Valuation of Lands in Southcentral Iowa," 108–9. See Appendix I for a map (taken from *ibid.*, 109) showing the years when the townships of Cession 262 were first offered for sale.
    [23] Lokken, *Iowa Public Land Disposal,* 85–86.
    [24] Bayard to Lyon, Nov. 17, 1844, May 23, 1843, Lucius Lyon Papers.
    [25] See Appendix II for maps (taken from Barlowe and Hammar, "Valuation of Lands in Southcentral Iowa," 91, 93) showing the years of establishment and organization of each of the cession counties.

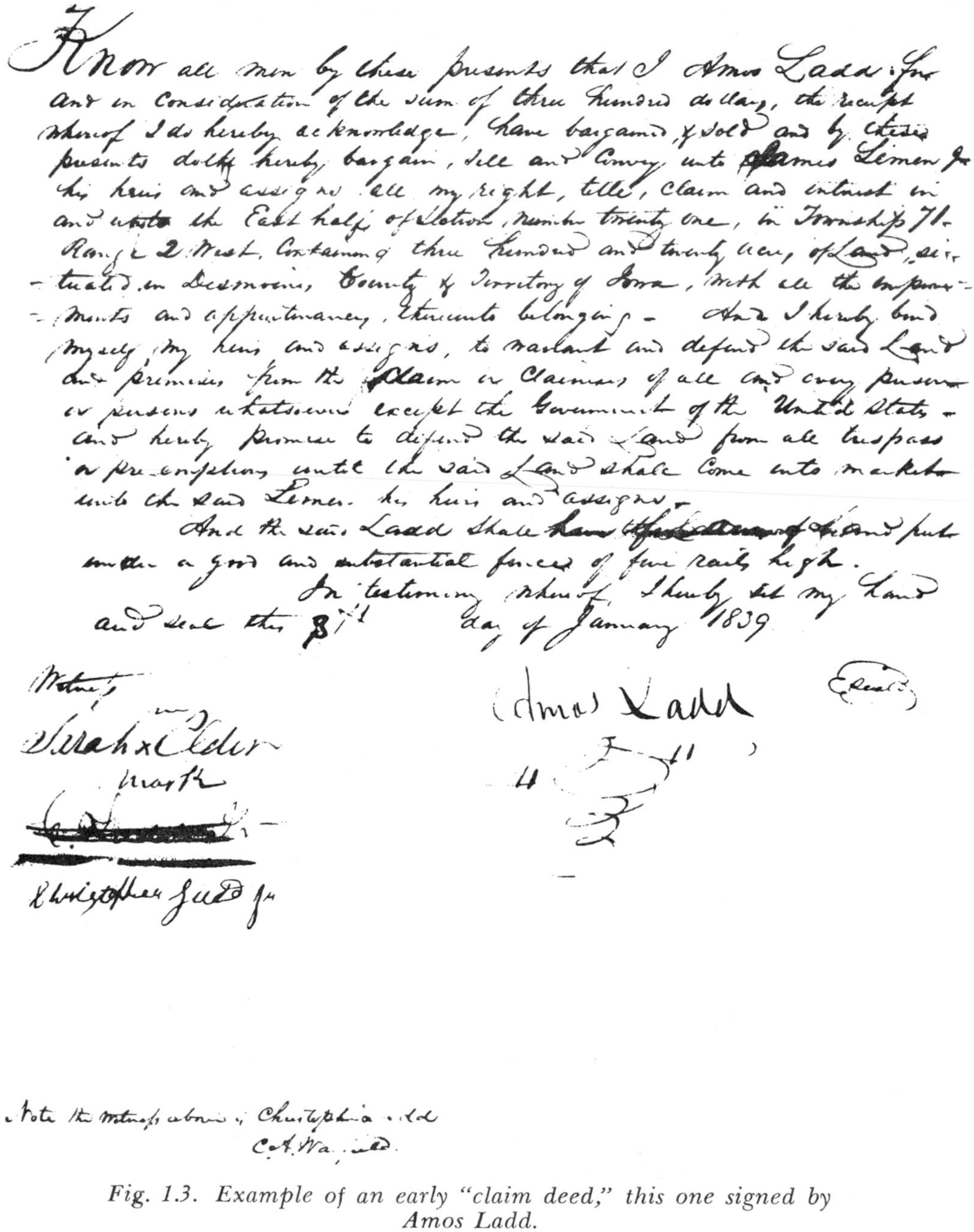

Fig. 1.3. Example of an early "claim deed," this one signed by
Amos Ladd.

time.[26] Richard F. Barrett, one of these capitalists from Springfield, Illinois, had previously advertised in the local paper: "I will attend the land sale at Burlington in November—will buy any lands that may be designated to me, and then sell back to the settlers, on a reasonable advance on a credit of from one to five years. The settlers may rely on my appearance with ample means to supply all demands in that way."[27]

At least one Iowa land agent, Daniel Smith Lee of Keokuk, insisted, however, that "the largest amount of money could be made" and without any "corresponding risk" by investing in claims for future speculation. He explained:

> Many persons came to this country squat down upon their choice of lands, Prairie, timber, water etc. combined and then go to work, break, fence, build cabins, dig wells etc. and then are unable to enter [i.e., to pay the preemption price at the land office] and yet are partially protected by their neighbors and the claimants law of the country, now these claims can be bought in many instances very low ranging from $50 to $350— a land warrant is now [1852] worth from $130 to 150—say the latter, and the farm the day it is entered will command and bring from $4 to $6 pr acre, there is no difficulty in selling these again as improved farms.[28]

The opinion that claims were abundant and a profitable investment was expressed by other Iowans besides Lee. Fairfield land officer Bayard reported to a Michigander that 160 townships in central Iowa would be put on the market within a year and that *"choice selections* might be made, . . . [since] the *claims* of the squatters, to mill scites, coal beds, Town scites etc. etc. will be for sale cheap."[29] In 1842, Cyrus Sanders of Iowa City

---

[26] Hawkins Taylor, "Squatters and Speculators at the First Land Sales," *Annals of Iowa, 1st Ser.,* VIII (July, 1870), 271; "Address of Edwin Manning of Keosauqua," *Semi-Centennial of Iowa: A Record of the Commemoration of the Fiftieth Anniversary of the Settlement of Iowa, Held at Burlington, June 1, 1883* (Burlington, 1883), 53–54; Louis Pelzer, "The Public Domain as a Field for Historical Study," *Ia. J. Hist. and Pol.,* XII (Oct., 1914), 574.

[27] Burlington *Iowa Territorial Gazette and Burlington Advertiser,* Sept. 15, 1838.

[28] Lee to Nathaniel Gordon, Apr. 2, 1852, Nathaniel Gordon Papers, Manuscript Division, Baker Library, Boston. Lee offered to pay one-half the cost of the claims and attend to the subsequent legal entry of the land at the government land office. In return, he demanded an equal division of any profits over and above the current value of the land warrant (used for the purchase) at the time of entry, the cost of the claim, and the other incidental expenses. Or, for every two warrants that the eastern investor supplied, Lee agreed to purchase the claims and allow the investor to take title to the one of his choice. Lee also mentioned the "popular method" of selling warrants on time, taking a mortgage on the land as security. Quarter section warrants, he added, could then be sold on one year's time for $175 to $200. Again, the agent offered his services for one-half of the net profits.

[29] Bayard to Lyon, July 4, 1843, Lucius Lyon Papers.

informed his brother in Ohio that one of the claims he had sold
a little more than a year ago for $300 was subject to entry at the
government minimum price by any person who had the money
to do it—"and there will be fifty chances perhaps as good or better than that."[30] Opportunities such as this were in the mind of
a Cincinnati investor, Milton N. W. Leace, when he queried
Jesse Williams, a Burlington real estate agent, about land in
Johnson County: "Write me at large on the subject of lands etc
& tell me when money can be made without fail. What do you
know of the preemption claims in that part of your Territory?"[31]

Newspaper advertisements indicate the magnitude of speculation in claims. In 1837, fully a year before the first public
land sales in Iowa, Fort Madison postmaster James Douglas and
attorney Henry Eno hung out their shingle as a general land
agency. To attract nonresident investors, they bought space in
the territorial journal with the largest eastern circulation—the
Burlington *Wisconsin Territorial Gazette and Burlington Advertiser*—and offered their services "for purchasing or disposing
of any lands situated in the Territory of Wisconsin west of the
Mississippi, or in the State of Illinois (particularly in the Military Tract)." Information about local real estate, they added,
would readily be sent upon request anywhere in the United
States.[32] James M. Morgan opened a "General Land Agency"
in Burlington in 1838, and his card read simply: "Land claims,
bought and sold." Morgan's local competitor, the firm of James
W. Grimes and Henry W. Starr, similarly announced that "particular attention will be paid to claims for lands."[33] That these
notices brought results is attested by another advertisement of
Grimes, a future Iowa governor and U.S. Senator, in which he
offered for sale in 1840 a list of 43 tracts owned by one of eastern Iowa's largest nonresident investors, Lewis Benedict of Albany, New York. The holdings, totaling 10,880 acres and spread
over seven counties, were represented as "select lands, eligibly
situated & somewhat improved," indicating that most had been
purchased from claimants.[34]

---

[30] Cyrus Sanders to Richard B. Sanders, Dec. 16, 1842, Cyrus Sanders Papers, State Historical Society of Iowa, Iowa City.

[31] Leace to Williams, Feb. 1, 1841, Jesse Williams Papers, Iowa State Department of History and Archives, Des Moines.

[32] Dec. 16, 1837.

[33] Burlington *Iowa* (formerly *Wisconsin*) *Territorial Gazette and Burlington Advertiser*, Nov. 3, 1838, Dec. 8, 1839; Burlington *Hawkeye and Iowa
Patriot*, Jan. 7, 1841.

[34] Burlington *Hawkeye and Iowa Patriot*, Oct. 29, 1840. Two advance
agents of the Mississippi Emigration Society, Toronto, Canada, after an extensive tour of eastern Iowa in the summer of 1838 just prior to the initial land
sales, reported to their society that claims of 320 acres or more were very common. "Many young men," the agents added, "have also made claims and some

Apart from newspaper advertisements, claim speculation by both residents and nonresidents is perhaps best illustrated in the few surviving records of Iowa claim clubs. In the land register of the Johnson County Claim Association, members recorded 233 claims and 179 claim transfers in the space of three years, and, since the club's record is not complete, this may well be only part of the actual claims registered and traded.[35] Further evidence of speculation is the frequent transfer of land by a relatively few members. Sixteen individuals deeded five or more quitclaims apiece and were involved as either buyers or sellers in 98 (54.7 per cent) of the 179 registered transfers. The record for the most activity belongs to Samuel Bumgardner with 17 transfers. John A. Street and William Sturgis were close behind with 11 transfers apiece, while Henry G. Reddout and Samuel B. Mulholland both had 10. These speculations could be very profitable. On February 15, 1839, for example, Bumgardner paid $100 for a claim which he sold a week later for $150. Altogether in the space of two years, 1839 and 1840, Bumgardner established 7 claims himself, purchased several more for the sum of $165, and sold 14 for a total price of $1,066.

That not all club members were impecunious squatters is also indicated by the fact that at least twenty subsequently speculated widely in government land. Territorial treasurer Morgan Reno and territorial auditor Jesse Williams, for example, each recorded one claim with the club. These two capitalists eventually entered over 105,000 acres of public land in eastern and central Iowa. One nonresident speculator, Stephen S. Phelps of Warren County, Illinois, played his role as capitalist to the hilt. He not only recorded a claim but placed a tenant on the land—an action that was the very antithesis of the club's supposed function. Phelps later entered 1,695 acres of Congress land in eastern Iowa.[36]

---

have made improvements on their claims and find themselves unable to pay for the land. Some [of these] claims sell very high according to their location. $8,000 was paid for half a section (320 acres) last summer. . . ." The lengthy report of the agent covers two full pages of the Davenport *Iowa Sun and Davenport & Rock-Island News,* Nov. 17, 1838.

[35] Data presented in this and the following paragraph were compiled from Benjamin F. Shambaugh (ed.), *Constitution and Records of the Claim Association of Johnson County, Iowa* (Iowa City, 1894). For a careful analysis of the records of this club and those in Webster and Poweshiek counties, which shows that they served largely as a facade for speculators, see Allan G. Bogue, "The Iowa Claim Clubs: Symbol and Substance," *Miss. Vy. Hist. Rev.,* XLV (Sept., 1958), 231–53.

[36] In addition to Phelps, ten other non-Iowans from Illinois, Indiana, and Ohio recorded either claims or transfers with the Johnson club. Claim club officers in Iowa also speculated widely in government land. Chester W. Cowles and Seth Richards, officers in a club in Van Buren County, entered 15,201 acres in central Iowa. Calvin J. Price and William Patterson, officers

Between July, 1854, and June, 1856, residents of Fort Dodge on the upper Des Moines River also organized a claim association while awaiting initial government land sales. In this short span of less than two years, 255 individuals registered claims totaling over 83,000 acres, or an average of 320 acres per member —the maximum allowed in the club's by-laws.[37] Minor improvements on each claim amounting to no less than $5.00 per month were required but residence was not compulsory. Consequently, claims were not infrequently filed for nonresidents by local agents. Luther L. Pease acted as the agent for R. P. Spear, a Cedar Falls realtor, and two other nonresidents;[38] E. N. Hulbert, another resident, filed claims for six different individuals. The practice apparently reached such proportions that the club felt compelled to act. On April 19, 1856, the minutes contain the following resolution:

> All persons holding clames and not living in this nabourhood
> but having thare clames attended to by Agents Must bee here
> in person by the 15th of June next or thare Clames will be
> Struck from this clame book.

Nonresidents not only controlled land in the Fort Dodge area through the club but they also purchased the claims of several club members. The club register lists quitclaims to L. S. Coffin of New York, Wm. Frederick Booth and Elliott H. Colburn of Ohio, and Jesse Williams of Fairfield, Iowa. Resident members also speculated in claims. Fifty-eight, or more than one in five, sold all or part of their claims before the land sales. At least eight claims were traded from two to four times during the 23 months of the club's activity. As soon as a claim was sold, the grantor generally registered a new claim without delay in hopes of another chance to capitalize on the golden opportunity at hand.

Some who were on the scene at the time further attested that the Fort Dodge claim association was a tool of speculators.

in a Lee County club, purchased 3,832 acres in eastern and central Iowa. Hiram C. Smith, an officer in a Henry County club, secured 1,095 acres in central Iowa. Charles Mason, chairman of a Des Moines County club, entered 1,912 acres in eastern Iowa. The names of the officers of these clubs are in the Burlington *Iowa Territorial Gazette and Burlington Advertiser,* Sept. 15, 1838, Mar. 30, and Sept. 21, 1839, and the Burlington *Iowa Patriot,* June 27, 1839. The acreage figures were compiled from the books of original entry. Yet more striking is the fact that George Weare, Sioux City's leading banker, speculator, and moneylender, served as the secretary of the local club (Sioux City *Journal,* Dec. 27, 1905).

[37] The data in this and the following paragraph were compiled from a manuscript entitled "Fort Dodge Claim Club," Iowa State Department of History and Archives, Des Moines.

[38] This fact was publicized in a Democratic campaign "white paper" of the late 1850's, entitled "A Plain Statement of the Facts," William Williams Papers, Iowa State Department of History and Archives, Des Moines.

Charles B. Richards, one of the city's pioneers, when requested to jot down for possible publication his recollections of the local claim club in 1855 and 1856, declared that:

> Most of the residents of Fort Dodge Were Speculators Land Agents and proffesional Men, Who Were Waiting for the Lands West of the Des Moines River to be brought into market. . . . To prevent these lands being taken by actual Setlers Who Wanted to improve and live on them the residents of the town formed this Claim Club. . . . It Asserted and Advertised that no one would be allowed to take up and Setle on any of the Lands So claimed, and Every New Emigrant . . . Were advised that any one attempting to Settle on any Lands Claimed by any Member of the Club Would be dealt With by the Club and his life Would not be Safe in that Comunity.[39]

Andrew J. Sterrett, a Pennsylvania speculator who was scouting for land at the time in the Fort Dodge and Des Moines land districts, also candidly confirmed that nonresidents participated in local claim associations. In a letter to his brother back home, Sterrett observed: "If I can find anything desirable, when I get a chance to look around, I will avail myself of this club arrangement." Although the clubs allowed only one free claim, Sterrett noted happily, a man can buy "as many more as he chooses," and the club "guarantees to protect him in getting them all . . . merely in consideration of his becoming a member. There's a barrier against speculation for you!"[40]

In addition to the Fort Dodge and Johnson County associations, at least a dozen other claim clubs were active in frontier Iowa.[41] Thus, one observer apparently approached the truth when he reported to relatives in the East: "Everybody speculating, nobody raising."[42]

V

ROYCE CESSION 262, or the New Purchase, the region chosen as the main focus of this book, is the largest of the Indian cessions in Iowa, embracing an area of approximately 11,776,000 acres

---

[39] Chas. B. Richards, "Recollections of the Fort Dodge Claim Club, 1855–1856." This manuscript was included in a letter to Cyrus Aldrich, dated Oct. 15, 1896, now in the Iowa State Department of History and Archives, Des Moines.

[40] Andrew Jackson Sterrett to David Brice Innis Sterrett, Oct. 20, 1856, Andrew Jackson Sterrett Papers, Manuscript Division, Minnesota Historical Society, St. Paul.

[41] Bogue, "Iowa Claim Clubs," 233.

[42] George C. Geaton to Nathaniel Gordon, Apr. 27, 1857, Nathaniel Gordon Papers.

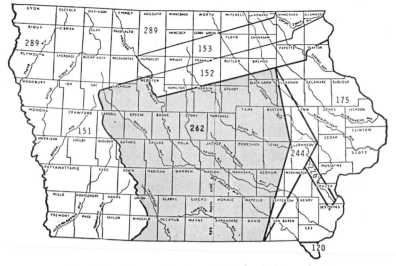

Fig. 1.4. Royce Cession 262 (shaded portion).

located in the central and southcentral part of the state.[43] As Figure 1.4 shows, the cession area includes either all or the major part of 34 of Iowa's 99 counties as well as smaller parts of 11 other counties.[44]

A gentle and rolling topography with good natural drainage, sufficient vegetation, and excellent soil quality were the major physical features that interested land buyers. And by these criteria, central Iowa scored high. "The whole country undulates beautifully," exclaimed one enthusiast in referring to the New Purchase: "The soil is dry & timber occurs in groves sufficient—water is got by digging from 12 to 20 feet. Coal abounds."[45] "Certainly nature has done all for the prairies of Central Iowa," added another: "The soil is a rich sandy loam, and its warmth brings forward vegetation with great rapidity. Its nature prevents the drowning of plants in wet seasons, as the

---

[43] The cession number is derived from the consecutive numbering of all Indian land cession treaties by Charles C. Royce (see n. 13 above), the noted authority on the subject. Hereafter the term "central Iowa" is used synonymously with Cession 262 and the 34 counties located entirely or mostly within the cession area are referred to as the major counties of Cession 262.

[44] The map is adapted from Royce, *Indian Land Cessions*, Map Plate CXXXI. It differs in two particulars from other government sources. The "Red Rock Line" is a few miles to the west in the map accompanying the 1845 report of the surveyor general to the commissioner of the General Land Office (U.S. Congress, *Senate Documents*, 29th Cong. 1st Sess., III, Doc. 16). The northwestern boundary of Royce Cession 262 is some miles to the south in the map prepared by the Bureau of Land Management in May, 1959.

[45] Bayard to Lyon, July 4, 1843, Lucius Lyon Papers.

soil absorbs the moisture only to return it to the surface when needed to nourish the plants in the absence of rain."[46] Topographic conditions vary throughout the cession, but viewed in modern scientific terms, almost 90 per cent of the area is level to moderately sloping (with slopes up to 13 per cent), while only 1.3 per cent has slopes of 25 per cent or more.[47] Thus most of Cession 262 is ideally suited to the cultivation of grain crops, while the remaining portion, rolling and hilly, is suitable for grazing and dairy farming, although some parts can also be cultivated.[48]

A number of medium-sized rivers traverse the cession area, flowing generally in a southeasterly direction toward the Mississippi River. The Des Moines, with its major tributaries the Raccoon and South Raccoon, is by far the most important river in the area; it more or less bisects the state. As the largest river, the Des Moines served as an important avenue of transportation in presettlement and early settlement days. For more than a century and a half it served the fur traders as the only uninterrupted path of canoe travel between St. Louis and the Hudson Bay and Saskatchewan fur county. Even in the early days of Iowa's statehood (until the advent of the railroad), the Des Moines River carried sufficient water during the spring freshets to allow Mississippi River steamboats to ply their trade as far up-river as the Raccoon Forks at the capitol city of Des Moines. Smaller steamboats were able to navigate between that point and the Lizard Fork at Fort Dodge.[49] To the northeast the Skunk, North Skunk, Iowa, Cedar, and Wapsipinicon rivers flow generally parallel to the Des Moines while to the southwest, the Chariton and Thompson rivers drain by a more southerly course into the Missouri River in the state of Missouri.

Most of the woodland and prairie area of central Iowa is well drained. The intricate network of streams and rivers (depicted in Figure 1.5) generally allowed for adequate run-off and also afforded opportunities for development of mill sites.[50] Availability of water similarly posed few problems for settlers. Early observers, as noted previously, frequently commented on

[46] *Mills Circular,* quoted in *The North-Western Rev.,* I (Feb., 1858), 50.
[47] Compiled from data in R. W. Arnold, L. E. Tyler, F. F. Riecken, "Estimate of Slope Classes by Counties in Iowa," *Ia. Acad. Sci. Pro.,* LXVII (1960), Table 1, 265–67.
[48] Information in this and the following paragraphs is summarized largely from Frank F. Riecken, "Soils and Related Physical Features of Cession 262 in Iowa" (typescript in possession of the author), and from Barlowe and Hammar, "Valuation of Lands in Southcentral Iowa," 2–12.
[49] See Charles Keyes, *Annotated Bibliography of Iowa Geology and Mining* ("Iowa Geological Survey," Vol. XXII, [Ames, 1913]), 32–37.
[50] Jacob A. Swisher, *Iowa—Land of Many Mills* (Iowa City, 1940), 110–12, 122–26, 133–45, 150–54.

Fig. 1.5. Forested land in Iowa at the time of the original survey begun March 23, 1832 and completed August 17, 1859.

the "well-watered" nature of the area.[51] Surface water from streams and natural springs was often convenient, and as Albert M. Lea observed in his comments concerning the Des Moines River country, "when there are no natural springs, there is no difficulty in obtaining water, by digging, at almost any point in the highland-prairies."[52]

Figure 1.5 also shows the general location and distribution of the forest resources of Iowa. This map, prepared originally by the staff of the Iowa State Planning Board, indicates the areas reported as timbered in the notes of the original land surveyors. Apart from scattered patches in the northwestern part of Cession 262, almost every township in the cession claimed timber suitable for fuel, fencing, and often for building materials.[53]

---

[51] See for example Caleb Atwater, *Remarks Made on a Tour to Prairie Du Chien* (Columbus, 1831), 51–52, 199–201.

[52] Albert M. Lea, "Notes on Wisconsin Territory, with a Map," *Annals of Iowa, 3rd Ser.,* XI (July–Oct., 1913), 138. See also John B. Newhall, *Sketches of Iowa, or the Emigrant's Guide* (New York, 1841), 9.

[53] Further examination of the field survey notes for 526 of the 527 (notes for one township were not available) townships located wholly or mainly within Cession 262 shows that the surveyors observed timber in at least 491 townships. Favorable comments were recorded concerning the quality or quantity of the timber found in approximately half of these townships. In only 12 townships did the surveyors report no timber while in 23 others their scanty notes make no mention of either its presence or absence. Altogether, timber was found in 93.3 per cent of the townships for which surveyors' notes and comments were available. For the above data, I am indebted to George B. Pletsch and Ruth K. Crum, who summarized some 11,000 pages of surveyors' notes preserved at the National Archives.

In terms of quantity, however, natural timber amounts varied widely from county to county. Computations derived from planimetric measurement of the forested area indicated on the map reveal that five counties in the cession area (Davis, Wapello, Appanoose, Marion, Decatur) had over 120,000 forested acres each while only four had less than 20,000 acres (Hamilton, Carroll, Calhoun, Grundy). Altogether, the 34 major counties of the New Purchase contained 2,304,052 acres of woodland, or 18.9 per cent of the total land area.[54] The kinds of trees included sycamore, oak, hard maple, elm, walnut, cherry, hickory, cottonwood, butternut, ash, poplar, and hackberry. Local entrepreneurs began commercial cutting and sawing of this timber at several sites within a few years after the area was opened for settlement.[55]

As is evidenced today by dark-colored, fertile topsoil, some 88 per cent of Cession 262 was covered with prairie vegetation at the time of settlement. The remaining 12 per cent, comprising forest soils, bordered the major rivers or was found in the forested areas of the southeastern and southcentral counties. Those timber-formed soils consisting of bottomlands along the rivers are exceptionally fertile but the remainder are generally best suited for grazing.

In natural fertility and productive potential, the soils of central Iowa ranked equal with the rest of the state but were far above average for the nation. In the early 1930's a U.S. government study made under the direction of Dr. Curtis F. Marbut, an outstanding soil scientist at the time in the Bureau of Chemistry and Soils of the U.S. Department of Agriculture, divided the nation's soils into five classes ranging from the best soils (Grade 1) to the poorest and least productive (Grade 5). The scientists classified about 75 per cent of Iowa soil as Grade 1—indeed almost one-fourth of all the Grade 1 soil in the continental United States.[56] Central Iowa boasted the same proportion as the remainder of the state. In short, central Iowa offered every natural advantage for agricultural settlement that a prospective settler could desire.

---

[54] See Appendix X for a table showing the approximate acreage of forest land in each of the central Iowa counties at the time of the survey. The acreage totals are in Robert R. Davidson, "Comparisons of the Iowa Forest Resource in 1832 and 1954," *Ia. St. J. Sci.*, XXXVI (Nov., 1961), 133–36.

[55] See George B. Hartman, "The Iowa Sawmill Industry," *Ia. J. Hist. and Pol.*, XL (Jan., 1942), 57–59 and *passim;* Charles E. Hall, "Pen Sketches of the Big Woods," *ibid.*, XXIX (July, 1931), 402. The Fort Des Moines *Gazette* reported that 8 sawmills were operating near Des Moines in 1850; the census of 1860 listed 114 flour and grist mills and 216 sawmills in 25 of the Cession 262 counties, while Jacob Swisher's research uncovered mills established in all of the remaining cession counties in the 1840's or early 1850's, *Iowa—Land of Many Mills*, 67, 245–72, 287–90.

[56] National Resources Board, *Report*, Dec. 1, 1934 (Washington, 1934), 127.

VI

HEAVY IMMIGRATION into eastern Iowa occurred in the 1830's and, given the excellent reports about the Des Moines valley of central Iowa, land seekers grew understandably eager for the government to press negotiations with the Indians. As early as four years before the New Purchase opened, the Indians were being pressed by white settlement. A Methodist circuit rider, Reuben Gaylor, reported in 1839 that due to the "immense" tide of immigration "the country is full back to the Indian line and more are coming every day." He ministered to a congregation only four miles from Indian territory.[57] In 1840 Fort Madison lawyer William E. Mason, a nephew of Iowa Chief Justice Charles Mason, reported to his father back in Pompey, New York, that "emigration at this time into the territory is absolutely astonishing. I suppose there are at least 20 wagons of emigrants crossing at this place every day. The same is true of every point on the Mississippi river where a ferry boat is run."[58]

As soon as Iowa territorial governor John Chambers received instructions in the fall of 1842 to negotiate a land purchase treaty with the Sac and Fox Indians, he ordered a full company of dragoons from Fort Atkinson to "protect the Indians" and keep overeager whites from pouring across the cession boundary. Chambers requested that the troops be outfitted to remain along the border until spring. It would be impractical, he explained, even if the negotiations were completed quickly, to remove the Indians before spring, and "it will in the meantime be equally impractical to Keep their country from being overrun by white people."[59] Despite precautions, however, "boomers" managed to scout the new territory long before its formal opening and mark off their claims on trees with ax heads smuggled past the border patrols in their boots.[60] To ensure their

---

[57] Walter R. Houf (ed.), "American Home Missionary Letters from Iowa," *Annals of Iowa, 3rd Ser.,* XXXVII (Summer, 1963), 53, 66.

[58] From Charles Mason Remey (ed. and comp.), "Life and Letters of Charles Mason, Chief Justice of Iowa, 1804–1882," (12 vols., typescript; Washington, D.C., 1939) I, 91. I used typescript "Copy C," owned by the State Historical Society of Iowa, Iowa City.

[59] As soon as the treaty is signed, Chambers declared, "it will be impossible to keep the whites (who are waiting along the boundary for the negotiation) from rushing into the country in great numbers, without the presence of an efficient military force, which will also be necessary to protect the Indians" (Chambers to Commanding Officer, Fort Atkinson, Iowa Territory, Sept. 16, 1842, Governor's Files, Indian Correspondence, Vol. II, Iowa State Department of History and Archives, Des Moines).

[60] Western Historical Company, *History of Marion County, Iowa* (Des Moines, 1881), 304–5. Cf. Jacob Van Der Zee, "The Opening of the Des Moines Valley to Settlement," *Ia. J. Hist. and Pol.,* XIV (Oct., 1916), 521–22; "Iowa Territory" in *The Home Missionary,* XVI (Dec., 1843), 172–73. That

claims, the eager settlers formed a giant claim club, with rules and regulations covering the entire New Purchase. The club boasted 800 members and allowed claims of 320 acres, which it pledged to protect "up to the termination of the land sales."[61] The climax to this first great land rush in American history[62] came a few seconds after midnight on May 1, 1843, when the troops opened the eastern part of the cession for occupation. At the echoing report of the soldiers' rifles, the boomers surged forward to claim the choice tracts they had previously scouted.[63]

Although the exact extent of the first inundation cannot be verified, firsthand observers reported that whole counties, particularly Wapello and Mahaska, seemed to be populated overnight. Doubtless with some exaggeration, Willard Barrows asserted that between midnight and daylight on May 1 "almost the whole country was settled up by claims."[64] Gaylor, the circuit-riding pastor, reported that 10,000 people staked claims in the New Purchase in the first two weeks.[65] Land officer Bayard confirmed the preacher's estimate. He reported to a friend on May 23 that "the Des Moines Country is represented as very desirable and about 10,000 squatters are already there upon the best locations."[66] By mid-June, 20,000 claims already had been staked out, a newspaperman wrote, and, he predicted, the population would soon reach the "immense number of 80 or 100,000 souls."[67] Another observer noted that the New Purchase was filling with "incredible celerity" at a rate "equalled by nothing but pigeons

---

the governor's request for troops was based on an accurate appraisal of the situation is evident from the later report of pioneer surveyor Willard Barrows, who noted that "for weeks and months previous, the dragoons from the forts were stationed upon the line, to keep off the settlers who had made their encampments with their families, near the promised land, so great was their anxiety to secure a good portion for their future homes"; from his *Notes on Iowa Territory With a Map* (Cincinnati, 1845), 19.

[61] A lengthy description of the club by a participant is in the Keokuk *Register*, Sept. 28, Oct. 5, 1848.

[62] Ray A. Billington makes this claim in *Westward Expansion, A History of the American Frontier* (3rd ed., New York, 1967), 478. Walter Havighurst, on the other hand, in *Wilderness for Sale; The Story of the First Western Land Rush* (New York, 1956), claimed that Ohio witnessed the first rush.

[63] For vivid descriptions of the eventful night of May 1, 1843, see Uriah Biggs, "Sketches of the Sac and Fox Indians, and the Early Settlement of Wapello County," *Annals of Iowa, 1st Ser.,* III (Oct., 1865), 535–36; G. D. R. Boyd, "Sketches of History and Incidents Connected with the Settlement of Wapello County, from 1843 to 1859, Inclusive," *ibid.,* V (Oct., 1867), 940–41; Harrison L. Waterman, *History of Wapello County, Iowa* (2 vols.; Chicago, 1914), I, 55; *The Home Missionary,* XVI (Dec., 1843), 172–73.

[64] Barrows, *Notes on Iowa Territory,* 19.

[65] *The Home Missionary,* XVI (July, 1843), 53.

[66] Bayard to Lucius Lyon, May 23, 1843, Lucius Lyon Papers.

[67] Davenport *Gazette,* June 15, 1843. For additional comments see *The Home Missionary,* XVI (June, Dec., 1843), 39, 172–73; Davenport *Gazette,* Oct. 7, 1847.

or blackbirds."[68] The western half of the cession was opened at midnight, October 11, 1845, and the scene of May 1 was repeated.[69]

While eager squatter-speculators located many choice tracts, tens of thousands of prime acres remained unclaimed, awaiting the rapid influx of the large-scale speculators.[70] Encouraged by the glowing reports, they or their agents were not only on hand at every public auction to purchase tracts not claimed by squatters and to enter land for those who lacked the necessary funds, but they subsequently flocked to the land offices and purchased most of the remaining unclaimed land. The agricultural resources of the area and the prospect of a continuing heavy immigration, these farsighted businessmen realized, spelled impending success for their ventures.

[68] Charles Mason to Edwin Mason, July 12, 1843, "Life and Letters of Charles Mason," II, 99. Mason eventually purchased about 6,560 acres of Iowa land, largely with land warrants (*ibid.,* III, 298).

[69] H. B. Turrill, *Historical Reminiscences of the City of Des Moines* (Des Moines, 1857), 16–17.

[70] Allan G. Bogue estimated that local farmers seldom claimed as much as half the available farm sites at the time of the land sale; in his *From Prairie to Corn Belt: Farming on the Illinois and Iowa Prairies in the Nineteenth Century* (Chicago, 1963), 39.

Chapter Two

PUBLIC LAND SPECULATION:
THE QUANTITATIVE EVIDENCE

THE EXTENT of speculation in government land can never be known exactly but existing public records enable one to make reasonably precise estimates. The books of original entry, safeguarded in the vaults of the county courthouses of Iowa, contain the legal description and acreage of each tract in the county, its purchaser, date of entry, entry price, patentee, and date of the final patent. The manuscript decennial federal agricultural census for Iowa, beginning in 1850, lists the names of all who were operating farms in the census years, the improved and unimproved acreage on each farm, and figures on the crop and livestock production. Beginning in 1847 the state auditor annually published the total acres assessed for taxation in each of the organized counties of the state. In 1864 the secretary of Iowa's state agricultural society requested the county secretaries to submit estimates of the extent of unimproved land owned by nonresidents and corporations in their respective counties. Between 1865 and 1869 many secretaries responded. From these records there are at least five ways to estimate the extent of speculation in Iowa. These are:

(1) analysis of the original entry books to determine the number of large buyers;
(2) census year comparisons of original entry acreage and total farm acreage in 1850, 1856, and 1860;
(3) census year comparisons of acreage assessed for taxes and total farm acreage in 1850, 1856, 1859, and 1862;
(4) Estimates of county agricultural society secretaries and other contemporaries of the extent of unimproved land held by nonresidents—that is, by speculators;
(5) comparisons of original entrants with farm operators enumerated in the manuscript federal agricultural censuses of 1850 and 1860.

I

BEFORE we examine the records of central Iowa we can give ourselves a basis for comparison by looking briefly at developments a decade earlier in the eastern counties (Royce Cession areas 175, 226, and 244) where the land auctions began in the fall of 1838.

Contemporaries disagreed on the extent of speculation in the early years; the weight of evidence, however, indicates that speculation was an important factor in public land sales from the first. Local newspaper editors, possibly in the vain hope of forestalling excesses, repeatedly returned from the auctions to report that there was "not a speculator in the crowd."[1] But other observers, and indeed the land records themselves, prove otherwise. Hawkins Taylor and Edwin Manning, both participants in the initial auction at Burlington, for example, later recalled that speculators and moneylenders had jammed the town and several had invested more than $100,000 apiece.[2] As early as 1840 voices were also raised in the territorial legislature against nonresident speculators. Typical of the continuing complaints was the following:

> Non-residents who have had capital to spare have invested largely in Iowa land on speculation only. Their wish is, and their course will be, as it ever has been with this grade of people, to let the land be vacant until the actual settler has so improved the county that they [the nonresidents] will realize profits from the toil of the actual settler.[3]

The land records alone can provide conclusive evidence of the prevalence of speculation, and they corroborate the observations of Taylor and Manning. Three large nonresident capitalists singled out by these participants were Richard F. Barrett of Springfield, Illinois; Lewis Benedict of Albany, New York; and Lyne Starling of Franklin County, Ohio. Tabulations of land entry records for 19 eastern Iowa counties revealed that Barrett purchased more than 29,000 acres of public land, Bene-

---

[1] Burlington *Iowa Territorial Gazette and Burlington Advertiser*, Aug. 8, Dec. 1, 8, 1838; June 6, 1840. See also Burlington *Hawkeye and Iowa Patriot*, Dec. 10, 1840. Only once did an editor admit that "a great number of strangers are in town" *(Iowa Territorial Gazette*, Nov. 24, 1838).

[2] Taylor, "Squatters and Speculators at the First Land Sales," *Annals of Iowa, 1st Ser.*, VIII (July, 1870), 271; "Address of Edwin Manning, of Keosauqua," *Semi-Centennial of Iowa: A Record of the Commemoration of the Fiftieth Anniversary of the Settlement of Iowa, Held at Burlington, June 1, 1883* (Burlington, 1883), 53–54; and Taylor's reminiscences in Benjamin F. Shambaugh, "From the Standpoint of a Pioneer," *Ia. Hist. Rec.*, XIV (July, 1898), 310–17.

[3] Bloomington (later Muscatine) *Herald*, Oct. 23, 1846; John E. Brindley, *History of Taxation in Iowa* (2 vols.; Iowa City, 1911), I, 8.

TABLE 2.1
Large Entrymen in Eastern Iowa*

Name	Residence	Acreage
Barney William J.	Dubuque	30,135
Barrett, Richard F.	Springfield, Ill.	29,046
Benedict, Lewis	Albany, N.Y.	20,599
Berryhill, Charles H.	Iowa City	28,904
Berryhill, James B.	Iowa City	18,981
Bissell, Frederick E.	Dubuque	14,981
Buckingham, Alvah	Zanesville, Ohio	18,957
Byington, LeGrand	Iowa City	16,210
Churchill, Alfred	Davenport	10,745
Cook, Ebenezer	Davenport	41,859
Culbertson, John C.	Iowa City	16,879
Daniels, Frances	Windsor, Vt.	22,999
Downey, Hugh D.	Iowa City	21,215
Gower, James H.	Iowa City	28,149
Higginson, John C.	Dubuque	16,289
Lamson, Ward	Fairfield	14,835
McDaneld, John M.	Dubuque	12,492
Phelps, Alexis	Warren Co., Ill.	10,041
Reno, Morgan	Iowa City	24,099
Sanford, Horatio W.	Dubuque	212,456
Sargent, George B.	Davenport	13,035
Starling, Lyne	Franklin Co., Ohio	27,199
Thompson, John	Muscatine Co.	16,153
White, Miles	Baltimore, Md.	12,862
Williams, Jesse	Fairfield	15,017
Willingham, William W.	Halifax Court House, Va.	10,837
Wilson, David S.	Dubuque	20,289
Wilson, Thomas S.	Dubuque	13,789
Total acres		739,052

*Compiled from books of original entry.

dict over 20,000, and Starling more than 27,000 (Table 2.1).[4] Nor were these three men the only large investors. Nine other individuals entered more than 20,000 acres, paced by Dubuque banker Horatio W. Sanford with 212,456 acres. Another 16 men purchased between 10,000 and 20,000 acres. This group included Alvah Buckingham, a Zanesville, Ohio merchant; Frances Daniels of Windsor, Vermont; Alexis Phelps of Warren County, Illinois; banker Miles White of Baltimore; and William W. Willingham, a merchant of Halifax Court House, Virginia. Altogether, the 28 entrants with more than 10,000 acres accounted for nearly 740,000 acres or 12.1 per cent of all Congress land in

---

[4] By 1849, or within 11 years, over 35,000 of these acres had been sold. This figure is based on tabulations of all resale data between the dates of original entry and the end of 1849 in the 19 full counties of the 3 cession areas of eastern Iowa, in Raleigh Barlowe and Conrad H. Hammar, "Valuation of Lands in Eastern Iowa, 1833–1839; Royce Cession Areas 175, 226, 244," 2 vols., presented before the Indian Claims Commission, Doc. 158, 209, 231, *Sac and Fox and Iowa Tribes v. The United States of America* (1962), I, 98–99. The authors also found that 249 grantors sold more than 500 acres each and 62 grantors each conveyed title to 1,000 acres or more.

TABLE 2.2

ACREAGE OF THE TEN LARGEST ENTRANTS AS A PERCENTAGE OF TOTAL ORIGINAL
ENTRY ACREAGE, EASTERN IOWA *

County	Original entry acreage	Acreage of 10 largest entrants	Per cent
Buchanan.................	351,960	28,560	8.1
Cedar....................	348,678	45,370	13.0
Clayton..................	437,455	81,314	18.6
Clinton..................	392,091	57,051	14.6
Delaware.................	345,717	61,761	17.9
Des Moines..............	241,059	29,722	12.3
Dubuque.................	359,854	67,752	18.8
Henry...................	266,718	22,721	8.5
Jackson..................	387,070	98,433	25.4
Jefferson................	260,304	21,543	8.3
Johnson.................	376,582	53,702	14.3
Jones...................	321,581	61,345	19.1
Lee.....................	198,947 †	25,645	12.9
Linn....................	429,862	49,948	11.6
Louisa..................	225,143	27,517	12.2
Muscatine...............	262,936	32,789	12.5
Scott...................	291,223	56,706	19.5
Van Buren...............	278,876	33,591	12.0
Washington..............	345,747	34,994	10.1
Total acres.............	6,121,803	890,464	
Arithmetic mean........			14.2

*Compiled from books of original entry.
†Does not include 119,183 acres comprising the Half-Breed Tract.

eastern Iowa. An additional 318 individuals secured between 1,000 and 10,000 acres. Their entries added to those of the other large investors totaled 1,445,511 acres, or 23.6 per cent of all public land sold in the three eastern cession areas.[5]

Considering only the entries of the ten largest buyers in each county (Table 2.2), the concentration of purchasing is still more apparent. The acreage of the ten largest entrymen as a percentage of total original entries ranged from 8.1 per cent in Buchanan County to 25.4 per cent in Jackson County. For all 19 counties the arithmetic mean was 14.2 per cent. In short, on an average, ten men secured almost one-sixth of the entire public domain in each of the eastern counties. In Jackson County, however, Horatio W. Sanford alone accounted for 66,680 acres or 17.3 per cent of the entire county total.

Census marshals canvassed the Iowa countryside periodically and, according to law, recorded the amounts of land (both improved and unimproved) included in farms.[6] Registers at the

[5] For a complete list of the individuals and their total entries, see Robert P. Swierenga, "Pioneers and Profits: Land Speculation on the Iowa Frontier" (Ph.D. dissertation, University of Iowa, 1965), Appendix I, 343–46.

[6] See Appendix VIII for the specific instructions to the census marshals. Improved acreage consisted of land which produced crops or in some manner

government land offices, meanwhile, methodically recorded all public land entries. Assuming that all but a small fraction of these entries (those exploited as townsites, for example) were best suited for agricultural development, and making allowance for farms carved out of land granted by the federal government to the state or to private transportation companies, one would expect the amount of federal (or "Congress") land sold to approximate the acreage reported in farms—that is, unless speculation was rife.

To test this possibility, the original entry acreage of eastern Iowa was tallied for each of the census dates of 1850, 1856, and 1860 and compared with acreage in farms, both improved and unimproved, at those times. As Table 2.3 indicates, 66.5 per cent of the land sold prior to January 1, 1850, was in farms while in 1856 and 1860 the percentage dropped to 59.1 and 63.0 per cent. (See also Figures 2.1, 2.2, and 2.3.) Conversely, therefore, between 33.5 and 40.9 per cent of the Congress land sold in eastern Iowa in the 1850's did not go directly into farms but was likely used for speculation. These percentages, of course, can serve only as a *minimum* estimate of the extent of speculation since they do not reflect any public land sold by the state or private transportation companies.

Measuring farm acreage against nonurban land assessed for taxes (instead of original entry acreage) further corroborates the prevalence of speculation. Indeed, the tax lists approximate more accurately than any other source the actual amount of public land that had passed into private hands.[7] Unlike the

---

added to the production of the farm. Unimproved acres consisted of land belonging to those farms from which productions were returned but which was not cleared. This explanation is in the *Report of the Superintendent of the Census for December 1, 1852* (Washington, 1853), 47–48. Although the specific instructions to the census marshal in 1860 could not be located, apparently the same definitions were applied. See the comments in *Eighth Census of the United States, Agriculture* (Washington, 1864), viii.

[7] Since the financially hard-pressed state government obtained its operating revenue almost entirely from a percentage of county property taxes, the first state auditor, Joseph T. Fales, began the practice in 1847 of hiring the registers of the federal land offices in Iowa to compile abstracts of all lands sold in the various counties of their district in each calendar year (Iowa *Senate Journal*, 1848, 277). In January, 1848, the legislature made this practice mandatory (Iowa *Laws*, 1848 [Extra Sess.], 63–64). These abstracts, furnished to local officials, enabled the county assessors to prepare reasonably accurate and complete lists of land subject to taxation. Not only were thousands of dollars added to the infant state's coffers in this way, but, fortunately for the historian, the amount of rural acreage assessed for taxes in each county was published by the state auditor in his annual reports to the governor. The registers charged $114 in 1847 for the initial list of lands sold (Iowa *Senate Journal*, 1848, 280). The territorial auditor, Jesse Williams, had suggested this system as early as 1840 but his idea had apparently been ignored (Iowa *House Journal*, 1840, 29).

TABLE 2.3
FARM ACREAGE AS A PERCENTAGE OF ORIGINAL ENTRY ACREAGE, EASTERN IOWA, 1850, 1856, AND 1860*

County	1850			1856			1860		
	Original entry acreage	Farm acreage	Per cent	Original entry acreage	Farm acreage	Per cent	Original entry acreage	Farm acreage	Per cent
Buchanan	11,382	8,781	77.1	349,838	115,464	33.0	351,960	121,340	34.5
Cedar	113,610	71,071	62.6	348,559	160,603	46.1	348,678	237,006	68.0
Clayton	121,153	47,650	39.3	420,299	251,342	59.8	437,455	243,583	55.7
Clinton	66,199	47,942	72.4	391,971	194,735	49.7	392,091	244,027	62.2
Delaware	51,577	29,100	56.4	344,357	187,834	54.5	345,717	156,460	45.3
Des Moines	218,885	151,613	69.3	240,899	161,631	67.1	241,059	189,973	78.8
Dubuque	255,485	160,524	62.8	359,814	204,628	56.9	359,854	278,760	77.5
Henry	203,957	130,892	64.2	266,678	172,983	64.9	266,718	188,457	70.7
Jackson	168,867	150,015	88.8	386,472	321,889	83.3	387,070	285,030	73.6
Jefferson	240,253	208,440	86.8	260,304	194,180	74.6	260,304	208,440	80.1
Johnson	126,723	80,535	63.6	375,990	194,083	51.6	376,582	154,406	41.0
Jones	76,519	39,439	51.5	321,461	191,180	59.5	321,581	228,082	70.9
Lee†									
Linn	149,809	111,765	74.6	427,542	222,121	52.0	429,862	252,318	58.7
Louisa	141,294	80,588	57.0	225,103	132,463	58.8	225,143	129,175	57.4
Muscatine	154,140	74,589	48.4	262,220	187,134	71.4	262,936	186,565	71.0
Scott	141,313	70,497	49.9	290,235	174,650	60.2	291,223	194,262	66.7
Van Buren	250,573	188,867	75.4	277,702	223,957	80.6	278,876	213,478	76.5
Washington	119,782	84,131	70.2	344,388	190,731	55.4	345,747	222,906	64.5
Totals	2,611,521	1,736,439		5,893,833	3,481,608		5,922,856	3,734,268	
Weighted averages			66.5			59.1			63.0

*Original entry totals include acres entered prior to Jan. 1, 1850, 1856, and 1860. Acreage in farms (improved and unimproved) was compiled from manuscript federal agricultural censuses of 1850 and 1860 and township totals published in the state census of 1856.

†Lee County could not be included because the book of original entry contains no data on the 119,183 acres of the Half-Breed Tract.

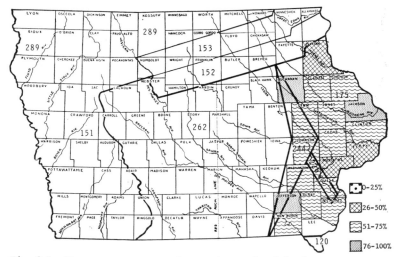

Fig. 2.1. Farm acreage as a percentage of original entry acreage, eastern Iowa, 1850.

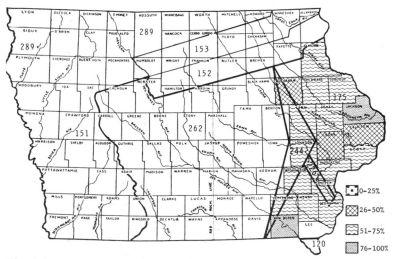

Fig. 2.2. Farm acreage as a percentage of original entry acreage, eastern Iowa, 1856.

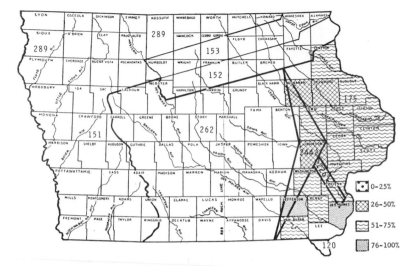

Fig. 2.3. Farm acreage as a percentage of original entry acreage, eastern Iowa, 1860.

original entry records, tax lists included not only federally alienated land but also land sold by the state and private transportation companies as part of their public land grants; that is, all land in private hands. Table 2.4 contains data on farm acreage as a percentage of rural acreage taxed for the census years of 1850, 1856, 1859, and 1862.[8] In 1850, 58.1 per cent of the nonurban land that was taxed was in farms (either improved or unimproved). During the decade the figure decreased slightly to 55.3 per cent in both 1856 and 1859, but by 1862 it increased again to 57.8 per cent. In short, based on the more accurate tax assessment method of computation, it appears that 42 to 45 per cent of the public land alienated in eastern Iowa in the 1850's was entered for speculative purposes. And of the remainder, designated as farm acreage and supposedly acquired for farming, almost one-half was yet uncleared and nonproductive in 1860, a hint that some of it was held by farmer-speculators.

---

[8] The years for which comparisons could be made in Iowa in the period through 1865 were limited because government officials, either national or state, collected statistics on farm acreage only in 1850, 1856, 1859, 1860, and 1862. The 1860 total could not be used because the tax assessment lists were not published for the period 1860–62; and the 1865 census reported only the farm acreage enclosed. In each case the tax assessment figures used were those of the year immediately succeeding the census year. (For instance, the 1850 census data were compared with the 1851 assessment lists.) This was necessary because the census data were collected in the fall of the year while the tax lists only included land in private hands on January 1 (prior to 1857 the assessment date was March 1).

TABLE 2.4
FARM ACREAGE AS A PERCENTAGE OF ACREAGE ASSESSED FOR TAXES, EASTERN IOWA, 1850, 1856, 1859, AND 1862[a]

County	1850 Acres assessed	1850 Acreage in farms	Per cent	1856 Acres assessed	1856 Acreage in farms	Per cent	1859 Acres assessed	1859 Acreage in farms	Per cent	1862 Acres assessed	1862 Acreage in farms	Per cent
Buchanan	23,695	8,781	37.1	360,236	115,464	32.1	358,845	97,893	27.3	354,212	118,138	33.4
Cedar	142,750	71,071	49.8	360,707	160,503	44.5	360,103	172,131	47.8	360,350	209,779	58.2
Clayton	154,759	47,650	30.8	467,973	251,342	53.7	474,298	240,719	50.8	491,045	252,137	51.3
Clinton	95,608	47,942	50.1	398,581	194,735	48.9	426,571	218,532	51.2	428,472	257,027	60.0
Delaware	80,087	29,100	36.3	366,034	187,834	51.3	358,709	158,061	44.1	362,333	114,040	31.5
Des Moines	229,942	151,613	65.9	280,817	161,631	57.6	245,223	173,869	70.9	252,420	173,757	68.8
Dubuque	317,344	160,524	50.6	379,392	204,628	53.9	380,956	238,155	62.5	380,623	265,770	69.8
Henry	215,090	130,892	60.9	268,845	172,983	64.3	268,842	145,202	54.0	272,030	143,608	52.8
Jackson	225,431	150,015	66.5	399,376[c]	221,889[d]	55.6	398,353	213,000	53.5	406,921	284,433	69.9
Jefferson	253,921	208,440	82.1	275,058	194,180	70.6	258,393	200,702	74.8	244,276	190,639	78.0
Johnson	160,132	80,535	50.3	385,000	194,083	50.4	382,990	184,306	48.1	388,912	198,978	51.2
Jones	100,666	39,439	39.2	362,436	191,180	52.7	358,676	169,841	47.4	361,573	219,924	60.8
Lee	326,576[b]	235,514	72.1	318,500	214,988	67.5	313,036	215,210	68.7	322,907	215,586	66.8
Linn	176,234	111,765	63.4	438,659	222,121	50.6	449,393	280,383	62.4	449,175	231,699	51.6
Louisa	162,006	80,588	49.7	249,134	132,453	53.2	228,768	155,451	68.0	245,254	125,125	51.0
Muscatine	172,603	74,589	43.2	265,888	187,134	70.4	265,888	143,783	54.1	300,451	174,458	58.1
Scott	163,142	70,497	43.2	274,005	174,630	63.7	262,397	172,670	65.8	281,193	213,446	75.9
Van Buren	262,809	188,867	71.9	292,462	223,957	76.6	298,556	204,191	68.4	304,677	204,798	67.2
Washington	134,127	84,131	62.7	357,552	190,731	53.3	355,107	188,655	53.1	356,944	199,609	55.9
Totals	3,396,922	1,971,953		6,500,655	3,596,596		6,455,104	3,572,754		6,563,768	3,792,951	
Weighted averages			58.1			55.3			55.3			57.8

[a]Assessed acreage figures are in *House Journal*, 1852, app., 18–19; *Report of the Auditor of State*, 1857, 24–25; 1859, 23–26; 1863, 25–28. Acreage in farms, including improved and unimproved acreage, compiled from manuscript federal agricultural census of 1850 and state agricultural censuses of 1856, 1859, and 1862.
[b]No figures given in 1850 assessment, 1852 substituted.
[c]Erroneously given as 299,376.
[d]Erroneously given as 321,889.

This, at least, was the contention of contemporary publicists who frequently included unimproved farm acreage in their estimates of the extent of speculation.[9]

II

STATE GEOLOGIST Charles A. White observed in 1867 that speculators had increased their activity as the Iowa frontier moved westward.[10] Judging by the central Iowa experience, the record bears him out.

Large-scale speculation can first be demonstrated by the distribution of land ownership in central Iowa. According to tabulations of original entries for the 33 major counties of Cession 262 (Table 2.5),[11] over 12,000 buyers, or almost one-third of the original entrants, purchased more than a quarter section (160 acres), their total entries absorbing 72.7 per cent of the Congress land in the area. Given the state of mechanized agriculture in the ante bellum years, few farm families could put to optimum use a tract larger than a quarter section. Indeed, 80 acres was the standard farm size used by most authors of travel guides and immigration pamphlets when they estimated the amount of capital needed to open an Iowa farm.[12] One could

---

[9] William Duane Wilson, *Description of Iowa and Its Resources* (Des Moines, 1865), 41 and *passim*. A present day authority who followed this approach is Paul W. Gates, *The Illinois Central Railroad and Its Colonization Work* ("Harvard Economic Studies," Vol. XLII [Cambridge, 1934]), 110. Farm acreage figures in the 19 counties of eastern Iowa, based on the manuscript federal agricultural census of 1860, are as follows: improved, 2,014,951; unimproved, 1,946,240. The fact that almost one-half of the land in farms was still uncultivated does not necessarily indicate that farmers held all of it for speculation. Some farmers developed their raw land at a leisurely rate and undoubtedly some also found small portions that were unfit for cultivation. But Iowa had less unsuitable land than any other state. In 1920, only 14.5 per cent of Iowa farm acreage was unimproved; the national average was 47.4 per cent. Illinois had 14.6, Missouri 28.6, Minnesota 28.9, Kansas 32.6, Wisconsin 43.8, and Nebraska 45.3 per cent unimproved (U.S. Bureau of the Census, *Fourteenth Census of the United States, Agriculture* [Washington, 1922], Pt. 1, 33, 523).

[10] White, "Some Characteristic Features in the Early and Present History of South-Western Iowa," *Annals of Iowa, 1st Ser.,* V (Apr., 1867), 835–36.

[11] Original entries in Decatur County, the 34th major county within the cession area, are not included in the tabulations in this table nor in tables 2.6, 2.7, and 2.8 below because a courthouse fire destroyed the original entry book.

[12] John B. Newhall, *A Glimpse of Iowa in 1846* (Burlington, 1846), 59; American Emigrant Co., *Two Thousand Families Wanted for Iowa* (n.p., n.d.), 1. Forty acres is considered optimum in John Regan, *Western Wilds of America* (Edinburgh, 1859), 353; while a prominent Iowan, John F. Dillon, declared that 80 acres was "a quantity more than sufficient for the cultivation of one man." See his agricultural address of Sept. 9, 1864, in Iowa State Agricultural Society *Report, 1864* (Des Moines, 1865), 114. For most settlers in central Iowa it required at least a decade to develop fully an 80-acre farm.

TABLE 2.5

ORIGINAL ENTRANTS AND ORIGINAL ENTRY ACREAGE BY ACREAGE GROUPING IN
33 COUNTIES OF CENTRAL IOWA (CESSION 262) *

Groups	Number of original entrants	Per cent			Total acreage	Per cent		
1–160 acres	26,833	68.5			2,582,689	27.3		
161–599	9,886	25.2	}	} 31.5	3,000,399	31.7	}	} 72.7
600–999	1,467	3.7	} 6.3		1,077,614	11.4	} 41.0	
1,000 and over	1,008	2.6			2,798,401	29.6		
Totals	39,194	100.0			9,459,103	100.0		

*These tabulations exclude joint-ownership purchases, town lots, and dupli-
cate claims. Because the spelling of entrants' names in the government records
was not entirely consistent, some buyers (ca. 5 per cent) may have been counted
more than once.

thus conclude with some justice that nearly three-fourths of the
Congress land in central Iowa was purchased for speculation
rather than for cultivation.

Within the group of 12,000 buyers entering more than a
quarter section, 9,886 individuals—mainly farmer-speculators—
procured up to 600 acres; and 2,475 buyers, many of whom
were nonresidents, secured 600 acres or more, accounting altogether for 41 per cent of the original entry acreage.[13] Of this
latter group, fully a thousand buyers each entered over 1,000
acres, totaling together 2.8 million acres, or almost one-third
(29.6 per cent) of all Congress land in Cession 262.[14] Forty-one
men entered over 10,000 acres (Table 2.6). Their purchases
numbered 973,387 acres or 10.3 per cent of the Congress land in
central Iowa. Twenty-four of these obtained between 10,000
and 20,000 acres; twelve entered between 20,000 and 40,000
acres; and five men amassed larger amounts, including James S.

In fact, it was 1870 before the average improved acreage per farm in Iowa
reached 80 acres (*Iowa Historical and Comparative Census, 1836–1880* [Des
Moines, 1883], 269).

[13] General evidence of the speculative activities of many early Iowa farmers
can also be deduced from the census reports on average size of farms. The
average Iowa farm contained 185 acres in 1850 and 165 in 1860, areas considerably larger than the average farmer was equipped to handle. By 1870,
after numerous settlers had had time to dispose of their surplus land to relatives or others, the average-sized farm dropped to 134 acres.

[14] Because of spelling inconsistencies in the tract books the buyer total
of 1,008 for the "1,000 acres and over" group includes at least 42 cases (4.2
per cent) of duplicate listings. An extreme case is Benjamin F. Allen, listed
also as B. F. Allen, Benj. F. Allen, and Benja. F. Allen. Fully as many large
entrymen, however, were deleted from the tabulation because their entries
were recorded under various spellings, none of which singly totaled 1,000
acres. The acreage totals for this group of buyers exclude all tracts of less
than 1,000 acres where the spelling does not conform exactly to the major
usage. From a careful check of nine counties this loss is estimated at 2 per
cent. For a complete list of the individuals and their total entries see
Swierenga, "Pioneers and Profits," Appendix IV, 348–58.

TABLE 2.6
Large Entrymen in Central Iowa*

Name	Residence	Acreage
Allen, Benjamin F.	Des Moines	35,308
Barney, William J.	Dubuque	28,429
Berryhill, Charles H.	Iowa City	14,397
Berryhill, James B.	Iowa City	10,686
Branner, John	Jefferson Co., Tenn.	11,732
Byington, LeGrand	Iowa City	19,989
Cook, Ira	Des Moines	37,359
Culbertson, John C.	Iowa City	48,833
Downey, Hugh D.	Iowa City	50,576
Easley, James S.	Halifax Court House, Va.	61,762
Eckert, David E.	Fairfield	12,843
Fowler, Samuel	New Orleans, La.	20,661
Gower, James H.	Iowa City	29,727
Greene, George	Cedar Rapids	10,983
Hager, William H.	Washington Co., Md.	13,309
Henn, Bernhart	Fairfield	13,465
Howe, George W.	Osceola	22,852
Ives, Robert H.	Providence, R.I.	16,669
Johnson, James	Muskingum Co., Ohio	10,471
Kirk, John W.	Hamilton Co., Ohio	11,425
Lamson, Ward	Fairfield	34,085
Morris, Jenkin W.	Des Moines	10,868
Neal, Jairus E.	Knoxville	13,773
Patterson, Ezekiel M.	Middlesex, N.J.	10,103
Reno, Morgan	Iowa City	27,426
Rice, Byron	Des Moines	19,740
Richards, Seth	Bentonsport	10,698
Roebling, John A.	Trenton, N.J.	14,145
Sanford, Horatio W.	Dubuque	19,251
Scholte, Henry P.	Pella	12,540
Sherman, Hoyt	Des Moines	22,441
Sternberg, Lambert	Herkimer Co., N.Y.	16,114
Stevens, Andrew J.	Des Moines	16,581
Temple, Edward A.	Chariton	60,841
Tousey, Omer	Dearborn Co., Ind.	10,068
White, Elias A.	Baltimore, Md.	36,332
White, John	Oskaloosa	12,175
White, Miles	Baltimore, Md.	53,372
White, William W.	Des Moines	12,128
Williams, Jesse	Fairfield	39,337
Willingham, William W.	Halifax Court House, Va.	39,893
Total acres		973,387

*Compiled from books of original entry.

Easley of Halifax Court House, Virginia, with 61,762 acres and Edward A. Temple of Chariton, with 60,841 acres. This great concentration of real estate in relatively few hands indicates that much of the public domain in central as in eastern Iowa first went to speculators who served as middlemen between the government and the settler.

It might be interesting at this point to establish whether investors in the central part of the state were the same who operated earlier in eastern Iowa. A search of the land entry

TABLE 2.7

ORIGINAL ENTRY ACREAGE OF CENTRAL IOWA LARGE ENTRYMEN IN 19 EASTERN
IOWA COUNTIES *

County	Total acres (all years)	Total acres (1838–42)
Buchanan	23,520	.....
Cedar	72,953	2,487
Clayton	99,728	560
Clinton	69,805	.....
Delaware	69,297	703
Des Moines	8,276	1,880
Dubuque	56,321	400
Henry	14,068	4,085
Jackson	106,858	472
Jefferson	14,846	1,268
Johnson	88,239	915
Jones	81,635	876
Lee	11,425	10,444
Linn	50,830	224
Louisa	21,967	3,623
Muscatine	22,565	3,142
Scott	30,892	1,175
Van Buren	5,953	3,017
Washington	49,576	80
Total acres	898,754	35,351

*Compiled from books of original entry.

records in the eastern counties revealed that 284 large entrymen
in central Iowa, or approximately one in three, invested previously in eastern Iowa.[15] Their acquisitions, moreover, were
sizeable—totaling nearly 900,000 acres, or about 15 per cent of
the original entry acreage in eastern Iowa (Table 2.7). More
than 35,000 acres of this amount was entered during the earliest
period of government land sales in the state, from 1838 to 1842.
During these same years the speculators in turn sold 5,779 of
these acres (17.1 per cent) at an average price of $3.21 per acre
(see Appendices VI and VII). It is clear that many speculators in
central Iowa had previously invested in the eastern counties,
apparently with some success.

The investors with experience in both the eastern and
central counties might well have testified to the greater competition for land in central Iowa. Of the 6 million acres of Congress
land in eastern Iowa, 346 individuals entered a thousand acres
or more. In central Iowa, on the other hand, 984 investors, or
almost triple the number in the east, acquired a thousand acres
or more, although the land area (11.8 million acres) was less than
double the amount in the east.

The acreage totals of the largest entrymen arranged by
county tell the same story. In the 33 counties of central Iowa,

[15] For a complete list see *ibid.*, Appendix V, 359–61.

the acreage of the ten largest entrants as a percentage of total
original entry acreage ranged from 7.6 per cent in Wapello
County to 20.5 per cent in Carroll County (Table 2.8). For all
of the counties the arithmetic mean was 12.1 per cent, as con-
trasted to a mean of 14.2 per cent in eastern Iowa (Table 2.2).
No ten men in any central Iowa county could hope to enter a
quarter of the land in a county, as had been done in Jackson
County. Nor could any one man—no matter how strong his desire and financial condition—duplicate Horatio Sanford's feat of
entering over 17 per cent of all Congress land in a county.

TABLE 2.8

ACREAGE OF THE TEN LARGEST ENTRANTS AS A PERCENTAGE OF TOTAL ORIGINAL
ENTRY ACREAGE, CENTRAL IOWA *

County	Original entry acreage	Acreage of 10 largest entrants	Per cent
Appanoose.................	264,712	37,931	14.3
Benton....................	411,933	44,429	10.8
Blackhawk.................	302,268	33,488	11.1
Boone.....................	228,938	30,173	13.2
Calhoun...................	153,005	26,418	17.3
Carroll...................	192,958	39,589	20.5
Clarke....................	234,990	31,275	13.3
Dallas....................	312,880	33,402	10.7
Davis.....................	282,233	25,075	8.9
Greene....................	299,550	41,975	14.0
Grundy....................	295,103	47,569	16.1
Guthrie...................	324,080	35,466	10.9
Hamilton..................	265,640	34,696	13.1
Hardin....................	299,709	32,188	10.7
Iowa......................	321,089	48,993	15.3
Jasper....................	397,257	42,481	10.7
Keokuk....................	341,657	33,876	9.9
Lucas.....................	224,239	34,876	15.6
Madison...................	324,917	32,877	10.1
Marion....................	257,588	41,265	16.0
Marshall..................	325,713	28,980	8.9
Mahaska...................	282,790	27,114	9.6
Monroe....................	240,765	27,711	11.5
Polk......................	241,278	30,416	12.6
Poweshiek.................	341,389	50,756	14.9
Ringgold..................	321,516	41,733	13.0
Story.....................	318,482	28,648	9.0
Tama......................	409,754	42,311	10.3
Union.....................	233,649	25,271	10.8
Wapello...................	178,043	13,582	7.6
Warren....................	312,995	26,661	8.5
Wayne.....................	300,423	26,392	8.8
Webster...................	205,388	22,751	11.1
Total acres.............	9,446,931	1,120,368	
Arithmetic mean........			12.1

*Compiled from books of original entry.

III

STRONG COMPETITION among speculators for central Iowa real estate is further attested by noting the acreage in farms as a percentage of all Congress land sold at each of the census dates of 1850, 1856, and 1860. As Table 2.9 and Figure 2.4 reveal, of the 19 counties included in the 1850 census, the percentage ranged from 100 per cent in Wapello County to only 20.7 per cent in Warren County, the weighted average for the whole area being 69.7 per cent. The amount of speculation, of course, should be approximately the reverse of these figures. Since Lucas County farms, for instance, comprised only 21.2 per cent of all Congress land sold by 1850, the remaining 78.8 per cent of the alienated acreage was being held either for speculation or by nonresident farmers planning to migrate in the near future.

Comparison of land entry with census data at this early date, however, leads to serious underestimation of the extent of speculation. This is clearly indicated by the Wapello County figures which show more than 142,000 acres in farms as of August 1, 1850, whereas only 135,441 acres had been entered at the federal land offices by December 31. Two factors skew the results, squatting and state land sales. It was a time-honored practice among pioneer farmers to settle on vacant public land and farm it for some time before taking title at the land office.[16] Census marshals included these squatter's tracts in their farm acreage statistics but federal land officers did not list them as sold until the claimants "proved up" and took title. The state of Iowa also alienated thousands of acres of land donated to it under various Congressional public land grants. Such sales were not registered in federal land entry books because U.S. patent titles had already passed to the state. In Wapello County, to return to our previous example, 53,000 acres adjoining the Des Moines River, donated to finance its navigational improvement, were sold by the end of 1850 in addition to about 7,000 acres of school land.[17] If these 60,000 acres are added to the original entry totals by that date, the acreage in farms as a percentage of land sold drops sharply to a more realistic 72.7 per cent. In addition, the largest part of the farm acreage in 1850 in Wapello (and all the counties for that matter) was unimproved and likely held for resale by farmer-speculators. The method used in

---

[16] A scanning of the books of original entry for individuals enumerated as farmers in the 1850 agricultural census showed that many entered their land in the following years.

[17] See Chapter 3 for data on the state lands.

TABLE 2.9
FARM ACREAGE AS A PERCENTAGE OF ORIGINAL ENTRY ACREAGE, CENTRAL IOWA, 1850, 1856, AND 1860[a]

County	1850 Original entry acreage	1850 Farm acreage	1850 Per cent	1856 Original entry acreage	1856 Farm acreage	1856 Per cent	1860 Original entry acreage	1860 Farm acreage	1860 Per cent
Appanoose	57,581	23,090	40.1	260,876	188,108	72.1	264,552	217,131	82.1
Benton	25,824	14,897	57.7	410,839	119,494	29.1	411,933	136,594	33.2
Blackhawk	2,751	2,304	83.8	301,163	87,720	29.1	302,268	96,033	31.8
Boone				226,363	91,878	40.6	228,938	56,040	24.5
Calhoun				87,640	1,055	1.2	150,109	2,997	2.0
Carroll				81,503	5,443	6.7	187,738	5,513	2.9
Clarke				228,972	106,013	46.3	234,910	96,346	41.0
Dallas				310,062	86,189	27.8	312,370	122,715	39.3
Davis	175,548	121,795	69.4	281,701	206,587	73.3	282,233	228,887	81.1
Decatur[f]	2,400	10,131	100.0	213,975	137,446	64.2	271,469	181,658	66.9
Greene				280,060	38,046	13.6	299,390	28,087	9.4
Grundy				282,702	13,035	4.6	292,301	19,409	6.6
Guthrie				305,957	63,548	20.8	322,775	57,789	17.9
Hamilton				240,727	27,776	11.5	262,126	28,552	10.9
Hardin				279,647	94,116	33.7	299,629	74,911	25.0
Iowa	31,611	13,582	43.0	320,529	109,303	34.1	321,089	141,614	44.1
Jasper	44,695	30,520	68.3	395,492	155,200	39.2	397,177	162,463	40.9
Keokuk	112,973	85,009	75.2	340,793	214,243	62.9	341,572	257,838	75.5
Lucas	32,285	6,829	21.2	220,261	57,383[b]	26.1	224,239	88,171	39.3
Madison	14,529	13,988	96.3	319,012	129,639	40.6	324,837	163,160	50.2
Mahaska	142,455	99,588	69.9	282,280	197,280	70.0	282,750	170,869	60.4
Marion	110,044	69,749	63.4	254,715	165,361	64.9	257,548	202,592	78.7
Marshall	5,854	3,473	59.3	322,667	121,997	37.8	325,429	113,747	35.0
Monroe	79,358	56,465	71.2	236,155	151,043	64.0	240,765	134,651	55.9
Polk	81,961	76,279	93.1	240,161	135,086[e]	56.2	240,958	118,513	49.2
Poweshiek	22,715	14,996	66.0	341,196	90,991	26.7	341,389	97,615	28.6
Ringgold				301,965	38,030	12.6	319,520	55,950	17.5
Story				315,921	60,529	19.2	318,482	73,385	23.0
Tama				406,028	96,641	23.8	409,194	95,906[d]	23.4
Union				228,695	31,488	13.8	233,249	42,596	18.3
Wapello	135,441	142,307	100.0	177,797	164,676	92.6	178,043	148,308	83.3
Warren	65,404	13,521	20.7	309,600	161,042[e]	52.0	312,995	144,836	46.3
Wayne	8,476	4,459	52.6	291,812	119,604	41.0	299,898	138,086	46.0
Webster				135,439	48,808	36.0	202,570	30,888	15.2
Totals	1,151,905	802,982		9,232,705	3,514,798		9,694,445	3,733,850	
Weighted averages			69.7			38.1			38.5

[a]Original entry totals include acres entered through July 31, 1850, and May 31, 1856, and 1860. Acreage in farms (improved and unimproved) was compiled from the manuscript federal agricultural censuses of 1850 and 1860 and township totals published in the state census of 1856.
[b]Erroneously given as 157,383.
[c]Erroneously given as 235,086.
[d]Erroneously given as 15,906.
[e]Not reported; 1859 census figures substituted.

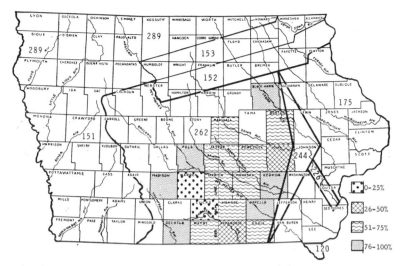

Fig. 2.4. Farm acreage as a percentage of original entry acreage, central Iowa, 1850.

compiling Table 2.9, in short, leads the researcher to under-estimate the extent of speculation, particularly in the early years.

From the state agricultural census of 1856 one can construct a more accurate index of speculation in the cession area.[18] This census is particularly useful for our purposes since the marshals commenced work on June 1, 1856, just as much of the public domain in Iowa was withdrawn from private entry (as it turned out, for nearly two years) until the railroads could make their land-grant selections.[19] Moreover, this date was immediately after the peak years of the mid-Fifties when buyers bought up most of the land in central Iowa; yet it was before the depression of 1857 with its resulting shrinkage in farm acreage.[20]

On May 31, 1856, the acreage in farms as a percentage of

[18] *Census of Iowa, 1856.* This printed volume, containing a summary of the data in the manuscript copy of the census, gives the total farm acreage, improved and unimproved, by townships. Compilations can also be made from the manuscript records on file in the Census Division, Iowa State Department of History and Archives, Des Moines.

[19] Richard C. Overton, *Burlington West: A Colonization History of the Burlington Railroad* (Cambridge, 1941), 83. The actual order was given on May 10. The printed census returns are undated but contemporary newspapers confirm that the enumeration began on June 1, 1856 (Iowa City *Daily Evening Reporter,* July 21, Aug. 4, 1856).

[20] In all but 50 of the 527 townships in Cession 262, 90 per cent or more of the total original entry acreage was in private hands by 1856. In 21 of the remaining 50 townships, over 75 per cent was sold. See Appendix IV for a series of maps showing biennially from 1842 through 1860 the proportion of original entry township land area sold in eastern and southcentral Iowa.

land sold varied from 1.2 per cent in Calhoun County to 92.6
per cent in Wapello with an all-county weighted average of 38.1
per cent (Table 2.9). Illustrated graphically by Figure 2.5, it is
obvious that large-scale speculation was prevalent in all but the
southeastern quarter of the cession. In ten counties less than 25
per cent of the land sold was in farms; in fourteen it was between 26 and 50 per cent; and in nine between 51 and 75 per
cent. The 1860 figures only confirm the general reliability of
the 1856 estimates. From county to county the amount of land
in farms as a percentage of original entry acreage (see Table 2.9
and Figure 2.6) varied from 2.0 per cent in the western county
of Calhoun to 83.3 per cent in the southeast county of Wapello.
The 33-county weighted average was 38.5 per cent, only .4 per
cent higher than the 1856 percentage. Thus, in 1860 as in 1856,
the amount of land in farms in central Iowa in proportion to
land sold was only about one-third.

IV

FIGURES ON the amount of rural land assessed for taxes in central
Iowa, as noted earlier, provide a more accurate measure of the
acreage actually in private hands than do federal land entry
records. As Table 2.10 indicates, the farm acreage as a percentage
of acreage assessed for taxes in the 34 full counties of Cession 262
stood at 53.3 per cent in 1850 and then dropped sharply to 34.7

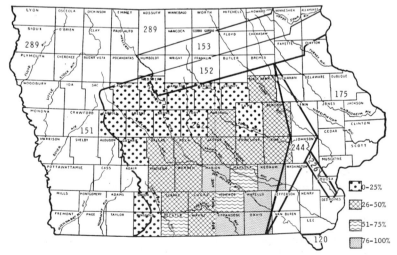

*Fig. 2.5. Farm acreage as a percentage of original entry acreage,
central Iowa, 1856.*

TABLE 2.10

FARM ACREAGE AS A PERCENTAGE OF ACREAGE ASSESSED FOR TAXES, CENTRAL IOWA, 1850, 1856, 1859, 1862[a]

County	1850 Acreage assessed	Farm acreage	Per cent	1856 Acreage assessed	Farm acreage	Per cent	1859 Acreage assessed	Farm acreage	Per cent	1862 Acreage assessed	Farm acreage	Per cent
Appanoose	88,404	23,090	26.1	280,970	188,108	67.0	302,828	192,371	63.5	317,436	176,060	55.5
Benton	27,082	14,897	55.0	454,399	119,494	26.3	453,764	127,552	28.1	448,715	135,251	30.1
Blackhawk	.....	.....	.....	332,733	87,720	26.4	330,584	92,104	27.9	347,351	107,507	31.0
Boone	.....	.....	.....	229,623	91,878	40.0	336,921	64,635	19.2	362,888	57,384	15.8
Calhoun	.....	.....	.....	94,579	1,055	1.1	160,841	3,132	6.9	297,908	5,300	1.8
Carroll	.....	.....	.....	32,822	5,443	16.6	124,000[d]	6,046	4.9	218,280	6,318	2.9
Clarke	.....	.....	.....	256,534	106,013	41.3	271,372	89,554	33.0	269,107	81,508	30.3
Dallas	.....	.....	.....	299,666	86,189	28.8	354,604	94,572	26.7	350,012	95,191	27.2
Davis	200,716	121,795	60.7	311,478	206,587	66.3	304,830	222,961	73.1	338,686	220,692	65.2
Decatur	24,840[b]	10,131	40.8	302,551	137,446	45.4	319,812	153,247	47.9	337,541	114,040	33.8
Greene	.....	.....	.....	294,897	38,046	12.9	304,837	31,211	10.2	312,162	23,819	7.6
Grundy	.....	.....	.....	196,926	13,035	6.6	317,254	14,678	4.6	313,115	21,611	6.9
Guthrie	.....	.....	.....	301,163	63,548	21.1	346,180	51,229	14.8	341,270	41,891	12.3
Hamilton	.....	.....	.....	.....	.....	.....	302,592	27,776	9.2	325,430	26,618	8.2
Hardin	.....	.....	.....	200,426	94,116	47.0	337,125	113,489	33.7	315,320	75,215	23.9
Iowa	37,020	13,582	36.7	345,677	109,303	31.6	363,795	136,086	37.4	362,668	119,216	32.9
Jasper	54,263	30,520	56.2	552,032	155,200	28.1	444,059	144,418	32.5	437,491	140,178	32.0
Keokuk	132,639	85,009	64.1	353,235	214,243	60.7	369,446	195,687	53.0	367,872	161,047	43.8
Lucas	27,985	6,829	24.4	241,408	57,383[e]	23.8	262,375	101,752	38.8	263,717	90,203	34.2
Madison	35,315	13,988	39.6	366,640	129,639	35.4	354,802	154,600	43.6	395,662	146,196	40.6
Mahaska	179,544	99,588	55.5	356,200	197,280	55.4	347,083	199,396	57.4	347,940	190,555[o]	54.8
Marion	145,151	69,749	48.1	321,440	165,361	51.4	347,771	167,595	48.2	347,529	163,266	47.0
Marshall	8,379	3,473	41.4	351,988	121,997	34.7	364,816	108,907	29.9	324,201	83,645	25.8
Monroe	95,700	56,465	49.0	253,408	151,045	59.6	255,662	130,936	51.2	266,044	122,458	46.0
Polk	144,781	76,279	52.7	297,539	135,086[f]	45.4	339,507	112,757	33.2	349,458	110,582	31.6
Poweshiek	24,488	14,996	61.2	365,321	90,991	24.9	268,821	75,476	28.1	371,362	82,046	22.1
Ringgold	.....	.....	.....	233,061	38,057	16.3	338,755	60,244	17.8	336,593	57,692	17.1
Story	.....	.....	.....	356,106	60,529	17.0	340,411	99,686	29.3	340,719	70,225	20.6
Tama	.....	.....	.....	458,399	96,641	21.1	456,052	87,360	19.2	459,554	107,698	23.4
Union	.....	.....	.....	253,889	31,483	12.4	269,854	41,734	15.5	260,333	33,136	12.7
Wapello	213,491	142,307	66.7	278,675	164,675	59.1	209,397	146,811	70.1	210,503	181,775	86.4
Warren	47,428	13,531	28.5	Not given			351,455	161,042	45.8	360,337	145,208	40.3
Wayne	15,134	4,459	29.5	313,497	119,604	38.2	333,447	134,798	40.4	324,470	93,880	28.9
Webster	.....	.....	.....	289,652	48,808	16.9	313,592	51,999	16.6	402,988	36,397	9.0
Totals	1,502,360	800,688		9,576,934	3,326,007		10,898,644	3,595,841		11,338,662	3,323,808	
Weighted averages			53.3			34.7			33.0			29.3

[a] Assessed acreage figures are in *House Journal*, 1852, app., 18–19; *Report of the Auditor of State*, 1857, 24–25; 1859, 23–26; 1863, 25–28. Acreage in farms (improved and unimproved) was compiled from manuscript federal agricultural census of 1850 and state agricultural censuses of 1856, 1859, and 1862.

[b] Erroneously given as 4,840.

[c] Erroneously given as 90,555.

[d] 1859 figure not given, interpolated from 1858 return.

[e] Erroneously given as 157,383.

[f] Erroneously given as 235,086.

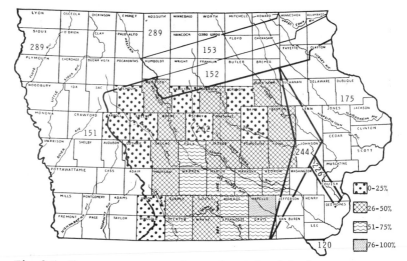

*Fig. 2.6. Farm acreage as a percentage of original entry acreage,
central Iowa, 1860.*

per cent in 1856, 33.0 per cent in 1859, and 29.3 per cent in 1860.
In other words, in 1850 approximately one-half of all land on
central Iowa tax rolls was not included in either the improved
or unimproved portions of local farms nor in town lots, and was
therefore likely in the hands of speculators. Moreover, between
1850 and the end of the decade the possible acreage held by speculators increased from one-half to more than two-thirds. In the
boom years of the 1850's, speculators apparently absorbed land
at a much faster rate than farmers.

Comparing the percentages of farm acreage to acreage
taxed in central Iowa with the figures for the counties of eastern
and western Iowa (Table 2.11), it is evident that the incidence
of speculation in the central area by the mid-1850's was considerably greater than in eastern Iowa but somewhat less than

TABLE 2.11

FARM ACREAGE AS A PERCENTAGE OF ACREAGE ASSESSED FOR TAXES BY FULL
COUNTIES OF ROYCE CESSION AREAS IN IOWA, 1850, 1856, 1859, AND 1862*

Area	1850	1856	1859	1862
Eastern..............................	58.1	55.3	55.3	57.8
(Cessions 175, 226, 244)				
Central..............................	53.3	34.7	33.0	29.3
(Cession 262)				
Western & Northern...................	15.8	22.8	34.1	17.3
(Cessions 151, 152, 153, 289)				
Entire State........................	55.9	36.8	38.8	31.5

*See Appendix IX for actual frequencies on which this table is based.

in the western counties. In 1856, 55.3 per cent of the land in private hands in eastern Iowa was in farms, 34.7 per cent in central Iowa, and only 22.8 per cent in the western and northern cession areas. In the state as a whole, the percentage of farm to taxable acreage declined steadily from 55.9 per cent in 1850 to 31.5 per cent by 1862. In sum, by 1862 approximately two-thirds of the privately owned land in Iowa was included in neither the improved nor unimproved portions of the state's farms and could only have been held for speculation.

Although this ratio may seem incredibly high, the estimates of men who were on the scene reporting from close observation seem to substantiate it. Iowa publicist William Duane Wilson, in his pamphlet *Description of Iowa, and Its Resources,* reported in 1865 that more than 5,000,000 out of 7,500,000 acres in 21 counties of central Iowa were owned by nonresidents. For the whole state, he set the figure conservatively "at not less than 15,000,000 acres," or two-fifths of the entire area.[21]

In September of 1865, at the specific request of J. M. Schaffer, secretary of the State Agricultural Society, various secretaries of county agricultural societies also estimated the amount of raw land and its value per acre held by nonresidents in their respective counties in the immediate postwar years.[22] Not all responded, but Table 2.12 contains the estimates of central Iowans who did. The figures are impressive. The secretary in Franklin County, which lies partly within Royce Cession 262, reported a startling nine-tenths of all land in the county held by nonresidents. Secretaries in Tama, Marshall, Jasper, and Jefferson all reported a ratio of one-half to two-thirds. Buchanan, Hardin, Iowa, and Story had between one-quarter and two-fifths. Only Davis, among the counties for which reports came in, had less than one-quarter of its lands held by nonresidents. Correspondents for Fayette and Ringgold vaguely recorded a "large amount" and "great portion" respectively.

The distribution of the counties reporting is not balanced. Most lie between the Skunk and Iowa rivers in the eastcentral part of the state or along the Missouri border to the south. Notwithstanding the lack of a representative sample, these figures show a surprisingly large amount of land owned by nonresidents twenty years after the land sales commenced. Most of

---

[21] *Description of Iowa,* 37–38, 45, 82; Rufus Blanchard, *Handbook of Iowa* (Chicago, 1867), 24–25, estimated 12 million acres of raw land was held by speculators. A correspondent of the Boston *Post* noted in 1857 that enough land had been bought for speculative purposes in the previous ten years "to supply immigration for the ten years next to come" (Davenport *Gazette,* Aug. 27, 1857).

[22] *Report of the Secretary of the Iowa State Agricultural Society for the Year, 1865* (Des Moines, 1866), 16.

TABLE 2.12

SPECULATION AND RAW LAND PRICE ESTIMATES OF COUNTY AGRICULTURAL
SOCIETY SECRETARIES, CENTRAL IOWA, 1865–69 *

County	Proportion of land held by nonresidents	Raw land price estimates (in dollars per acre)
Benton	....	$ 6.00
Bremer	....	5.00
Buchanan	1/3	6.00
Butler	....	2.50–10.00
Davis	1/10	....
Decatur	1/2	3.00– 4.00
Fayette	"large amount"	2.00–15.00
Franklin	9/10	2.00–10.00
Hamilton	....	3.00–10.00
Hardin	1/4	5.00
Iowa	2/5	6.00
Jasper	2/3	6.00
Jefferson	2/3	10.00
Madison	....	7.00
Marshall	1/2	4.00–20.00
Poweshiek	1/3	8.00
Ringgold	"great portion"	3.00–10.00
Story	1/3	2.50–10.00
Tama	1/2	5.00

*Compiled from annual reports of the Iowa Agricultural Society, 1865–69.
Acreage figures were transposed into fractions for Decatur, Jefferson, and Poweshiek counties.

this acreage, of course, was not in the hands of the speculators
who had purchased it originally from the national and state
governments but had passed to numerous secondary speculators.

V

IN ADDITION to estimates of speculation based on acreage totals,
there are several other ways to measure speculation using original
entry and agricultural census lists. One is to determine the percentage of original entrants who, at the time of the censuses,
were operating farms in the same county in which they entered
Congress land. Another technique is to isolate the farm operators in the census years who had never entered any public land.
In both methods, farm operators holding land under credit
arrangements are not counted as original entrants unless their
lands were entered in their own names. In the paragraphs
which follow, these techniques are applied to selected counties
of central Iowa for the census years of 1850 and 1860.

The names of farm operators in 12 counties in 1850 were
checked against the record of land entries prior to the census
enumeration. The counties selected were those which fell within an approximate checkerboard pattern imposed upon the
cession area as a sampling device. Table 2.13 contains the

TABLE 2.13

ORIGINAL ENTRANT FARM OPERATORS AS A PERCENTAGE OF TOTAL ORIGINAL
ENTRANTS IN SELECTED CENTRAL IOWA COUNTIES, 1850

County	Total original entrants as of July 31	Original entrant farm operators	Per cent
Appanoose	284	42	14.8
Benton	146	35	24.0
Blackhawk	15	2	13.3
Iowa	156	31	19.9
Keokuk	695	202	29.1
Lucas	105	13	12.4
Madison	45	12	26.7
Marion	489	176	36.0
Marshall	31	10	32.3
Polk	295	96	32.5
Poweshiek	107	35	32.7
Wapello	872	270	31.0
Totals	3,240	924	
Weighted average			28.5

results. On July 31, 1850, the percentage of original entrants who were operating farms in the county ranged from a low of 12.4 per cent in Lucas County to a high of 36.0 per cent in Marion. The weighted average for all the counties was 28.5 per cent. In other words, less than one-third of all entrants by 1850 were actually farming their land although probably a small minority were eastern farmers who had not yet immigrated to develop their land.

In the 1860 records, evidence of speculation is even more apparent. Table 2.14, comprising data from 18 counties, shows much lower percentages of original entrants who were actual farmers, ranging from 1.1 per cent in Calhoun to 28.2 per cent in Wapello County.[23] By 1860, therefore, less than one entrant in six was reported by the census marshal as a resident farmer on his land.

Two factors which bear somewhat on conclusions to be drawn from these tables are the death rate and the mobility of farm population in a frontier community. Undoubtedly, some original entrants did break sod, improve their farms, and subsequently die or sell and move on before they could be recorded in the decennial census. But removal from the census by death

---

[23] Seven of the 18 counties include data only for selected townships. The basis of selection was determined by the source materials. The federal agricultural census listed townships by name only, while the books of original entry gave only the township and range number. The *Iowa Historical and Comparative Census, 1836–1880*, Table LXXXII, 423–610, lists both, as constituted in 1880. Some township boundaries, however, had shifted frequently prior to 1880 making it impossible to connect township names with land office numbers. Hence, the only townships that could be analyzed were those whose boundaries remained unchanged after 1859. The seven partial counties included in Table 2.14 contain all 33 such townships.

TABLE 2.14

ORIGINAL ENTRANT FARM OPERATORS AS A PERCENTAGE OF TOTAL ORIGINAL
ENTRANTS IN SELECTED CENTRAL IOWA COUNTIES, 1860

County	Total original entrants as of July 31	Original entrant farm operators	Per cent
*Appanoose	138	24	17.4
Benton	2,062	224	10.9
*Blackhawk	715	65	9.1
Boone	928	125	13.5
Calhoun	563	6	1.1
Carroll	631	8	1.3
Dallas	1,440	229	15.9
Greene	1,036	44	4.2
Hardin	630	64	10.2
Keokuk	1,932	331	17.1
*Lucas	845	106	12.5
Madison	1,598	287	18.0
Marion	1,490	287	19.3
Marshall	1,354	190	14.0
*Polk	359	28	7.8
Poweshiek	1,024	77	7.5
Union	1,047	116	11.1
*Wapello	177	50	28.2
Totals	17,969	2,261	
Weighted average			12.6

*Denotes data based only on selected townships.

is of a different order than moving from the county. Those settlers who moved were in a sense speculators, taking their profits and clearing out early. There certainly was no lack of purchasers for their improved lands.

Another way of determining the extent of speculation, which indirectly eliminates the factors of mortality and mobility, is to note the percentage of census year farm operators who did not buy any of their land from the national government. In the 12 counties listed for 1850, three out of every five farm operators, on an average, bought none of their land from the federal government and more than four out of five obtained all or part of their farm land from private sources (Table 2.15). In actual numbers, of the 2,379 farm operators recorded in the 1850 census in the 12 counties, 1,455 (61.2 per cent) bought no land from the national government and an additional 401 (16.9 per cent) bought only a part of their reported farm holdings from that source.

The figures from 1860 are yet more extreme (Table 2.16). In the 18 counties analyzed, approximately seven out of every ten farmers (72.2 per cent) bought no land from the national government and an additional 13.5 per cent bought only a portion of their farm land from that source. Stated another way, less than one farmer in seven bought as much land from the federal

TABLE 2.15

NON- AND PARTIAL ORIGINAL ENTRANT FARM OPERATORS AS A PERCENTAGE OF
CENSUS YEAR FARM OPERATORS IN SELECTED CENTRAL IOWA COUNTIES, 1850

County	Farm operators	Non-original entrants	Per cent	Partial original entrants	Per cent
Appanoose	95	53	55.8	22	23.2
Benton	80	45	56.3	16	20.0
Blackhawk	9	7	77.8	...	....
Iowa	73	42	57.5	15	20.5
Keokuk	415	213	51.3	72	17.3
Lucas	38	25	65.8	8	21.1
Madison	53	41	77.4	5	9.4
Marion	343	167	48.7	82	23.9
Marshall	49	39	79.6	6	12.2
Polk	318	222	69.8	50	15.7
Poweshiek	84	49	58.3	22	26.2
Wapello	822	552	67.2	103	12.5
Totals	2,379	1,455		401	
Weighted averages			61.2		16.9

government as he reportedly was farming in 1860. In sum,
Tables 2.15 and 2.16 demonstrate that between one-half and
three-quarters of the census farmers of 1850 and 1860 in central
Iowa acquired their lands from private owners or from the state
rather than at the federal land sales. Between 80 and 90 per
cent bought at least part of their holdings from private sources,
and only slightly over 10 per cent farmed as much land as their

TABLE 2.16

NON- AND PARTIAL ORIGINAL ENTRANT FARM OPERATORS AS A PERCENTAGE OF
CENSUS YEAR FARM OPERATORS IN SELECTED CENTRAL IOWA COUNTIES, 1860

County	Farm operators	Non-original entrants	Per cent	Partial original entrants	Per cent
*Appanoose	79	55	69.6	17	21.5
Benton	997	773	77.5	121	12.1
*Blackhawk	221	156	70.6	49	22.2
Boone	401	276	68.8	77	19.2
Calhoun	20	14	70.0	5	25.0
Carroll	32	24	75.0	4	12.5
Dallas	536	307	57.3	106	19.8
Greene	147	103	70.1	17	11.6
*Hardin	211	147	69.7	43	20.4
Keokuk	1,449	1,118	77.2	119	8.2
*Lucas	281	175	62.3	44	15.7
Madison	1,059	772	72.9	131	12.4
Marion	1,445	1,158	80.1	138	9.6
Marshall	513	323	63.0	81	15.8
*Polk	107	79	73.8	17	15.9
*Poweshiek	171	94	55.0	35	20.5
Union	311	195	62.7	60	19.3
*Wapello	153	103	67.3	36	23.5
Totals	8,133	5,872		1,100	
Weighted averages			72.2		13.5

*Denotes data based only on selected townships.

original entries totaled. One can only conclude from these and all the other indices presented in this chapter that the speculator, not the national government, provided the major source of land for the frontier Iowa farmer. Certainly the commissioner of the General Land Office was incorrect when he asserted in 1859: "We have the fact shown that our whole operations, sale and locations, have generally been for actual settlement and cultivation, and not for speculation."[24]

---

[24] Commissioner of the General Land Office, *Annual Report*, 1859, 171. For a similar assertion two years previous see *ibid.*, 1857, 80. Either these officials were misinformed or their definition of speculation was not that of Horace Greeley or modern economists!

Chapter Three

SPECULATION IN STATE LANDS

T HE NATIONAL GOVERNMENT was only one of several dis-
pensers of public land in Iowa. Between 1840 and 1864
Congress donated to the state of Iowa approximately 8.5
million acres, which made up almost one-fourth of the public
domain in the state (Table 3.1). The proceeds of these land
grants were designated for financing public education, swampland drainage, and internal improvements. The latter included
projects for making the Des Moines River navigable and for encouraging railroad construction.[1]

Land subsidies to aid education were of two kinds. Some
grants Congress specifically designated for schools. These were
the sixteenth section allotments and the state university and agricultural college grants. Other donations were not originally intended to promote education but the state legislature diverted all
or part of the proceeds to that use. These were the internal improvement, saline, and five-section grants, and part of the swamp
grant.

Large investors were strongly attracted to the state-owned
lands, particularly because the state offered such liberal credit.
The disposition of these lands in central Iowa in the 1840's and
1850's, therefore, invites comparison with speculative activity
in the sale of Congress land in the same area. The six grants,

[1] Table 3.1 does not include approximately 121,000 acres reserved for
the benefit of Indians or located with Indian scrip. Background material on
the special grants in Iowa can be found in Hugh S. Buffum, "Federal and
State Aid to Education in Iowa," *Ia. J. Hist. and Pol.*, IV (Oct., 1906), 554–98,
and V (Jan., 1907), 3–45; Roscoe F. Lokken, *Iowa Public Land Disposal* (Iowa
City, 1942), chaps. v, vii–x. For general information on federal land grants
to the states, see Matthias N. Orfield, *Federal Land Grants to the States with
Special Reference to Minnesota* ("Studies in the Social Sciences, University of
Minnesota," No. 2 [Minneapolis, 1915]), 1–44; George W. Knight, "History
and Management of Land Grants for Education in the Northwest Territory
(Ohio, Indiana, Illinois, Michigan, Wisconsin)," *Am. Hist. Assn. Papers*, I, No.
3 (1885), 3–175.

TABLE 3.1

NATIONAL LAND GRANTS TO THE STATE OF IOWA

Grant	Total acreage	Total acreage in 34 major counties of Cession 262	Per cent
School Land (sixteenth section)....	1,013,824[a]	343,543[b]	33.8
Internal Improvement (500,000 acre)...............	526,640[b]	238,656[b]	45.3
University.....................	46,127[b]	44,001[b]	95.4
Saline........................	46,114[b]	45,474[b]	98.6
Five Section....................	3,200[b]	3,200[b]	100.0
Des Moines River Improvement...	1,161,513[e]	539,690[f]	46.5
Swamplands...................	1,195,833[d]	174,314[f]	14.6
Railroad......................	4,360,046[e]	538,233[f]	12.4
Agricultural College............	204,167[b]	12,980[b]	6.4
Totals....................	8,557,464	1,940,091	
Weighted average...........			22.7

[a]*Report of the Secretary of State to the Governor of Iowa, of the Transactions of the Land Department* (1905), 1–2.
[b]Compiled from tract books of the state of Iowa, Off. of the Secy. of State, Des Moines.
[e]*Report of the Department of the Interior* (1907), I, 148.
[d]*Report of the Commissioner of the General Land Office* (1921), 71.
[e]Roscoe L. Lokken, *Iowa Public Land Disposal* (Iowa City, 1942), 267.
[f]Compiled from listings in the county books of original entry.

alienated largely in this period, which will be considered are: the four that aided education (the sixteenth section, internal improvement, university, and saline lands), the Des Moines River navigation improvement lands, and the swamplands.[2] Of these grants, 1,385,678 acres (34.7 per cent) fell within the 34 counties of Royce Cession 262. Together with the other three grants—the five-section, railroad, and agricultural college—which were alienated largely after the Civil War and thus are not considered here, the state lands comprised approximately one-sixth of the total land area in central Iowa.

I

The School Land Grant. On March 3, 1845, Congress followed its usual policy when a new state prepared to enter the Union and granted the sixteenth section in each township to the future state of Iowa for establishing and maintaining common schools. Eventually the grant totaled 1,013,824 acres, one-third

[2] Tract books showing the complete disposition of these grants (except the swamplands) are located in the office of the secretary of state, Des Moines, Iowa. These typewritten books, compiled by W.P.A. teams in 1936 under the sponsorship of Mrs. Alex Miller, Iowa secretary of state (who also certified their accuracy), are the basic source for the tables in this chapter.

of which lay in the 34 counties of Cession 262. In 1847 the state lawmakers outlined legislation for the sale of this land. Apparently they were sympathetic to the desires of local residents and somewhat intimidated by the established national policy of allowing preemption rights. Their legislation provided not only for the sale of the land at public auction to the "highest and best bidder," with a minimum price of $1.25 per acre, but also allowed squatters to preempt as much as 160 acres of their claims at the appraised value, calculated by excluding the value of improvements. Terms of sale in all cases were one-fourth in cash and up to ten years' credit at 10 per cent per annum on the balance.[3]

Analysis of the land entry records indicates that speculators as well as local residents took full advantage of this liberal state land policy. The preemption right, however, gave settlers a distinct advantage. This is evident first from the relatively low price obtained for the school land in the early years, as Table 3.2 indicates. Average annual prices in the first nine years of sales climbed less than fifty cents per acre above the minimum and sometimes, as in 1850 and 1853, exceeded the minimum by only ten to fifteen cents. In 1856, however, the state legislature tightened its sales policy and thereafter prices climbed steadily from an average of $2.23 per acre in 1856 to $8.00 in the 1880's and 1890's. The overall average price in all of central Iowa was $2.80 per acre. Small buyers of a quarter section or less also were in the large majority. Of the 2,872 individual purchasers, only 368 or 12.8 per cent secured more than 160 acres. Over 87 per cent of all buyers, therefore, could have been preemptors, although this was likely not the case.

Despite the preponderance of small preemptors, larger investors did not shy away from the sixteenth sections. The 368 purchasers with more than a quarter section obtained a total of 139,611 acres, or 40.6 per cent of the entire grant acreage in central Iowa. Of this group, 61 individuals or partners secured over 500 acres; 12 had more than double that amount. The largest buyer by far was Walter B. Beebe with a whopping 4,720 acres spread over nine different counties (see Table 3.3). Beebe, of Harrison County, Ohio, not only entered over 11,500 acres of Congress land in eastern and central Iowa but he also purchased nearly 2,000 acres of the internal improvement grant in the Hawkeye State. At least two Iowa realtors were among the larg-

---

[3] Iowa *Laws*, 1847, 160–64. After January 24, 1848, all preemptors who settled on school land subsequent to the survey were required to pay an advance of 50 per cent above its appraised value (*ibid.*, 1848 [Extra Sess.], 59–60). The $1.25 minimum remained in effect until 1858 when it was doubled. In 1870, $6.00 per acre became the established minimum (Buffum, "Federal and State Aid to Education," 574–75).

est buyers, LeGrand Byington of Iowa City and John Scott of
Nevada. Given the relative scarcity of the sixteenth sections and
scattered as they are among more than 500 townships, it is noteworthy that buyers could amass such large acreages. Yet more
instructive is the fact that 110 of the major speculators in Congress land in Cession 262 were among the purchasers of school
land in the area. In addition to Beebe, Byington, and Scott,
there were such noted investors and realtors as Josiah B. Grinnell
of Poweshiek County; John A. L. Crookham of Oskaloosa;
Phineas M. Casady, Robert L. Tidrick, and Francis R. West of

TABLE 3.2

DISPOSAL OF SCHOOL LAND (SIXTEENTH SECTION) GRANT IN CENTRAL IOWA *

Year[a]	Acres sold	Per cent sold	Acres sold price given	Net sale price	Avg. price per acre[b]
1847	1,484	.4	1,484	$ 2,345	$ 1.58
1848	4,125	1.6	4,125	6,378	1.55
1849	6,753	3.6	3,560	5,744	1.61
1850	8,521	6.1	4,850	6,736	1.39
1851	10,343	9.1	6,450	9,835	1.52
1852	10,993	12.3	5,943	9,266	1.56
1853	22,638	18.9	16,828	22,774	1.35
1854	68,657	38.9	52,617	86,063	1.64
1855	30,792	47.8	19,620	33,871	1.73
1856	27,153	55.7	17,013	37,903	2.23
1857	16,905	60.7	16,745	45,653	2.73
1858	4,194	61.9	4,194	13,469	3.21
1859	1,707	62.4	1,387	3,352	2.42
1860	1,796	62.9	1,575	2,649	1.68
1861	1,490	63.3	1,410	3,964	2.81
1862	2,475	64.1	2,475	9,080	3.67
1863	3,752	65.1	3,672	12,259	3.34
1864	7,420	67.3	6,940	19,555	2.82
1865	18,780	72.8	18,780	49,884	2.66
1866	19,740	78.5	19,500	43,338	2.22
1867	10,603	81.6	10,603	34,480	3.25
1868	29,940	90.3	29,940	117,394	3.92
1869	10,992	93.5	10,992	54,138	4.93
1870–79	6,305	95.3	6,265	43,506	6.94
1880–89	12,659	99.0	12,659	101,573	8.02
1890–99	960	99.3	880	6,973	7.92
1900–27	510	99.5	330	4,040	12.24
Unpatented	1,856[c]	....	.....	.....	.....
Totals	343,543[d]		280,837	$786,222	$ 2.80

*Compiled from "School Lands, 16th Section, Tract Book (65–100), State of
Iowa."

[a]When sale dates are not given, patent dates are substituted.

[b]Obtained by dividing the net sales price by the acreage sold for which the
sale price was given.

[c]Includes 160 acres in Decatur and Tama counties described as "Mortgage
School Land."

[d]Report of the Secretary of State to the Governor of Iowa, of the Transactions of the
Land Department (1905), 1–2, gives 343,384 acres as the official amount of the
grant. The difference of 159 acres can be accounted for by the inclusion of 160
acres of "Mortgage School Lands" (see below) and the rounding of fractional
acreages.

TABLE 3.3

LARGE BUYERS (OVER 1,000 ACRES) OF SCHOOL LAND GRANT IN CENTRAL IOWA

Purchasers	Acres	Avg. price per acre	Year	County
Bayless, James L. & Dement, W. C.	1,120	$1.86	1866	Union
[a]Beebe, Walter B.	4,720	1.56	1851, 1854–56	See below[b]
Boise, Leander	1,960	1.36	1856	Guthrie
Brown, S. E. & Sully, Alfred	1,120	2.65	1868–69	Guthrie, Hardin, Jasper
[a]Byington, LeGrand	1,260	1.25[c]	1854, 1856	Lucas, Poweshiek
Eldridge, M. H.	1,760	1.85	1868	Guthrie
Given, Robert	1,440	3.75	1868	Greene, Guthrie
Granger, Henry S. & Mary J.	1,240	1.48	1866	Carroll
Hill, Robert & Jane L.	1,920	1.45	1865–67	Carroll
Kellogg, Ozro N.	1,200	1.30	1854–55, 1860	Decatur, Wayne
[a]Scott, John	1,600	2.29	1855, 1868–69	Hardin, Hamilton, Story, Webster
Wetmore, George H.	1,640	4.49	1868	Guthrie
Total acres	20,980			
Per cent of grant	6.1			

[a]Denotes large buyers of Congress land in Cession 262.

[b]Beebe purchased land in Clarke, Guthrie, Iowa, Jasper, Madison, Marshall, Polk, Tama, and Warren counties.

[c]No selling price given on some purchases.

Des Moines; John H. Leavitt of Waterloo; George Greene of Cedar Rapids; and Edward A. Temple of Chariton. Although 11 of the large speculators entered over 500 acres of school land, the total acquisitions of the group were not very extensive, totaling in fact less than 10 per cent of the grant acreage. The disposition policy, despite some exceptions, seemingly favored the local preemptor rather than the capitalist desiring an investment outlet.

The place of residence of school land buyers is not recorded in the tract index, but some non-Iowans were among the group. Beebe is the notable example. Others were John Dunn of Vernon Center, Connecticut; Thaddeus H. and Hiram W. Walker of Salem, New York; William Murray of Freeport and Abraham J. Rockafellow of Henry County, Illinois; and David N. Smith of Miami County, Ohio.[4] These few examples indicate that nonresident as well as resident speculators could surmount the handicaps of dealing with dozens of unknown county officials and invest their funds successfully.

[4] John Dunn to Cook, Sargent & Downey, Dec. 16, 1856; Thaddeus H. Walker to same, Dec. 4, 1856; John A. Clark to same, Dec. 23, 1856, Cook, Sargent & Downey Papers, State Historical Society of Iowa, Iowa City.

II

The Internal Improvement Land Grant. Beginning in the early nineteenth century the national government allotted to new states created from the public domain grants of land to aid in the development of internal improvements. On September 4, 1841, Congress standardized this practice by providing a donation of 500,000 acres of public lands to each future public land state.[5] Upon admission into the Union, Iowa also received this inheritance, but promptly diverted it from internal improvements to education.

The act of 1841 entitled Iowa officials to select from the surveyed public lands within the state's borders, not reserved or occupied by claimants, parcels of not less than 320 acres in the aggregate amount of 500,000 acres. A dispute with the national government over the meaning and intent of the law delayed the selection of the lands for a number of years.[6] Finally in 1849, shortly after the surveyors had run their lines in much of central Iowa, the state legislature named one agent in each of the three land districts then in operation (Dubuque, Fairfield, and Iowa City) to make the all-important selections. These men worked with dispatch and by 1852 the task was nearly completed.[7]

Meanwhile, on September 3, 1851, Iowa's superintendent of public instruction, Thomas H. Benton, Jr., proclaimed for sale nearly 100,000 acres of the grant, on which the commissioner of the General Land Office had given his stamp of approval. Only the legal provision that restricted sales to tracts in the organized counties prevented Benton from ordering the entire grant into market. In this, the superintendent reflected official policy which had long favored disposal of the grant as rapidly as possible. In fact, until thwarted by legal complications, the initial expectations were to sell the entire grant within the first year, 1848.[8]

The policy of rapid sales ostensibly was justified on the threefold grounds of replenishing the impoverished school fund, preventing "an undue interference with the settlement of the

[5] U.S. *Statutes at Large,* V, 455.

[6] The dispute centered on the decision of the state legislature to allow squatters to designate up to 320 acres of their preemption claims as part of the internal improvement grant, the state agreeing to sell at the Congress minimum of $1.25 per acre. The act of Congress of 1841, however, specifically provided that the land selections must be unoccupied by claimants. For correspondence in the dispute see Iowa *House Journal,* 1848 (Extra Sess.), 82–98.

[7] For the acreages selected in the various land districts see Iowa *Senate Journal,* 1850, appendix, 157; Iowa *House Journal,* 1852, appendix, 106; 1854, appendix, 242–45.

[8] "Report of the Superintendent of Public Instruction, January 14, 1848," Iowa *House Journal,* 1848 (Extra Sess.), 79. For all of the sale proclamation dates and acreages involved, see "School Lands, 500,000 Acre Grant, Part 2, Abstract," in the office of the secretary of state, Des Moines.

country," and forestalling "depredations" and "waste" on the
lands.[9] Judging, however, by the fact that dozens of prominent
Iowans later borrowed privately from the school fund on easy
terms and at rates of interest below the prevailing cost of money
in the market, the desire to create a source of easy capital may
have been a factor of equal importance in hurrying sales.[10]

Since the selections of the internal improvement grant were
made with care and at a time when much of the land in the districts was still available, they were considered more valuable, acre
for acre, than those arbitrarily located in the sixteenth sections.[11]
Despite this fact, the lands were sold on even more generous terms
than the regular school land. Buyers could gain possession with
a cash payment of only one-fifth (instead of one-fourth) of the
purchase price, with ten years to pay the balance at an interest
rate of 10 per cent per annum. More important, unlike the school
land which, barring preemptions, had first to be offered at public
auction to the "highest and best bidder," the lands in the internal
improvement grant were never offered at public sale. Buyers were
allowed to buy any quantity of unclaimed land at private entry,
"at any rate per acre which the said Superintendent of Public Instruction may determine, not less than the minimum fixed there-
on by the selecting agent." [12]

The three selecting agents, apparently intimidated by local
opinion, fixed the minimum price of all but one-tenth of the half-
million acres at the Congress minimum of $1.25 per acre. To no
avail was the protest of Superintendent Benton that the valuation was too low for such choice lands.[13] As a result, at least
in the 34 counties of Cession 262 which contained nearly half
(45.3 per cent) of the entire 500,000 acre grant, only 40,978

---

[9] Iowa *Senate Journal*, 1850, appendix, 159–61; 1852, appendix, 106.

[10] Benton expressed the hope in 1848 that the school lands would yield
close to a million dollars if sold immediately and that "this immense fund
would have been invested in the different counties at an interest of nine or
ten per cent, furnishing capital for the business operations of the country"
(Iowa *House Journal*, 1848 [Extra Sess.], 79–80). The state superintendent of
public instruction or local school fund commissioners could loan school funds
at their own discretion for as long as ten years with interest of 10 per cent
per year, "upon bond and mortgage of real estate of the clear unincumbered
value of at least twice the value of the sums thus respectively secured" (Iowa
Laws, 1851, 229). For lists of borrowers see *Report of the Auditor of State*,
1857 (Des Moines, 1858), 34–36; *Report of J. M. Beck, Agent for Investigating
the Disposition of the School Fund, During the Administration of James D.
Eads* (Des Moines, 1858), 4–31.

[11] The superintendent of public instruction reported to the legislature in
1850: "I am advised from various sources that the land selected is of the *very
best quality,* generally combining the advantages of timber, water and prairie.
In many of the selections . . . coal and plaster of Paris is found in abundance" (Iowa *Senate Journal*, 1850, appendix, 159–60).

[12] Iowa *Statutes Relating to Common Schools* (Iowa City, 1849) 28, 34–35.

[13] The final 40,000 acres, selected in 1852, were valued at from $2.00 to

acres or 16.7 per cent yielded more than $1.25 per acre. Indeed, in the first seven years of sales, 1848–54, when nearly 60 per cent (140,211 acres) of the land was sold, a mere 4,040 acres (2.9 per cent) brought more than the Congress minimum. Not until 1856 following a legislative investigation and a reappraisement of the lands yet unsold, did the average price begin a steady ascent from $1.51 per acre in 1856 to $6.76 in the 1890's (Table 3.4). The average per acre price realized for the entire grant in the Cession 262 counties was only $1.82 compared with $2.80 for school land. The sale prices of the land in the internal improvement grant therefore reflected the actual productive value of the land even less than did the sixteenth sections.

That the lax sales policy encouraged speculation is indicated by an analysis of the tract book. Of the 1,931 individuals obtaining land in central Iowa under the 500,000 acre grant, 338 (17.4 per cent) purchased more than a quarter section, their entries totaling 110,291 acres or 46.2 per cent of the grant acreage in the cession area. Nearly half of the choice grant lands, therefore, went to buyers in quantities larger than the quarter section considered maximum for efficient agricultural use. Comparison of the names on the sale certificates with those on the patents further confirms the speculative nature of these entries. Fully one-half were patented to individuals other than the original entrant; that is, the land had been alienated before the patent issued—a process that normally required several years. Of the 64,391 acres for which both the name of the purchaser and patentee is recorded, the governor signed patents for 31,992 acres or 49.7 per cent in the name of individuals who had not been initial entrants. In short, buyers entered the internal improvement grant as much for speculation as for agriculture.

Isolating the very largest entrants further illustrates this fact. Thirty-seven individuals secured over 500 acres (Table 3.5), accounting for 12.8 per cent of the grant in the central counties.

$3.00 per acre (Iowa *House Journal*, 1854, appendix, 242–45). For Benton's views see Iowa *Senate Journal*, 1850, appendix, 159. Interestingly enough, Ohio's internal improvement grant had also been sold indiscriminately and in unlimited quantities at the same price ($1.25 per acre), due to the insistence of the governor who wanted to follow Congressional precedent. To charge more, the governor had warned, would discourage purchasers, divert immigration, and impede development of the districts where the lands lay (Harry N. Scheiber, "State Policy and the Public Domain: The Ohio Canal Lands," *J. Econ. Hist.*, XXV [Mar., 1965], 91). Kansas and Wisconsin similarly offered their half-million acres hastily and at the Congress minimum, according to Thomas LeDuc, "State Administration of the Land Grant to Kansas for Internal Improvements," *Kan. Hist. Quart.*, XX (Nov., 1953), 548–51, and Joseph Schafer, "Wisconsin's Farm Loan Law, 1849–1863," *Wisc. St. Hist. Soc. Publ.* (1920), 179.

TABLE 3.4

DISPOSAL OF THE INTERNAL IMPROVEMENT (500,000 ACRE) LAND GRANT IN
CENTRAL IOWA *

Year	Acres sold	Per cent sold	Acres sold price given	Net sale price	Avg. price per acre[a]
1848	3,890[b]	1.6	3,804	$ 5,030	$1.32
1849	1,892[b]	2.4	.....	.....	....
1850	2,348[b]	3.4	.....	.....	....
1851	3,781[b]	5.0	2,781	3,476	1.25
1852	21,405	14.0	11,686	14,683	1.26
1853	33,020	27.8	22,936	28,832	1.26
1854	73,875	58.7	42,082	55,119	1.31
1855	26,521	69.9	4,993	6,910	1.38
1856	18,039	77.4	2,825	4,258	1.51
1857	12,832	82.8	12,072	35,448	2.94
1858	14,504	88.9	14,324	34,891	2.44
1859	1,060	89.3	740	1,550	2.09
1860	1,661	90.0	1,541	2,976	1.93
1861	1,275	90.6	855	1,216	1.42
1862	787	90.9	747	934	1.25
1863	1,649	91.2	1,498	2,844	1.90
1864	2,204	92.2	2,204	3,653	1.66
1865	5,275	94.4	5,195	14,025	2.70
1866	2,402	95.4	2,402	8,207	3.42
1867	1,460	96.0	1,460	3,366	2.31
1868	2,149	96.9	2,149	6,726	3.13
1869	760	97.2	760	1,533	2.02
1870–79	1,261	97.7	1,221	6,628	5.43
1880–89	1,040	98.2	1,000	4,715	4.72
1890–99	1,241	98.7	1,241	8,395	6.76
1900–25	360	98.8	160	250	1.56
Undated	1,965[c]	....	....	.....	....
Totals	238,656[d]		140,676	$255,665	$1.82

*Compiled from "School Lands, 500,000 Acre Grant, Tract Book, Part I,
State of Iowa."

[a]Obtained by dividing the net sale price by the acreage sold for which the
sale price was given.

[b]Totals in most cases are patent dates; sale dates are not given.

[c]Includes 440 acres in Decatur and Madison counties described as "Mortgage
School Land."

[d]*Report of the Secretary of State to the Governor of Iowa, of the Transactions of the
Land Department*(1905), 4, gives 248,905 total acres as the official amount of
the grant. Of the difference of 10,249 acres, all but 460 acres can be accounted
for by the fact that the Hamilton and Webster county totals in the official *Report*
include 10,709 acres known as "Des Moines River School Lands."

Ozro N. Kellogg led all buyers with 1,966 acres in the extreme
southcentral counties of Decatur and Wayne where the large buyers seemingly concentrated their attention. Kellogg was followed
closely by Francis R. West and Benjamin F. Allen, Des Moines
bankers and realtors, with 1,960 and 1,560 acres respectively; and
by the 1,907 acres of Walter B. Beebe of Ohio, one of the large
school land investors cited in the previous discussion. Nine of
the largest entrants (denoted in the table by an asterisk) were
also among those entering more than a thousand acres of Congress

TABLE 3.5

LARGE BUYERS (OVER 500 ACRES) OF THE INTERNAL IMPROVEMENT GRANT IN
CENTRAL IOWA

Purchasers	Acres	Avg. price per acre	Year	County
*Allen, Benjamin F........	1,560	$1.25	1853	Madison
Bacon, William..........	563	1.25 †	1853–54, 1864	Clarke, Union
*Beebe, Walter B..........	1,907	1.25	1855	Clarke, Union
Blodgett, Miron..........	620	1.25 †	1854, 1856	Tama
Bone, John..............	671	....	1851–52	Monroe
Boone, Wm. D..........	767	1.25 †	1852–53, 1857	Dallas
Butterworth, Hiram......	520	1.33 †	1854, 1856	Hamilton, Webster
Buttles, Joel B...........	800	3.93	1857	Poweshiek
*Byington, LeGrand.......	992	1.25	1853	Tama
Caney, Charles..........	520	1.25	1854	Clarke
Clark, Libbeus..........	778	....	1855	Decatur
Duncan, Harvey B........	1,086	1.25 †	1854–55, 1857	Decatur, Wayne
Duncan, Thomas H. P....	845	1.25 †	1854–55	Wayne
Dunlavey, Harvey........	640	1.25	1854	Decatur
Emery, Jesse............	620	1.25 †	1853–54, 1864	Clarke
Fisher, Richard..........	520	1.50 †	1853–54	Wapello, Webster
Graves, Elijah M.........	985	3.35	1857	Poweshiek
*Grinnell, Josiah B.......	839	2.51	1857, 1867	Poweshiek
Gwinn, Ephraim J........	644	....	1854	Wayne
Hawley, George A........	720	1.25	1854	Decatur
*Judd, Eli P..............	678	4.48	1857	Poweshiek
Kellogg, O. A...........	571	1.39	1854, 1856	Decatur
Kellogg, Ozro N.........	1,966	1.25	1851, 1854–55	Decatur, Wayne
Kelly, Joseph...........	640	4.10	1857	Poweshiek
Logan, John E...........	543	1.25 †	1854–55	Decatur, Wayne
*Mc Mullen, Thomas......	818	1.25 †	1853	Dallas, Polk
*Moore, Thos. and Stevens, A. J...........	1,190	1.25 †	1853–54	Dallas
Notson, Henry B.........	760	1.25	1852–54	Decatur
Sleeper, Isaiah H........	760	....	1853, 1856	Mahaska
Stephen, Andrew O.......	600	1.36 †	1852, 1862	Benton, Iowa
Stoner, John E...........	560	2.50	1858	Iowa
Thornton, Isaac..........	560	1.25 †	1852, 1856	Dallas
*Voris, Geroge W.........	870	1.25	1851–52	Marshall
West, Francis R..........	1,960	1.25	1853, 1860	Madison, Warren
*West, William B.........	640	2.09 †	1853, 1854, 1856	Clarke, Decatur
Young, John L...........	880	....	1853	Decatur
Total acres	30,593			
Per cent of grant	12.8			

*Denotes large buyers of Congress land in Cession 262.
†No selling price given on some purchases.

land in Cession 262. These nine were joined by another 70 of
their fellow speculators in the cession area who entered lesser
amounts of the grant acreage. Together, the speculators in Congress land purchased over 30,000 acres of the 500,000 acre grant
in central Iowa. Included in addition to Kellogg, Beebe, West,
and Allen, were such prominent real estate dealers as LeGrand
Byington of Iowa City, Andrew J. Stevens and Thomas McMul-
len of Des Moines, George W. Howe of Osceola, and Jesse Williams of Fairfield. At least six of the entrants were nonresident
speculators: these were Beebe of Ohio; Sanford Allen of Bath

County, Kentucky; John M. Gates of Switzerland, Indiana; George W. Lyttle of Fulton County, Illinois; David N. Smith of Miami County, Ohio; and William B. West of Kane County, Illinois. Thus, as in states to the east such as Ohio, the role of the speculator, both resident and nonresident, was an important one in the disposal of the internal improvement land grant.[14]

III

The University Land Grant. In July, 1840, Congress granted two townships of land (approximately 72 sections) to the territory of Iowa to aid in fianancing a future university in the state.[15] The land was to be selected by agents of the United States Secretary of the Treasury, but the several agents, named as early as 1840, procrastinated in making their selections. As late as 1849, only three sections (about 1,920 acres) had been designated. Finally in 1849 the first diligent agent, John W. Whitaker of Van Buren County, selected 35,603.30 acres, all but 1,725 in Royce Cession 262.[16] Meanwhile, the University of Iowa was founded in 1847 and located in Iowa City.

The board of trustees of the university determined the sales policy of their grant. Intending not to sacrifice their lands at the Congress minimum, the trustees wisely decided to ban all pre-emptions. Instead, they provided that the lands must be sold at public sale at the state capital for a sum not less than their appraised value. The minimum appraisement was $5.00 per acre. Terms of sale were identical to those of the school land— one-fourth in cash and the balance within ten years at 10 per cent interest per annum.[17]

The first sale was held on November 1, 1851. Despite extensive advertising and the advantageous central location for the auctions, only two bidders purchased any land, and that a mere 645 acres. Undaunted, the trustees raised the minimum price to $10.00 per acre.[18] During 1852 and 1853 only two 40-acre tracts were sold, as Table 3.6 indicates. Squatters meanwhile demanded

---

[14] In the two-year span (1835–36), of 123,000 acres sold of the Ohio Canal Lands (500,000-acre grant), five individuals and one land company obtained one-fifth of the amount (Scheiber, "Ohio Canal Lands," 93–94). In Wisconsin, speculators acquired at least 50 per cent of the half-million acres, concluded Joseph Schafer ("Wisconsin's Farm Loan Law," 182).

[15] U.S. *Statutes at Large*, VI, 810.

[16] Vernon Carstensen, 'The State University of Iowa: The Collegiate Department From the Beginning to 1878" (Ph.D. dissertation, State University of Iowa, 1936), 16–29; Iowa *Senate Journal*, 1850, appendix, 142.

[17] Iowa *House Journal*, 1852, appendix, 89. For a copy of the minutes of the meeting of the board of trustees on June 27, 1851, see Andrew *Western Democrat*, July 16, 1851.

[18] Iowa *House Journal*, 1852, appendix, 89–90.

TABLE 3.6
Disposal of the University Land Grant*

Year	Acres sold	Per cent sold	Total appraised value	Avg. appraised value per acre	Net sale price	Avg. price per acre
1851	645.16	1.4	......	....	$ 3,261.00	$ 5.05
1852	40.00	1.5	$ 200.00	$ 5.00	200.00	5.00
1853	40.00	1.6	400.00	10.00	400.00	10.00
1854	16,572.91	37.5	47,858.66	2.89	50,869.65	3.07
1855	20,289.69	81.5	63,134.44	3.11	71,200.26	3.51
1856	160.00	81.8	260.00	1.63	434.00	2.71
1863	1,200.00	84.4	6,160.00	5.13	7,550.00	6.29
1864	2,589.38	90.0	15,001.83	5.79	16,168.11	6.24
1865	841.92	91.9	7,055.36	8.38	8,175.36	9.71
1866	1,208.27	94.5	6,559.26	5.43	7,211.57	5.97
1867	776.82	96.2	3,633.41	4.68	4,168.59	5.37
1868	960.00	98.3	5,220.00	5.44	6,038.00	6.29
1873	40.00	98.3	......	....	....	....
1875	160.00	98.7	1,280.00	8.00	2,400.00	15.00
1888	240.00	99.2	900.00	3.75	1,000.00	4.17
1889	83.26	99.4	269.58	3.22	253.14[a]	3.02
1890	200.00	99.8	560.00	2.80	570.00	2.85
1891	40.00	99.9	80.00	2.00	200.00	5.00
1893	40.00	....	80.00	2.00	160.00	4.00
Totals	46,127.41[b]		$158,052.54	$3.44	$180,259.68	$ 3.91

*Compiled from "University & Saline Lands, Tract Book, State of Iowa."
[a]Probably erroneous since the sale price is less than the appraised price.
[b]Report of the Secretary of State to the Governor of Iowa, of the Transactions of the Land Department (1905), 7, gives the total acreage as 45,928.96.

their "right" to buy university land at the government minimum of $1.25 per acre. The board finally buckled under pressure from both the settlers and the state legislature and in early January, 1854, allowed preemptors to buy 2,280 acres at the double minimum price of $2.50 per acre.[19]

Spurred by the General Assembly the board also reduced the appraised value on the remainder of the land from $10.00 to between $3.00 and $4.00 an acre and staged more frequent public auctions.[20] Buyers were quick to take advantage of the policy changes. During the next two years, 1854 and 1855, over 80 per cent of the entire grant was sold at an average price of about $3.30 per acre.[21] The major sale was at Iowa City from

[19] Carstensen, "University of Iowa," 31.

[20] Iowa Laws, 1855, 200–201; Carstensen, "University of Iowa," 33, 432.

[21] The 9,793 acres sold at public auction in 1854 were appraised at $3.64 per acre and returned a price of $3.72 per acre. By January 15, 1855, 18,651 acres had been sold at an average price of $3.34 per acre. This included the preempted acreage sold at $2.50 per acre. See Iowa House Journal, 1854, appendix, 218–19. The price Iowa received for its university land ($3.91 per acre) was three times as much as the neighboring state of Illinois received on its 46,080 acres and twenty cents per acre above Wisconsin's average on 92,160 acres (Knight, "Land Grants for Education," 172).

TABLE 3.7
LARGE BUYERS (OVER 500 ACRES) OF UNIVERSITY LAND GRANT

Purchaser	Acres	Avg. price per acre	Year
*Benson, John................	800	$4.08	1854
*Connelly, Edward............	2,200	3.23	1855
*Downey, Hugh D.............	1,298	3.64	1855
*Gower, James H.............	2,265	3.22	1855
Gower, Robert H. & Alexander.................	1,076	2.52	1855–56
*Hart, Anson.................	2,010	2.78	1855
Kellogg, C. L................	720	2.17	1855
Lathrop, Henry W...........	1,992	3.36	1855
*Morsman, Moses J...........	2,231	3.31	1855
Ross, M. M. & T. J..........	654	2.48	1864
Sanderson, Luther F.........	520	2.51	1854
Total...................	15,766	$3.12	
Per cent of grant..........	34.2		

*Denotes large buyers of Congress land in Cession 262.

June 14 to 18, 1855, when 18,500 acres were sold. Of this amount six trustees of the university purchased over 11,000 acres at an average price of $3.00 per acre.[22] Interestingly enough, four of the six men—James H. Gower, Moses J. Morsman, Hugh D. Downey, and Edward Connelly—were prominent speculators in Congress land in Iowa. Gower, Downey, and Connelly, in fact, were land agents in the university town.[23] But the six trustees were only part of a larger group of heavy investors. Forty-eight buyers (16.5 per cent of all purchasers) secured more than a quarter section from the board of trustees, ranging from Edward A. Temple's 168 acres to James H. Gower's 2,265 acres. Together these few individuals accumulated 26,421 acres, 57.3 per cent of the entire grant.

More strikingly, as few as 11 men acquired 15,766 acres or over one-third (34.2 per cent) of the acreage in the grant, as Table 3.7 shows. Their selections, made mainly in 1854 and 1855, ranged over all the counties included in the grant (except Iowa County which had only 647 acres). Federal land entry records show that 6 of the 11 buyers (denoted by an asterisk) also entered over 1,000 acres of Congress land in central Iowa. In addition to these 6, the names of 24 other large speculators in Cession 262

[22] Compiled from the "University & Saline Lands, Tract Book, State of Iowa." Carstensen ("University of Iowa," 33) also gives these figures, citing *Minutes of the Board of Trustees,* Book A, 67–69.

[23] Although some have charged these men with fraud, Carstensen feels that they can at most be charged with a failure to use due discretion, as the Iowa legislature had reappraised the lands prior to the 1855 sales at an average price of $2.50. The board member-speculators had paid an average of $3.00 per acre on their purchases or 50 cents per acre above appraised value. But Carstensen also notes that they paid proportionately *less* above the appraised price than did other buyers ("University of Iowa," 42).

appeared in the tract book of the university lands. Together these
30 investors acquired 14,872 acres, or almost one-third of the
university grant. At least a few of the buyers were nonresidents.
Crawford Baker of Freeport, Illinois, paid $3.73 per acre for 240
acres in Hardin County in 1854 and 1855 and Lipman Mayer of
Saline County, Missouri, bought 360 acres in Polk County for
$3.00 per acre in 1854.[24]

IV

The Saline Land Grant. Beginning in 1802 with the admission
of Ohio to the Union, new public land states received title to
their salt springs and certain adjacent lands. Bound by precedent, Congress usually donated twelve salt springs with six sections of land adjoining each. Accordingly, on March 3, 1845,
as part of the supplemental enabling act granting statehood to
Iowa, the state received her 72-section allotment.[25] All of the
land lay in six counties of central Iowa except for one section in
Van Buren County.

     Until May 27, 1852, the national government allowed the
state of Iowa to lease *but not sell* these lands. On that date, after
a petition from the Iowa General Assembly, Congress granted the
lands to the state in fee simple. The legislature in early 1853
authorized the sale of all of the approved lands "by the same
officer, and under the same regulations" as the school land.[26]
The proceeds were designated first for a "lunatic asylum" but
ultimately were diverted into the school fund of the state. Thus,
the saline land, like the internal improvement grant, financed
Iowa schools although that was not the original intention of the
congressional donation.

     It was 1853 before the legal questions and administrative
problems were solved and a part of the lands were thrown open
for sale. In that first year (see Table 3.8), buyers acquired over
11,500 acres or 25 per cent of the grant at an average price per
acre of $1.30. By the end of 1854, 60 per cent of the land that
had been offered was alienated. The remainder went on the
block in 1855. Sales continued brisk and by 1860, 80 per cent
of the saline lands were in private hands. Thereafter, annual
sales dwindled, continuing into the twentieth century. The
average sale price per acre for the entire grant was $2.16 per
acre.

     [24] See John A. Clark to Cook, Sargent & Downey, Dec. 23, 1856; L. & W.
Mayer to same, Dec. 28, 1855, Cook, Sargent & Downey Papers.
     [25] Lokken, *Iowa Public Land Disposal,* 176–77; U. S. *Statutes at Large,*
V, 790.
     [26] Iowa *Laws,* 1851, 246; 1853, 126–27; U.S. *Statutes at Large,* X, 7.

TABLE 3.8
DISPOSAL OF THE SALINE LAND GRANT*

Year	Acres sold	Per cent sold	Acres sold price given	Net sale price	Avg. price per acre†
1850	120.00	.3	120.00	$ 150.00	$1.25
1853	11,507.09	25.2	10,147.09	13,155.92	1.30
1854	16,099.36	60.1	11,779.36	14,726.20	1.25
1855	920.00	62.1	920.00	1,250.00	1.36
1856	4,201.29	71.2	400.00	709.60	1.77
1857	120.00	71.5	120.00	150.00	1.25
1858	160.00	71.8	160.00	201.68	1.26
1860	3,574.74	79.6	3,574.74	4,691.85	1.31
1861	40.00	79.7	40.00	150.00	3.75
1862	240.00	80.2	240.00	300.00	1.25
1863	1,260.00	82.9	1,140.00	1,425.00	1.25
1864	945.31	85.0	945.31	1,881.65	1.99
1865	920.00	87.0	920.00	1,590.00	1.73
1866	680.00	88.4	680.00	1,280.00	1.88
1867	240.00	89.0	240.00	550.00	2.29
1868	320.00	89.7	320.00	1,160.00	3.62
1869	85.69	89.8	45.69	57.11	1.25
1870–79	1,273.52	92.6	1,113.52	5,617.70	5.04
1880–89	1,711.22	96.3	1,351.22	7,365.42	5.45
1890–99	160.00	96.7	120.00	550.00	4.58
1900–48	1,055.69	99.0	815.68	18,878.50	23.14
Unpatented	480.00		. . . . . .	. . . . . .	. . . . .
Totals	46,113.91		35,192.61	$75,840.63	$2.16

*Compiled from "University and Saline Lands, Tract Book, State of Iowa," Office of the Secretary of State, Des Moines. The above total is 88.63 acres less than the total cited in *Report of the Register of the State Land Office* (1871), 13.
†Obtained by dividing receipts by acreage sold for which the price was given.

Concentration of ownership among the purchasers of the grant again indicates considerable speculative activity. Of the 374 individual buyers, 68 (18.2 per cent) acquired more than a quarter section, their entries totaling 23,384 acres or over half (51.2 per cent) of the total grant area. Eight of the 68 large buyers, listed in Table 3.9, entered over 500 acres each, for a

TABLE 3.9
LARGE BUYERS (OVER 500 ACRES) OF SALINE LAND GRANT

Purchaser	Acres	Avg. price per acre	Year	County
*Byington, LeGrand.	600†	$1.25	1856	Lucas
*Crow, Wayman.	1,200	. . . .	1853	Lucas
Francis, Silas J.	520	1.25	1853	Lucas
*Myers, Jacob.	600	2.25	1856	Lucas
Palmer, Oliver L.	600	. . . .	1856	Lucas
Ragsdale, Amos.	560	1.25	1853–54	Lucas
*Smith, David N.	1,945	1.25	1854	Lucas
Waynick, Peter.	560†	1.25	1853–54	Lucas
Total.	6,585†	$1.40		
Per cent of grant.	14.3			

*Denotes large buyers of Congress land in Cession 262.
†No selling price given on some purchases.

total of 6,585 acres or 14.3 per cent of the land. David N. Smith of Ohio and Wayman Crow of St. Louis paced the group with entries of 1,945 and 1,200 acres respectively. These two men alone acquired nearly 7 per cent of the entire grant. Smith and Crow were also active speculators in Congress land in central Iowa, entering over 11,000 acres. These men were not alone among the large speculators in the public domain who acquired saline land. Thirty-four others, led by LeGrand Byington and Jacob Myers, joined them to purchase 9,182 acres of saline land or fully one-fifth (20.2 per cent) of the grant acreage.

V

The Des Moines River Navigation Improvement Grant. Incessant local demands for navigation improvements on the Des Moines River, together with a widespread belief that a simple system of locks and dams could make the river completely navigable up to the Raccoon Forks in Polk County, finally induced Congress in 1846 to donate to the territory of Iowa alternate sections within five miles of the river to finance a construction program.[27] Although it was generally assumed at the time that the grant stretched only to the Raccoon Forks—the extent of the river specified for navigational improvement—Iowa officials soon argued that Congress had intended the donation to include land along the entire length of the river to the Minnesota border. The state eventually won its claim to the disputed northern area but not before many years of dispute and much litigation.[28]

Construction on the improvement project, meanwhile, began in 1848 under a board of public works. But the board made only halting progress and finally in 1854, the discouraged state legislature contracted with a New York firm, the Desmoines Navigation & Rail Road Company, to complete the enterprise in exchange for all of the grant lands not sold by December 23, 1853—the date when all sales were suspended pending the negotiation of the contract.[29] Wisconsin and Michigan had previously made such

---

[27] U.S. *Statutes at Large,* IX, 77–78.

[28] See Lokken, *Iowa Public Land Disposal,* 210–35; Leonard F. Ralston, "Iowa Railroads and the Des Moines River Improvement Land Grant of 1846," *Ia. J. Hist.,* LVI (Apr., 1958), 97–128; Jacob A. Swisher, "The Des Moines River Improvement Project," *ibid.,* XXXV (Apr., 1937), 142–80.

[29] *Report of the Register of the State Land Office,* 1865, 36, 39, 44. For a copy of the contract see Iowa *House Journal,* 1854, appendix, 39–47. See also the letter of J. Brown, Land Commissioner of the D.N. & R.R. Co. to Gov. Ralph P. Lowe, Mar. 27, 1858, in "Governor's File, Correspondence" (hereafter cited as G.F. Corr.) Des Moines River Grant, Fold. 1, Iowa State Department of History and Archives, Des Moines.

agreements with New York capitalists like Erastus Corning, and it was hoped that a similar step would benefit Iowa.[30] The company proceeded for awhile with the project and in return received title to 266,108 acres, but its work was felt by many to be slow and unsatisfactory.[31] In 1858 the state lawmakers declared the contract forfeited and turned over the remainder of the grant to an Iowa railroad company. Thus, the dreams of local promoters to make the Des Moines River the central highway of the state were dashed, but the iron horse with its tracks paralleling the river more than compensated for the loss.

The location of the Des Moines River grant within Cession 262 is shown graphically on Figure 3.1.[32] Settlers occupied and claimed over two-thirds of the grant area south and east of the Raccoon Forks by the time Congress made the donation. Supposedly to avoid doing an injustice to these squatters and to prevent the lands "from falling into the hands of speculators, whose only design would be to hold them in reserve for speculation," the legislature allowed all claimants who were on their land before the first of January, 1847, to buy it at the Congress minimum of $1.25 per acre. This preemption privilege, however (which also included the usual year of grace for "proving up" claims), was later extended to all who filed claims on river grant land prior to February 9, 1853—a decision hardly justifiable on the pretext of protecting early squatters.[33] Since the original law of 1847 was silent on the maximum preemption allowed, the board allowed up to 320 acres, double the usual amount under

---

[30] Irene D. Neu, *Erastus Corning: Merchant and Financier, 1794–1872* (Ithaca, 1960), chap. ix.

[31] The contract with the state proved to be most advantageous for the company. An investigating committee of the Iowa legislature appraised the lands at $6.00 to $7.00 at the time (Iowa *House Journal,* 1856, 576–77). Indeed, analysis of Boone County "Deed Record Book 3D," located in the office of the county recorder at Boone, showed that the company sold 7,985 acres of its holdings in that county in 1858 at prices ranging between $5.80 and $11.25 per acre, with the average being $7.81 per acre. For company circulars advertising the land offering, see Bloomfield *True Flag,* Nov. 17, 1855; Vernon *Democratic Mirror,* May 30, 1856, Nov. 27, 1857. Pennsylvanian James Murray Clark, who purchased river land north of the Forks from the company, noted that its lands "were resold at *high* and *advanced* prices" (Clark to Gov. Wm. Stone, Nov. 23, 1863, G.F. Corr., Des Moines River Grant, Fold. 3). The company reportedly sold its Polk County river land at $6.00 per acre, one-fourth cash down, the balance within nine years at 8 per cent interest per annum (Peter Shepps to Lowe, Jan. 1, 1858, *ibid.,* Fold. 1). See also Charles E. Snyder, "Curtis Bates," *Ia. J. Hist. and Pol.* XLIV (July, 1946), 304.

[32] From Raleigh Barlowe and Conrad H. Hammar, "Valuation of Lands in Southcentral Iowa: 1839–1843: Royce Cession Area 262," presented before the Indian Claims Commission, Doc. 153, *Sac and Fox and Iowa Tribes v. the United States of America* (1965), 122.

[33] Iowa *House Journal,* 1846, 18; "Report of the Board of Public Works, December 2, 1850," Iowa *Senate Journal,* 1850, appendix, 55; Iowa *Laws,* 1847, 168–69; 1848, 40; 1853, 163.

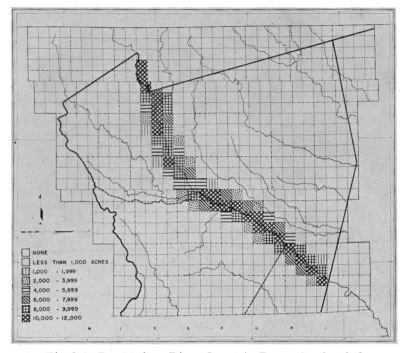

NONE
LESS THAN 1,000 ACRES
1,000 - 1,999
2,000 - 3,999
4,000 - 5,999
6,000 - 7,999
8,000 - 9,999
10,000 - 12,000

Fig. 3.1. Des Moines River Grant in Royce Cession 262.

federal law. None would want more than that, declared the board secretary with tongue in cheek, unless one wished to gain the "obnoxious . . . title of 'land speculator.'" In 1848, the legislature legalized the 320-acre maximum—which itself allowed for small-scale speculation—and only reduced it to a quarter section in 1853 after most of the grant south of the Forks was sold.[34]

Congress in its initial act of August 8, 1846, geared land sales to the rate at which funds were disbursed for actual construction of the improvement. Initially, only $30,000 worth of land could be sold. Thereafter with each $15,000 expended, the state could sell the equivalent amount of land.[35] Because of delays in the improvement program, this stipulation undoubtedly retarded sales. As Table 3.10 shows, between October 11, 1847, and December 23, 1853 (when all sales were permanently suspended), the register of the board was able to sell only about 328,000 acres. Of this amount almost 59,000 acres were located above the Raccoon Forks, mainly in Polk, Boone, and Webster counties. The

[34] Iowa *House Journal,* 1848, 68, 70; Iowa *Laws,* 1848 (Extra Sess.), 39: 1853, 64, 163.
[35] U.S. *Statutes at Large,* IX, 77–78.

Fig. 3.2. Original patent from the State of Iowa to Henry H. and Wopke H. De Haan, Marion County, under the Des Moines River Improvement Land Grant.

THE STATE OF IOWA.

No. 3405

TO ALL TO WHOM THESE PRESENTS SHALL COME, GREETING:

KNOW YE, That, whereas, the United States of America, by Act of Congress, approved August 8th, 1846, entitled "An act granting certain lands to the Territory of Iowa, to aid in the improvement of the navigation of the Desmoines River, in said Territory," has granted to the State of Iowa "One equal moiety in alternate sections of the public lands remaining unsold, and not otherwise disposed of, encumbered or appropriated, in a strip five miles in width, on each side of said river: And, whereas, H. H. & M. H. De Haan of the County of Marion and State of Iowa has, on the 13th day of April 1855, purchased of the Register of the Des Moines River Land Office in Ottumwa under the provisions of the several Acts of the General Assembly of the State of Iowa, the North West quarter of the North East quarter of Section No. Thirty five Township No. Seventy Seven N. of Range No. Nineteen West of the 5th Principal Meridian, containing Forty Acres, being a part of the grant aforesaid. And it appearing that the said H. H. & M. H. De Haan has made payment thereof in full, as required by law: **NOW, KNOW YE,** That in consideration of the premises, and in conformity with the several acts of the General Assembly of the State of Iowa, and of all acts in such case made and provided, **the State of Iowa hath given,** and by these presents **does give and grant** unto the said H. H. & M. H. De Haan his heirs and assigns, the land above described, **to have and to hold the same,** together with all the rights, privileges, immunities and appurtenances, of whatever nature thereunto belonging, unto the said H. H. & M. H. De Haan

IN TESTIMONY WHEREOF, I, Stephen Hempstead Governor of the State of Iowa, have caused the Great Seal of the State of Iowa to be hereto affixed.

GIVEN UNDER MY HAND, at Iowa City, this First day of June in the year of our Lord, one thousand, eight hundred and Fifty four and of the State of Iowa the Eighth.

S. Hempstead

Geo. W. McCleary Secretary of State.

This is to Certify, that the foregoing DEED was received from the Governor, July 10 1855 and was recorded in DES MOINES RIVER RECORDS, Book F, Page 309 July 15 1855.

T. S. Parvin Register of the D. M. R. L. O.

TABLE 3.10
DISPOSAL OF DES MOINES RIVER LAND GRANT, 1847–53*

Year	Acres sold at $1.25	Acres sold at $1.30	Acres sold at $2.00	Acres sold at $3.00
1847 (from Oct. 11).......	6,959.99	.....	......	.....
1848....................	35,856.77	.....	120.00	.....
1849....................	68,426.59	40.00	40.00	.....
1850....................	65,779.86	.....	......	.....
1851....................	28,393.79	.....	......	.....
1852....................	35,059.72	.....	440.00	80.00
1853 (to Dec. 23).........	86,199.76	.....	478.21	.....
Totals..............	326,676.48	40.00	1,078.21	80.00
Grand total.........	327,874.69			

*Compiled from monthly sale figures in "Report of Investigating Committee of Iowa Legislature," submitted June 14, 1853, reprinted in Iowa *House Journal*, 1854, appendix, 282, 512–17, and financial statement of the register of the Des Moines River Improvement, Nov. 30, 1854, in *ibid.*, appendix, 37.

remaining 269,000 acres embraced 84 per cent of the total grant of 321,000 acres lying below the Forks.[36] The average sale price of the 328,000 acres was only four mills above the Congress minimum.[37]

An average sale price so close to the legal minimum for valuable Des Moines River frontage and rich alluvial lands adjacent to it would seem to indicate that all entrants were preemptors. While many were, analysis of the tract book shows that individuals who could not have been preemptors were also prominent among the purchasers. Two counties in southcentral Iowa, Wapello and Marion, containing together 161,061 acres or one-half of the entire grant area south of the Forks, were chosen for detailed study. In Wapello, 17 buyers acquired more than 320 acres accounting in the aggregate for 10,237 acres or 15.7 per cent of the total grant area. In Marion, 26 buyers entered more than a half section, covering 15,121 acres or nearly one-quarter (22.0 per cent) of the grant. Table 3.11 contains the names of 15 of these large buyers whose combined entries in the two counties exceeded 500 acres. State Senator Jairus E. Neal and Henry P. Scholte, leader of the Dutch immigrant colony at Pella, head

[36] *Report of the Register of the State Land Office*, 1865, 39, 44. A typed copy of the General Land Office list of August 8, 1848, describing all lands below the Raccoon Forks is in "Miscellaneous Conveyances from the United States to the State of Iowa, Vol. 'A', State of Iowa," 90–107, office of the secretary of state, Des Moines. The exact total given is 321,028.03 acres, but see Iowa *Senate Journal*, 1850, 43, and Iowa *House Journal*, 1864, 172.

[37] Other midwestern states sold their donation lands adjoining internal improvements at considerably higher prices and without allowing preemption rights. The lowest grade of Wabash and Erie canal lands in Indiana was priced at $3.50 per acre. Illinois canal lands were sold at auction in August, 1847, at appraised values ranging from $7.00 to $20.00 per acre. Ohio canal lands remaining unsold at the time were similarly appraised at $2.50 to $10.00 per acre. See Iowa *House Journal*, 1848, 85–86.

TABLE 3.11

LARGE BUYERS (OVER 500 ACRES) OF DES MOINES RIVER LAND GRANT,
MARION AND WAPELLO COUNTIES *

Purchaser	Acres	Year	County
Allison, George..........	600	1850	Marion
Ames, Pleasant, Sr.......	560	1851–52	Marion
Brand, Calvin W.........	525	1849, 1853	Marion
†Cowles, Chester W......	694	1850–51	Marion
DeHaan, Jacob..........	620	1849–51, 1853	Marion
†Howe, George W........	659	1850–51, 1853	Marion
Inskeep, David P........	558	1849	Wapello
McCune, Charles T......	599	1851	Wapello
Manning, Edwin........	1,993	1850–51	Marion & Wapello
Meek, Robert...........	1,926	1851	Marion & Wapello
†Neal, Jairus E...........	2,730	1851–53	Marion
Price, James...........	520	1849–50	Marion
†Richards, Seth..........	1,805	1849–52	Marion & Wapello
†Scholte, Henry P........	1,178	1849–50	Marion
VanDam, Herman.......	570	1849–50, 1852–53	Marion
Total acres..........	15,537		
Per cent of grant.....	9.7		

*Compiled from "Des Moines River Grant, Tract Book, State of Iowa."
†Denotes large buyers of Congress land in Cession 262.

the Marion County list with purchases of 2,730 and 1,178 acres respectively. Edwin Manning, Robert Meek, and Seth Richards, all of whom entered land in both counties, were the largest Wapello County buyers with acreage totals of 1,993, 1,926, and 1,805 respectively. Together the purchases of these 15 men totaled 15,537 acres or nearly 10 per cent of the grant area in the two counties.

Significantly—except for Manning, who was the commissioner of the Des Moines River Improvement agency, and Robert Meek, one of the contractors on the project (who might well have been paid in land)—the five largest investors were also major speculators in Congress land in central Iowa. In addition to these five, twelve other large speculators acquired varying lesser amounts of river grant land in Marion and Wapello, including Benjamin H. Buckingham of Zanesville, Ohio. The Congress land speculators in Cession 262 obtained en toto 9,960 acres or about 8 per cent of the river grant in the two counties. Enterprising Iowa land agents likely encouraged these investors. In October, 1849, pioneer Des Moines realtor Barlow Granger announced by an advertisement in a leading capital city newspaper with a wide eastern circulation that he had an agent in Ottumwa at the office of the Board of Public Works to locate river land for nonresident clients. As with Congress land, all river land once offered at public auction was available for promiscuous entry in unlimited quantities at $1.25 per acre.[38]

[38] Granger's ad and a notice by George Gillaspy, register of the Board, outlining the sale policy are in the Des Moines *Iowa Star*, Feb. 1, 1850, July 8, 1852.

Analyses of land sales in the other river counties falling within the grant would undoubtedly uncover similar evidence of speculation. At $1.25 per acre, this land in the rich Des Moines River Valley was obviously a genuine bargain. Jesse Williams, a partner in the land agency of Henn, Williams & Company at Fairfield, realized this fact. He accepted 720 acres, calculated at $2.00 per acre, in lieu of cash owed him for previous services as secretary of the Board of Public Works. George Gillaspy, register of the Improvement's land office, took 218 acres, also in lieu of a debt. State Representative Alfred Hebard, a member of the legislative committee that examined the books of the river agency in 1853, valued Williams' and Gillaspy's lands at $5.00 per acre.[39] With this opportunity for profit awaiting them, speculators obviously needed no prompting to secure as much of the Des Moines River land as preemptors left unclaimed. That they got more than their share, despite the frequent pronouncements from the Board of Public Works about not selling to speculators, is evidence of their determination to share with the squatters in the state's bounty.

VI

The Swampland Grant. Congress, on September 28, 1850, granted all unclaimed "swamp and overflowed lands made unfit thereby for cultivation" to the respective public land states where the land lay, the proceeds to be used by the state for reclamation projects.[40] The act did not define the ambiguous word "swamp" or specify the basis for selection of the land. The states were given the option of preparing their own lists upon personal inspection or accepting those lands designated as swampy in the surveyors' field notes.[41] Iowa legislators, much to their later regret, chose to compile their own lists in the vain hope of obtaining a larger land donation. The elected surveyor in each of the organized counties was requested to make a thorough inspection and designate those lands unfit for cultivation.[42] But no provision was made to reimburse the surveyors. They were therefore reluctant to act. As a consequence, the compilation of the swampland lists was unduly delayed. In Lucas County, for instance, seven years passed before a county official completed the task.[43]

---

[39] Iowa *House Journal,* 1854, appendix, 512.

[40] U.S. *Statutes at Large,* IX, 519–20.

[41] J. Butterfield to Gov. Stephen Hempstead, Nov. 21, 1850, in G.F. Corr., Swamp Lands, Fold. 1; C. H. Booth to Hempstead, Feb. 26, 1851, *ibid.*

[42] Iowa *Laws,* 1851, 169–71; Hempstead to C. H. Booth, Feb. 22, 1851, G. F. Corr., Swamp Lands, Fold. 1.

[43] Robert Coles to Lowe, Feb. 10, 1859, G.F., Corr., Swamp Lands, Fold. 2.

An inefficient selection system was not the only obstacle, however. Once selected, the surveyor-general of Iowa and Wisconsin and the Secretary of the Interior in Washington had to approve and certify the lists. But these officials had become overly suspicious due to the many lists containing fraudulent selections that reached their desk daily from the public land states. Unless the state selections conformed rather closely to their compilations based on the original field notes, they usually withheld their approval until the completion of a time-consuming investigation.

It was 1858 before the Secretary of the Interior certified the first list of Iowa swampland selections. By that time, however, much of the grant was in jeopardy. For in 1855 Congress had opened for private sale all tracts that county officials had designated as swampy and buyers had quickly purchased approximately 50 per cent of them.[44] Many of the remaining swampland selections were claimed by Iowa's railroads under the congressional land grant of 1856. Figure 3.3 graphically illustrates the extent of the grant in Cession 262 to which the state ultimately received title.[45]

The experience of Lucas County in central Iowa is a good illustration of the obstacles confronting state officials who hoped to benefit from the swamp grant. Robert Coles of Chariton, the county's swampland agent, forwarded to the surveyor general's office in 1858 a list of lands totaling 8,340 acres which he had selected that summer. Of this amount, however, only 197 acres were still vacant. Buyers had previously entered 5,342 acres at the Chariton land office (56 per cent with land warrants and the remainder in cash at $1.25 per acre) and 2,800 acres had been transferred to the saline land grant.[46] Eventually, only 80 acres were patented in Lucas County under the swamp grant, although the county received indemnity land in western Iowa totaling 2,200 acres.[47]

While Iowa officials were making their swampland selections and dickering with federal officials for certification, the state legislature laid down policy for the sale of the land. The basic decision was to give full administrative control to the respective counties in which the land lay. Each county, however, must adhere to state regulations which required that the land be sur-

[44] *Report of the Register of the State Land Office*, 1857, 17.

[45] From Barlowe and Hammar, "Valuation of Lands in Southcentral Iowa," 128.

[46] See "A List of Swamp Lands in Lucas County, Iowa. Selected by R. Coles, agent for the State of Iowa for Said County," in Coles to Lowe, Feb. 10, 1859, G.F. Corr., Swamp Lands, Fold. 2.

[47] See "Swamp Land Patents from State of Iowa, Vol. 1 & 2, Tract Book, State of Iowa," and "Indemnity Swamp Lands, Record of United States Patents, Tract Book, Part 2, State Land Office."

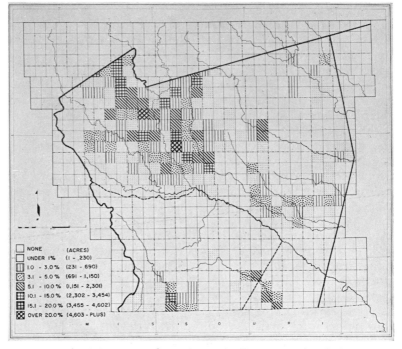

Fig. 3.3. Swampland Grant in Royce Cession 262.

veyed, appraised, and sold at public auction for not less than the
appraised value. The initial minimum valuation was set at
twenty cents per acre but before any lands were sold at that price,
the minimum was raised to $1.25. It was under this law that
much of the swampland in central Iowa was sold. In 1864, the
minimum valuation was permanently reduced to $1.00 per acre.

Regulations governing claims and preemption rights were
also formulated. At first only squatters who could prove that they
were cultivating the land were allowed to preempt a maximum
of 160 acres at its appraised value. In 1855, the law was liber-
alized to allow all claimants *or their assignees* to enter up to a
quarter section at the minimum appraisal. Under this law thousands of acres were claimed by both large-scale investors and local
farmers. In 1858 all further right to claim or preempt swampland at the minimum valuation was abrogated. By this time,
however, claimants had already "proved up" much of the land.[48]
As a result a large portion of the grant sold at the minimum
valuation of $1.25 per acre.

---

[48] For legislation pertaining to swampland sales see Iowa *Laws*, 1851,
169–71; 1853, 29–37; 1855, 173–74, 228–31; 1857, 127–28; 1858, 198–99; 1864
(Extra Sess.), 74–75.

Analysis of swampland disposal in two counties in central Iowa, Appanoose and Boone, will serve to illustrate the significance of the state's preemption policy. In Appanoose County, when the swamp grant lands were first offered in 1858, preemptors or their assignees deposited in the office of the county judge certificates of preemption for 6,040 acres out of the 8,643 acres offered, or nearly 70 per cent. By state law all of these claimants secured their tracts for $1.25 per acre.[49] Of the 46 claimants presenting certificates, 21 were assignees who accounted for 2,960 acres, or almost one-half of all acres sold. Two of the assignees, Barzilla Bowen and Daniel P. Sparks, were large speculators in Congress land in central Iowa. Most of the swamp tracts were sold in quarter sections or less, but five men, by buying assignments from preemptors, were able to enter 200 or more acres each. Their purchases totaled 1,200 acres or one-fifth of the county's swampland grant. Three preemptors who had originally claimed 160 acres sold a part of their claim to assignees before the initial public sale, thereby acquiring funds to pay for the land that they retained.[50]

In Boone County, which obtained more land under the swamp grant than any other county in Cession 262—a total of 26,990 acres—preemptors played almost as large a role as in Appanoose. During the first year of sales (1858) preemptors (or their assignees) entered at the legal minimum of $1.25 per acre 6,356 acres on which they had filed their claims in 1856 under provisions of Iowa law. About one-third of the entrants were assignees.[51]

Squatters were not the only active traders in swampland claims. Large speculators also invested, but not uniformly, as is indicated by a survey of swampland disposal in four counties of central Iowa—Blackhawk, Boone, Iowa, and Mahaska.[52] The state of Iowa patented to Blackhawk County 2,711 acres designated as swampland. Sales began in 1861 and within a decade virtually the entire grant had been alienated at an overall average price of $2.12 per acre. All of the 36 buyers were county residents

[49] Total acreage of the swamp grant was compiled from Appanoose County "Book of Original Entry" and total acres sold from "Deed Record Book F," in the office of the county recorder, Centerville.

[50] Data were not compiled on the 2,600 acres sold after 1860.

[51] Total acreage of the swamp grant was compiled from Boone County "Book of Original Entry," in the office of the county recorder, Boone. For swampland sales of 1858 see the various deed registers. The exact acreage entered by assignees was not computed.

[52] Blackhawk, Iowa, and Mahaska are included because they are the only counties in Cession 262 in which "Swamp Land Registers" have survived. In the other counties receiving grants of swampland, the swamp deeds must be extracted from the voluminous deed records. This task was completed only for Boone County.

and only three men acquired more than 160 acres. But one of
these was John H. Leavitt, a Waterloo realtor and major investor
in Congress land in Cession 262.[53]

Boone County's massive grant of 26,990 acres was first offered
in 1858.[54] By 1869, buyers had purchased 18,884 acres, or almost
70 per cent of the grant. The average yearly price ranged from
$1.25 in the first two years, when most of the buyers were pre-
emptors or their assignees, to $2.51 in 1867; the average for the
entire grant was $1.84 per acre.[55] In contrast to Blackhawk
County land, analysis of the purchasers in Boone indicates strong
speculative activity. Of the 147 buyers, 27 (18.4 per cent) obtained more than a quarter section, their total purchases absorbing 11,707 acres, or 55.4 per cent of the grant. As few as eight
men (see Table 3.12), paced by Charles Rowlings of Boone with
1,240 acres, amassed a total of 6,266 acres, about one-third (33.2
per cent) of the grant. One of these, Thomas W. Ward, was
also a large investor in government land in Cession 262. In addition to Ward, two other speculators in Congress land in central
Iowa bought Boone County swampland. Evidently, the land was
an attractive investment.

Iowa County received approximately 2,000 acres in 1860 and
1861 under the swampland grant. Beginning in 1864 the county
swampland commissioners offered the tracts for sale. By 1869
when the commission disbanded, local residents had purchased
1,052 acres at an average price of $2.07 per acre.[56] As in Black-
hawk County, seemingly little speculation was involved, for 13
local residents secured the entire 1,052 acres. Seven men bought
40-acre tracts, four acquired 120-acre pieces, one bought a quarter
section, and one entered 240 acres.

Mahaska County was fortunate to acquire almost 6,500 acres
under the swampland grant. Under the jurisdiction of the board
of supervisors, the local drainage commissioner surveyed and
examined all of the donated land and classified it by first, second,
and third grades.[57] The board valued grade one land at $2.00
per acre, grade two at $1.50, and grade three at $1.25 and offered
all of it at public auction. Terms were one-half cash and a credit
of one year on the remainder at 6 per cent interest. No credit

[53] Compiled from information in the "Swamp Land Record, Blackhawk
County, Iowa," in the office of the county recorder, Waterloo.

[54] For list of swampland in this and all other counties see "Swamp Land
Patents from State of Iowa, Vol. 1 & 2, Tract Book, State of Iowa."

[55] Compiled from information in the Boone County deed record books in
the office of the county recorder, Boone.

[56] Compiled from information in "Swamp Land Record, Vol. I, Iowa
County," in the office of the county recorder, Marengo.

[57] Minutes of Jan. 8, 1861, in "Minute Book, 1859–64, Mahaska County,"
165, 169, in the office of the county clerk, Oskaloosa.

TABLE 3.12

LARGE BUYERS (OVER 500 ACRES) OF BOONE COUNTY SWAMPLAND GRANT*

Buyer	Acres	Years
Alexander, Joseph F.	785	1858, 1865
Ballinger, R. H.	533	1858
Beal, Cornelius	916	1858
Hamilton, C. W.	508	1858, 1863
Lindsey, Edmund	640	1868
Pomeroy, Charles	924	1859–60, 1863, 1868
Rowlings, Charles	1,240	1867, 1869
†Ward, Thomas W.	720	1858, 1861
Total acres	6,266	
Per cent of grant	33.2	

*Compiled from Boone County deed registers, Office of the County Recorder, Boone, Iowa.
†Large buyer of Congress land in Cession 262.

was allowed, however, on tracts which were mostly timbered. All claimants of swampland were given the privilege of buying their lands at their appraised value prior to the public auction.[58] Annual sales were slow but steady over a 15-year period from 1860 to 1874. Although all of the 41 buyers were county residents, a tabulation of their entries revealed that four men monopolized over 60 per cent of the entire grant. Indeed, John A. L. Crookham, a prominent Oskaloosa realtor and a major investor in government land in central Iowa, purchased 2,784 acres or one-half of the entire county grant.[59]

Swampland sales in the central counties, outlined above, seemingly were no different than the pattern in eastern Iowa. For example, the eastcentral county of Johnson sold its grant of 3,531 acres in the years 1858 through 1871 at average yearly prices ranging between $1.25 and $3.19 per acre with the overall average being $1.34 per acre. Again, local capitalists were conspicuous among the 39 buyers. In fact, five men acquired 1,731 acres or 49 per cent of the entire grant. And all five were major speculators in Congress land in Cession 262, including such prominent Iowa City land investors as Charles H. Berryhill, Thomas J. Cox, and James A. Woods.[60]

Not all large buyers of swampland were Iowans. At least one interstate corporation, the American Emigrant Company

[58] Minutes of June 3, 5, 1861, and Jan. 9, 1862, *ibid.*, 187, 199–200, 246.
[59] Compiled from information in the "Swamp Land Record, I, Mahaska County," in the office of the county recorder, Oskaloosa. When the swampland register ends in 1874, 810 acres remained unsold. Neither the sale price nor the grade classification was recorded in the deeds. A biographical sketch of Crookham is in Edward H. Stiles, *Recollections and Sketches of Notable Lawyers and Public Men of Early Iowa* . . . (Des Moines, 1916), 712–13.
[60] Compiled from information in the "Swamp Land Register, Johnson County," in the office of the county recorder, Iowa City.

of Hartford, Connecticut, acquired 300,000 acres of Iowa swamp-land, almost one-fifth of the total swampland donation.[61] As a land-selling agency the company began activities in Iowa in 1861. Among the original incorporators were several prominent citizens of Des Moines—F. C. D. McKay who became the company's chief agent in the Hawkeye State; James C. Savery, who headed the company's land department; and Tallmadge E. Brown. Savery and McKay secured most of the land by contracting with individual county officials to build needed public improvements in exchange for the county's swamplands. Adams, Audubon, Calhoun, Crawford, Greene, Monona, Montgomery, Page, and Taylor were a few of the counties agreeing to such an arrangement.[62]

State officials who claimed personal knowledge of the facts charged that Savery and Brown induced county clerks to call special meetings of the boards of supervisors and then "by false and fraudulent representations as to the condition of the swamp land, etc., are inducing the boards to make ruinous contracts with them." Contracts already signed with Franklin and Cerro Gordo counties, it was claimed, would net the company $14,000.[63]

In 1864 the company asked $2.50 per acre for its Iowa land but lowered the price to $1.50 in 1865. If sold in 40-acre tracts, only $20 cash was required with credit up to six years. Every contract, supposedly, contained a stipulation restricting sales only to actual settlers.[64] In its annual statement filed for 1867 the company listed as assets 138,000 acres of Iowa valued at $3.00 per acre. By 1868, its holdings were 292,000 acres, valued at from $1.00 to $5.00 per acre. Thereafter, the land was slowly sold until 1887 when the remaining 80,000 acres were signed over to the Des Moines land speculators, Savery and James Callanan, Jr.[65]

---

[61] For accounts of the company's history and activities see Charlotte Erickson, "The Recruitment of European Immigrant Labor for American Industry from 1860 to 1865" (Ph.D. dissertation, Cornell University, 1952); Daniel F. Clynch, "An Introduction to Swamp Land Disposal in Iowa: 1850–1880" (M.A. thesis, State University of Iowa, 1957); *Report of the Register of the State Land Office*, 1865, 86–87 and appendix, 178–85. For the company's prospectus, advertising circulars, and rather extensive correspondence with Iowa governors see G.F. Corr., Swamp Lands, Fold. 5–7.

[62] Clynch, "Swamp Land Disposal," 61–66.

[63] For the specifics, see letters of Shubeul P. Adams and William Baker to Gov. Samuel J. Kirkwood, dated May 20 and May 21, 1863, in G.F. Corr., Swamp Lands, Fold. 6. For Savery's rejoinder see Savery to Kirkwood, June 24, 1863, *ibid.*

[64] Circular, Feb., 1865, signed by F. C. D. McKay, and Circular, Jan., 1865, signed by J. S. Maughlin, Burlington Papers, cited in Erickson, "Recruitment of European Immigrant Labor," 102, n. 2; S. P. Lyman, Secretary of the American Emigrant Company, New York, to Gov. Kirkwood, Dec. 16, 1862, G.F. Corr., Swamp Lands, Fold. 5; Savery to Kirkwood, June 24, 1863, *ibid.*, Fold. 6.

[65] See the annual statements of the American Emigrant Company for the years 1867–91, filed with the Connecticut secretary of state, Hartford. I used photocopies of these records owned by the Iowa State Department of History and Archives, Des Moines. See also Clynch, "Swamp Land Disposal," 67–68.

Iowa's railroads also managed to inveigle various counties into deeding their swamp grant to aid in railroad construction. Story County, for example, bargained her swampland interest in its entirety to the Cedar Rapids & Missouri River Railroad Company during the Civil War.[66] Thus, Iowa's swamp grant seems to fit the general conclusion reached by land historian Benjamin H. Hibbard many years ago, when he declared that "no better bait was ever thrown to speculators than the swamplands of the various states."[67]

In the disposal of Iowa's land grants, both local speculators and nonresident capitalists played an important role. Large investors in central Iowa did not restrict their activities to Congress land alone. They secured a sizeable amount of the state's public domain as well, despite the special handicaps often involved. Their total acquisitions, however, were not on as large a scale as their dealings in Congress land. They faced stiffer competition from small investors who could bid more readily due to the state's liberal preemption and credit policy. Nor did the decentralized administration of land sales serve the convenience of the large buyers, particularly nonresidents. Until the creation of the state land office in 1857 only investors who were in close contact with local officials in the various townships and county seats could hope to make purchases. But even these obstacles did not deter determined investors, as is proved by the fact that hundreds of the large investors in Congress land in Cession 262 were able to enter a substantial amount of state land.

---

[66] Jno. M. Brainard to R. C. Orwig, May 31, 1865, G.F. Corr., Swamp Lands, Fold. 7.

[67] *A History of the Public Land Policies* (New York, 1924), 280. In eight Illinois counties with extensive swamp grants, Margaret B. Bogue discovered that speculators acquired about 56 per cent of the donation ("The Swamp Land Act and Wet Land Utilization in Illinois, 1850–1890," *Agr. Hist.*, XXV [Oct., 1951], 172–73). Iowa, however, seemingly obtained higher prices than neighboring states. See Knight, "Land Grants for Education," 171.

Chapter Four

THE SELECTION
OF SPECULATOR LANDS

T HE VALUE of a piece of land," declared an Iowa realtor
in one of his advertising circulars, "depends upon Quality and Location, and whether Timbered or Prairie,
Slough or Upland."[1] To veteran land speculators this was hardly
startling news. As knowledgeable buyers, they had long considered in their selection policies such vital factors as soil quality,
proximity to budding towns, and timber and water resources.[2]
Indeed, most Hawkeye realtors engaged full-time surveyors and
land scouts to map new terrain and record their findings in
copious notes for the benefit of prospective customers. In the
great rush for government land, however, one wonders whether
large investors were able to satisfy their desires for choice land.
That question has never been systematically explored—in Iowa
or any other public land state. This chapter presents such an
analysis based on the actual experience of several dozen of the
largest investors in central Iowa.

I

SOME who have studied Iowa settlement patterns have concluded
that early settlers, at least before the 1850's, preferred timbered

---

[1] J. U. Perry to James S. Easley, Aug. 8, 1868, James S. Easley Papers,
Alderman Library, University of Virginia, Charlottesville.

[2] Dozens of letters from eastern investors to the Iowa City real estate
firm of Cook, Sargent and Downey illustrate this point. One asked for several
thousand acres "of good land as near the centre of the counties as possible
also with runing Streams of water or mill Seats if Such can be had" (Alexander
Koster to H. D. Downey, Dec. 29, 1855). Another requested land "near county
Towns, or on central lines, & points laying between on[e] grate laeding point
to another, which might open up someday to advantage" (John Sherrick to
Cook, Sargent and Downey, Dec. 5, 1855). See also Jonathan W. Bonnel to
same, Dec. 13, 1855; I. C. Spencer to same, Dec. 6, 1855; James B. Brace to
same, Dec. 8, 1855, all in the Cook, Sargent & Downey Papers, State Historical
Society of Iowa, Iowa City.

tracts along the streams.[3] Speculators, often among the latecomers, supposedly were willing to buy off sections where the open prairies were dominant which the earlier settlers had bypassed.[4] While this broad generalization has some support, there is much evidence that contradicts it. Many early settlers did not avoid the prairies and many speculators were able to acquire large tracts of woodland. One distraught prospector, after a diligent but unsuccessful search for timberland, exclaimed in obvious frustration: "Speculators have every where Secured the best of the Woodland."[5] Eight hundred Dutch immigrants, fleeing economic and religious difficulties in the Netherlands, deliberately spurned Michigan, where a major Dutch settlement already existed, and settled instead in central Iowa. Explaining the refusal to join his compatriots, the immigrant leader remarked that heavily forested Michigan lacked "sufficient prairie adapted to agriculture. . . . To the farmer who had already spent a part of his life in the level hay lands and fields of Holland, the unusual battle with trees and the constant view of stumps in the midst of meadows and cultivated fields could not be agreeable. . . . I knew that the Dutch farmers . . . were especially eager to be able early to possess pastures and milk-cows, to use plow and harrow on the land, and that they were not at all inclined to prefer ax to spade or to become dealers in wood."[6]

While the Dutch preferred to farm prairie land, a contemporary native American family, the Wilkinsons of nearby Madison County, cleared a piece of timberland to plant their first corn crop.[7] In 1860, Charles Lindsey, describing his extensive

[3] Karl K. Keffer, "Original Land Entry in Eastern Iowa" (M.A. thesis, State University of Iowa, 1954), 59–61; Gordon B. Schilz, "Rural Population Trends of Iowa as Affected by Soils" (Ph.D. dissertation, Clark University, 1948) 58–59; Leslie Hewes, "Some Features of Early Woodland and Prairie Settlement in a Central Iowa County," *Ann. of the Assn. of Am. Geog.*, XL (Mar., 1950), 44–48; Clare C. Cooper, "The Role of Railroads in the Settlement of Iowa: A Study in Historical Geography" (M.A. thesis, University of Nebraska, 1958), 38–43; Harriet M. Heusinkveld, "The Historical Geography of Population in Mahaska, Marion, and Monroe Counties in Iowa" (Ph.D. dissertation, State University of Iowa, 1958), 32–46.

[4] Allan G. Bogue, *From Prairie to Corn Belt: Farming on the Illinois and Iowa Prairies in the Nineteenth Century* (Chicago, 1963), 39; Paul W. Gates, "Land Policy and Tenancy in the Prairie States," *J. Econ. Hist.*, I (May, 1941). 66, and *The Farmer's Age: Agriculture, 1815–1860* (New York, 1960), 180–83.

[5] "Major William Williams' Journal of a Trip to Iowa in 1849," *Annals of Iowa, 3rd Ser.*, XII (Apr., 1920), 251.

[6] Henry Peter Scholte, *Eene Stem uit Pella* (Amsterdam, 1848) translated by Jacob Van Der Zee as "The Coming of the Hollanders to Iowa" in *Ia. J. Hist. and Pol.*, IX (Oct., 1911), 531. The Dutch were by no means a unique case; see Bogue, *Prairie to Corn Belt*, 21. Terry D. Jordan, "Between the Forest and the Prairie," *Agr. Hist.*, XXXVIII (Oct., 1964), 212, 214–16, cites similar comments by English, German, and Swiss immigrants in the Midwest.

[7] W. S. Wilkinson, "A Pioneer Settlement in Madison County," *Annals of Iowa, 3rd Ser.*, VI (July, 1904), 448.

tour through the Midwest, best summed up the issue when he declared: "You find everywhere some who prefer prairie to woodland, and others who prefer woodland to prairie; the latter generally coming from hard-wood portions in other States."[8] Sometimes even brothers could not agree. "For as much as I have ploughed among stumps I still prefer timbered land before prairie," declared Cyrus Sanders of Iowa City. But his brother, still at the family homestead in Highland County, Ohio, insisted meanwhile that Cyrus stake out for him a half section of of "smooth level Prairie of the richest kind of soil with not a tree or bush on it."[9]

The weight of evidence both in contemporary writings and recent scholarly analyses seems to indicate that the choicest locations were those that contained a judicious combination of prairie and wood (a ratio of three acres of prairie to one of timber was considered ideal), and, of course, water. This usually meant a farmstead on the edge of the woods, with the home built in the shelter of the timber and the fields laid out on the adjoining prairie.[10] As ideal locations were rapidly claimed, buyers chose land farther and farther out in the open prairies. "Tim-

---

[8] Lindsey, *The Prairies of the Western States: Their Advantages and Their Drawbacks,* (Toronto, 1860), 46. Gottfried Duden had previously reached the same conclusion. Describing the advantage of western settlement in southern Missouri in the 1820's he wrote: "It is most enticing to settle in a region, where one can be absolutely free in one's choice . . . to select one's land, wholly according to one's taste, in the forest or on the prairie" ("Gottfried Duden's 'Report' 1824–1827, The Thirteenth Letter," William G. Bak, trans., *Mo. Hist. Rev.,* XII [Jan., 1918], 86).

[9] Cyrus Sanders to Richard B. Sanders, June 22, 1839, Cyrus Sanders Letters, State Historical Society of Iowa, Iowa City.

[10] An English immigrant leader explained: "My object . . . was to find prairie, timber, and water power in conjunction, within a moderate distance of good markets" (Grant Foreman, "English Emigrants in Iowa," *Ia. J. Hist. and Pol.,* XLIV [Oct., 1946], 405). Another Iowan wrote: "I have a small farm under way and shall add to it from the contiguous prairie [sic] as my means allow" (Samuel J. Bayard to Lucius Lyon, Oct. 23, 1843, Lucius Lyon Papers, William L. Clements Library, University of Michigan, Ann Arbor). The first settlers in Marshall County, the Davidsons, explained that in 1846 they pushed into the new area "for then we could have first choice of prairie and with timberland adjoining; which would be a great object to us" (Mary Ann Ferrin, "An Autobiography and a Reminiscence," *Annals of Iowa, 3rd Ser.,* XXXVII [Spring, 1964], 244). An earlier settler in Clayton County noted: "The claim which I now possess consists of 40 acres of timber and ¼ Sec. of smooth prairie adjoining. There are two beautiful springs on the edge of the prairie" (David Olmsted to Samuel D. Gifford, Feb. 12, 1844, David Olmsted Letters, photostatic copy at State Historical Society of Iowa, Iowa City). A Johnson County pioneer reported: "When I first came it was impossible to get timber and prairie adjoining without paying a high price for the claim on it" (Cyrus Sanders to Richard B. Sanders, June 22, 1839, Cyrus Sanders Letters). See also C. L. Lucas, "Recollections of Early Times in Iowa," *Annals of Iowa, 3rd Ser.,* VI (Apr., 1904), 384; "Letters of Jerome Carskaddan, 1843–1854," *Ia. J. Hist.,* XLVIII (July, 1950), 251. For analyses by modern geographers, see Hewes, "Some Features of Early Woodland and Prairie Settlement," 40–57, and Jordan, "Between the Forest and the Prairie," 205–16.

ber lots" of 10 to 40 acres, staked out in the nearest woodland, soon became common accessories of such farms.[11] At least one family, the Byerses, in 1841 settled "on the sea of prairie," ten miles from timber.[12] But most settlers probably did not have to locate nearly so far from timber anywhere except in parts of western Iowa. One Iowan summed up the situation in 1849 by remarking that "the only plan is to select good Prairie Land, well watered & buy 20 or 40 acres of Wood Land to Supply it, any quantity can be bought at $5 p Acre. The Wood land is generally on bluffs. The Prairie Land is far preferable for farming purposes."[13]

It goes without saying that most Iowans by the early 1840's realized the greater productivity of prairie soil. In 1829, Caleb Atwater in his *Remarks Made on a Tour to Prairie Du Chien* vehemently defended Iowa's prairies: "We are often told by eastern scientific empirics who have seen them, of the sterility of the soil where the prairies are, but the very reverse is the fact."[14] Lieutenant Albert M. Lea reemphasized the point in 1836. "Wheat is produced with a facility unknown except in the west," he wrote. "I have known the sod of the prairie to be simply turned over, the seed harrowed in, and thirty bushels per acre to be harvested."[15] Lea's remark about turning the prairie sod also indicates that by the mid-1830's farmers had perfected machinery such as "breaking plows" for opening prairie land.

II

AN EXAMINATION of specific speculator-held tracts gives an indication as to whether or not these entrepreneurs responded to settler preferences. All of the land entries of the ten largest speculators in nine representative counties of central Iowa were

---

[11] John W. Taylor, *Description of Iowa: Information for Those Seeking New Homes or Profitable Investments* (Dubuque, 1860), 8–9. If sufficient wood was unavailable, farmers soon learned to substitute sod banks or hedges for fencing and coal for fuel. On sod fencing see "Fort Des Moines Land District," *Mills Circular* as cited in *The North-Western Review*, I (Feb., 1858), 50. For statements on feasibility of hedging see Willard Barrows, "Letters on the West," Davenport *Commercial*, 1854, cited in N. Howe Parker, *Iowa As It Is in 1855* (Chicago, 1855), 65–67; John G. Wells, *Wells' Pocket Hand-Book of Iowa* (New York, 1857), 48–49. An excellent survey of these problems for the entire prairie triangle is Bogue, *Prairie to Corn Belt*, 74–80.

[12] S. H. M. Byers, "Out West in the Forties," *Ia. Hist. Rec.*, V (Oct., 1889), 366. A prairie farmer in Knox County, Illinois, reported in 1855 that settlers often owned woodlots "six to seven miles distant" from their prairie homesteads (Jordan, "Between the Forest and the Prairie," 212).

[13] "Major William Williams' Journal of a Trip to Iowa in 1849," 251.

[14] (Columbus, 1831), 51.

[15] "Notes on Wisconsin Territory, with a Map," *Annals of Iowa*, 3rd Ser., XI (July–Oct., 1913), 123.

chosen for analysis.[16] Altogether, these entries totaled 304,680 acres, or 7,617 "forties," spread over 138 townships. The technique is quite simple. Each 40-acre tract was plotted on township graphs which were in turn superimposed on county soil maps. This permitted the classification of each "forty" according to major soil type and land type.[17] The numerous soil types were grouped into four major land type categories—prairie, woodland, alluvial, and swamp/overflow.[18]

A recognized tool of soil scientists, the designation of soil types carries with it inferences with respect to timber. Soils develop differently under trees than under grass, so that a "forty" made up of Clinton silt loam is known as having originally been timbered. Similarly, a "forty" composed of Carrington loam indicates land developed under prairie grasses. The soil type carries additional inferences. Such soils as Wabash, Genessee, La Moure, Bremer, and so on, are all alluvial soils that developed along stream courses. Carrington, Muscatine, Grundy, Clarion, and so on, all occupied broad plateau-like areas between the streams. These latter have gentle slope gradients in contrast to timbered soils which generally have strong and even steep

---

[16] Appanoose, Benton, Boone, Carroll, Hardin, Madison, Marion, Poweshiek, and Wapello counties were chosen as being most truly representative of Royce Cession 262 in terms of soil types. The large buyers undoubtedly entered under the time-entry system a portion of the lands included in this analysis. In such cases the buyer, not the speculator, selected the land. The moneylender, however, by allowing the entry to be made in his own name, faced the ever-present risk of having to repossess the land in case of default. His willingness to extend a loan, therefore, implied tacit approval of the type of land selected.

[17] I am grateful to Professor Conrad H. Hammar, former agricultural economist at the universities of Minnesota and Missouri, for assisting in the task of classifying the soil type of the speculators' acreage. "Soil type" is, in strict scientific parlance, a technical term designating a textural class, such as Clarion *loam* or Carrington *sandy loam*. Clarion and Carrington, on the other hand, are soil series. In this book, however, soil series will be referred to as soil types. Soil scientists also commonly transpose these terms.

[18] The soil types, as found in the county soil maps published by the U.S. Department of Agriculture's Bureau of Soils in cooperation with the Iowa Agricultural Experiment Station, were classified as follows:

Prairie type—Carrington, Clarion, Clyde, Fargo, Grundy, Muscatine, Putnam, Shelby, Tama, Webster soil series;

Woodland type—Clarion R, Clinton, Conover, Lindley, Marion, Weller soil series;

Alluvial type—Bremer, Buckner, Cass, Chariton, Genessee, La Moure, O'Niell, and Wabash soil series;

Swamp/Overflow type—Riverwash and Pierce soil series.

Professor Hammar's methodology described in his letter to the author of January 13, 1964, is as follows:

(1) The classification was done by visual inspection since no other method is possible. No planimeter would be accurate with the small scale maps used.

(2) Only the two dominant soils in any given "forty" determine the final classification although others are considered at the time of classification.

(3) No effort was made to allow for distorted descriptions. All "forties" are assumed to be regular, although they are not.

TABLE 4.1
ACREAGE BY LAND TYPES OF TEN LARGEST ENTRANTS IN NINE COUNTIES
OF CENTRAL IOWA

County	Prairie acres	Woodland acres	Alluvial acres	Swamp/ overflow acres
Appanoose	30,750	2,420	3,390	...
Benton	32,940	3,550	5,990	...
Boone	24,980	2,420	1,310	90
Carroll	35,010	50	3,980	200
Hardin	28,560	1,110	2,610	80
Madison	18,350	8,450	4,400	...
Marion	21,870	7,320	6,870	300
Poweshiek	31,490	6,630	7,360	...
Wapello	5,060	5,950	1,190	...
Totals	229,010	37,900	37,100	670
Per cent	75.2	12.4	12.2	0.2

slopes.[19] Also each soil has a well-known fertility complex and certain of the upland soils such as Webster contain some "potholes."[20] By classifying each 40-acre tract by soil type, therefore, one can determine whether speculators bought prairie or timbered lands, level rather than strongly sloping terrain, and fertile rather than thin soils.

Based on the soil and land type classifications, the total acreage of the speculators' entries by each of the four major land types was calculated.[21] The results, summarized in Table 4.1, make it readily apparent that the speculators overwhelmingly purchased the prairie. Over 75 per cent of all entries were prairie land, compared to a low 12.4 and 12.2 per cent respectively for woodland and alluvial land. Only in Wapello County did the speculators favor woodland over prairie. Overall, the largest buyers entered three acres of prairie to every one of woodland and alluvial land.

Gauged on a relative rather than an absolute basis, the speculators also entered more of the prairie. In Table 4.2 the percentages of land types purchased by the speculators are compared with percentages of total land types in the nine counties. Comparing weighted averages for the entire area, the largest

[19] See R. W. Arnold, L. E. Tyler, and F. F. Riecken, "Estimate of Slope Classes by Counties in Iowa," Ia. Acad. Sci. Pro., LXVII (1960), 260–67.

[20] Potholes are saucerlike basins or depressional areas which range in depth from a few inches to several feet and contain ponded water much of the time. Although only about 5 per cent of the Webster soil association contain these depressional areas, they understandably caused unique soil management problems (D. F. Slusher, R. W. Arnold, and R. Protz, "Extent and Distribution of Soils in Depressional Areas in the Clarion-Nicollet-Webster Soil Association in Iowa," ibid., LXVIII [1961], 380–96).

[21] If a tract contained more than one land type the dominant type was weighted at 75 per cent and the minor type at 25 per cent.

TABLE 4.2

ACREAGE BY LAND TYPE OF THE TEN LARGEST ENTRANTS AS A PERCENTAGE OF LAND TYPE IN NINE COUNTIES OF CENTRAL IOWA*

County	Prairie			Woodland			Alluvial		
	Per cent of area	Speculator entries	Per cent of differential	Per cent of area	Speculator entries	Per cent of differential	Per cent of area	Speculator entries	Per cent of differential
Appanoose	73.6	84.1	+10.5	13.0	6.6	−6.4	13.4	9.2	−4.2
Benton	73.6	77.6	+4.0	9.2	8.3	−.9	17.0	14.1	−2.9
Boone	81.7	86.7	+5.0	11.7	8.4	−3.3	5.7	4.6	−1.1
Carroll	82.7	89.2	+6.5	1.4	.1	−1.3	15.9	10.1	−5.8
Hardin	85.4	88.3	+2.9	3.9	3.4	−.5	10.3	8.1	−2.2
Madison	74.2	58.8	−15.4	16.6	27.1	+10.5	9.1	14.1	+5.0
Marion	53.3	60.1	+6.8	24.9	20.2	−4.7	20.1	18.8	−1.3
Poweshiek	74.0	69.2	−4.8	8.9	14.6	+5.7	17.0	16.2	−.8
Wapello	31.6	41.5	+9.9	54.8	48.8	−6.0	11.9	9.7	−2.2
Weighted average	71.2	75.2	+4.0	14.9	12.4	−2.5	13.5	12.2	−1.3

*Percentages do not total 100 because of the omission of swamp/overflow land type acreage.

entrants purchased 4.0 per cent more prairie, 2.5 per cent less woodland, and 1.3 per cent less alluvial land than the relative amounts of such land in the area as a whole. Among individual counties the percentage differential between the land types of speculator entries and the all-county percentages varied considerably. In Appanoose and Wapello counties, both in the southeast corner of Royce Cession 262, the large investors purchased respectively 10.5 and 9.9 per cent more prairie land, but in Benton and Hardin counties in the northeast, they acquired only 4.0 and 2.9 per cent more prairie. On the other hand, in Madison and Poweshiek counties the large entrants obtained respectively 15.4 and 4.8 per cent less prairie and 10.5 and 5.7 per cent more woodland.

How can one explain these variations? Why did the large speculators buy more prairie land, proportionately, in Appanoose and Wapello and less in Madison and Poweshiek? Since Appanoose and Wapello were settled early, one's first reaction is to resort to the standard interpretation—namely, that the settlers arrived first, acquired all the wooded tracts along the streams and rivers, and forced latecomers, among whom were the speculators, to satisfy themselves with the open prairies. This simple formula may be true for Wapello but not for Appanoose where several of the ten largest buyers were among the earliest purchasers, and they deliberately chose prairie land. John White began entering land in 1848, only one year after the land offices opened; while William Wallace White completed his purchases in 1850 and 1851 when less than one-third of the land was sold. (See Table 4.3.)

Another possible explanation for the seeming preference for prairie lands in both Appanoose and Wapello may be that both counties had great amounts of timbered land, which reduced its desirability as compared to the less abundant prairies. Timber, of course, was not a *sine qua non* but was desired only because its resources could be combined with the fertile prairie lands in farm-making.[22] Conversely, it is quite plausible that the large buyers in Poweshiek tended to favor forested tracts because timber was relatively scarce—only about 9 per cent at the time of survey. Abundance of timber or lack of it, however, is not a universal formula for explaining the variations between counties found in Table 4.2. In Madison County, which was approximately 20 per cent forested in the 1840's, speculators bought more woodland and alluvial land. In Hardin, on the other hand, only

---

[22] Over 40 per cent of Appanoose and 53 per cent of Wapello lands were covered with timber at the time of the original survey. See Appendix X for the approximate acreages of forest land in each of the central Iowa counties at the time of survey.

TABLE 4.3

ACREAGE BY LAND TYPE OF SELECTED LARGE BUYERS IN COMPARISON WITH ALL-COUNTY AND LARGE BUYER LAND TYPES IN SELECTED COUNTIES *

County	When entered	Total acres	Prairie	Wood-land	Allu-vial
				(Per cent)	
Appanoose					
All county.............	.....	....	73.6	13.0	13.4
10 largest buyers.......	1848–56	....	84.3	6.3	9.3
Sel. buyers					
Barzilla Bowen......	1851–55	3,720	96.0	1.3	2.7
Ward Lamson.......	1850–55	9,360	75.0	8.4	16.6
John White.........	1848–53	1,800	88.3	7.8	3.9
William W. White...	1850–51	1,840	94.5	0.0	5.4
Benton					
All county.............	.....	....	73.6	9.2	17.0
10 largest buyers.......	1849–61	....	77.6	8.3	14.1
Sel. buyer					
Horatio W. Sanford..	1849–61	13,700	70.3	10.9	18.8
Boone					
All county.............	.....	....	81.7	11.7	5.7
10 largest buyers.......	1853–56	....	86.9	8.5	4.6
Sel. buyers					
Benjamin F. Allen...	1853–55	2,880	78.8	18.1	3.1
Miles White........	1853–55	2,740	81.6	15.7	2.6
Carroll					
All county.............	.....	....	82.7	1.4	15.9
10 largest buyers.......	1854–64	....	89.2	0.1	10.1
Sel. buyer					
Benjamin F. Allen...	1855–56	1,640	59.9	3.0	27.4
Hardin					
All county.............	.....	....	85.4	3.9	10.3
10 largest buyers.......	1854–58	....	89.0	3.4	7.3
Sel. buyers					
Elias A. White &					
Miles White.......	1854–58	7,720	81.0	6.1	13.0
Madison					
All county.............	.....	....	74.2	16.6	9.1
10 largest buyers.......	1850–56	....	58.8	27.1	14.1
Sel. buyers					
Benjamin F. Allen...	1853–56	2,800	47.1	31.4	21.4
Alvah H. Buck-					
ingham..........	1851	1,880	41.5	38.3	20.2
John C. Culbertson...	1850–51	7,160	53.8	27.9	18.3
Marion					
All county.............	.....	....	53.3	25.9	20.1
10 largest buyers.......	1847–58	....	60.1	20.2	18.8
Sel. buyers					
Samuel Fowler......	1848	4,560	71.9	18.4	9.6
John A. Graham.....	1847	7,640	60.6	19.5	15.7
Ward Lamson.......	1849–53	1,840	37.5	35.9	26.6
Edward A. Temple					
& Jesse Williams...	1851–58	3,640	53.3	34.6	12.1

TABLE 4.3 (*continued*)

ACREAGE BY LAND TYPE OF SELECTED LARGE BUYERS IN COMPARISON WITH
ALL-COUNTY AND LARGE BUYER LAND TYPES IN SELECTED COUNTIES *

County	When entered	Total acres	Prairie	Wood-land	Allu-vial
				(*Per cent*)	
Poweshiek					
All county			74.0	8.9	17.0
10 largest buyers	1851–57		69.2	14.6	16.2
Sel. buyers					
Charles H. Berry-hill	1851–55	2,400	47.1	25.0	27.9
Omer Tousey	1853	3,280	87.2	5.5	7.3
John C. Culbertson & Morgan Reno	1851–55	8,080	57.4	23.5	19.1
Wapello					
All county			31.6	54.8	11.9
10 largest buyers	1846–55		40.8	48.9	10.3
Sel. buyers					
Ward Lamson	1849–53	1,040	5.8	90.4	3.8
Seth Richards	1849–53	1,880	8.0	75.0	17.0

*The buyers selected were those who purchased earlier than the other individuals among the ten largest purchasers. Percentages do not total 100 because of the omission of swamp/overflow land type acreage.

12 per cent of it forested, they purchased the prairie. Rather than seek explanations in timber resources or settlement patterns, it seems wise to acknowledge the human variable—the individual buyer and his preferences.

To illustrate this variability in land type preferences among the large investors, and at the same time to take into account the land entry dates, the data on land type of those individuals who began entering their land earlier than the majority were recast and are presented separately in Table 4.3. Presumably, these early buyers had a larger measure of choice between prairie and timbered tracts than their competitors. Their entries, therefore, should more accurately reflect their prejudices rather than the land market situation.

The striking fact in the table is the absence of any uniform pattern. Some large speculators favored timber, others prairie. In Appanoose County, Barzilla Bowen and Ward Lamson began entering land together in 1850 and 1851, yet Lamson secured only 75 per cent prairie while Bowen bought 96 per cent. Since their entries coincided almost exactly in time, one can only conclude that personal preferences varied. In Marion County, Samuel Fowler and John A. Graham acquired far more than their proportionate share of the county's prairies, although they were among the very first entrants. While land agent Charles H. Berryhill of Iowa City entered 47.1 per cent prairie in Poweshiek

County, his hometown rivals, John C. Culbertson and Morgan Reno, secured 57.4 per cent prairie. Omer Tousey of Dearborn County, Indiana, on the other hand, seemingly could not purchase enough prairie: 87.2 per cent of all his purchases were prairie acres.

III

ALTHOUGH it has been demonstrated that preferences for timber or prairie land varied, the data in Table 4.3 also suggest a tendency among the earliest large speculators to prefer timbered land in combination with open areas over prairie without timber when both types of land were available. To test this factor more accurately, each year's land sales were analyzed by individual "forties" in the one township in each county where speculators concentrated most of their entries. In this way their selections could be related to the amount of each type of land available at the time of purchase. The findings in two townships —Washington (T69N–R16W) in Appanoose County and Dodge (T85N–R26W) in Boone County—can serve to illustrate the patterns.[23]

In Washington, the government first offered the 535 full "forties" of Congress land in 1850 (Table 4.4). Of these 21,400 acres, 77 per cent comprised prairie land and 23 per cent woodland. Before the year passed, buyers snapped up 221 "forties" (41 per cent), 40 (18 per cent) by the ten largest speculators and 181 (82 per cent) by the other entrants. Both groups acquired proportionally less prairie land than was offered for sale, the largest buyers slightly less than the others. The prairie-woodland acreage proportions were: for the largest speculators 70–30 per cent, for the other entrants 74–26 per cent. Altogether, the buyers entered 39 per cent of the available prairie acreage and 47.5 per cent of the woodland. In the second year, with 315 "forties" (79 per cent prairie land and 21 per cent woodland) remaining for sale, the largest entrants stepped up their buying pace to 54 "forties" (35 per cent of sales), and also increased their proportion of prairie land entries from 70 to 78 per cent—a figure nearly equal to the relative amount of prairie land available. The other buyers, however, seemed more conscious of the dwindling timber land and increased their proportion of woodland entries from 26 to 39 per cent. Only 14

---

[23] I am again indebted to Professor Hammar for classifying by major soil type the nine special townships, from which group Washington and Boone Twps. were arbitrarily selected. See Appendix XI for the total acreages by townships of the ten largest original entrants in the nine counties.

TABLE 4.4

DISPOSITION OF 535 FULL "FORTIES" OF CONGRESS LAND IN WASHINGTON
TWP., APPANOOSE CO., 1850–55

Buyer group	Land type	1850		1851		1852–55		All years	
		(*No.*)	(%)	(*No.*)	(%)	(*No.*)	(%)	(*No.*)	(%)
10 largest	P	28	70	41	78	53	93	122	81
entrants	W	12	30	13	22	4	7	29	19
All other	P	134	74	60	61	95	91	289	75
entrants	W	47	26	38	39	10	9	95	25
Totals		221	41	152	28	162	31	535	100

woodland "forties" remained unsold at the end of the second
year, and these were alienated along with the final 162 prairie
"forties" in the succeeding four years. Thus, in Washington
Township, comparison of land entry data and soil type confirms
the fact that the large speculators first on the scene shared a slight
preference for woodland. Seemingly, however, the large buyers
had as much choice in the second year of sales as in the first, and
then they entered more prairie land. Indeed, over 80 per cent of
their total entries were prairie.

The findings in Dodge Township of Boone County substantiate the Washington conclusions. The national government
offered for sale 333 "forties" in Dodge and donated an additional
243 under various land grants. Of the 13,320 acres of Congress
land, 88 per cent consisted of prairie acreage and only 12 per
cent woodland. In the first year of sales, 1853, 61 "forties" (18
per cent) were sold, 13 (21 per cent) by the ten largest speculators
and 48 (79 per cent) by the other entrants (Table 4.5). As in
Washington, both groups acquired relatively less prairie land
than was offered for sale, and the largest buyers again entered less
prairie acreage than the others. But the variance was more pro-
nounced. Compared to the slight 4 per cent difference in Washington, the largest speculators in Dodge entered 15 per cent less

TABLE 4.5

DISPOSITION OF 333 FULL "FORTIES" OF CONGRESS LAND IN DODGE TWP.,
BOONE CO., 1853–56

Buyer group	Land type	1853		1854		1855–56		All years	
		(*No.*)	(%)	(*No.*)	(%)	(*No.*)	(%)	(*No.*)	(%)
10 largest	P	8	62	34	92	57	93	99	82
entrants	W	5	38	3	8	4	7	12	18
All other	P	37	77	53	91	105	91	195	88
entrants	W	11	23	5	9	11	9	27	12
Totals		61	18	95	29	177	53	333	100

prairie land than the other buyers in the initial year of sales. In the three succeeding years, however, the difference between the two groups disappeared as they purchased the remaining prairie and woodland in almost identical proportions. Overall, 82 per cent of the largest speculators' entries were prairie acres compared to 88 per cent for the other buyers. In Dodge as in Washington Township the largest speculators purchased more woodland and less prairie than the other entrants in the first year of sales, but in the remaining years they aquired as much as or more prairie than the rest. In the end, both groups overwhelmingly purchased prairie land.

Evidently the type made little difference; all seemingly was a bargain at the land office price.[24] If timber had been an object in itself, the large investors could readily have turned to other states. Iowa's largest nonresident investor, James S. Easley of Virginia, ostensibly favored partially wooded land; yet when he found that this was not available in large quantities in western and westcentral Iowa, he channeled his funds into the Hawkeye State regardless. Only when the government temporarily closed the state's land offices in 1856 did Easley turn to Wisconsin pine lands.[25]

IV

THAT the large investors assaulted the prairies none can doubt, but did they distinguish between various kinds of prairie soils? Specifically, did they favor the rolling Shelby soils with their scattering of trees, or the flat, treeless Grundy-Putnam combinations? And did they avoid upland soils such as the Webster series which contained occasional potholes?

Appanoose is a good prairie county in which to test the first question; the counties of Boone, Carroll, and Hardin, all with large amounts of Webster soils, can serve to illustrate the second. In Appanoose, the Shelby soil series covered 131,584 acres, or 40.1 per cent of the county's surface, while the Grundy-Putnam series included 101,016 acres, or 33.5 per cent. The ten largest pur-

---

[24] As one speculator remarked about the rush for government land in Fort Dodge, Webster County, in 1855: "No matter what the quality or value, people only seem intent upon getting the number of acres or quantity of Surface, be it land or water." Referring to the many entries of wet lands, he added facetiously, "I know a great many people who are prepared to go to raising geese & ducks in this county—having ponds & pasture too in great abundance for that business." (Andrew Jackson Sterrett to William Sterrett, July 8, 1855, Andrew Jackson Sterrett Papers, Manuscript Division, Minnesota Historical Society, St. Paul.)

[25] See Chapter 7 for a discussion of Easley's business.

chasers secured 35,560 acres in the county. Of these, 14,970 acres (41.4 per cent) contained primarily Shelby soils, only 1.3 per cent more than the all-county percentage, and 16,000 acres (44.1 per cent) were of the Grundy-Putnam soils, or 10.6 per cent more than the all-county ratio. Speculators bought large quantities of both types of land but apparently did not discriminate significantly between the two major prairie soil series. The percentage differential of 9.3 per cent may suggest a tendency to favor the flat, treeless Grundy-Putnam soils over the rolling, tree-clumped, Shelby prairies, but it hardly permits any concrete generalization.

The findings on the question of whether Webster soils went begging at the land office likewise indicate that the large speculators were relatively unconcerned about the various types of prairie soils. In Boone County where 27.5 per cent (100,032 acres) of the county land area consisted of Webster soils, the largest buyers included this type in 24.6 per cent (7,000 acres) of their purchases. In Hardin County, 14.4 per cent (4,640 acres) of the speculators' entries were Webster soils although the county-wide percentage was only 13.6 per cent (49,344 acres). In Carroll County, 49,792 acres (13.6 per cent) were Webster soils and only two of the large speculators—John J. Burtis and Andrew L. Cadmus—entered any of it (2,280 acres, or 5.8 per cent).

One might suspect that Burtis and Cadmus were the latecomers of the group and therefore had to be satisfied with what was left. But this was not true. The dates of entry in the tract book show that these men were among the earliest of the ten largest buyers to purchase land in Carroll County (January, 1856). Only Benjamin F. Allen had preceded them by a few months. All of the other large speculators bought their land in 1858 and 1859 but entered no Webster soils, probably because the largest amounts of such soils were in the northern half of the county which was selected as part of a railroad grant in 1856 and 1857.[26] Judging from the experience in Boone, Hardin, and (if the railroad holdings are taken into account) Carroll counties, we can conclude that the large speculators bought their share of Webster soils. Potholes apparently were a matter of no greater concern than flat or rolling topography.

V

Since the earlier analysis of soil types (Table 4.3) showed that the large speculators varied in their purchasing habits, it may be

[26] The railroads obtained 137,051 acres in Carroll County, according to tabulations from the Carroll County "Book of Original Entry," Carroll.

that factors other than simply soil cover influenced their decisions. Such factors might be direction of settlement, proximity to
growing towns and county seats and actual or projected transportation facilities, and nearness to rivers, mill sites, roads, a
stagecoach line, timber tracts, schools, and churches. As Daniel
Rider, a Fairfield realtor, noted in one of his advertisements:

> Having six years experience in selecting and entering Lands in
> this State, and personally examined most of the Land in and
> out of market, I flatter myself that I am well qualified to make
> choice and valuable selections. Persons at a distance desiring
> my services may transmit to me by mail, their Land Warrants,
> scrip, or Eastern Drafts, and their Orders shall be promptly
> attended to. . . . Plats containing the Prairie, Timber, Streams,
> Mills, Churches, Roads, Railroad Surveys, etc., will invariably
> accompany each certificate of location free of charge.[27]

It is impossible now for us to evaluate location factors as
accurately as a local realtor like Rider. But such important things
as towns, roads, rivers, mill sites, and major variations of soil
types can be pinpointed by the use of soil survey maps, surveyors'
notes, county histories, and especially contemporary maps.[28]

In Appanoose County, the large buyers selected almost one-
third of their total entries in two townships—Wells (T68N–
R16W) and Washington (T69N–R16W). (See Appendix XI for
a list by county and township of the total acreages of the ten
largest entrants. All figures presented hereafter are based on this
table.) Both Wells and Washington were on the eastern border,
eight to fifteen miles from the county seat. The Chariton River
courses through the southwest corner of Wells Township, which
also boasted the first saw and grist mill in the county. Washington Township seemingly had little to recommend it other than
a stage coach route inaugurated in 1855 after much of the land
had been sold. The large buyers purchased rather evenly in the
remaining townships except for the four bordering the state of
Missouri. These were probably avoided because of the boundary
dispute with Missouri and the Lindley soils concentrated there—
soils best suited for pasture and hay land.[29] In the two townships

---

[27] Fairfield *Iowa Sentinel*, May 14, 1857.

[28] The U.S. Surveyors' Notes for all of Iowa are in the National Archives.
Two contemporary maps of Iowa published in 1855 by Ensign, Bridgman &
Fanning of New York City, and Henn, Williams & Company of Fairfield pic-
ture towns, state roads, rivers, and projected railroads. Also helpful were two
charts in Cooper's "The Role of Railroads in the Settlement of Iowa"—Fig. 6,
"Passenger Stagecoach Routes in Iowa," and Fig. 7, "Navigable Waterways in
Iowa in 1860." A detailed map of the early mills in Iowa, constructed by L. C.
Belthius, is in Schilz, "Rural Population Trends of Iowa," 75.

[29] Ia. Agr. Exp. Sta., *Soil Survey of Iowa, Appanoose County* (Ames, 1938),
43.

where the Grundy-Shelby prairie soils were concentrated (T69N–R16W and T69N–R19W), on the other hand, the large entrants bought almost 10,000 acres.

In Benton County the largest purchasers concentrated one-fifth of their selections in two prairie townships, Kane (T83N–R12W) and Eldorado (T83N–R10W). Both are more than ten miles from the county seat, and Kane, which had the greatest number of entries, was supposedly where timber was most scarce.[30] The townships are on the opposite side of the county from the major river, the Cedar, and neither could boast of a major town, mill, or road, until 1856 when a main road bisected Kane. Of Eldorado, the government surveyor could only remark in his field notes (September 23, 1841): "This Township is all rich rolling prairie and nothing can be said of it worthy of notice or that would excite public curiosity." No comments at all are recorded for Kane Township.

Almost three-fifths of the entries of the largest buyers in Boone County were in three townships, Dodge (T85N–R26W), Union (T82N–R28W), and Amaqua (T84N–R28W). Dodge, which had the heaviest buying, was directly north of Boonesboro (now Boone), the county seat, and lay along the east bank of the Des Moines River. This is a clear instance of speculative buying near the county seat and the major river of the county. Although the large buyers favored Dodge, their combined purchases in Union and Amaqua townships were actually far greater. These two legal subdivisions are in the extreme southwestern section of Boone County along Beaver Creek where the Carrington loam soils lie in larger blocks than elsewhere in the county. The surveyor described the area as "moderately rolling prairie, with generally 1st rate soil."[31] Hence, although some large buyers preferred the county seat locale, the majority selected the better agricultural lands to the south.

The ten largest purchasers in Carroll County bought almost one-half of their land in two townships, Eden (T82N–R35W) and Warren (T82N–R36W). Both are in the extreme southwest and are drained by the East Nishnabotna and the Nishnabotna rivers respectively. The county seat was eight to seventeen miles distant. Carroll had no stagecoach service and no major state thoroughfare until after 1860. A sawmill may have been located at Coon Rapids on the Middle Raccoon River in Union Township. Although John J. Burtis purchased almost 4,000 acres in

[30] Western Historical Company, *History of Benton County, Iowa* (Chicago, 1878), 308.

[31] Ia. Agr. Exp. Sta., *Soil Survey of Iowa, Boone County* (Ames, 1924), 43; "General Remarks," Oct., 1849, Township 82 North, Range 28 West, U.S. Surveyors' Notes.

this district, most of the other speculators were forced to confine their activity to the southwest. The determining factor in this case, as noted above, was the railroad grant which absorbed more than 137,000 acres in the northern townships.

In Hardin County the large purchasers secured almost one-third of their acreage in two townships, Sherman (T87N–R22W) and Grant (T86N–R21W). Both are in the southwestern part of the county at the farthest distance from what was then the county seat, Iowa Falls, in the extreme northcentral township, and from the Iowa River which cuts through the county from northwest to southeast. In addition, neither township had any state roads, stagecoach service, major town, or mills although Honey and Tipton creeks meandered through the region. Both are prairie townships, predominantly of Carrington and Clarion drift soils, and in the poorest drainage area in the county.[32] This is an instance where the speculators were willing to buy what land remained unentered.

The large buyers in Madison County acquired over one-fourth of their purchases in Center Township (T75–76N–R27W) which, as the name implies, lies in the center of the county and boasts the county seat, Winterset. The Middle River and Cedar Creek drain the township but the area did not contain the best farmland.[33] It will be recalled, however, that Madison and Poweshiek were the only two counties of the nine analyzed by soil types in which the largest holders secured relatively more timbered land than prairie.

The large buyers in Marion County entered almost one-half of all their land in one township, Lake Prairie (T76–77N–R18W). This was definitely related to the decision of some 800 Dutch immigrants to settle in the township in 1847. Henry Peter Scholte, leader of the immigrant band, and John A. Graham, mayor of Keokuk—the Mississippi River town through which the immigrants had passed en route to central Iowa—purchased 15,840 acres in the township for the use of the settlers. The Lake Prairie entries were on the plateau or divide between the Des Moines and Skunk rivers. The soil in the area, said the surveyor, "is generally very fertile and lies beautifully. It is proportionally timbered and the timber is of the most valuable kind. . . . The township is also very well watered."[34] The major Des Moines Valley state road from Keokuk to Des Moines passed through the

---

[32] Ia. Agr. Exp. Sta., *Soil Survey of Iowa, Hardin County* (Ames, 1925), 11, and Surveyors' Notes.

[33] Ia. Agr. Exp. Sta., *Soil Survey of Iowa, Madison County* (Ames, 1922), 9.

[34] "General Remarks," Sept., 1845, Township 76 North, Range 18 West, U.S. Surveyors' Notes.

town of Pella, the center of the colony. Six sawmills and one saw and grist mill were soon constructed to utilize the extensive water power. Another large buyer in Marion, Samuel Fowler of New Orleans, Louisiana, secured almost 5,000 prairie acres in the southern part of the county in the townships of Indiana (T74N–R19W) and Washington (T74N–R20W).[35] The area around the county seat at Knoxville was largely neglected.

In Poweshiek County the large buyers concentrated one-third of their purchases in two key townships, Bear Creek, now Scott, (T79N–R14W), and Grinnell (T80N–R16W). Bear Creek included the county seat, Montezuma, and Grinnell Township encompassed the town and immigrant colony of Grinnell, founded in 1855 by the New England clergyman Josiah B. Grinnell. Grinnell and Iowa City realtor Hugh D. Downey purchased almost 8,000 acres between them to ensure sufficient land for the settlers who followed Grinnell to Iowa.[36]

As already observed, Poweshiek and Madison were the only two counties where large buyers acquired less prairie than the relative amount of such land in the areas, and these are also the two counties where major purchasers concentrated their buying around the county seat and key towns. One reason for this seeming coincidence may be that the county seats and key towns were often platted near major streams where wood for lumber and fuel would be available, provided, of course, that the location was reasonably near the geographic center of the county.

Finally, in Wapello County, the bulk of the large buyers' selections were in the northeast townships of Competine (T73N–R12W) and Highland (T73N–R13W). These were decidedly judicious purchases because the northeastern part of Wapello had the best prairie acreage in the county ("a dark loam," said the surveyor) while the watersheds of Competine and Cedar creeks provided water, scrub timber, and drainage.[37] Both are eight to fifteen miles from Ottumwa, the county seat, and the Des Moines River which courses through that city. The main appeal of the eastern area, therefore, must have been the prairie soil, which was relatively scarce in Wapello County. Interestingly, many of the large buyers were preceded in the county by earlier

[35] Fowler died in 1850 leaving an estate inventoried at $1,480,689.60. Included in this huge inventory was real estate valued at $328,900.00. For the detailed inventory and extended commentary on it, see Davenport *Gazette*, Dec. 18, 1851.

[36] For information on Grinnell see his *Events of Forty Years: Autobiographical Reminiscences of an Active Career from 1850 to 1890* (Boston, 1890).

[37] Harrison L. Waterman (ed.), *History of Wapello County, Iowa* . . . (2 vols.; Chicago, 1914), I, 335–37; "General Remarks," Nov. 17, 1843, Township 73 North, Range 12 West, U.S. Surveyors' Notes.

settlers who had elected to remain near the Des Moines River, a
main transportation artery in the early years.

VI

FROM these analyses regarding land selection by speculators, we
may safely conclude that soil type and topography were apparently more important than proximity to the county seat, major
towns, or important rivers. The large buyers seemed to prefer
prairie land near lesser watercourses, but they also entered prairie
land in areas deficient in water and timber by some contemporary
standards, as in Kane and Eldorado townships of Benton County
or Sherman Township of Hardin. In any case, as with the analysis of soil types and selected large buyers, the most striking fact
of all is the failure of stereotyped patterns to emerge. Because
of this it is difficult to generalize. The assumption that speculators always sought out the county seat locations is, however,
simply not true. It would be more accurate to affirm that they
usually entered the best agricultural areas—namely the fertile
prairie soils.

Chapter Five

THE MECHANICS
OF LAND SPECULATION

FRONTIER LAND SPECULATION in the nineteenth century was a complex business. In its simplest form it consisted of buyers entering vacant government land with the objective of reselling at a profit. Not as simple but equally as common, was the "professional" squatters' trade in claims already described in Chapter 1. Protected by extralegal organizations known as claim clubs, such petty entrepreneurs frequently did not buy a tract of land at the land office until they had given quitclaim deeds on a number of previous claims. For many this was a way to accumulate enough gold to pay for government land which they wished to keep for themselves. For others, the process was itself a means of livelihood. Willard Barrows, veteran government surveyor, recalled from his firsthand knowledge of frontier Iowa that "great speculations were carried on by pioneer 'claim makers,' a class of men who no sooner than they had sold one claim to some newcomer, would proceed to make another, and commence improvements."[1]

As prevalent as the professional squatter was the more permanent settler who likewise used "claim law" to preempt a half section or more although the government allowed him only 160 acres. The intention was to sell the second quarter section and use the proceeds to pay for the first quarter section—where the homestead stood—thus securing one's farm for little or no cash outlay.[2]

This book, however, is primarily concerned not with the small speculator, important though he was, but with the large capitalists who acquired vast amounts of Iowa land. With no

---

[1] "History of Scott County, Iowa," *Annals of Iowa, 1st Ser.*, I (Jan., 1863), 59. See also Thomas LeDuc, "History and Appraisal of U.S. Land Policy to 1862," in Howard W. Ottoson (ed.), *Land Use Policy and Problems in the United States* (Lincoln, 1963), 14–15.

[2] Thomas LeDuc, "Public Policy, Private Investment, and Land Use in American Agriculture, 1825–1875," *Agr. Hist.*, XXXVII (Jan., 1963), 5–6.

88853

intention of farming in the Hawkeye State, these individuals and corporations were simply interested in attractive investments for surplus or borrowed funds. Iowa real estate, it was commonly believed, could provide such an outlet. Even recent immigrants were aware of this fact. A Marion County newcomer, for example, writing to his friends in the Netherlands in 1848, urged men with means who intended migrating to the United States to buy "uninhabited" land rather than lend their funds (at the legal interest limit of 10 per cent) if they wished to maximize profits. Monied Americans, the immigrant explained, had already learned this lesson. "In Iowa," he wrote, "we have speculators who, five years ago . . . bought large areas of government land in the eastern part of our state, at one dollar and twenty-five cents per acre. These people are again selling it for ten dollars or more. This is better than tying up your money at interest."[3]

I

IN THE BROAD SENSE only three components are needed in a system of land speculation—the seller with land to offer, the buyer with capital to invest, and the realtor or middleman to bring buyer and seller together. In the situation considered here, the seller was either the national or state government, the commodity was unimproved or "wild" land on the Iowa frontier, and the investors were from every part of the Union. The interchange was complicated by the interstate nature of Iowa land investment, the involvement of the national government, and the fact that the general business picture and prosperity of the nation influenced the amount of available investment capital. Frequently the speculator's final decision to invest hinged on his assessment of a wide variety of factors: among other things, the amount of immigration into the state; the agricultural potential of the soil; and the prospects for transportation outlets. Unless the buyer had gained his information at firsthand by a visit to the West, even such a thing as the extent of eastern newspaper coverage of western conditions might influence his ultimate decision.

To obtain a clearer picture of the larger investors, biographical information was culled from county histories, newspapers, and manuscript population census rolls for the 984 individuals who entered a thousand acres or more of land in

[3] Sjoerd Aukes Sipma, *Belangrijke Berigten uit Pella* (Dockum, Netherlands, 1849), 23–24. An original copy of this pamphlet is in the State Historical Society of Iowa, Iowa City. For a complete English translation, see Robert P. Swierenga (ed.), "A Dutch Immigrant's View of Frontier Iowa," *Annals of Iowa, 3rd Ser.*, XXXVIII (Fall, 1965), 81–118.

TABLE 5.1
LARGE ENTRYMEN IN CENTRAL IOWA BY OCCUPATIONAL GROUPING

Iowans		Non-Iowans	
Major occupation	No.	Major occupation	No.
Realtor-banker-lawyer	118	Merchant-manufacturer	27
Farmer-stock raiser	86	Realtor-banker-lawyer	24
Merchant-manufacturer	37	Farmer-stock raiser	15
County, township, city		Attorney	7
official	12	Physician	4
Physician	10	State legislator	2
Attorney	9	U.S. Congressman	1
Carpenter	5	Insurance executive	1
U.S. official	5	Newspaper editor	1
Clergyman	3	Carpenter	1
"Gentleman"	2		
Clerk	2		
Newspaper editor	1		
Horticulturalist	1		
Railroad executive	1		
Total	292	Total	83

central Iowa (Royce Cession 262).[4] A search of the county deed registers, which usually contain the county or city of residence of the grantor, indicated that 648 (65.9 per cent) lived in Iowa while 308 (31.3 per cent) resided in 24 other states and territories plus the District of Columbia. Only nine states in the Union were not represented, seven in the Deep South.[5]

The occupations were as varied as the places of residence. Of the 292 investors living in Iowa for which data could be uncovered, 118 (40 per cent) were primarily engaged as realtor-bankers or realtor-lawyers (Table 5.1). Many of these, of course, also doubled as government officials, merchants, farmers, and even clergymen. The 86 local farmers who comprised the second largest occupational group speculated on a comparatively smaller scale; all but eleven entered less than 2,000 acres.[6] Most of the

[4] See Chapter 2, n. 14. Michael D. Green, Michael Cunningham, and Charles Bowman assisted in the collection and compilation of the data on which this section is based. The largest repository of county histories is, of course, the Library of Congress, but the excellent collections in the libraries of the State Historical Society of Iowa, Iowa City, and the Wisconsin State Historical Society, Madison, also proved helpful. Although the works consulted are not cited here or in the bibliography, a nearly complete list is available in Clarence Stewart Peterson (comp.), Consolidated Bibliography of County Histories in Fifty States in 1961, Consolidated 1935–1961 (2nd ed., Baltimore, 1963).
[5] The place of residence could not be determined for 28 (2.8 per cent) entrants. The breakdown by state for the 308 out-of-state investors is as follows: Ohio 85, Ill. 48, Ind. 42, N.Y. 30, Pa. 25, Md. 17, Mo. 9, Ky. 7, Mass. 7, Va. 7, Neb. 4, Tenn. 4, Wis. 4, Conn. 3, N.H. 3, N.J. 3, Vt. 3, Calif. 1, D.C. 1, Kan. 1, Minn. 1, N.C. 1, Ore. 1, and R.I. 1.
[6] A brief investigation into the occupations of investors in the 640–1000-acre group similarly disclosed a very high proportion of local farmers.

remaining investors were principally employed as merchants or manufacturers, government officials, physicians, and attorneys (trial and legal counselors), with a scattering of tradesmen, clergymen, "gentlemen," clerks, and a newspaper editor, horticulturalist, and railroad executive. These figures, it should be noted, represent only what seems to have been the major occupation of the individuals. For example, although only seventeen Iowans indicated they were in full-time government employ, at least 150 held elective or appointive posts in national, state, and local governments at some time in the ante bellum period.

Whether dealing in raw land led to financial success for these investors is a matter discussed in later chapters. A comparison of the net worth of their real property as listed by the federal census marshals in the decennial censuses of 1850 and 1860 suggests, however, that such investments were profitable. Of the 49 Iowans for which such data were found (Table 5.2), the average net worth climbed from $4,648 in 1850 to $31,029 by 1860. Significantly, 20 were Iowa realtor-bankers and their net worth increased most markedly. For example, the value of Morgan Reno's real estate rose from only $1,700 in 1850 to $200,000 in 1860. Benjamin F. Allen, William F. Coolbaugh,[7] Bernhart Henn, and LeGrand Byington each saw their net worth climb from less than $10,000 in 1850 to $100,000 and above by 1860. As a group, the value of the real property of the realtors increased nearly tenfold during the decade of the 1850's, from an average of $6,316 in 1850 to $56,375 in 1860.

Of the 83 out-of-state investors for which biographical information was found (Table 5.1), a third were merchants and manufacturers; realtor-bankers and realtor-lawyers comprised another one-third. Only 13 were farmers and stock-raisers—a much smaller proportion than among Iowans. The remainder were mostly attorneys, physicians, and government officials. Frontier real estate for most of these business and professional men, it would appear from their biographies, was not the major source of their income but rather provided a profitable outlet for surplus capital. For instance, Alvah Buckingham and his son Benjamin H. of the Ohio firm of Buckingham & Sturgis used funds earned in their successful grain warehouse business in Zanesville, Toledo, Chicago, and New York to enter 230,000 acres of Congress land in the prairie states from Indiana to Kansas.[8]

---

[7] For an account of Coolbaugh's success story, see J. T. Remey, "William F. Coolbaugh," *Annals of Iowa, 3rd Ser.*, VII (July, 1906), 401–12.

[8] The other partners were Solomon Sturgis and his son William. See J. F. Everhart & Co., *History of Muskingum County, Ohio* . . . (n.p., 1882), n.p. The acreage figure is in Paul W. Gates, "Land Policy and Tenancy in the Prairie States," *J. Econ. Hist.*, I (May, 1941), 70.

TABLE 5.2
Value of Real Estate of 49 Large Entrymen in Central Iowa*

Investor	Value 1850	1860
†Allen, Benjamin F.	$ 6,000	$130,000
Beard, Andrew	2,600	5,000
Benson, John	9,000	10,000
†Berryhill, Charles H.	6,830	50,000
Bird, William	2,000	3,600
Bowman, Samuel H.	1,800	8,000
†Byington, LeGrand	16,000	100,000
Campbell, James	3,000	10,000
Carpenter, Anthony	10,000	25,000
†Casady, Phineas M.	300	36,000
Chase, Hiram	600	5,000
†Coolbaugh, William F.	15,000	100,000
Delay, Joseph	5,000	15,000
Dicks, Jesse S.	2,000	30,000
†Downey, Hugh D.	3,500	20,000
Fenton, Joel	2,000	3,000
†Granger, Barlow	1,500	4,000
†Grimes, James W.	30,000	75,000
†Hamilton, William L.	500	15,000
Hart, James B.	1,000	6,000
†Henn, Bernhart	7,500	100,000
†Langworthy, James L.	21,200	80,000
Lowe, Obediah	6,000	92,000
Luther, Samuel	3,200	30,000
Lyons, William H.	2,000	2,500
McCall, Samuel	1,500	4,000
†McDaneld, John M.	1,000	50,000
McKinley, Abner	2,400	5,000
McMillen, Thomas	1,500	23,000
Miller, Admiral B.	800	10,000
Mitchell, Thomas	5,000	2,000
Mize, Fleming	3,000	10,000
†Ogg, Elias B.	300	15,000
†Reno, Morgan	1,700	200,000
†Rider, Daniel	1,800	23,500
†Sanford, Horatio W.	5,000	40,000
Saylor, John	4,000	8,000
Schaeffer, David L.	2,000	7,000
†Scholte, Henry P.	2,096	40,000
Stutzman, Conrad	2,200	3,000
Sypher, Reuben W.	4,000	10,000
†Temple, George D.	600	7,000
Thomas, Younger	400	1,800
Thompson, Andrew McF.	10,786	25,000
†Tidrick, Robert L.	1,500	25,000
Walker, George G.	3,000	4,000
†White, John	4,000	17,000
Williams, Benjamin	3,500	5,000
Workman, Samuel M.	2,500	30,000
Totals	$223,112	$1,520,400

*Source: manuscript federal population censuses of 1850 and 1860. The 1850 census did not distinguish between realty and personalty; the totals therefore include both kinds of property.

†Denotes an Iowa realtor-banker.

Omer Tousey of Lawrenceburg, Indiana, likewise diverted into western land the capital that had accumulated in his dry goods business.[9] So too did John A. Roebling of Trenton, New Jersey, inventor of the wire cable and famed builder of the Brooklyn Suspension Bridge.[10] Dr. Hiram H. Little of Cleveland turned to real estate from a successful medical practice, while a Pennsylvania state senator, Henry Johnson, dabbled in western lands between his legislative duties and law practice.[11] Most of the farmers and stockmen on the list were "gentlemen farmers" who likewise found their diversion in real estate and politics. Benjamin G. Herr of Lancaster County, Pennsylvania, for example, is described in his published biographical sketch as a "farmer," yet the account blithely goes on to report that he had served three terms in the state legislature and spent the last 35 years of his life in "reading, study, and travel, and writing his various works over a dozen of which he published."[12]

The incoming letter files of one important real estate and banking firm, Cook, Sargent & Downey of Iowa City, also reveal the national scope of Iowa land investments as well as provide insights of the motivations and goals of investors. For a three-year period in the mid-1850's, nearly a hundred letters survive from citizens of 15 states pertaining to buying, selling, or the payment

---

[9] F. E. Weakley & Co., *History of Dearborn and Ohio Counties, Indiana* (Chicago, 1885), 949. Benjamin Franklin Murphey, who later accepted Des Moines banker-realtor Benjamin F. Allen as a silent partner in his Chicago commission house, was another Indiana merchant who invested in Iowa land in the 1850's. (See George Hazzard, *Hazzard's History of Henry County, Indiana, 1822–1906, Military Edition* [2 vols.; New Castle, Ind., 1906], I, 163–65. See also the sketches of New York merchant, Charles Clement Sheppard, in Lewis Cass Aldrich (ed.), *History of Yates County, N.Y.* . . . (Syracuse, 1892). 524–25: of Illinois grocer Gilbert Woodruff in Biographical Publishing Company, *Portrait and Biographical Record of Winnebago and Boone Counties, Illinois* . . . (Chicago, 1892), 237–38; and of Ohio merchant James Stockdale in C. O. Owen & Co., *Portrait and Biographical Record of Guernsey County, Ohio* . . . (Chicago, 1895), 323–24.

[10] For some of Roebling's Iowa real estate correspondence see the John A. Roebling Papers, Rutgers University Library, New Brunswick, N.J.

[11] Lewis Publishing Company, *Memorial Record of the County of Cuyahoga and City of Cleveland, Ohio* (Chicago, 1894), 725; John F. Meginnes (ed.), *History of Lycoming County, Pennsylvania* (Chicago, 1892), 752–55. Another large nonresident investor in Iowa land who deserted the medical profession for real estate was John Warner of Clinton, Ill. (See S. J. Clarke Publishing Company, *Biographical Record of DeWitt County, Illinois* [Chicago, 1901], 26–29.)

[12] J. H. Beers & Company, *Biographical Annals of Lancaster County, Pennsylvania* (Chicago, 1903), 205. Two other examples of investors like Herr were William Miller of South Bend, Ind., and Stephen M. Brinton of Allegheny County, Pa. (See Lewis Publishing Company, *Biographical Record and Portrait Album of Webster and Hamilton Counties, Iowa* . . . [Chicago, 1889], 267–68, and Western Biographical Publishing Company, *A Biographical History of Eminent and Self-Made Men of the State of Indiana* . . . [2 vols.; Cincinnati, 1880], II, 42–43.)

of taxes on Iowa land.[13] Illinois, Ohio, New York, and Pennsylvania residents contributed the most correspondence, with Maryland and Massachusetts close behind. Typical of these investors was the Gettysburg, Pennsylvania, farmer who with a wealthy neighbor wanted to enter several thousand acres in Iowa "to make some money," since his funds commanded only 6 per cent per year at home and "this way of doing business I am geting tyred of." I. A. Tilsby, proprietor of the Winthrop House of Boston, wanted a section and a half located as an investment. "I hope it will be . . . a good location," he wrote, "both for a Rise and for good Farming land."[14] What the Bostonian desired, of course, was land with fine agricultural possibilities plus a strategic location near a growing town or transportation artery.

Quite surprisingly, not a few of the eastern customers of the Iowa City agency had visited Iowa in person and knew the land market situation intimately. Frequently their letters specified the exact counties where they wished to invest. Joshua L. Baily of Philadelphia was one such buyer, demanding land in either Marshall or Hardin County. As he put it: "From what I saw myself of the country westward from Toledo to Marietta and as far as the northern townships of Hardin County my impression is very favorable, and I will therefore direct the selection . . . to be made somewhere in the region designated, according to your best judgment."[15] Speculators desiring to sell could likewise spell out in great detail the particular advantages of a given tract. An Ohioan offered an unimproved 160-acre tract in Johnson County in 1857. He reported not only that the land was good quality rolling prairie, located seven miles from Iowa City in a Quaker settlement, and surrounded on all four sides by improved farms, but also went on to name each of the farm neighbors and the exact length in rods of their fences.[16] Such information, obviously, could only have been gained by a personal visit. All this is not to deny that many investors had little or no firsthand knowledge of Iowa lands and consequently had to rely fully on the integrity of agents. Common were such hopeful re-

---

[13] The letters are in the Cook, Sargent & Downey Papers, State Historical Society of Iowa, Iowa City. A tract book of Abraham Tuston Hay, a Burlington land agent, labeled simply "Bounty Lands," lists land warrants entered in eastern and central Iowa for a brief period in 1856 and 1857. Again, the owners (almost all assignees) who sent the warrants for location lived in all parts of the Union, with 36 men from eleven different states in addition to many Iowans. The volume is in the A. T. Hay Collection, Iowa State Department of History and Archives, Des Moines.

[14] Alexander Koster to H. D. Downey, Dec. 29, 1855; Tilsby to same, Dec. 25, 1855, Cook, Sargent & Downey Papers.

[15] Dec. 14, 1855, Cook, Sargent & Downey Papers.

[16] Letter from Jesse Embree, Feb. 28, 1857, Cook, Sargent & Downey Papers.

marks as these from an Albany, New York, newspaper editor: "I trust you may be able to make such a selection as will prove remunerative as an investment."[17]

Eastern capitalists often contracted together and invested as a group, the Cook, Sargent & Downey correspondence also disclosed. One of the men might serve as secretary or agent, manage the land selections, pay taxes, and sell when favorable, the net proceeds being divided proportionately.[18] One such business contract outlining what was probably a common arrangement was signed in New York on June 30, 1853, by Joseph Stuart of New York, Wayman Crow of St. Louis, and Abraham Lincoln's friend and future U.S. Supreme Court appointee, David Davis of Bloomington, Illinois. Stuart agreed to furnish the capital sum of $15,000 for investment in western lands in Illinois, Iowa, or Wisconsin—or all three states. Crow and Davis guaranteed to return the money in three years with 7 per cent annual interest. Davis agreed to proceed to the West (in return only for his expenses), invest the funds in government land "whereever the most desirable investments may be found," pay taxes, sell the lands, and make collections. The three men agreed to enter the lands in the name of Wayman Crow and to sell a sufficient amount within three years to reimburse Stuart for his initial investment and Davis for tax payments. They planned to sell the remaining lands gradually when the price was advantageous with an equal division of the proceeds.[19]

Some easterners expressed interest in special types of land. Several Pennsylvanians, for example, inquired about undeveloped central Iowa coal lands. One asked if government land was available containing thick coal veins near transportation outlets and growing towns like Des Moines or Council Bluffs. He had in mind "a district where an Iron Foundry would be profitable, that is in good settlement . . . , with coal convenient and Pig Iron not too high price[d] or too great expense in getting it to the Foundry with some advantages in shipping manufacturing arti-

---

[17] V. Ten Eyck to H. D. Downey, Dec. 5, 1855, Cook, Sargent & Downey Papers.

[18] Letter from Thomas Harbine, Dec. 17, 1855; from L. Woodburn, Dec. 24, 1855, Cook, Sargent & Downey Papers.

[19] A copy of the memorandum is in the David Davis Papers, Illinois State Historical Library, Springfield. Land records of all the central and eastern counties in Iowa indicate that a total of 7,586 acres were entered in the name of Wayman Crow, with more acres possibly entered on the western slope. Davis, in any case, elected to sink at least two-thirds of the total capital of the partnership in Iowa land. Apparently, he felt the best investment opportunities lay in that state. Davis, on his own account, entered over 2,100 acres in eastern and central Iowa. For a brief account of the career of Wayman Crow as St. Louis merchant, state senator, railroad promoter, and philanthropist, see William Hyde and Howard L. Conrad (eds.), *Encyclopedia of the History of St. Louis* . . . (4 vols.; New York, 1899), I, 530–32.

cles." Another wanted from four to eight hundred acres "tolerable convenient to timber or coal."[20]

II

WITHOUT resident professionals to guide them, nonresident investors would have been severely handicapped. The major real estate agencies were found in the larger cities and land office towns where they usually doubled as frontier banks and law offices. These houses—the hub of the land business in the state— were linked to one another by a remarkable network of branch offices. The organizational pattern was a replica of the typical private banking house of the mid-nineteenth century such as E. W. Clark & Company, which began in Philadelphia and soon had branches in St. Louis, New Orleans, New York, and Burlington, Iowa. Based on a system dating back to medieval Italy, the original partners (those of the parent office or at least one or several of them) became partners in all the branches, whereas each branch had in addition a managing partner who participated in the profits of that branch only.[21]

There were in Iowa by the mid-1850's at least three principal land agencies with multiple branches based on this pattern. One was the pioneer agency in the state, Cook & Sargent of Davenport, established in 1847 as central Iowa lands were first being offered for sale.[22] Beginning with but a few thousand dollars of capital it was destined in the next years to play an important part in the real estate and banking operations of the state. Its founders were Ebenezer Cook, a Davenport attorney, and George B. Sargent, United States deputy surveyor and later surveyor-general for the

[20] John L. Smith to Cook, Sargent & Downey, Dec. 14, 1855; John Sherrick to same, Dec. 5, 1855, Cook, Sargent & Downey Papers. John A. Roebling of Trenton, New Jersey, was another eastern speculator who leased coal lands in central Iowa (John H. Leavitt to John A. Roebling, Feb. 27, 1861, John A. Roebling Papers).

[21] Fritz Redlich, *The Molding of American Banking, Men and Ideas, Part II, 1840–1910* (New York, 1951), 71.

[22] Cook & Sargent's advertisement announcing the opening of their agency is in the Davenport *Gazette*, Oct. 21, 1847. For general information on the firm see Rand McNally & Co., *History of the First National Bank in the United States* (Chicago, 1913), 16–24; Clarence R. Aurner, *Leading Events in Johnson County, Iowa, History* (Cedar Rapids, 1912), 446–47. Although Cook & Sargent are usually recognized as the first general land and banking agency in Iowa (see, for example, Earle D. Ross, "George Barnard Sargent, Western Promoter," *Ia. J. Hist. and Pol.*, XLV [Apr., 1947], 117, 121), local land agents advertised their services as early as 1837 when Iowa was still part of Wisconsin Territory. See the cards of Joshua Aiken and Robert E. Little of the Des Moines Land Company at Montrose, and James Douglas and Henry Eno of Fort Madison in the Burlington *Wisconsin Territorial Gazette and Burlington Advertiser*, July 20, Dec. 16, 1837.

Fig. 5.1. New business card of Cook & Sargent, Davenport Gazette, *October 21, 1847.*

Iowa-Wisconsin district. Within a year they were dealing heavily in land warrants while on the side they sold life insurance, laid out new additions to the city of Davenport, and operated a general banking business.[23] In January of 1853 they founded branch agencies under new partners at Dubuque, Iowa City, and Rock Island, Illinois.[24] When government land offices opened in cen-

[23] Davenport *Gazette,* Apr. 6, Aug. 3, 1848, Nov. 20, 1851, Feb. 12, 1852. Ebenezer Cook practiced law in Davenport as early as 1842. He also served as an insurance agent for two eastern companies and held a directorship on the boards of the Rock Island and Burlington railroads. See *ibid.,* Aug. 26, 1842, Apr. 18 and Nov. 21, 1850, May 6, 1852. Sargent, like Cook, was an insurance agent and railroad advocate but, unlike his partner, was not satisfied to remain an Iowa entrepreneur. After a stint as mayor of Davenport he left Iowa during the Civil War for Boston, New York, and finally European financial circles, where as a member of Jay Cooke & Co., he marketed railroad bonds. For a sketch of his business career see Ross, "George Barnard Sargent," 115–32.

[24] Iowa City partner Hugh D. Downey of Pennsylvania was the most influential of Cook & Sargent's associates. He came to Iowa City in 1842 only two years out of college with his law degree, and within a decade, had become the leading banker of the then capital city. In 1859, when the parent house in Davenport failed, Downey's books showed a $150,000 surplus of assets over liabilities. Downey took on Walter Curtis of Boston as his new partner, changing the style of the firm to Downey & Curtis. Curtis, the son of ex-U.S. Supreme Court Justice Benjamin R. Curtis, brought $25,000 in cash to the reorganized firm. The extended depression of the late Fifties finally discouraged the partners, and the firm liquidated its liabilities, paid all

---

COOK & SARGENT, - - *Davenport, Iowa.*
COOK, SARGENT, BARNEY & CO., Dubuque, "
COOK, SARGENT & DOWNEY, - Iowa City, "
COOK, SARGENT & PARKER, - Rock Island, Ills.

BANKERS AND DEALERS IN EXCHANGE,

AND LAND AGENTS.

Notes and Bills collected and proceeds remitted to any part of the United States.

Bills of Exchange on all the principal Cities of the United States and Europe,
Bought and Sold.

Money remitted to Europe in Sight Bills, which can be cashed in any town in
England, Ireland, or Wales, in sums £1 upwards.

LAND WARRANTS,

FOR CASH, OR ON TIME, TO SUIT PURCHASERS, CONSTANTLY ON -
HAND. DEALERS SUPPLIED ON LIBERAL TERMS.

—REFER TO—

E. W. CLARK & BROS., St. Louis.	E. W. CLARK, DODGE & CO., New York.
E. W. CLARK & CO., Philadelphia.	J. W. CLARK & CO., Boston, Mass.
GEORGE SMITH & CO., Chicago.	HATCH & LANGDON, Cincinnati, Ohio.
HARRIS & CO., Philadelphia.	SAMUEL HARRIS & CO., Baltimore.

Fig. 5.2. Advertisement of Cook & Sargent and branch agencies,
Davenport Gazette, *June 30, 1853.*

tral and western Iowa they also established houses at Des Moines
and Florence, Nebraska.[25]

Their real estate offerings increased as rapidly as their
branches. Before 1853 their largest advertisement boasted only
5,000 acres in Scott, Clinton, and Cedar counties; but by the end
of the year they offered almost 25,000 acres in five eastern counties. In 1856 they advertised 27,000 acres in nine central Iowa
counties. At this time their net worth was reputed to be over
one million dollars. In 1858 they published a catalogue of first-

its creditors, and closed permanently on July 8, 1861 (Iowa City *Republican,*
June 13, 1856, Mar. 9, 1859, July 10, 1861, Oct. 2, 1867; Davenport *Gazette,*
Dec. 29, 1859).

[25] See advertisement in Davenport *Gazette,* Jan. 27, 1853. The Nebraska
agency was designed more to issue paper money, called "Florence money,"
than to sell land (Nebraska law allowed banks of issue banned by Iowa law).
Capitalized at $100,000, the bank eventually issued $236,000 in paper notes.
In the depression of the late Fifties, Florence money, along with most paper
currency, fell into disrepute. The firm was finally forced into suspension in
December of 1859 but all the notes were ultimately redeemed at par and destroyed. Meanwhile, in June, 1860, Sargent reopened his land agency and
resumed dealing in Iowa real estate. See Ruth A. Gallaher, "Money in Pioneer Iowa, 1838–1865," *Ia. J. Hist. and Pol.,* XXXII (Jan., 1934), 28–29;
Iowa City *Republican,* July 6 and 31, 1856, Mar. 17 and Apr. 7, 1858; Davenport *Gazette,* Nov. 12, 1857, Jan. 7, 1858; Ross, "George Barnard Sargent,"
124–25.

class unimproved lands for sale listing 300,000 acres spread over 51 Iowa counties and several in Nebraska, Minnesota, and Wisconsin. "That advertisement tells its own story," an Iowa newspaper editor remarked about this huge inventory. "It attests the enormous wealth of the firm and it conveys some idea of the extent to which the lands of this State are held by speculators."[26]

Another major statewide land agency was that of Greene & Weare, founded in 1851 in Cedar Rapids. George Greene, an immigrant from England, came to Davenport in 1838 and assisted David Dale Owen in making a government geological survey of the new territory of Iowa. By 1841 Greene owned the land on which the future town of Cedar Rapids was platted, and in 1842 successfully lobbied in Washington to get a United States land office located in Marion, near his interests. He was also a lawyer, newspaper editor, and territorial legislator. In 1847, at only thirty years of age, he was appointed to the Iowa supreme court. Greene's partner, John Weare, Jr., came to Cedar Rapids in 1845 from Vermont, via Michigan. He was a man of great practical ability—"one of the shrewdest financiers in Iowa," boasted a biographer—and he handled most of the daily operations of the real estate and banking house. Something like three million dollars eventually passed between his hands and settlers via the time-entry route, it was claimed. Within a few years Greene & Weare had established seven branch agencies throughout Iowa on the same pattern as Cook & Sargent. Their houses were located at the major land office towns of Marion, Des Moines, Fort Dodge, Sioux City, and Council Bluffs, as well as at Cedar Falls and Vinton.[27]

A third major agency and one that figured most prominently in central Iowa was Henn, Williams & Company of Fairfield. Bernhart Henn, the senior member of the firm, was a native of New York State who began his career in Iowa in 1839 as a clerk in the Burlington Land Office. In 1844 he won a coveted appointment as register in the new Fairfield Land Office. By August of 1849, his apprenticeship complete, Henn launched into the land

[26] *Catalogue of Lands in Iowa, Wisconsin, Minnesota, etc., for Sale by Cook & Sargent* (Davenport, 1858). For representative newspaper advertisements see Davenport *Gazette*, Oct. 2, 1851, June 9 and Dec. 13, 1853, Jan. 14, 1858; Iowa City *Republican*, June 11, 1856, June 30, 1858. The editor's comment is in the Des Moines *Iowa Weekly Citizen*, Feb. 17, 1858. A rival realtor years later described the firm as the "Pierpont Morgans of the day" (L. A. Brewer and B. L. Wick, *History of Linn County, Iowa* [2 vols.; Cedar Rapids, 1911], I, 439).

[27] Western Historical Co., *History of Linn County, Iowa* . . . (Chicago, 1878), 680; American Biographical Publishing Co., *The United States Biographical Dictionary and Portrait Gallery of Eminent and Self-Made Men, Iowa Volume* (Chicago, 1878), 55–56; Brewer and Wick, *History of Linn County*, I, 435–36; George B. Carroll, *Pioneer Life in and around Cedar Rapids, Iowa, from 1839 to 1849* (Cedar Rapids, 1895), 142–45, 148–53; John S. Ely, *George Greene, Address of John S. Ely, Coe College Founders' Day, December 3, 1914* (Cedar Rapids, 1914), 5–24. For one of the firm's land advertisements see Cedar Rapids *Democrat*, June 24, 1856.

Fig. 5.3. George Greene, pioneer Cedar Rapids land agent.

business in Fairfield on his own. His shingle, hung over a store-front adjacent to the town's leading hotel, read simply "Land and Agency Office." With his choice location, intimate knowledge of the land district, and expertise in dealing with land office personnel, Henn's business boomed. His reputation rose accordingly, and in 1850, the citizens of the Second Congressional District elected their budding real estate promoter to the first of two successive terms in Congress. To free himself for service in Washington, Henn in 1851 reorganized his agency into a partnership with Jesse Williams and George and Edward Temple.[28]

[28] One of Henn's first advertisements, dated Aug. 9, 1849, is in the Des Moines *Iowa Star*, Feb. 1, 1850. The Fairfield *Ledger*, Dec. 10, 1851, contains the initial announcement of the new partnership, dated June 13, 1851. The firm offered the customary services: exchange, land warrants, tax paying, collections, locating government land, and selling second-hand lands. For biographical data on Henn, see *ibid.*, Aug. 14, 1895; Edward H. Stiles, *Recollections and Sketches of Notable Lawyers and Public Men of Early Iowa* . . . (Des Moines, 1916), 128–29; Lake City Publishing Co., *Portrait and Biographical Album of Jefferson and Van Buren Counties, Iowa* . . . (Chicago, 1890), 282–83.

Henn's partners proved as capable as he was. Williams, a native of Cincinnati, had migrated to Iowa in 1838 after a stint as clerk in the office of the Ohio surveyor-general. As early as 1836 he had entered lands in Indiana on joint account with a Cincinnati capitalist and by 1838 he was engaged in a land agency in Burlington. However, his appointments as Iowa territorial agent and then as territorial auditor and finally his election as the first secretary of state kept him from Iowa real estate affairs for almost a decade.[29] George D. Temple came to Burlington in 1836 from New Hampshire. He practiced law and notarized legal documents, served in the territorial legislature, and ultimately became mayor of the city. Edward Ames Temple, George's younger brother, also joined the firm, taking charge of its new Chariton branch in 1853. In 1860 he went into the banking business in Ottumwa and became a financier of the first rank.[30]

Henn, Williams & Company expanded rapidly. The original partners established branches under resident partners as fast as new land offices were opened at Chariton, Council Bluffs, Fort Dodge, and Sioux City. In 1854 one of their newspaper advertisements boasted of 40,000 acres of "Choice Lands" for sale. The firm was also one of the first to publish a detailed map of Iowa, hopefully designed to lure eastern investors and settlers (see endpapers).[31]

Besides the three major chains, many other land agencies flourished in the 1850's. Dubuque claimed Horatio W. Sanford, Iowa's largest land speculator and one of the state's first realtors and moneylenders. Beginning operations in 1846, he was so successful that within four years he had accumulated over $30,000 and by 1858 had made over $100,000. Eventually the title to over a million acres of land, largely in northern Iowa, passed through his hands.[32] Another important Dubuque agency was that of William J. Barney, originally the resident partner in the Cook &

[29] See Samuel Williams to Jesse Williams, May 19, 1838, Augustus Hopkins to same, Mar. 23, 1839, Milton N. W. Leace to same, Feb. 1, 1841, and a copy of the partnership agreement with John W. Cooper, dated July 13, 1836, all in the Jesse Williams Papers, Iowa State Department of History and Archives, Des Moines. See also Iowa *House Journal,* 1841, 38; 1843, 287; 1847, 27. An early real estate advertisement of Williams is in the Burlington *Iowa Territorial Gazette and Burlington Advertiser,* Mar. 30, 1839.

[30] E. A. Temple founded the Bankers' Life Assurance Company and served as its president until his death in 1912. For information on the Temples see State Historical Co., *History of Lucas County, Iowa* (Des Moines, 1881), 673–74; Thomas Hedge, "Installation of the Temple Tablet, June 17, 1913," *Annals of Iowa, 3rd Ser.,* XI (July–Oct., 1913), 168–79, 225–26; Fairfield *Ledger,* July 30, 1857.

[31] Fairfield *Ledger,* Mar. 2, 1854; Fort Dodge *Sentinel,* July 31, 1856; B. L. Wick, "Early Iowa Map Attracts Settlers," *Annals of Iowa, 3rd Ser.,* XXV (Oct., 1943), 135–36.

[32] Western Historical Co., *History of Dubuque County, Iowa* (Chicago, 1880), 873; Dubuque *Weekly Miners' Express,* May 3, 1848.

BERNHART HENN.   JESSE WILLIAMS.   G. D. TEMPLE.

LAND AND EXCHANGE
OFFICE.

HENN, WILLIAMS & CO.,
FAIRFIELD, IOWA,

Are pacpared to do a GENERAL EXCHANGE and LAND AGENCY business, as heretofore—receive DEPOSITES on the most favorable terms—Time and sight bills bought and sold. Collections made in any part of Southern Iowa, and proceeds promptly remitted by sight drafts on any of the cities East. Remittances, and orders for EXCHANGE from the surrounding country, will receive prompt attention.

They keep constantly on hand an ample supply of LAND WARRANTS, and SCRIP, and are prepared to fill any and all orders for the selection and purchase of Government land, in any part of Iowa.

March 9, 1854—tf   H W & CO

40,000 ACRES of choice lands, situate in the different counties of the State, for sale on the most liberal terms.

March 9, 1854—tf

Fig. 5.4. Advertisement of Henn, Williams & Co., in the Fairfield Iowa Sentinel, April 13, 1854.

Sargent chain, and Caleb H. Booth, former surveyor-general of Iowa; they also maintained branches at Fort Dodge and Decorah. Greene & Weare's major competitor in Cedar Rapids was B. S. Bryan, who with his brother-in-law from New Jersey opened an office in 1852 and soon had branches at Waterloo and Sioux City.[33]

In addition to Hugh D. Downey, agent for Cook & Sargent, Iowa City boasted three major realtor-bankers who entered large quantities of Iowa land: Morgan Reno, John C. Culbertson, and James H. Gower. Reno, who served as Iowa's first state treasurer (1842–50), was associated with Culbertson in a banking and real estate firm.[34] Gower was one of the most successful frontier Iowa

[33] Dubuque *Daily Miners' Express,* Feb. 1, 1854; Fort Dodge *Sentinel,* Apr. 23, 1857; Cedar Rapids *Democrat,* June 24, 1856; Brewer and Wick, *History of Linn County,* 436. The partnership of an Iowan and an easterner in local real estate agencies and banks was common. Cedar Rapids banker S. D. Carpenter joined in partnership with two Ohioans, L. H. Lehman of Wooster and E. C. Kreider of Lancaster. A. L. Yerby of Virginia and A. H. Barrow of the District of Columbia, described as "an old established firm at the East," established a Davenport agency in 1855, with Barrow moving to Iowa to manage the business. Davenport land agent Charles Powers was associated with John P. H. Tallman of Poughkeepsie, N.Y., while P. D. Turner of Iowa City was the resident agent for William H. Ward of Washington, D.C. See Brewer and Wick, *History of Linn County,* 438; Davenport *Democratic Banner,* Jan. 19, 1855; Davenport *Gazette,* Apr. 19, 1855.

[34] Iowa City *Republican,* July 14, 1859. See also Stiles, *Recollections and Sketches,* 765–66.

Fig. 5.5. Advertisement of James H. Gower in the Iowa City Weekly Republican. *Gower ran ads of this type continuously, 1858–60.*

businessmen. A native of Maine, he came to Iowa in 1838 and almost immediately began entering land. From 1845 until 1877, except for the Civil War interlude, he operated an agency in Iowa City. In the prewar period he combined real estate with a produce commission house, an extensive wholesale and retail dry goods store, and the first savings bank in Iowa. His newspaper advertisements by 1856 listed 40,000 acres of land for sale in over 30 counties. A portion of these lands, he noted, were selected as early as 1840 and were "the very oldest in the State." Ultimately Gower purchased and sold over 100,000 acres of government land in Iowa and boasted that more than a thousand men and families settled on lands purchased from him.[35] A friend of his best summed up Gower's career when he wrote: "In business he was great. That faculty in him seemed more the outgrowth of genius than of mere talent. All seasons were alike. His operations in real estate covered Iowa, Nebraska, Kansas and Missouri. Not in any sense a speculator[!] his improvements were planted with rare foresight in the path of settlement, where roads must go, where towns had to be. In a seaport he would have been the greatest merchant of his generation, with argosies on every sea. But Fate cast him inland and he gathered from every quarter the avails of his good judgment and happy foresight."[36]

Gower, the businessman's ideal, had his counterparts elsewhere in Iowa. In Des Moines the outstanding realtor-bankers were Benjamin F. Allen, Hoyt Sherman, Ira Cook, Byron Rice, and Andrew J. Stevens. Allen, Des Moines' first private banker, opened his offices in 1854, and was followed the same year by Hoyt Sherman and his partners Phineas M. Casady and Robert L. Tidrick. Byron Rice founded the third Des Moines institution in conjunction with the Cedar Rapids firm of Greene & Weare, and Ira Cook became the resident partner of Cook & Sargent. Andrew J. Stevens opened the fifth in partnership with two New Yorkers, Samuel R. Ingham and James Callanan.[37] In all, by

[35] Iowa City *Iowa Capitol Reporter*, Mar. 28, 1855; Iowa City *Republican*, Mar. 26 and June 5, 1856, Nov. 24, 1858, Nov. 25, 1868, Nov. 19, 1879; Iowa City *Daily Crescent*, Aug. 15, 1857.

[36] "Obituary of James H. Gower," Iowa City *State Press*, Nov. 19, 1879.

[37] For one of Sherman's advertisements of over 100,000 acres for sale in 13 central Iowa counties see Des Moines *Iowa Weekly Citizen*, June 10, 1857. Stevens at the same time offered 10,000 acres of the "choicest Farming Land" in central Iowa, "selected at the first sales," for $10 per acre and up (*ibid.*, June 24, 1857). Surviving records of Andrew J. Stevens & Co. consist of a journal (June 1, 1857–Aug., 1857), and James Callanan's letter book (1858–63) in the Iowa State Department of History and Archives, Des Moines. For biographical data on Allen, Callanan, Casady, Cook, Tidrick, Rice, Sherman, and Stevens, see L. F. Andrews, *Pioneers of Polk County, Iowa, and Reminiscences of Early Days* (2 vols.; Des Moines, 1908), I, 27–31, 55–65, 67–71, 79–83, 253–61, and 415–20.

1855, Iowa boasted 46 private banks in 18 cities across the state.[38]

III

TYPICALLY, young men operating financially on the proverbial "shoestring," but with some experience either as surveyors or land office officials, built the first real estate and banking concerns in Iowa.[39] George Weare, twenty-year-old employee in the Cedar Rapids firm of Greene & Weare in which his older brother John was the junior partner, found himself in 1855 staked with $1,000 and a few land warrants to open a branch office in Sioux City. In 1850 or 1851 Seymour D. Carpenter of Cedar Rapids, also in his early twenties, was offered a fourth interest in that city's first land agency for only $500—another indication of the limited capital required by pioneer realtor-bankers.[40] But more important for ultimate success than the amount of initial capital were the qualifications of the men involved. The most essential prerequisites were familiarity with the land of the district and with the field notes, maps, and operation of the land office. Helpful, too, was previous legal training for title and tax problems. Thus, lawyers, experienced surveyors, and former land office personnel proved to be the best equipped dealers in government lands. Henn, Williams, Downey, Tidrick, Casady, Thomas J. Cox, John Clark, and Joseph B. Stewart, to name only a few, all came into the real estate profession through positions in government land offices. On the other hand, Sargent, Booth, Greene, Ira Cook, and Willard Barrows were among those surveyors who parlayed their knowledge of Iowa land into profitable careers in real estate. Western attorneys, needless to add, almost all augmented their earnings by dabbling in realty, and every prominent banking and land agency included at least one lawyer.

Since the issuance of notes or paper money was banned by the Iowa constitution until 1858, land was the main avenue to

---

[38] For a listing see the *Bankers' Magazine and Statistical Register, New Ser.,* V (Dec., 1855), 471–72. On pioneer banking in Iowa see Hoyt Sherman's "Early Banking in Iowa," *Annals of Iowa, 3rd Ser.,* V (Apr., 1901), 1–13, and "The State Bank of Iowa," in *Iowa Bankers' Assn. Pro., 1894* (Cedar Rapids, 1894), 28–44; Howard H. Preston, *History of Banking in Iowa* (Iowa City, 1922), chap. iv; and Erling A. Erickson, "Banks and Politics Before the Civil War: The Case of Iowa, 1836–1865" (Ph.D. dissertation, University of Iowa, 1967), chap. iv. Erickson's excellent study supersedes Preston for the ante bellum period.

[39] Of the 358 large Iowa investors for which data on age were obtained, 240, or two-thirds, were under forty. Half (119) of this group, in turn, were under thirty years of age.

[40] Sioux City *Journal,* Dec. 27, 1905; Brewer and Wick, *History of Linn County,* 435.

prosperity.[41] And profits accumulated rapidly as the land market blossomed under the stimulus of the principal medium—the land warrant. As the following chapter outlines in detail, the government opened millions of acres for entry and at the same time granted to veterans thousands of acres of land warrants as reward for military service. The warrants, which quickly circulated among eastern brokers at varying rates of discount, were accepted at the western land offices at par. The realtor-banker always included these certificates among his assets, offering them for cash sale or on a year's credit with no down payment at rates of 40 to 50 per cent.[42] Most were sold on credit to speculators and to settlers who were eager for land but lacked the only alternative exchange medium accepted at land offices—hard cash. In such cases, the realtor would protect the loan by entering the land in his own name, giving the other party a title bond expressing an obligation to deed the land at the end of a specified time on the payment of the loan.

The practice of "entering land on time" was widespread. So, at least, one would conclude from the frequent appearance in the land records of the names of Iowa land agents and bankers. In the 33 counties of central Iowa for example, 118, or nearly one-fifth, of the 648 Iowans who entered 1,000 acres or more of government land advertised their services as land agents (see Appendix V). Together their original entries in the cession area totaled nearly 880,000 acres. More striking, of the 14 men who entered 25,000 acres or more, ten were Iowa realtors and bankers who dealt largely in land warrant credit entries; the remainder were eastern investors who followed the same practice through their local western agents.[43]

---

[41] Hoyt Sherman's land ventures, for example, apparently proved most remunerative, since he left an estate valued at $350,000 (Des Moines *Daily News,* Jan. 25, 29, 1904). George W. Howe, Osceola land agent and merchant, similarly accumulated an estate worth $200,000 (Lewis Publishing Co., *Biographical and Historical Record of Clarke County, Iowa* . . . [Chicago, 1886], 231). Benjamin F. Allen, on the other hand, was able to have an opulent $250,000 mansion constructed in Des Moines immediately after the Civil War for his residence (Andrews, *Pioneers of Polk County,* I, 59–60).

[42] Evidence to substantiate high interest costs in frontier Iowa is abundant. Andrew Jackson Sterrett, a Pennsylvania land buyer who spent several years in the mid-1850's at the land office towns of Fort Des Moines and Fort Dodge, reported in early 1855 to his brother in Pennsylvania that "money is now worth 40 pr ct a year here with the best of real estate security" (A. J. Sterrett to David Brice Innis Sterrett, Jan. 16, 1855, Andrew Jackson Sterrett Papers, Manuscript Division, Minnesota Historical Society, St. Paul). At the time of the Osage land sales in 1857 another agent reported that money "bears high interest here, the lowest at 2 per cent a month" (N. Boardman to Nathaniel Gordon, Apr. 7, 1857, Nathaniel Gordon Papers, Manuscript Division, Baker Library, Boston). See also Chapter 6, n. 55.

[43] The ten Iowa realtors who entered more than 25,000 acres were Benjamin F. Allen, William J. Barney, Ira Cook, John C. Culbertson, Hugh D. Downey, James H. Gower, Ward Lamson, Morgan Reno, Edward A. Temple,

Fig. 5.6. Hoyt Sherman, prominent Des Moines land agent and banker.

Fig. 5.7. Judge Phineas M. Casady, of the Des Moines land agency, Casady & Sherman.

Of course, some of these entries by local land agents involved only their own speculations. To gain an idea of the extent of such personal speculations a rule of thumb was devised to distinguish them from time entries made for others. At the standard interest rate on credit entries of 40 per cent per annum, the land office price of $1.25 per acre advanced approximately fifty cents per year. One or two years was the usual time allowed on credit sales after which the buyer paid his note and the creditor transferred title. Thus land held longer than two years, or sold within one year after entry at more than $2.00 per acre or within two years at more than $3.00 per acre, likely was not a credit entry. Guided by this rule, the holdings of the ten major Iowa real estate vendors whose entries exceeded 25,000 acres were traced in the deed registers of nine representative central Iowa counties. Of the sales recorded, comprising 127,150 acres, only 36,178 acres or 28.5 per cent were clearly not credit entries. Of the remaining 71.5 per cent, most had likely been entered for other buyers via the time entry system.

In addition to buying and selling land and dealing in land warrants, most Iowa realtor-bankers offered many other services, all related to land. Dealing in bills of exchange on St. Louis and the eastern cities was profitable. Since the government required payment for land in gold, land buyers would exchange their drafts on eastern banks for gold on which they paid a high premium. The frontier bankers would in turn sell the eastern drafts at an advance to local merchants who constantly needed eastern funds to pay for goods purchased. Realtors, of course, also bought and sold land for customers on commission, located government land and paid taxes for nonresidents, and collected notes and bills. Many of the notes were in the hands of settlers, the result of credit sales of land. When they fell due, the agent exchanged the patent title for the title bond upon the collection of the debt and remitted the funds to the investor.

Iowa financiers not only handled the bulk of the funds invested in Hawkeye real estate, they also played a major part in broadcasting the advantages of the state throughout the rest of the nation. To lure investors they ran extensive advertisements in key eastern newspapers and published detailed maps outlining new towns, cities, and transportation routes. In their circulars and advertisements the realtors stressed both the ease of acquiring land and the certain profits that would ensue. One such advertisement by Greene & Weare in *Thompson's Bank Note Reporter*

and Jesse Williams. The four easterners were James S. Easley and William W. Willingham of Halifax Court House, Va., and Miles and Elias A. White of Baltimore.

in the winter of 1856 caught the eye of a wealthy southerner, Israel G. Lash of Salem, North Carolina, and brought quick results. After a preliminary letter of inquiry, Lash began the practice of periodically sending $100 through the mail for investment in Iowa land. By the time the Civil War disrupted his program in 1861, he had entered nearly 5,000 acres of Congress land. These fortunately tided him over in the lean postwar years when he tried to recover from his wartime losses of a half million dollars.[44]

While some investors sent cash for their land entries, other easterners and southerners, especially war veterans, were urged to locate their land warrants in Iowa. John Clark, for example, a former register of the Iowa City Land Office, opened a "Land Warrant Agency" in Washington, D.C., in 1856 for this purpose. With local agents in every Iowa land office town, he offered warrant holders the opportunity to enter land anywhere in the state. When announcing the opening of his agency, Clark also assured prospective customers that profits were certain if they invested in Iowa land through his house. He declared in his circular:

> I *guarantee* that all selections made by them [his western agents] will be judicious, by actual inspection, and upon the best land vacant in the District at the time: such as will be worth I am confident from $2.50 to $5.00 per acre as soon as located, and will rapidly advance upon that price. Warrantees and other holders, cannot fail to realize at once in this way, a large advance on the face of their Warrants, instead of a sacrifice which they suffer upon cash sales.[45]

Clark's announcement that he had local agents throughout Iowa was typical, yet it illustrates an important fact: that Iowa land agencies constituted a vast network linking all land office towns and county seats. For instance, Cook, Sargent & Downey of Iowa City, a central agency, paid taxes through more than two dozen different subagents in the various counties of the Iowa City Land District. Their agencies at Des Moines and Council Bluffs had similar arrangements within their land districts. Thus, any firm in the chain could locate or sell land, pay taxes, and

---

[44] See Sioux City *Journal,* Dec. 27, 1905, and Paul W. Gates, "Southern Investment in Northern Lands before the Civil War," *J. So. Hist.,* V (May, 1939), 176.

[45] A copy of the circular, dated Jan., 1856, is with the James S. Easley Papers, Alderman Library, University of Virginia, Charlottesville. For information on Clark see Hawkins Taylor, "Early Men and Early Days Recalled," *Annals of Iowa, 1st Ser.,* X (Jan., 1872), 300.

make collections anywhere else in the state, certainly a boon for nonresident investors.[46]

Some jobs were "farmed out" by the large land agencies to the smaller real estate houses scattered across the state.[47] Almost every county seat had two or three realtors, who often doubled as county treasurers, recorders, or surveyors, while every town no matter how small boasted at least one. In the land office towns it was not uncommon to find several dozen real estate firms advertising their services in the local press.[48] Paying taxes was the most common task of the smaller agencies. The large urban agency realized very little profit on these onerous operations as fees were characteristically small (from fifty cents per tract to 5 per cent of the total tax amount). But this was a necessary service which had to be performed if the city realtor hoped to obtain the cream of the business—the privilege of locating and selling land for nonresidents.

Another of the important services offered by many local agencies was to maintain a "Register" containing full descriptions of all land for sale in the county or area.[49] At a cost of one dollar per tract the big speculators were well-advised to list their lands here, since prospective buyers and particularly immigrants likely scanned the register first. In this way the small town agent played a key role in bringing buyers and sellers together.

---

[46] James H. Gower of Iowa City had a similar network. In one of his advertisements listing 40,000 acres of raw land for sale in many eastern and central Iowa counties, the name of a local realtor was listed for each county where prospective buyers could inquire about the land (Iowa City *Weekly Republican*, May 26, 1858). See also advertisement of Eads & Stewart in Davenport *Democratic Banner*, Mar. 2, 1855.

[47] Fees had to be divided when business was farmed out. L. Parker & Co. of Fort Dodge, for example, charged the Iowa City firm $1.50 for cash entries and $3.00 for land warrant entries for 160-acre tracts entered at the Fort Dodge Land Office. Cook, Sargent & Downey, in turn, charged customers for whom these entries were made the rates of $6.00 for cash and $10.00 for land warrant entries of 160 acres (L. Parker & Co. to Cook, Sargent & Downey, Dec. 13, 1855, Cook, Sargent & Downey Papers).

[48] In the course of newspaper research I compiled a list of central Iowa realtors who advertised in local newspapers or promotional pamphlets in the 1840's and 1850's. For Fort Dodge the list totaled 45, Iowa City had 39, Des Moines 38, Fairfield 14, Cedar Rapids 10, with an additional 135 scattered among the various county seat towns of central Iowa. Dubuque headed the eastern Iowa list with 44 realtors, Davenport had 30, Keokuk 12, and Burlington 10. On the western slope, Council Bluffs had 24 realtors and Sioux City at least 10. This is only a partial list, but it does suggest the magnitude of the frontier land business.

[49] See the advertisement of John R. Needham, Mahaska County realtor, in the Oskaloosa *Herald*, Nov. 20, 1857. Needham's success story is related in his obituary in *ibid.*, July 16, 1868, and in Stiles, *Recollections and Sketches*, 713–14. As early as 1841, Burlington land agents James M. Morgan and Jesse Williams announced that they kept a register of vacant land in the district available for entry. See the Burlington *Iowa Territorial Gazette and Burlington Advertiser*, Mar. 28, 1840.

The connection between urban and small town agencies was of mutual benefit. While city agencies needed correspondents at the county seats, small town agencies with less capital and resources often had to rely on the larger houses. Not being able, for instance, to keep large supplies of land warrants on hand, local men would call on the city vendors if warrants were suddenly in great demand.[50] Or, again, if a smaller agency had a call for locations in a distant district, it could depend on the services of a larger company having permanent connections in the district. One such local agent was H. S. Monson of Muscatine, who asked Hugh Downey to select and locate a thousand acres at the Decorah Land Office "just as soon as you can do it to a good advantage. The land is for parties east who have sent there [sic] warrants to me and I want to get them as good selections as I would for myself (or better)."[51] Often the very existence of the local agencies may have depended on the patronage and good will of the larger firms. Similarly, when new agents entered the field, they frequently solicited business from established firms throughout the state. Grenville M. Dodge, erstwhile Iowa railroad surveyor, launched his brief but colorful career in the land business at Council Bluffs in 1855 with a mass mailing of the following appeal: "We have but little capitol [sic] to commence with but hope by being enterprising and industrious in connection with our many friends and acquaintances that we will succeed. Any business you may entrust to us will be promptly attended to."[52]

The large land agencies also dealt with eastern bankers and warrant brokers. They collected and remitted funds, bought and sold drafts, and circulated eastern bank note issues. Most interesting was the arrangement some Iowa land agencies had with large eastern bankers to sell the latter's land warrants on a commission basis. This enabled western firms pinched for capital to expand their businesses with little additional capital outlay. Hamilton G. Fant, a large Washington banker and land warrant broker, reported in 1855 having upwards of 10,000 acres of warrants in Iowa "on commission."[53] Frequently, eastern agencies also listed in their advertisements the Iowa land holdings of eastern speculators, thus giving them the benefit of wider markets.

[50] Skiff & Meek, agents in Newton, Jasper County, ordered a lot of two to three thousand acres of warrants from Cook, Sargent & Downey in 1855 when demand was heavy (Dec. 17, 1855, Cook, Sargent & Downey Papers).

[51] Monson to Downey, Jan. 7, 1856, *ibid.*

[52] One of these form letters of Baldwin, Dodge and Co., penned by Dodge's partner, John T. Baldwin to Hugh D. Downey, Dec. 17, 1855, is in the Cook, Sargent & Downey Papers. Dodge's career in the Iowa land business is described briefly in Stanley P. Hirshson, *Grenville M. Dodge: Soldier, Politician, Railroad Promoter* (Bloomington, Ind., 1967), 23–29, 49–62, 85.

[53] Fant asked Downey if he would sell warrants on commission and if so for what rates (Fant to Downey, Dec. 7, 1855, Cook, Sargent & Downey Papers).

IV

CATERING to nonresident land investors was a major aspect of the total business of all Iowa land agencies. As such, it was a relationship demanding mutual trust. The business correspondence of Virginia speculator James S. Easley reveals perhaps the typical investor-agent relationship. Easley dealt with more than 200 Iowa agents during the three decades of his land business. During this time he maintained continual relations with several men who matched him in longevity and found only three or four who proved untrustworthy.[54] One was agent Charles Amy of Sac City, who collected about $100 on land sales and, according to Easley, kept the money with the excuse that the draft had been sent and presumably was lost in the mail.[55]

The machinations of another agent were a trifle more subtle. I. J. McIntyre of Clarinda informed Easley that he had a buyer for some of the easterner's land and that the top price being offered was $4.50 per acre. Easley was instructed to send the deed signed but with the consideration left blank in case the buyer could be induced to raise his offer. McIntyre then inserted his own name in the deed as the buyer, recorded the instrument, and sold the tract the same day for $5.00 per acre. In addition to collecting his 5 per cent commission of $36 on the original sale, the dishonest agent made fifty cents per acre on the deed (by first selling to himself). Because both deeds were recorded the same day, Easley happened to discover the swindle when in Clarinda to pay taxes.[56]

Not infrequently it was the investor who defrauded the agent. One cause for complaint was the willingness of investors to connive with prospective buyers and deprive agents of their commissions. Nonresident speculators customarily sent a list of their lands for sale to local agents, with the understanding that the realtor's commission would be passed on to the buyer, if at all possible. (Although the fee was rightfully the seller's obligation,

---

[54] William J. Barney of Dubuque and later Chicago remained an agent from 1852 through 1879 when Easley died. Jefferson P. Casady of Council Bluffs served from 1853 through 1879. George Weare of Sioux City served from 1857 until 1879. The Civil War ruined Easley's friendship with at least one agent, Hoyt Sherman of Des Moines. For a complete discussion of Easley's business, see Chapter 7.

[55] James S. Easley to S. T. Hutchinson, July 20, 1871, James S. Easley Papers. This, of course, was Easley's contention. It was apparently not proved in a court of law that Amy kept the money.

[56] James S. Easley to Moore & McIntyre, Aug. 22, 1873; same to B. Moore, Sept. 15, 1873, *ibid.* A fraud similar to this was reported by the Iowa City *Daily Evening Reporter* on May 28, 1856. No other cases of dishonesty by Iowa land agents in the ante bellum period were reported in the press to my knowledge.

neither law nor convention regulated such matters on the frontier; whichever party was most eager to buy or to sell accepted
the obligation.) Wily buyers, aware of this intent, would contact
a local agent, tour the area with him, obtain plats and descriptions of available tracts, and submit bids to be forwarded to the
owners. After flushing out an owner's best counteroffer, they
would then write the owner privately and offer to buy at the
quoted price, if the deed was sent direct. Eager to sell, the owner
often complied, causing the agent who actually made the sale to
lose his fee.[57]

The most common source of friction between agent and investor stemmed from their differing objectives. The investors
coveted the highest possible selling price, while local agents desired a steady volume of business even if their commissions were
somewhat less on each sale. The usual practice was for investors
to give local agents exclusive listings of their land in a given
county or counties; but they seldom stated their lowest selling
price and always demanded the right to approve all sales before
issuing deeds.[58] The agent was thus left in the difficult position
of having to appraise the land, offer it for a price he thought
realistic, persuade a buyer, and then risk having the owner's
ideas differ as to the value of his land and decline the offer.
Agents sometimes refused to demand more money from the buyer,
claiming their "professional pride" was of greater concern than
a larger commission. Generally in such instances, the owner reluctantly sent the deed with the admonition to make no firm
commitments in the future without first obtaining written approval.[59]

Besides inconveniencing the realtors, the refusal of nonresident owners to establish fixed prices irritated prospective purchasers who were usually eager to buy and have the title in hand
as soon as possible. The length of time required to obtain an
owner's approval of an offer was often greater than a buyer's
patience, and the sale was lost. The agents' viewpoint was set
out in a printed circular by Mickel & Head, realtor-bankers of
Jefferson:

> We would respectfully call the attention of all non-resident
> land holders who desire to sell their lands, to the importance

---

[57] It was no trick for the purchaser to write to the nonresident speculator.
As an agent explained to a speculator, 'Your P.O. Address is Known to every
woman or child in this county," Weare & Allison to Easley, Aug. 27, 1875,
James S. Easley Papers.

[58] These were known as "positive" rather than "discretionary" instructions. See advertisement of James H. Gower in Iowa City *Republican,* Nov.
25, 1868.

[59] G. T. Kilburn to Easley & Willingham, Sept. 16, 1868; James S. Easley
to D. Carr Early, Feb. 17, 1871, James S. Easley Papers.

and necessity of sending us a list of their lands with prices, terms etc., in order that we may be able to answer promptly all inquiries made by those desiring to settle among us. We presume that you are aware that this, and adjoining counties are very sparsely settled, and that most of the lands are still held by nonresidents. . . . Many persons looking for farms could be induced to purchase and settle among us, if they could get a prompt and specific answer as to the prices etc., of such tract, or tracts as they might feel inclined to buy. We wish, therefore, to be furnished with the prices and terms of payment, at which owners *will sell,* so that we may be able to satisfy buyers that the land selected can be obtained on compliance with such terms, with as much certainty as if we had the deed here ready for delivery.

The length of time required to correspond with owners to find prices, etc., has often lost us the opportunity of making favorable sales, that could have been secured, had we the price and terms at the time applied for—the buyer being unwilling to remain so long on expense to receive an answer.

Some of our correspondents write us that they are anxious to sell their land, and complain of our hitherto moderate taxes, yet give us no prices at which they are willing to sell. To such we say, send your prices and terms at once, if you would avoid the payment of still higher taxes, as we have yet to build a Court House, and School Houses, and construct Roads and Bridges.[60]

Despite occasional grounds for complaint, relations between agents and investors in general appear to have been cordial and mutually beneficial. Personal friendships were built and periodically renewed by the frequent western excursions of eastern speculators. Good businessmen all, they tried to disregard political or social differences—even when such questions as slavery and secession became the burning issues of the day. Apart from the brief period of the Civil War, politics did not inhibit Iowa land investment by any Americans, from the North or South.

---

[60] This circular, dated 1868, is in the James S. Easley Papers.

Chapter Six

LAND WARRANTS AND SPECULATION

I
OWA LAND SPECULATORS, like their predecessors in Ohio, Indiana, and Illinois, capitalized on the land bonuses that Congress offered from time to time to encourage enlistments and reward service in the armed forces. This bonus policy, begun during the Revolutionary War, culminated in the mid-nineteenth century during the Mexican War and its aftermath.[1] Between 1847 and 1855 Congress enacted four major bounty warrant acts granting almost 61 million acres to veterans (or their heirs) of every war (including many an Indian skirmish) beginning with the Revolution. These liberal acts coincided with the opening of the land offices in central and western Iowa. As a result 14.1 million acres—approximately a fourth of the total land warrant acreage and an area equal to more than one-half (52.4) per cent) of all the Congress land in Iowa—was entered with land warrants instead of cash. This amount far exceeded that of any other state in the Union.[2]

---

[1] A definitive study of military bounty land warrants yet remains to be written. The genesis of the policy is explored in Rudolf Freund, "Military Bounty Lands and the Origin of the Public Domain," *Agr. Hist.,* XX (Jan., 1946), 8–18; Jean H. Vivian, "Military Land Bounties During the Revolutionary and Confederation Periods," *Md. Hist. Mag.,* LXI (Sept., 1966), 231–56. A brief survey of the bounty system is Jerry A. O'Callaghan, "The War Veteran and the Public Lands," *Agr. Hist.,* XXVIII (Oct., 1954), 163–68. The Revolutionary warrants are thoroughly covered by William T. Hutchinson, "The Bounty Lands of the American Revolution in Ohio" (Ph.D. dissertation, University of Chicago, 1927). Theodore L. Carlson has examined the warrants of the War of 1812 in *The Illinois Military Tract: A Study of Land Occupation, Utilization and Tenure* ("Illinois Studies in the Social Sciences," Vol. XXXII, No. 2 [Urbana, 1951]).

[2] In Iowa approximately 8.9 million acres were granted to the state for schools, internal improvements, and other purposes. Of the Congress land totaling 26.9 million acres, 11.9 million acres were sold for cash, 0.9 million acres were homesteaded, and 14.1 million acres were granted for military services (Roscoe F. Lokken, *Iowa Public Land Disposal* [Iowa City, 1942], 267). The total acreage in warrants issued under the various acts was: 13,213,640 in 1847; 13,168,480 in 1850; 694,400 in 1852; 34,151,590 in 1855 (Report of the Commissioner of the General Land Office, Sept. 30, 1907, in

I

SINCE most veterans preferred selling their certificates rather than
making new homes for themselves in the West, a market quickly
developed in warrants and military bounty land scrip. (Scrip
was issued by the Treasury Department beginning in 1830 to
veterans of the Revolution in exchange for land warrants of
various state governments, particularly Virginia.)[3] Veterans who
wanted to exchange their land paper for cash sought out the new
warrant brokers who went into business on a large scale in the
late 1840's.

Energetic dealers also pursued the veterans. Nathaniel Gordon of Exeter, New Hampshire, for example, worked systematically through old regimental muster rolls searching for veterans
who had not yet obtained or sold their warrants.[4] Other agents
were less scrupulous, at least if congressmen engaged in the heat
of debate can be trusted. Senator Jefferson Davis of Mississippi
described how soldiers discharged at New Orleans fresh from
the Mexican campaigns were inveigled by speculators into hypoth-
ecating their discharge papers "at fifty and sixty dollars." The
agents' tactics were to represent to the soldier "that it would
be difficult, and would require a long time to get their warrants
from the officers at Washington." Needing money immediately,
the soldiers found the argument persuasive. Senator James D.
Wescott of Florida noted that the buying price from the veterans
in January, 1849, ranged from $30 to $110 for quarter section
warrants. As he explained the procedure, "the soldier gave a
power of attorney, often in blank, and authority to enter the

---

U.S. Department of the Interior, *Report*, 1907, I, 259). Iowa's 14.1 million
acres of warrant entries compares with 9.5 (million) in Illinois, 6.8 in Missouri, 6.3 in Wisconsin, 5.9 in Minnesota, 4.2 in Kansas, 3.8 in Michigan, and
lesser amounts in the other public land states *(Annual Report of the Commissioner of the General Land Office, 1870, 504)*.

[3] In the scrip act of May 30, 1830 (U.S. *Statutes at Large*, IV, 422–24),
Congress authorized the exchange of Virginia land warrants for assignable
scrip for the purchase of lands open for sale in Ohio, Indiana, and Illinois.
Other scrip acts in 1832, 1833, and 1835, converted an additional one million
acres of warrants into scrip *(ibid.,* 578, 665, 770–71).

[4] Gordon held a Dartmouth law degree, served as captain of the local
militia, and was a small-time land warrant broker and speculator who entered
Congress land in Illinois, Iowa, Nebraska, and Minnesota in the 1850's. As
late as the 1870's he still held land in the Midwest. If the warrants he had
unearthed were not located on western land, Gordon sent them to his friend,
Amos Tuck, in Washington. Tuck, a New Hampshire Whig congressman,
sold the warrants on the Washington market mainly to the brokerage house
of Chubb & Schenck. This service the congressman provided without charge
in exchange for Gordon's political support in the home district. The
Nathaniel Gordon Papers, containing incoming correspondence for the period
1851 to 1871, are in the Manuscript Division, Baker Library, Boston.

land in his name."[5] Most senators who commented on the issue agreed that the soldiers sold their warrants or rights to their warrants for half their land office value or less.

Preying on war-weary campaigners was a short-lived practice. Reputable brokerage houses soon controlled the market and regularized it. Major firms in Boston, New York, Philadelphia, and Washington depended on local agents throughout the country to secure their supply of warrants. Wall Street became the hub of the trade, and *Thompson's Bank Note Reporter* the broker's bible. John Thompson had built his weekly circulation above 100,000 by 1855, which was by far the largest claimed by any periodical of this type up to that time.[6] *Thompson's Bank Note Reporter*, published at No. 2 Wall Street, quoted the buying and selling prices of warrants and scrip on the New York market. This determined the price level for all the other markets. Usually, however, the buying prices along the Atlantic seaboard fell in an inverse ratio to the distance from New York and Washington. Boston warrant prices were always at the bottom of the range quoted in the major centers. So too with the southern market in New Orleans, Louisville, parts of Tennessee, and southern Virginia.[7]

If a veteran was well informed of the current market situation, he could probably sell at close to the market price. It was more likely, however, that he sold in ignorance. Undoubtedly for this reason, some land speculators and brokerage houses sent junior partners or agents into remote areas to purchase warrants.

---

[5] *Congressional Globe,* 30th Cong., 2nd Sess., XVIII, 232, 263–65. Joseph Fowler, of New Orleans, bought claims from returning soldiers totaling 175 quarter sections or 28,000 acres and after securing the warrants located most of them in late 1848 in one large body in central Iowa at the junction of Marion, Lucas, and Monroe counties (William M. Donnel, *Pioneers of Marion County* [Des Moines, 1872], 107–8). Ward Lamson, a Burlington commission merchant who conducted a profitable exchange of products between the upper and lower Mississippi River during the Mexican War, was also on hand at New Orleans in the spring of 1848 investing in warrants. By the summer he had opened an office in St. Louis to sell and loan warrants, and quickly established branches in Burlington and Fairfield. (See Lake City Publishing Co., *Portrait and Biographical Album of Jefferson and Van Buren Counties, Iowa* (Chicago, 1890), 656.

[6] William H. Dillistin, *Bank Note Reporters and Counterfeit Detectors, 1826–1866, with a Discourse on Wildcat Banks and Wildcat Bank Notes* (New York, 1949), 78–93.

[7] Miss Natalie Disbrow to Allan G. Bogue, Aug. 16, 1963 (copy in possession of the author). Miss Disbrow researched the eastern land warrant market in preparation for her doctoral dissertation at Cornell University, Ithaca, N.Y. The projected title of her study is "Mexican War Bounty Land Warrants" (U.S. Department of the Interior, Bureau of Land Management, *Public Lands Bibliography* [Washington, 1962], 95). See also James S. Easley to G. D. Neal, Oct. 24, 1855, James S. Easley Papers, Alderman Library, University of Virginia, Charlottesville.

William W. Willingham, junior partner in the Virginia firm of Easley & Willingham, scouted distant Texas in 1853 in an attempt to buy cheaper warrants. Edward Sherman, of the New York brokerage house of Sherman Brothers, journeyed to southern Georgia in 1855.[8] But this source of supply was so unreliable that Easley & Willingham and Sherman Brothers, like all the other large-scale investors, had to rely mainly on the established markets of the major eastern centers for their supplies.

Warrant brokers such as Sherman Brothers, Greenway & Brothers, and John Thompson of New York; William H. Brown & Sons of Philadelphia; and Sweeny, Rittenhouse & Fant and Chubb & Schenck of Washington, sold land paper on a commission basis, usually of one cent per acre or one-half per cent of the total sale price.[9] Customarily, eastern land speculators placed purchase orders with their brokers and directed that the certificates when acquired be properly assigned in their name and sent directly to western land agents. A list of the names of the original assignees and the numbers of each warrant were then forwarded to the new owner, along with a notation of the charges for the warrants, brokerage fee, and postage that had been deducted from the investor's standing account. Since most brokers were also bankers, their clients usually found it convenient to maintain standing deposits, avoiding the cost of buying drafts or sending checks or specie for small amounts.

II

IN ORDER for land warrants and treasury scrip to be useful tools for land speculators, certain prerequisites had to be met. Most important, warrants had to be assignable and acceptable for entry anywhere on the public domain, including inhabited tracts. In the early National period, Congress and the several states reserved military districts where warrants were to be located. After 1842, however, land warrants and treasury scrip could be located upon any part of the public domain subject to private entry.[10]

---

[8] Easley & Willingham to Wm. H. Brown & Co., June 25, 1853; Sherman Bros. to James S. Easley, Nov. 1, 1855, James S. Easley Papers.

[9] James S. Easley to Jno. P. Stagg, Son & Co., June 14, 1853; same to Wm. T. Smithson, Aug. 1, 9, 1855; same to Hamilton G. Fant, Oct. 31, 1855. With the Richmond brokerage house of Younger & Smith, Easley offered either to pay one dollar for each warrant or to furnish the money for the firm to buy warrants on the best possible terms and divide equally the difference between the actual price paid and the Washington or New York buying price (Easley & Willingham to Wm. T. Smith, July 7, Aug. 7, 1855). All correspondence from the James S. Easley Papers.

[10] U.S. *Statutes at Large*, V, 497. Private entry was the right to purchase lands which had been offered at public sale, which were not sold, and which

Fig. 6.1. The front page of Thompson's Bank Note Reporter, *December 25, 1858. The buying and selling prices of warrants are shown in bottom left corner.*

N. Y. State Library
APR 7 - 1937

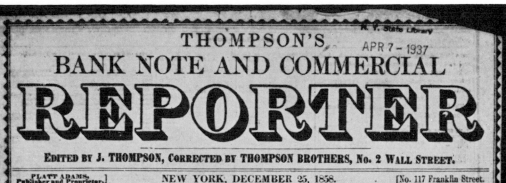

THOMPSON'S
BANK NOTE AND COMMERCIAL

REPORTER

EDITED BY J. THOMPSON, CORRECTED BY THOMPSON BROTHERS, No. 2 WALL STREET.

PLATT ADAMS, Publisher and Proprietor.] NEW YORK, DECEMBER 25, 1858. [No. 117 Franklin Street.

☞ WE HAVE NO TRAVELING AGENT. ☜

INDEX.

NEW COUNTERFEITS.

5s, on the **Traders' Bank**, Newport, R. I.—Vig. spread eagle, ship in full sail and city in distance.

5s, on the **National Bank**, Providence, R. I., altered—Vig. man in large V—5, female bust and FIVE on right end—5, female bust and 5 on left end.

2s, on the **Whitehall Bank**, Whitehall, N. Y.—photographed—Vig. man and woman, &c.

2s, on the **Conway Bank**, Mass., altered—Vig. man and woman standing by well—female supporting **2** on right end—two silver dollars on left end.

10s, on the **Farmers' Bank**, Troy, N. Y., altered—Vig. Controller's die with **10** on either side—Vulcan and females on right end—man in corn field on left end.

5s, on the **Rockville Bank**, Conn., altered—Vig. drove of horses—girl on right end.

5s, on the **Western Bank**, Philadelphia, Pa.—imitation of genuine—blue tint—Vig. group of Indians on rock, city, &c.—female, sheaf of grain, &c. on right end—large V and the engraver's name poor.

10s, on the **Bank of Cape Ann**, Mass., altered—Vig. female, eagle, &c.—bust of man each side of vig.—agricultural implements, &c. on right end—cattle on left end.

5s, on the **National Bank**, Boston, Mass., altered—Vig. hunter, squaw three nude children and five gold dollars—female bust on right end—unlike genuine.

10s, on the **Cambridge Valley Bank**, N. Y., raised from **1s**—Vig. smith's shop, man, &c—State arms on right end—farmer on left end.

2s, on the **Monson Bank**, Mass., photographed.

3s, on the **Union Bank**, New London, Conn.—Vig. **3** with five male busts—steamboat on right end—anchor and shield on left end—blue tint.

5s, on the **Laighton Bank**, Lynn, Mass.—two females, shield, &c. on upper left corner—bust of Webster on lower right corner.

50s, on the **Georgia Railroad and Banking Co.**—Vig. three faces, the middle one very indistinct—in the medallion head on right end the left eye is blurred—Indian on left end and dies on each upper corner—poorly engraved.

20s, on the **Eagle Bank**, Providence, R. I., raised—Vig. two females, safe, &c.—portrait of woman on right end—eagle on left end.

10s, on the **Bank of Lima**, N. Y., raised from **1s**—Vig. cattle, horses, sheep, &c.—drove of cattle on lower right corner—bust of man on upper right corner.

2s, on the **Thames Bank**, Norwich, Conn., altered—Vig. man and woman standing by a well—female supporting **2** on right end—two silver dollars on left end.

☞ Our new "DESCRIPTIVE LIST" is now ready for delivery and on sale.

☞ We call attention to the advertisement of GAYETTY, on the 3d page.

The old issue of bills of the HOLYOKE BANK, Mass., is being withdrawn from circulation, and new ones substituted, of a red tint.

LAND WARRANTS

We quote Land Warrants, Dec. 24, as follows:

	Buying		Selling
40 acres	$1.00	40 acres	$1.10
80 acres	0.83	80 acres	0.86
120 acres	0.78	120 acres	0.82
160 acres	0.82	160 acres	0.85

Warrants sold at this office are guaranteed in every respect.

THOMPSON BROTHERS.

THE REPORTER.

☞ **To Correspondents.**—ALL LETTERS AND COMMUNICATIONS intended for the "BANK NOTE AND COMMERCIAL REPORTER," must be addressed to the subscriber, or JOHN THOMPSON, Editor; and Correspondents are particularly requested to name the State, as well as the Town or City.

☞ Bank Officers are requested to inform us of all New Organizations, Change of Officers, New Counterfeits, &c.

PLATT ADAMS 117 Franklin-st. N. Y.

☞ THOMPSON BROTHERS ☜
buy all Money as herein quoted.

WESTERN BANKING.

The engraving and printing for the STATE BANK OF IOWA is completed, and the Branches will be put in possession of their circulating notes through the Board of Control forthwith. Our opinion of the STATE BANK OF IOWA is on record in former numbers of this paper; we will now only repeat in brief—It is like the STATE BANK OF OHIO, good, if ably and prudently managed; but it is susceptible of expansion to a bursting point. Banking in new States and Territories has ever been found to be doubtful, if not disastrous. We remember, as of yesterday, the old banks of Illinois, of Michigan, of Mississippi, of Arkansas, and of Florida. It might be well for the historical societies of Iowa, Kansas, Nebraska and Minnesota, to study the rise, progress and downfall of banking in the first-named States.

There are two prominent reasons why banking has a "downfall" in new States—1st. The bankers are generally young, headstreng and inexperienced. 2d. The population is speculative, revulsionary and reckless. It is quite evident to us that Illinois and Wisconsin are getting on too much steam, and that some of the banking machinery there will give out before long, very much to the chagrin of some promising financiers, who think they are making a fortune.

Michigan and Minnesota have inaugurated banking by general laws. To applaud Michigan and denounce Minnesota currency, issued under these laws, is our thankless duty. The reason we do this is—the Michigan law permits the deposit of the stocks of the following States only, at 95 cents on the dollar, as security for currency, all of which must be or be made equal to a six ℔ cent. stock, viz: New York, Michigan, Ohio, Kentucky, Indiana and Illinois—none of which can be bought except at a premium; hence, Michigan currency will be better secured than any free bank currency, except a few banks in New York, which have never used bonds and mortgages.

On the other hand, the Minnesota banking law has been designedly amended so as practically to exclude all stocks except those of her own State, viz: $250,000 issued last summer, bearing 8 ℔ ct. interest; and $5,000,000 now being issued for Railroad purposes, bearing 7 ℔ ct. interest. The first loan of $250,000 is admitted to be a legal, valid loan; but the Railroad bonds are of a more dubious character than the repudiated promises of Florida or Mississippi.

The argument that a Minnesota Bank *has* deposited only the good bonds should be regarded, but for the fact that the Bank *may* withdraw the good bonds and substitute the bad bonds any day.

☞ Another shinplaster mill has been started at Cannelton, Ind. The *Evansville Journal* says of this attempt to swindle;

A bank has been opened at Cannelton, Perry County, under the name of the FARMERS' AND MECHANICS' BANK of Cannelton, the managers of which are all strangers in this section of the State. As yet none of its bills have made their appearance in the vicinity of the Bank; and consequently no test of its ability to redeem its issues has been had. It is reported that large amounts of its bills have been circulated in the Northwest. Its bills are quoted in the mercenary Bank Note Lists as good, and at a half and one per cent. discount. As the Bank is unauthorized by law, and nothing is known of the responsibility of the owners and managers, it will be well for the public to be cautious in giving currency to its promises-to-pay.

FINANCIAL AND COMMERCIAL.

The official weekly statement of the city banks, last Saturday, shows a continued expansion of loans and discounts, amounting to over half a million, since the last report. Rumor says this increase is caused mostly by loans on hypothecations of the new issue of Treasury notes; very little, if any, on mercantile paper, unless for extensions.

There has been, unexpectedly, a falling off in the specie reserve of $586,645, instead of a gain, by the California remittances going into the account, as was anticipated last week. The deposits have run up over $700,000 during the same time.

The averages of the 18th inst. compare as follows with those of the previous week, viz:

	Dec. 11.	Dec. 18.		
Loans	$126,520,129	$127,055,010	Inc.	$534,881
Specie	27,193,522	26,606,877	Dec.	586,645
Circulation	7,750,166	7,710,629	Dec.	39,539
Deposits	88,981,966	89,690,087	Inc.	708,121

The Money Market presents no new features, being fully supplied, and call loans promptly responded to at 4@5 ℔ cent. but a more rigid circumspection in the selection of collaterals is adopted by the banks and by capitalists.

We hear of no change in the Money Market at any of the Eastern or Southern cities; all seems quiet and easy; whereas at the West there is good enquiry, and at more than legal rates, for accommodations; yet domestic Exchange ranges low.

Foreign Exchange is in fair demand, at slightly advanced rates. Sterling is held at 9⅛@9¼ by Bankers, and 9⅛@9⅛ for first class commercial houses. Francs, 5.18¾@5.15.

We note no alteration in Domestic Exchange, or important changes in the rates of Uncurrent Money. The amount offering for discount in the street is comparatively light. The small discount charged on home and Eastern paper gives the public confidence, and it consequently remains in circulation.

The Stock Market is without any marked cha[...] in rates. The tendency, however, is indic[...] growing weakness of the fancies, of [...]

Land historians disagree on when Congress made warrants and scrip assignable. One historian argues that warrants became legally transferable in 1788, another that speculation in warrants received its initial impetus from the Scrip Act of May 30, 1830, which authorized the exchange of Virginia warrants for assignable scrip. A third insists that Mexican warrants of 1847 "were clearly assignable," while yet others believe that they could be transferred legally only after the Warrant Act of 1852 specifically authorized assignment.[11] The fact is that from 1788 when Revolutionary warrants and scrip were made assignable, until the last land paper was issued in the twentieth century, warrants and scrip were usually transferable. Only the military bounty act of the War of 1812 had explicitly banned assignment—and for a brief time the act of 1850 was similarly interpreted—but the decision was reversed for both in 1852. Between these two issues, however, Congress enacted several warrant and scrip acts allowing transfer. The 1830 Scrip Act, for example, specifically stated that "all such certificates or scrip shall be assignable."[12]

The Mexican Bounty Act of February 11, 1847, was not this explicit, but nonetheless it clearly allowed assignment. Admittedly, during debate on the bill, reformers who were critical of the speculative use of warrants proposed a specific provision banning transfer. But the legislators, after a persuasive appeal by Senator Thomas Hart Benton of Missouri, beat down the amendment, satisfying themselves instead merely with prohibiting alienation or sale prior to the issuance of the warrant—a standard legal stipulation. At the same time—and this subterfuge is what has confused historians—the lawmakers refused to state explicitly that warrants were assignable because this would be tantamount to approving the activities of speculators, an action which no politically astute legislator would take. Thus, the warrants of 1847 were transferable after issue simply because the act did not specify to the contrary.[13]

---

had not since been reserved or otherwise withdrawn from market. See Thomas Donaldson, *The Public Domain, Its History, with Statistics* [47th Cong., 2nd Sess., H.R. Doc. 45, pt. 4] (Washington, 1884), 1159.

[11] Freund, "Military Bounty Lands," 18, defends the 1788 date; Benjamin H. Hibbard, *A History of the Public Land Policies* (New York, 1924), 121, 125, notes both the 1830 and 1852 dates; Margaret B. Bogue, *Patterns from the Sod: Land Use and Tenure in the Grand Prairie, 1850–1890* ("Collections of the Illinois State Historical Library," Vol. XXXIV, Land Series, Vol. I [Springfield, 1959]), argues for the 1847 date; O'Callaghan, "The War Veteran and the Public Lands," 166, insists on the 1852 date, as do Clarence Danhof, "Farm Making Costs and the 'Safety Valve': 1850–1860," *J. Pol. Econ.*, XLIX (June, 1941), 330, and Addison E. Sheldon, *Land Systems and Land Policies in Nebraska* (Lincoln, 1936), 60.

[12] U.S. *Statutes at Large*, II, 729; IX, 520–21; X, 3–4; IV, 422–24, 665, 770. All war bounty scrip, in fact, was assignable including that issued under the act of 1847. See *ibid.*, IX, 562–63.

[13] *Congressional Globe*, 30th Cong., 2nd Sess., XVIII, 262.

Statements of the commissioner of the General Land Office confirm this interpretation. In a general circular to all land office personnel explaining the provisions of the new act, the commissioner explained that warrants presented by assignees were valid if they bore dates of assignment subsequent to the warrant issuance date, were properly acknowledged before a notary public, and were accompanied by a properly authenticated power of attorney.[14] The commissioner's annual reports to Congress are equally clear. In 1847, for example, Commissioner Richard M. Young, referring to the act of February of that year, warned Congress to expect smaller land receipts in the future as "a large number of these warrants have and will, in the course of speculation, fall into the hands of persons desirous only of reconverting them into money at enhanced prices, by selling to those who wish to purchase for settlement."[15] Senator Sidney Breese of Illinois, chairman of the Committee on Public Lands, also stated flatly during congressional debate in 1849 that the 1847 warrants "have always been assignable."[16]

In 1850 Congress enacted another warrant act to include veterans passed over in the 1847 measure. The bill, as first proposed, was similar to the 1847 act in that it would have allowed the soldiers to alienate their warrants. However, the Senate Committee on Public Lands spearheaded a drive against assignability. A few legislators in both houses of Congress then mounted stiff opposition against the transfer feature, declaring that history had proven this a boon to speculators. As a result Congress amended one key word in the bill, making it illegal to assign warrants prior to the issuing of the *patents*, instead of prior to the issuing of the *warrants*.[17] The engrossing clerk, however, when writing the bill, either unintentionally or deliberately, deleted the words "of the patents," thereby making warrants assignable.

The Senate immediately corrected the error and returned the bill to the lower house on the final morning of the legislative session. At fifteen minutes before noon—the time of adjournment fixed by joint resolution—the House finally took up the matter. In a dramatic race against the clock, advocates of assignability cleverly applied such parliamentary delaying tactics as rising to

---

[14] The circular (No. 604) is reprinted in W. W. Lester (comp.), *Decisions of the Interior Department in Public Land Cases, and Land Laws Passed by the Congress of the United States; Together with the Regulations of the General Land Office* (Philadelphia, 1860), 576–77 (hereafter cited as Lester *Land Laws*).

[15] *Senate Executive Documents*, 30th Cong., 1st Sess., II, Doc. 2, 12. Further proof of assignability is in *ibid.*, 31st Cong., 1st Sess., II, Doc. 1, 6–7, 28, and 32nd Cong., 1st Sess., III, Doc. 1, 5; *House Executive Documents*, 30th Cong., 2nd Sess., III, Doc. 12, 23.

[16] *Congressional Globe*, 30th Cong., 2nd Sess., XVIII, 263.

[17] U.S. *Statutes at Large*, IX, 520–21. Cf. Act of Feb. 11, 1847, in *ibid.*, 125.

"a question of privilege" to demand the ejection from the galleries of the "many speculators in land warrants [who are] here interfering with the legislation of Congress." At two minutes to the hour, the lawmakers finally began to vote, only to have the speaker's gavel fall "precisely upon the hour of twelve" as the name "John A. King" was called.[18] Strangely enough, the bill became law with the controversial phrase reinstated despite the failure of the House to concur.

Because of the highly irregular origin of the law, the Commissioner of Pensions, whose task it was to issue the land paper to eligible applicants, expressed a reluctance to act until Congress had clarified the matter. The lawmakers determined to do this as soon as the new session convened. Grass-roots sentiment seemed overwhelming in favor of assignment. A joint resolution, introduced in both houses in early 1851, quickly passed the House by a two-to-one margin but a small minority of western senators stalled passage in the upper chamber until the last day of the session. Although the resolution then passed by a four-to-one margin, it contained an amendment (inserted by foes of transfer) which the House lacked time to approve. As a result, the assignability of the 1850 warrants remained an open question for another year.[19]

Meanwhile the Pension Office had issued the first 1850 certificates in February, 1851, and the Secretary of the Interior, with the concurrence of the commissioner of the General Land Office, had arbitrarily prohibited their transfer.[20] But legal justification for the Secretary's decision was tenuous at best. Representative Howell Cobb of Georgia, a leading member of the House Committee on Public Lands, declared that the Secretary had placed a "false construction" on the 1850 law, that congressional intent had clearly been to make the 1850 warrants assignable. "So satisfied am I," asserted Cobb on the floor of Congress, "that the construction of the Secretary of the Interior upon that point was wrong, that if I had been disposed to purchase a land warrant from an individual I should have done it, and relied upon the

---

[18] *Congressional Globe,* 31st Cong., 1st Sess., XIX, 2072, 2074. Debate on the warrant bill during this session filled over one hundred pages of the journal.

[19] *Congressional Globe,* 31st Cong., 2nd Sess., XX, 126, 792, 838 and *passim.* In the New York *Daily Tribune,* Mar. 8, 1851, Editor Greeley described the narrow margin by which assignment had been averted and warned that, of the estimated one-half million warrants to be issued, assignment would cause two-thirds to fall into the hands of a few land speculators "for a song."

[20] J. Butterfield to A. K. H. Stuart (Secretary of the Interior), Mar. 10, 1851, Records of the General Land Office, Miscellaneous Letters Sent, New Series, XXX, 460–62, National Archives, Washington, D.C. (hereafter cited as GLO Misc. Letters). See also *Senate Executive Documents,* 31st Cong., 2nd Sess., I, Doc. 1, 25.

courts of the country to sustain me in the position that these land warrants were truly and properly assignable under the original law."[21]

Cobb's suggestion to challenge the Secretary's ruling in the courts went unheeded, however, and the 1850 warrants remained legally nonassignable until Congress revised the law early in 1852.

But speculators were not to be thwarted by a mere law; they simply resorted to a diversionary tactic—the power of attorney. Instead of buying warrants outright, speculators paid the soldier for his power of attorney which allowed them to locate the land certificate and transfer title at any time thereafter. For the years 1850 to 1852, Iowa deed registers frequently contain such agreements, although most were probably never recorded.[22] One such instrument, found among the papers of an Iowa land agent, read as follows:

> Know all men by these presents that I Charles Stewart, late a private in Captain Lott's Company, in the 2nd regiment of Illinois (foot) volunteers, do here authorize and empower David C. March as my true and lawful attorney, to locate for me in his own name my land Warrant for 160 acres of land, for my services in Mexico in the company and regiment above named, I also Empower him hereby to sign my name to all papers necessary to enable him to enter the land under said warrant at any of the U.S. land offices, and to execute all transfers on the back of said Warrant, in my name which by law may be required in order to Enable him to locate said Warrant in his own name.[23]

A similar method of circumventing nonassignability—and probably more frequently used—was for the speculator to locate soldiers' warrants under a private contract that pledged the

---

[21] *Congressional Globe,* 32nd Cong., 1st Sess., XXI, 337, *House Executive Documents,* 32nd Cong., 1st Sess., II, Doc. 2, 247.

[22] For examples, see Marion County "Deed Record Books" D (627) and E (409). In the instrument recorded in Book D, Thomas Guyton, a Baltimore veteran, granted a power of attorney to Jesse Williams. Notarization was by Elias A. White of Baltimore. White was the largest Maryland speculator in Iowa lands, and Williams of the Fairfield firm of Henn, Williams & Co., was his western agent. Williams located the warrant in question and within a month the title was transferred to another buyer. The instrument recorded in Book E was identical except that White had his Des Moines agent, Benjamin Bryant, invested with the power of attorney. Some Iowa agents in their advertising circulars offered to supply proper forms accompanied by detailed instructions for granting attorney's powers. See LeGrand Byington, "Circular No. 4, Iowa General Land Agency, Iowa City," Iowa State Department of History and Archives, Des Moines (Fig. 6.2).

[23] Jesse Williams Papers, Iowa State Department of History and Archives, Des Moines.

IOWA GENERAL LAND AGENCY

BY LE GRAND BYINGTON,

AT IOWA CITY, IOWA.

$5.00
Cymmockux
Trading Co. 13.

SIR:—The assignability of the Bounty Land Warrants issued under the act of 1850, h rendered the forms and instructions which accompanied my former circulars unnecessary, and i duced me to modify the propositions therein submitted. I have also increased my facilities, wi a view to more extensive operations. I will now receive these warrants, (assigned in blank) my residence in Iowa City, Iowa, and, as directed by the sender, either—

I. Locate them upon the choicest land in the state (when the warrant holder desires the LAN for his own use, or for speculation) for the following fees in advance: for 40 acres, $5, 80 acre $7; 160 acres, $10; paying thereout all land office and other charges of selection and location; or—

II. Purchase them at 15 per cent. above their current price in the city New York; or—

III. Sell them to actual settlers, for cash or on time, for a commission of ten per cent. up the amount realized, besides conveyancing fees; or—

IV. Locate and sell the land, or sell the warrant in the first instance, to the very best advan age, for a moiety of the net profits, and, on time sales, allow the sender, in addition, interest up the cost of his warrants at the rate of 6 per cent. per annum, from the date of sale to the time h money is remitted.

Where warrants are sent to me regularly, by Eastern Agencies, I report sales and make settl ments monthly, and on all time sales, guarantee the payment of the money to the sender, up the expiration of the time given. All warrants, or packages of warrants, should be accompani by specific directions as to the manner of disposal; and, if sent under the 4th of the above prop sitions, by a statement of the exact cost of each warrant.

I attach, for your information, a schedule of the present selling prices of the warrants at Io City; remarking, however, that prices for the larger denomination of warrants, cannot, in my jud ment, be maintained at these figures, for any great length of time:

Warrants for 160 acres, Cash $135; On one year's time, $200;
      "   80 "   "   75; "   "   "   "   110;
      "   40 "   "   40; "   "   "   "   55;

As in my circular of September, (No. 3,) I offer the following considerations as inducemei to warrant holders to send me warrants, to-wit:—The large quantity of choice land subject to e try in Iowa; the wonderful rapidity with which settlements are being made; the rapid enhanc ment in the value of these lands; the unequalled demand here for warrants, whereby high prices a maintained; an intimate knowledge of the lands of the State; ready access to all the land offic and to their muniments; a confidential intercourse with the public surveyors and other local of cers; an extensive personal acquaintance and established legal reputation throughout the Weste States; and such arrangements with different banking houses as enable me to make remittanc without risk of loss from mail casualties.

The attention of regular dealers in warrants is particularly invited to the splendid opportuni which is here offered for safe and profitable investments, by locating these warrants, for settle upon their "improvements," so called, upon time.

My acquaintance at the east being quite limited, I refer, for my capacity, integrity and pec niary ability, to Governors Wood of Ohio, Wright of Indiana, and Hempstead of Iowa; and al to the State officers, including all the Supreme Court Judges and the Congressional delegatio of the first and last named States.   **LE GRAND BYINGTON.**

☞If you desire it, I will procure for you, from the Governor of Iowa, an appointment as Commissioner of Deeds, Depo tions, &c. for this State, and forward all necessary forms and instructions for the office. The cost, to you, of such appointme will be $1.00—that being the legal fee of the Secretary of State for issuing the commission.

If you accept the correspondence, please put this up in your office. If you decline it, do me the favor to hand this to so respectable person whom you suppose to be interested in the subject matter.

43437

soldier to convey title as soon as he received the government patent to the land.[24]

Whether by contract or by power of attorney, however, the machinery for making warrants transferable was sufficiently complicated to discourage a flourishing warrant market in the eastern cities. Warrants could not become a circulating medium without legal assignability.[25] As a result, market prices of land paper remained extremely low, to the dissatisfaction of veterans who wished to sell. Congress finally buckled under pressure from both speculators and veterans and in March, 1852, permanently settled the troublesome matter by declaring all warrants assignable "which have been or may hereafter be issued under any law of the United States."[26]

The liberal lawmakers granted another 694,400 acres of certificates in 1852; this in addition to the 13,213,640 acres allotted in 1847 and 13,168,480 in 1850. In terms of gross area, however, the act of 1855 was the most important. Under its provisions, veterans claimed 34,151,590 acres, or almost half of the 68,786,310 total acres conveyed as a bounty for war service.[27] The 1855 measure was of such large proportions because its framers entertained a broad interpretation of military service to include not only officers and fighting men but musicians, militiamen, marine clerks or landsmen, wagonmasters and teamsters, chaplains, and Indian-fighting volunteers—all as far back in time as the Revolution. Only fourteen days' service, or participation in one battle, was required for eligibility.[28]

Not all soldiers, it should be noted, elected to receive warrants. A few chose treasury scrip. In the act of 1847 Congress gave each veteran the option of a 160-acre warrant (worth $200 at the land offices) or treasury scrip in the amount of $100 bearing 6 per cent interest. For men who served less than one year, 40-acre warrants or $25 in scrip was offered.[29] On December 2, 1850, the Secretary of the Interior reported that only 3,332 men had selected scrip under the 1847 act, while 81,373 had desired warrants.[30] Most of the old campaigners shrewdly realized that

---

[24] *Congressional Globe,* 32nd Cong., 1st Sess., XXI, 312; *ibid.,* 31st Cong., 2nd Sess., XX, 175, 440.

[25] One Senator ascribed the lack of an active land paper market to the "risk" involved in circumventing the laws (*ibid.,* 32nd Cong., 1st Sess., XXI, 312).

[26] U.S. *Statutes at Large,* X, 3; XI, 309.

[27] U.S. Commissioner of the General Land Office, *Report,* 1907, 259.

[28] U.S. *Statutes at Large,* X, 701; XI, 8.

[29] *Ibid.,* IX, 125–26.

[30] *Senate Executive Documents,* 31st Cong., 2nd Sess., I, Doc. 1, 25. The Treasury Department in 1850 reported issuing warrants totaling 14.4 million acres or $18 million, whereas only $260,000 had been paid on commuted treasury scrip (*Congressional Globe,* 31st Cong., 1st Sess., XIX, 1707).

Fig. 6.2. Circular No. 4, issued by LeGrand Byington, Iowa General Land Agency, ca. 1851. (Courtesy of Iowa Dept. of History and Archives.)

the land warrant would usually bring a price above that of the treasury paper since the scrip was pegged at only half the land office value of the warrants. On the other hand, the scrip option feature of the act tended to place a floor under land warrant prices.[31]

III

WHILE ALLOWING assignment and promiscuous entry, Congress carefully circumscribed the use of warrants with many restrictions which also tended to depress their market prices. Originally the certificates could only be located on lands "subject to private entry" at the "usual minimum," "according to legal subdivisions," and "in one body." The law expressly forbade location of a warrant on any land to which there was a "preemption right," or "an actual settlement or cultivation"—unless the volunteer or soldier was entitled to a preemption in his own right.[32]

The warrants of 1847 were also unacceptable for entry on any lands where the minimum price was greater than $1.25 per acre.[33] In 1848, Congress extended to warrantees *but not to assignees* the privilege of locating warrants on public lands where the minimum price was above $1.25 per acre, the difference to be paid in cash.[34] When Senator Breese of the Public Lands Committee proposed in 1849 to extend to assignees the right to locate warrants on land held above the minimum, the Senate refused, following a bitter debate in which speculator-assignees were derided as "sharpies," "piratical picaroons," and "cormorants with gaping maws."[35] The result of the negative decision was to lower asking prices for warrants held by veterans, since warrants now were unusable for the choice alternate sections along rivers, canals, and ultimately railroads, many of which were part of special land grants and thus subject to private entry only

---

[31] Senator Truman Smith of Connecticut conjectured as much in 1850 in the course of debate. The reason that so few soldiers chose treasury scrip, he declared, was because "the soldier could obtain in the market more than the commutation price provided for in the [1847] bill" (*ibid.*, XIX, 1708).

[32] *Senate Executive Documents*, 30th Cong., 1st Sess., II, Doc. 2, 13. The decision was made by the Secretary of the Treasury in 1847 (Lester, *Land Laws*, 578; Commissioner Richard H. Young to Kemper and Lindwarm, Aug. 25, 1847, GLO Misc. Letters, XXIII, 22).

[33] As Commissioner Young explained, "The law intends to confine the location to the general class of *unclaimed, unsettled* public lands, subject to *private entry* at the *usual* minimum" (Lester, *Land Laws*, 576).

[34] *Ibid.*, 144–45; cf. 580, and Richard H. Young to I. F. Bringhurst, Sept. 27, 1848, GLO Misc. Letters, XXIV, 198.

[35] *Congressional Globe*, 30th Cong., 2nd Sess., XVIII, 217, 231–32, 263–65.

at $2.50 per acre. In 1852, Congress reversed its earlier decision and allowed assignees to locate on double minimum land but three years later again withdrew the privilege until May 23, 1858, when it was again reinstated.[36]

Such vacillating policy was typical of most congressional and administrative decisions regarding land warrants in the 1850's. Businessmen were therefore understandably reluctant to pay land office prices for warrants which did not give assignees full rights and privileges. Especially was this true in the period from 1855 to 1858 when warrants were abundant and the stifling restrictions on locations were in effect. Some registers and receivers in Iowa even misconstrued the commissioner's instructions regarding the 1855 act—that warrants were not an acceptable means of payment at a "public sale" (i.e., the initial public auction) nor on land held above the "minimum price"— and refused to accept warrants for private entries whenever buyers bid a tract above the government minimum. It was a year before the commissioner corrected such officers.[37] Warrants could after all be used for nothing but private entries.[38]

That warrants were worthless at land sales was undoubtedly the greatest drawback in their use. During the middle 1850's when demand for land was at its peak, most of the better tracts in a district were bid off at the two-week public auction. Warrants were applicable only after a district had been well picked over. Hence, when warrant prices declined as a result, contemporaries attributed this not to depression but to prosperity. An Iowa correspondent of the New York *Times* reported:

> At the recent sales in this State, all the good land was bid off, and paid for in gold, at from $1.50 to $4.00 per acre, leaving little or nothing upon which to apply the warrants. For instance, at Osage it is notorious that there was more gold than

[36] Lester, *Land Laws*, 179, 253, 296, 599, 608.

[37] *Ibid.*, 599; 615–16. By the mid-1850's the competition for Iowa land was so keen that many officials, instead of allowing promiscuous entry on a strict priority basis (the traditional practice) adopted a more systematic policy of "entering by ranges" and then allowing two or more persons desiring the same tract to bid against each other. This was interpreted by some to be a "public sale." See "Letters of J. W. Denison," *Ia. J. Hist. and Pol.*, XXXI (Jan., 1933), 121.

[38] Des Moines banker Hoyt Sherman notified his Virginia customer, James S. Easley, in late 1855, that the register at the Fort Dodge Land Office had "unexpectedly and without any precedent for his course," decided not to receive land warrants on the locations of land at private entry bid off at over $1.25 per acre. This "absurd and unreasonable" policy, Sherman complained, was proving "disastrous [for it] had the effect of ruling out nearly all our Warrants, and caused us to lose some (in fact a large portion) of our best entries." Most of these choice selections, Sherman noted, were struck off to cash buyers "who had bid $1.26 per acre on contested lands, even though they were willing to pay as high as $1.75 or two dollars per acre." Sherman to Easley, Nov. 23, Dec. 10, 1855, James S. Easley Papers.

there were unoccupied lands at those prices, three to one, and, consequently, scarcely a man who went there with warrants obtained a single foot of land, and was obliged to bring back and sell his warrants for what he could get, or send them to Sioux City or Fort Dodge with no better prospect of success. Any candid man must be ready to confess, therefore, that the depreciation in the price of warrants is owing to the great demand for land by men who have the money to pay for it. [39]

While this anonymous Iowan probably exaggerated the small amount of land available at private entry, he was essentially correct in reporting that lands auctioned at public sales in the period when the speculative boom was at its peak often sold above the government minimum, and also that land was available for private entry after the public sale for only a short time. In December of 1855, for example, a speculator reported that buyers had entered "scarcely any" land at the Des Moines Land Office "for some time past for less than $1.30 to $1.80 per acre" and by the next spring all the government land would be gone. Similarly, at the Sioux City Land Office in the spring of 1857, the land sales at the public auction averaged $1.40 per acre, with a top price paid of $3.05. In the months of May and June following the public sale, 347,857 acres were entered, mainly with warrants, and by the end of July there was no more land subject to entry in the district. [40]

Another confusing, yet crucial aspect of land warrants concerns the use of assigned warrants on preemption tracts. One of the major speculative uses of warrants was to sell them on credit to settlers. Under this arrangement the speculator would protect his investment by taking title to the land in his own name, giving his bond to transfer the title when the debt was paid. This eliminated mortgages which could be difficult and costly to foreclose if the borrower defaulted. But lenders had to be able to locate their certificates on occupied land in their own names for this arrangement to be valid.

At first glance, the land laws of the 1840's and 1850's seem to preclude any such procedure. The Preemption Law of 1841 stated explicitly that "no assignments or transfers of preemptive rights can be recognized. The patents must issue to the claim-

---

[39] Quoted in *The North-Western Rev.*, I (Aug., 1857), 13. Similar comments came from Iowa agents in 1855 in reference to the Dubuque and Decorah districts. At Decorah, Iowa City realtor Hugh D. Downey expected *"one grande rush"* which will last a month or two," and at the sale of 16 townships remaining in the Dubuque District, he reported land dealers were having a "sweet time—not less than about five applicants for each qr. Sec. left in the Dist." (Downey to Easley, Nov. 21, Dec. 15, 1855, James S. Easley Papers).

[40] "Letters of J. W. Denison," 120; *The North-Western Rev.*, I (Aug. 1857), 11.

ants, in whose names alone all entries must be made." As late as 1859, the commissioner of the General Land Office declared that preemptions could never be assigned to another by the original claimant.[41]

While these laws appear straightforward in denying to moneylenders the right to apply warrants in their own names on preempted or occupied land, a careful reading of subsequent administrative interpretations and legislation indicates that the arrangement was allowed, at least partially. To understand the laws one must distinguish between preemptions prior to the public sales and later preemptions, when a district was open for private entry.[42] Prior to the public sales, preemption rights could never be transferred. Only a mortgage instrument could be used in credit arrangements in such cases. For the period 1852 to 1855, however, Commissioner John Wilson of the General Land Office acquiesced in allowing preemptors on unoffered land to assign their rights to other parties. The act of 1852 making land paper assignable apparently was interpreted to apply also to preemption rights. Commissioner Thomas A. Hendricks, upon taking office in 1855, repudiated his predecessor's interpretation.[43]

When preemption declarations were filed on land subject to private entry (i.e., after the public sale) the settler could, under a decision of Congress in 1843, allow his preemption right to lapse after the twelve-month period and enter his claim at private sale. In this case the law which applied to all occupied land subject to private entry went into effect—namely, that with the settler's written consent or affidavit, the land could be entered in the name of the moneylender.[44] Speculators who dealt largely with warrants, therefore, could make satisfactory credit arrangements with all non-preemptive claimants and with all preemptors whose claims involved land that had already been offered at public auction. With all preemptors on unoffered land, however, a mortgage was the only alternative except during the period 1852 to 1855, when the commissioner misconstrued the law.

Several other restrictions on the locations of warrants should

---

[41] Lester, *Land Laws,* 364, 616.

[42] Contrary to common conceptions, preemption claims could be filed on land after the public auction as well as before. The only stipulation was that the claimant must file his notice of preemption within 30 days after settlement and pay for the land within one year, unless at that time he chose to let his preemptive right lapse and enter the land under private entry. He must, however, be the first applicant for private entry in order to retain possession of his homestead (Lester, *Land Laws,* 359, 362, 373). See also Thos. A. Hendricks to Register and Receiver at Osage, May 17, 1858, Governor's Incoming Correspondence, School Lands, Fold. I, Iowa State Department of History and Archives, Des Moines.

[43] Lester, *Land Laws,* 384, 599, 607, 616. See also J. Butterfield to G. W. Jones, July 17, 1850, GLO Misc. Letters, XXIX, 108.

[44] Lester, *Land Laws,* 86, 373, 582, 620.

also be noted. Warrants could only be located "according to legal subdivisions" and in one body "in as compact a form as possible." This restriction, designed to prevent speculators from entering the best "forties" in many different sections, was never removed in subsequent laws.[45] Thus, a 160-acre warrant could be located on only one tract, not on four noncontiguous tracts, whereas with the supposed equivalent of $200 cash in hand the entrant could select four choice 40-acre locations anywhere on the public domain. Conversely, an 80-acre warrant could not be located on a 40-acre tract held for sale at double the minimum price. Also when a tract was entered that contained a lesser number of acres than was specified in the warrant, the excess acres reverted to the government. For instance, if a 120-acre warrant was applied on a 100-acre tract, the excess 20 acres were forfeited. In short, the warrant holder had less freedom of choice than the cash buyer.

Subject as it was to the arbitrary whims of government officials, the land warrant market was obviously not a free market in the classical economic sense. Such a market is predicated on the assumption that an unlimited number of buyers and sellers were free to make bids and accept offers dictated only by their economic self-interest, the price being determined by the value which the good represented to the last buyer as either a productive or consumptive good. The land warrant was a claim to land but its price was not (even in the long run or on an average) dictated by the productive value of the land which the warrant might be used to buy. This was so because the government not only flooded the market with over 60 million acres' worth of warrants in less than a decade but, through its minimum sale price of $1.25 per acre, put an upper limit on the price which a rational buyer would pay for such land paper. On the other hand, the $100 treasury scrip which Congress offered in lieu of 160-acre warrants in the act of 1847 tended to place a floor under warrant prices, at least during the ante bellum period.[46]

---

[45] *Ibid.*, 576, 587, 595; J. Butterfield to Senator A. Felch, Feb. 10, 1852, GLO Misc. Letters, XXXIV, 129.

[46] Warrant prices hinged on supply and demand to such an extent that even a heavy snowstorm which delayed the mails for several days created temporary scarcity and resulted in a price rise (Sherman Bros. to Easley & Willingham, Jan. 14, 1856; Dec. 26, 1855, James S. Easley Papers). See also Sweeny, Rittenhouse & Fant to Easley & Willingham, Jan. 18 and 24, 1856, James S. Easley Papers. Strange as it may seem, warrant prices may even have been influenced by the religious scruples of Quakers, many of whom refused to countenance their use. Having entered land with a warrant for a nonresident investor, Barlow Granger, a Des Moines realtor, received this reply: "I think that if thee still pay for the land without the land warrent it would be more satisfactory to our friends and our selves as friends disapprove of Warrants[.] But it m[a]y make a difference has thee entered it for James[.] But had James entered himself with the land warrant he would be liable to dis-

IV

JUDGING from the seeming oversupply of warrants and the many restrictions on their use, it would be logical to assume that warrants were always cheap, as indeed most students of land policy have concluded. However, rather than systematically investigating warrant prices as they were reported faithfully in the major eastern markets, scholars have generally relied only on random quotes from newspapers and other sources to illustrate that warrants were always a bargain. Professor Benjamin H. Hibbard cited the *Ohio Statesman* of 1841 in which it was reported that scrip obtained in exchange for Revolutionary War military warrants was bought "for a mere song." Again, he noted that on February 26, 1852, the Andrew (Iowa) *Western Democrat* reported quarter section Mexican land warrants dull, selling at $110 to $115 (69 to 72 cents per acre), whereas they would have been worth $200 on the basis of $1.25 per acre at the land office. Finally, he found Greeley's *Tribune* reporting on October 24, 1857, that New York City brokers were quoting warrants "as low as 60 cents per acre," or less than half-price. The highest quotation on one day, "taken as a sample," was 85 cents per acre.[47]

However, Hibbard's "samples" were misleading because he cited warrant prices at two of their weakest points in the decade of the 1850's. In early 1852 the question of assignability had not been settled by congressional action and warrants were not yet accepted at the land offices on preemptions. Thus, few brokers were willing then to buy warrants. The October, 1857, market quotation reflects the break in the market caused by the financial crash which struck Wall Street on August 29 with the collapse of the Ohio Life Insurance Trust Company.

Professor Roscoe Lokken attempted to correct the mistaken notion created by Hibbard. Lokken, after citing the October, 1857, New York City warrant market quotations added a sentence noting that in 1855 when demand had been stronger, *Thompson's Bank Note Reporter* quoted warrants at $1.08 per acre for 120-acre warrants and $1.11 per acre for 160-acre denominations with the brokerage fees in addition.[48] If the brokerage fee of $1.60

onement [disownment?]." (Deborah Wrigley to Barlow Granger, "1st day morning," Barlow Granger Papers, Iowa State Department of History and Archives, Des Moines.) Quaker associates of Baltimore speculator Miles White similarly expressed religious scruples against the use of military warrants and White accordingly discontinued the entry business. (See Paul W. Gates, "The Homestead Law in Iowa," *Agr. Hist.*, XXXVIII [April, 1964], 69.)

[47] Hibbard, *History of the Public Land Policies*, 125–27. Sheldon, *Land Systems and Land Policies in Nebraska*, 60, similarly cited low warrant prices in 1858 and 1861, not realizing that these were atypical dates.

[48] Lokken, *Iowa Public Land Disposal*, 140–41.

(one cent per acre), the western land office fee of $4.00 ($1.00 per forty acres), and the customary real estate agent's fee of $6.00 for locating a 160-acre warrant are added to the initial investment (as they must be for all but those veterans who located their own warrants), it will be obvious that the warrant buyer paying $177.60 ($1.11 per acre) in New York City for a 160-acre warrant, plus a total of $11.60 in fees, actually was investing $189.20, or $1.18 per acre, to secure a quarter section of land, a figure very near the land office cash price.[49] Even this higher 1855 quotation of $1.11 per acre, however, is noticeably below the prevailing prices of the two previous years because congressional debate on a new warrant act—an act that promised to be more lavish than all previous ones combined—thoroughly unsettled the market throughout 1855. During 1853 and 1854, on the other hand, when purchasers acquired the great bulk of central Iowa land, warrant quotations ranged as high as $1.18½ per acre in New York and Washington; and from July, 1853, to September, 1854, prices were never below $1.11¼ per acre, as Table 6.1 indicates.[50] At $1.18½ per acre, a 160-acre warrant bought in New York would actually cost the owner $201.20 by the time land was secured.

That these stiff prices did not deter purchasers is obvious from the books of original entry and the official statistics on Iowa

---

[49] Until May 17, 1848, warrants were located free of charge. At the urging of the commissioner of the General Land Office, Congress thereafter allowed the land officers to collect fees of fifty cents on 160-acre warrants and twenty-five cents on "forties." Soldiers, however, retained the privilege of locating free. Believing these fees to be "wholly inadequate," the commissioner induced Congress on Mar. 22, 1852, to raise the fee to $1.00 for each 40 acres. Only warrant holders, not cash entrants, had to pay these fees, however (Lester, *Land Laws,* 179, 588, 603; *House Executive Documents,* 30th Cong., 2nd Sess., III, Doc. 12, 23; *Senate Executive Documents,* 32nd Cong., 2nd Sess., I, Doc. 1, 61–62).

[50] The statistics in Table 6.1 were supplied by Miss Natalie Disbrow (see n. 7). These quotations, it should be noted, are based on dealer's *advertised* rather than *actual* selling prices. As the spread between these figures was relatively fixed, brokers were often tempted to quote artificially low selling prices so as to have an excuse to buy at a lower price from their correspondents. William T. Smithson, Washington, D.C., broker, in a confidential letter to his friend, James S. Easley of Virginia, in late 1855, reported that dealers refused to sell warrants under $1.00 per acre for 160's whereas their advertised selling price was only 93 cents per acre. These quotations "amount to nothing," Smithson concluded. "Several dealers have (I say it [in] confidence) put in those quotations for the purpose of having an excuse to make *such returns* to their correspondents. They are making a desperate effort to bring down the price of warrants in the Country and sell them at the best rates they can" (Smithson to Easley, Dec. 11, 1855, James S. Easley Papers). These comments, however, must be weighed in the knowledge that Smithson was engaged at this time in strong competition with Hamilton G. Fant and other brokers in soliciting Easley's business. That Easley continued to place orders with both Smithson and Fant indicates that Smithson's charge of chicanery must be discounted somewhat.

TABLE 6.1

DEALERS' ADVERTISED SELLING PRICES OF MILITARY BOUNTY LAND WARRANTS, BASED ON 160-ACRE WARRANTS, NEW YORK AND WASHINGTON, 1848–60*

Year	Price range	Jan.	Feb.	Mar.	Apr.	May	June	July	Aug.	Sept.	Oct.	Nov.	Dec.
							(*Cents per Acre*)						
1848	High	88¼	78⅛	78⅛	81¼	75	78⅛	71⅞	88¾	70	70	69 1/16	68⅛
	Low	78⅛	76¼	70	78⅛	73⅝	71⅞	62½	62½	66⅞	65⅝	62½	65⅝
1849	High	70	68¾	66⅞	66⅞	68⅜	81¼	82½	80	79⅜	79⅜	78⅛	81¼
	Low	65	63¾	64⅜	63¾	63¾	65⅝	78⅛	75	78⅛	75	68¾	73¾
1850	High	84⅜	83⅛	82½	82½	81¼	76 9/16	78⅛	81¼	78⅛	87½	81¼	78⅛
	Low	75	75	78¼	75	70⅛	62½	62½	71⅞	68⅝	78⅛	75	68¾
1851	High	72½	81¼	90⅝	90⅝	89⅜	96⅞	96⅞	96⅞	96⅞	96⅞	93¾	93¾
	Low	65⅝	68¾	81¼	81¼	81¼	84⅜	87½	90⅝	92½	87½	84⅜	71⅞
1852	High	87½	81¼	88¾	81¼	81¼	83¾	90	96⅞	96⅞	93¾	93¾	93¾
	Low	68¾	68¾	62½	62½	75	75⅝	78⅛	78⅛	87½	87½	87½	89½
1853	High	100	104⅜	106¼	103¾	109⅜	115⅜	118¾	118¾	117½	118¾	116¼	117½
	Low	91⅞	100	103⅛	100⅝	104⅜	107½	115⅝	115	115	115⅝	112½	113¾
1854	High	115	118¾	118¾	118¾	118¾	.....	120	118¾	117½	.....	.....	.....
	Low	111¼	115⅝	116¼	116¼	116¼	.....	117½	115⅝	112½	109⅜	.....	.....
1855	High	.....	.....	103⅛	110	114	114	112½	112	112½	116½	114	111
	Low	.....	.....	100	100	103⅛	107	109	110	90	108	100	85
1856	High	108	109	116	112	109	100	104	106	100	97	97	96
	Low	100	105	108	108	85	85	90	94	92	90	90	91
1857	High	98	105	105	104	101	96	99	98	94	85	84	82
	Low	90	96	98	99	87	88	92	87½	83	60	60	78
1858	High	95	92	99	92	92	92	94	95	95	85	88	86
	Low	80	87	85	87	87	89	89	92	83	80	81	82
1859	High	88	88	90	87	87	88	92	95	90	85	76	76
	Low	83	80	82	80	80	81	84	88	85	78	60	70
1860	High	75	77	77	77	78	86	88	84	91	96	88	..
	Low	66	68	67	71	65	71	78	73	75	86	70	..

*The data for this table were supplied by Miss Natalie Disbrow, St. Petersburg, Fla., and represent part of her study of the military bounty warrants. Most citations are from the Riggs and Corcoran Collections, Library of Congress.

acreage acquired by warrants. As stated previously, buyers laid out warrants rather than cash on more than one-half of all Congress land in Iowa. As early as 1851, when the warrants issued under the acts of 1847 and 1850 had been circulating only a short time, Iowa land offices reported that 2.6 million acres had already been located in the state with warrants, compared with 2.7 million acres in cash entries since the offices first opened in 1838.[51]

Eastern capitalists were willing to invest $200 or more for 160-acre land warrants for sound economic reasons. Warrants could more easily, safely, and cheaply be shipped through the federal mails than could bulk gold or silver, which was virtually the only alternative acceptable at the land offices.[52] When available, gold could be purchased at western banks, but the cost was often prohibitive. Similarly, sight drafts and bills of exchange were always discounted at 1 per cent or more. Since warrants could be sold for cash in the West at an advance above the current New York prices, speculators also could usually make moderate profits with rapid turnover of their funds by selling their warrants rather than entering land with them.[53]

Convenience, safety, economy, and a modest return through quick cash sales were by no means the only attractions of warrants and scrip. Investors purchased high-priced warrants mainly because they anticipated much larger profits by locating the warrants for other buyers on credit. Given the stringent specie supply in all western land districts, settlers often faced land sales with little or no gold to secure their claims. With Davis County settlers anticipating the first land sale in early 1845, for example,

[51] The acreage located with warrants of 1847 was 1,987,049 on Nov. 30, 1850, and 2,475,960 on Sept. 30, 1851, with an additional 168,220 acres of the warrants of 1850 (Iowa *Senate Journal*, 1850, appendix, 156; J. Butterfield to Sen. A. C. Dodge, Jan. 28, 1852, in GLO Misc. Letters, XXXIV, 63). By June 30, 1856, the total warrant entries in Iowa had climbed to 10,692,300 acres (Iowa *House Journal*, 1858, 24).

[52] Notes of a very few western banks had been accepted at the land offices in the 1830's and 1840's. John B. Newhall's *Sketches of Iowa, or the Emigrants Guide* (New York, 1841), 50, reported that payments at the land sales in Iowa must be in Missouri bank notes of $20 or more, silver and gold coins, United States treasury notes, and, under certain conditions (removed in 1842), Virginia military land scrip. From the initial Iowa land sales in Nov., 1838, until Mar., 1839, notes of the State Bank of Illinois and the Bank of Mineral Point, Wis., and their branches, in denominations of $20 or more, were also acceptable at the government's repository—the Bank of Missouri at St. Louis (Burlington *Iowa Territorial Gazette and Burlington Adviser*, Oct. 6, 1838, Mar. 9, and Aug. 10, 1839).

[53] LeGrand Byington, Iowa City land agent, offered in late 1852 to purchase any quantity of warrants at 15 per cent above their current price in the city of New York. (See his "Circular No. 4.") Jesse W. Denison, Iowa agent for the Providence Western Land Co., noted in 1855 that warrants, "a ready cash article," were worth from five to eight cents an acre more in Iowa than in Boston and New York ("Letters of J. W. Denison," 96).

a local minister reported that "not one in 10 or 15 was prepared to pay for his land, and much anxiety was felt."[54]

Neither the United States government nor commercial banks would extend credit on land during the middle decades of the nineteenth century. Settlers and would-be speculators, consequently, had to rely on private individuals, eastern corporations, and private frontier "banks" for land credit. Because specie was generally scarce in the West and credit facilities were limited, interest rates were correspondingly high, from 25 to 50 per cent per annum. At the initial public auction at Marion in 1843, for instance, a settler reported a great "want of money." As a result, "a great many people were crazy to get money at 50 per cent."[55]

With interest rates as appealing as these, speculators eagerly grasped all the warrants available. None explained the craving for warrants despite high prices as succinctly as did Cyrus Woodman, a prominent and highly successful Wisconsin land agent. Writing to one of his local agents in 1855, he stated: "I have only time to enclose an 80 and 160 [acre warrant] before the mail closes. These are all I have. I write to New York today for 1000 acres, though I dislike to buy at the present high prices. Warrants are worth in New York from [$]1.14 to [$]1.20 per acre."[56]

A letter penned the same day to his brother and supply agent, George Woodman of New York, continued the theme: "I

---

[54] Walter R. Houf (ed.), "American Home Missionary Letters from Iowa," *Annals of Iowa*, 3rd Ser., XXXVII (Fall, 1963), 108. The sale was subsequently postponed for another year.

[55] Cyrus Sanders to Richard B. Sanders, Mar. 24, 1843. During the previous year 50 per cent had also been the prevailing rate at Iowa City (Cyrus Sanders to Richard B. Sanders, Dec. 16, 1842 [Cyrus Sanders Papers, State Historical Society of Iowa, Iowa City]). As early as Aug. 28, 1841, Sanders noted that he had loaned all of his available capital "at from thirty-three to forty per cent and could loan ten times as much if I had it at the same rate." For further documentation on this point see Henry Eno to William Eno, Oct. 17, 1840, Henry Eno Papers, Special Collections Department, Library, University of Iowa, Iowa City. "The moneylender normally gets thirty to forty per cent yearly," explained [Jan Nollan], *De Hollanders in Iowa: Brieven uit Pella, van een Gelderschman* (Arnhem, Netherlands, 1858), 176. Charles Lindsey reported that in Iowa "in spite of the usury laws, which restrict the rate of interest to ten per cent, from three to five cents per month had been the actual rates in the previous winter" (*The Prairies of the Western States* [Toronto, 1860], 46). Judge Arden B. Holcomb of Boonesboro cited interest of 40 per cent as the "lowest sale last week" at the Fort Dodge land sales in July, 1855. In 1856 he lent money at 7½ per cent per month and in one extreme case at 7½ per cent for 20 days (John M. Brainard, "Opening an Iowa County," *Annals of Iowa*, 3rd Ser. II [Jan., 1896], 261, 270). The editor of the Burlington *Iowa Territorial Gazette and Burlington Advertiser* reported standard interest rates of 25–50 per cent and even as high as 70 per cent (Nov. 3, 24, 1838; Aug. 31, 1839).

[56] Cyrus Woodman to Ephraim Brown, Nov. 12, 1855, Cyrus Woodman Papers, Wisconsin State Historical Society, Madison.

am sorry that warrants keep up so high, *but let the price be as it may*, please send me 1,000 acres more."[57] On November 24, Woodman asked his brother for another 2,000 acres' worth. With the warrants, he explained to a prospective investor: "I can invest, I think, from $10,000 to $20,000 in Government land so that I can afford to pay the taxes and double the amounts of the cost per acre in 7 years. The entries can be made in your name and you giving a bond for a deed. Nothing can be safer on your part."[58]

It is a well-documented fact that moneylenders could extend credit with warrants with such profitable returns. G. L. Tremaine was one such borrower. "My first banking," he recalled before a meeting of the Iowa Bankers' Association, "was at Dubuque, when I negotiated a $200 loan on 160 acres. I contracted to pay and paid, at the end of one year, $320, the modest rate of 60 per cent. Not having the $1.25 per acre Uncle Sam wanted, I paid this rate to H. W. Sanford to get my 160 entered."[59]

The customary credit arrangement between a moneylender-speculator and purchaser such as Sanford and Tremaine, was to effect a time-entry contract. The lender entered the land at the land office in his own name, thus gaining possession of the title deed himself, and delivered to the purchaser a bond for the deed. This required the lender to transfer title to the buyer as soon as the terms of the contract were fulfilled. Typically, the contract provided that at the expiration of the designated time period (generally one but sometimes two years) the buyer must pay an agreed-upon sum. Customarily, no interest charge was mentioned. The contract price, however, was usually 40 per cent (or 80 percent if a two-year loan) higher than the land office price (the amount actually loaned) in order to offset the low interest ceiling imposed by Iowa law.[60] For instance, instead of selling a 40-acre land warrant for $1.25 per acre plus 40 per cent interest per annum, the moneylender would sell it for $1.75 per acre.

---

[57] Cyrus Woodman to George Woodman, *ibid*. (italics supplied).

[58] Cyrus Woodman to John S. Haywood, Dec. 20, 1855, *ibid*.

[59] Iowa Bankers' Association, *Proceedings*, 1888, 10.

[60] In the early years before warrants replaced cash in time-entry loans, that is, before 1852, contracts often stipulated the maximum legal interest rate of 10 or 20 per cent (see below), in which cases the 40 per cent mark-up on the land price would be reduced by the equivalent amount. For instance, a 40-acre warrant worth $50 at the land office would be sold on one year's time for $62.50 plus 10 per cent interest or $58.50 plus 20 per cent. For various references to such contracts, see George W. Hight's advertisement in the Burlington *Hawkeye and Iowa Patriot*, Mar. 25, 1841; Henry Eno to William Eno, Oct. 17, 1840, Henry Eno Papers; *The North-western Rev.*, I (Oct. 1857), 35.

V

IN 1838, the Iowa territorial legislature allowed interest charges no greater than 20 per cent if explicitly stated in the contract. To charge interest above the legal limit was to invite forfeiture of the usurious portion of the interest and a fine of 25 per cent of the contract's value. The borrower could initiate court proceedings without penalty to himself for being a participant in the usurious transaction.[61] On February 9, 1843, the legislature revised the legal interest rate downward to 10 per cent and continued in force the penalty clauses of the 1838 act, although the amount of the penalty was likewise reduced to 10 per cent. The reduction came despite an impassioned plea by the judiciary committee to leave the legal interest rate maximum at 20 per cent because "in a new country of vast undeveloped resources, it is the dictate of wisdom to offer inducements for men of wealth to send their money among us; and a less rate of interest . . . would not have the desired effect of diverting the capital of the east to the far west."[62] The house concurred in the suggested amendment but the council, the upper chamber, refused. The lower house reluctantly acquiesced on the 10 per cent figure. In the revised code of 1851 the interest ceiling was temporarily abrogated, but in January, 1853, the Fourth General Assembly reinstated the prevailing 10 per cent limit although requiring that it be expressed in writing. Otherwise, 6 per cent was the maximum. Governor Stephen Hempstead allowed the bill to become law without his signature. Until the post-Civil War era, 10 per cent remained the legal maximum interest in Iowa.[63]

That the "bond for a deed" arrangement either based on cash or land warrant transactions was designed to evade these Iowa usury laws can be conclusively proved. Henry Eno, an

[61] Iowa *Statute Laws*, 1838, 293–94. The original bill set the legal interest rate at 10 per cent but this was quickly raised to 20 per cent. Thereafter, the majority beat down numerous proposals to revise the maximum legal interest downward to 15 per cent or 12 per cent. George D. Temple, later a partner in the real estate firm of Henn, Williams & Co., Fairfield, tried unsuccessfully to delete the penalty clauses. For the debates see Iowa *House Journal*, 1838, 35, 40, 45–56, 68, 73, 97–98, 104, 107, 138, 152, and 170. From 1833 to 1838, while Iowa was a part of Michigan Territory, the maximum legal interest had been 7 per cent (Michigan *Territorial Laws*, III, 1094).

[62] Iowa *Revised Statutes*, 1843, 293–94. For the debate see Iowa *House Journal*, 1842, 107, 109, 111, 118, 252–53, 271–72. For the full text of the judiciary committee's appeal, see *ibid.*, 252–53. Opponents of usury laws also cited their ineffectiveness. See, for example, editorials in the Burlington *Iowa Territorial Gazette and Burlington Advertiser*, Nov. 3 and 24, 1838; and Davenport *Gazette*, Jan. 2, 1851.

[63] Iowa *Revised Code*, 1851, 148–49; *ibid.*, 1860, 316–17; Iowa *Laws*, 1853, 67–79.

aspiring Fort Madison lawyer and land agent, wrote his brother in 1840: "If my health had permitted I should have went east this summer as . . . I had hopes that by representing matters & things in this Country in their true light I might perhaps have induced some capitalist to make me an agent for him here, as I can now loan money on the very best & safest security at from twenty-five to fifty per cent, the laws of the Country allow of twenty per cent, *but property can be purchased on a deed of trust executed so to make every thing safe and in many cases the very highest rate of Interest secured.*"[64]

While Eno outlined the standard technique for evading Iowa usury laws in the case of cash loans in the 1830's and 1840's, others were quick to realize the possibilities afforded by the Mexican bounty land warrants which had flooded the market by the late 1840's. "Have you ever talked to Gen. [Simon?] Cameron on the subject of a Land Warrant speculation?" former Iowa Governor James Clarke queried Senator Augustus C. Dodge in early 1849. "Jesse Williams says that fifty warrants might be *loaned* at their face [i.e., their inflated sale price], with 10 per cent interest for one or two years, and he would like to be interested in such a speculation."[65] LeGrand Byington of Iowa City had the same idea as Williams. In the early 1850's he issued circulars inviting warrant dealers to avail themselves of "the splendid opportunity which is here offered for safe and profitable investments, by locating these warrants, for settlers, upon their 'improvements,' so called, upon time." Byington's definition of "profitable investments" was a 50 per cent rate of return on 160-acre warrants sold on one year's time.[66]

---

[64] Henry Eno to William Eno, Oct. 17, 1840, Henry Eno Papers (italics supplied). Eno was one of the first to open a land agency in Iowa in 1837. See his card in the Burlington *Wisconsin Territorial Gazette and Burlington Advertiser,* Dec. 16, 1837. When one eastern investor expressed concern that his funds had been loaned at usurious rates, the western agent replied: "Loaning on long time in violation of usury laws is not safe—Short time will do when it is done with care" (S. S. Jones to Nathaniel Gordon, Mar. 23, 1857, Nathaniel Gordon Papers). Another westerner explained: "There is a perfect understanding between the borrower and lender that the use of money is worth more than our legal rates of interest, and no mention is ever made of usury, or apparently ever thought of" (*The North-Western Rev.,* I [June, 1857], 31). Editor Alfred Sanders of the Davenport *Gazette* (Jan. 2, 1851) likewise noted that the usury law in Iowa "is violated with impunity."

[65] James Clark to A. C. Dodge, Feb. 14, 1849, William Salter (ed.), "Old Letters," *Annals of Iowa, 3rd Ser.,* VIII (July, 1908), 439.

[66] His "Circular No. 4" quoted 160-acre warrants as selling in Iowa City for cash at $135 and on one year's time for $200. The $65 difference represented the mark-up, which was almost half the cash price of the warrant. Daniel Smith Lee, a Keokuk land agent, similarly advised Nathaniel Gordon of New Hampshire to sell warrants on time and take a mortgage on the land as security. "Mexican Warrants can be sold now for from $175 to $200 on 12 months time," Lee informed Gordon (Apr. 2, 1852, Nathaniel Gordon Papers). It should be noted that the price quotations cited above are in early 1852 before the assignability question was settled. Consequently, these prices are far below average for the decade of the Fifties.

In early 1850 the use of land warrants under a bond for a deed arrangement to evade Iowa usury laws was brought to the attention of the entire nation by senators Truman Smith of Connecticut and George W. Jones of Iowa. Observed Smith in the United States Senate chamber,

> These speculators, or rather capitalists, who are desirous of loaning money at a higher rate than the ordinary interest allowed by the laws of the land, go into the market and purchase this scrip [i.e., warrants] at a reduced price, from something over $100 for a quarter section of land up to the present market price, which I have understood is about $125. They purchase this scrip in very large quantities. They then go with it to the western country, and seek out that portion of the people who are in possession of public lands—those who are entitled to preëmption rights; and they make a contract with them. They take out the patent in their own names, and give them a contract to transfer the title at the minimum price: $1.25 cents per acre. I understand that in the State of Iowa the legal rate of interest is ten per cent per annum. These speculators will purchase scrip for a quarter section at, say, $125; and go to Iowa and make a contract with the party entitled to preëmption, take the title in their own name, stipulate for ten per cent interest, and then enter into an agreement to transfer the land when it is paid for. In this way, they will succeed in obtaining 15, 20, and 30 per cent per annum on their money.

"And sometimes fifty per cent," added Jones from his seat, which Smith conceded to be correct.[67]

It may appear incredible that a purchaser who lacked funds to buy his land from the government could borrow money at 40 or 50 per cent and repay at the end of a year. Minnesota territorial banker Jason C. Easton, one of the largest warrant dealers and loan brokers of the Northwest and a man who often received returns of 60 per cent on his warrant loans, recognized this seeming paradox. "I am aware," he wrote, "that these figures will surpris[e] our Eastern friends. They wonder how men can run in debt for a farm and contract to pay such rates of interest. But this is so & the borrower is frequently making more money than the lenders."[68] The secret in Iowa as in Minnesota, of course, lay in the land boom and continued immigration. Land was advancing in price, an Iowan wrote in 1853, "from 12% to 25% every month, and in many cases 100%, and will continue to do so as

---

[67] *Congressional Globe,* 31st Cong., 1st Sess., XIX, 1708. Smith, in his example, is obviously referring to preemptors on offered land, not unoffered. See previous discussion.

[68] Easton to H. W. Moon, Aug. 30, 1856, cited in Rodney C. Loehr, "Jason C. Easton, Territorial Banker," *Minn. Hist.,* XXIX (Sept. 1948), 226. The best study of Easton is Robert R. Jost, "An Entrepreneurial Study of a Frontier Financier, 1856–1863" (Ph.D. dissertation, University of Minnesota, 1957).

long as emigration continues to flow in as at present."[69] One of
the many who profited was S. D. Carpenter, a Cedar Rapids
physician. Years later he recalled that: "Being in the practise of
medicine, I became familiar with all the surrounding country.
When I discovered a choice location as regarded timber, water,
etc., I went to the bank, bought a land warrant at $1.25 per acre,
gave my note at three per cent per month, with a cast iron mortgage, and took my chances in the hope of selling at an advance
before the maturity of the note. I was so successful in these
ventures that I soon abandoned my profession and devoted my
whole time to real estate."[70]

Just as some buyers were able and willing to pay usurious
interest rates because the increments in their land values were
greater than the interest charges, so some large investors were
convinced that laying warrants on land was a better investment
than selling them on credit. "I have found so many *choice selections*," wrote the Reverend Jesse W. Denison, resident agent for
the Providence Western Land Company of Rhode Island, to his
partners, "and where you could hardly avoid coining the massive
gold from them, that I can hardly persuade myself that I *must*
leave them for others. I could invest for you $100,000 on the
same terms and about to the same advantage that I can $10,000.
You never will make money faster than by buying up Land
Warrants at less than $1 an acre, as you can now, and have me
locate them."[71]

Hundreds of other investors must have shared in Denison's
glowing optimism, for his subsequent letters throughout 1855
and 1856 reiterated the tremendous hunger for land. "You can
have no conception of the amount of lands that have been entered
in this state during the last 6 months and that are now continually being entered," Denison reported from Des Moines. "I had
no idea of it myself, though I knew that there was a *great rush*,
into this state; but the extent of it, is almost incredible."[72] Having spent the previous Sunday at Grinnell in Poweshiek County,

[69] Isaac Lane Usher to his father, Oct. 16, 1853, in "Letters of a Railroad
Builder," *Palimpsest*, III (Jan., 1922), 18.

[70] L. A. Brewer and B. L. Wick, *History of Linn County, Iowa* (2 vols.,
Cedar Rapids, 1911), I 435–36. Nels Omstead of Webster City was another
who reported borrowing money at 40 per cent to buy land and profiting on
the deal. See Sarah Brewer Bonebright, *Reminiscences of Newcastle, Iowa,
1848: A History of the Founding of Webster City, Iowa* (Des Moines, 1921),
107.

[71] Denison to Phetteplace and Hoppin, Jan. 10, 1856, in "Letters of J. W.
Denison," 125. The warrants were purchased in New York and Boston but
mainly from Horatio Woodman of Boston who pledged to supply as many
warrants as the firm needed at one-half cent less per acre than the current
prices quoted in *Thompson's Bank Note Reporter*. Agent Denison's contract called for dividing the profits on a ⅓–⅔ basis with Denison receiving
the one-third (Sept. 27, 1856, *ibid.*, 92–93).

[72] Oct. 30, 1855, *ibid.*, 100. Andrew Jackson Sterrett of Erie, Erie County,

he also learned that the 1,000 acres fellow minister Josiah B. Grinnell had entered the previous year were already worth $10 an acre.

Finding nothing in the Fort Des Moines Land District except "a few quarter sections, scattered around in different places," Denison went to Chariton in Lucas County. Here, too, he found nothing "that will suit our purpose," but he added an optimistic note: "My hopes of making a 'handsome thing' for you grow more sanguine as I ride over these Prairies."[73] Arriving in Council Bluffs the agent found land that looked good. "It is truly astonishing to see how rapidly the land is being taken up," he wrote, adding this complaint: "I waited at the Land Office all this forenoon for an opportunity to even examine the Plats of Townships to see what was still vacant, and was then told that there would probably not be any time even in the afternoon, because of the crowd waiting to make entries."[74] During the noon hour, however, Denison made the acquaintance of the register "and he very kindly gave me the first hearing this afternoon [and] . . . all the information I desired." Subsequently, Denison sent 4,440 acres' worth of warrants to the officer (plus a sufficient commission) with specific instructions for locating the warrants in the center of Crawford County.[75] How Denison gained the favor of the land officer is not known but the practice of paying "something" to obtain special consideration was not uncommon in Iowa land offices.[76]

Pa., a speculator who entered land at Fort Dodge, Des Moines, and other Iowa land offices in 1855 and 1856, recorded a reaction similar to Denison's. In a letter to his brother, he noted: "I write in the midst of the babble & confusion of a barroom, with fifty different persons from fifty different parts of the world, all jabbering at once. Land, with all is the topic. Nobody talks about anything else here. Nobody thinks about anything else here—nobody knows anything about anything else here, but *land*. Such a rush, & such a hue & cry for land, I never dreamed of." (A. J. Sterrett to David Brice Innis Sterrett, May 27, 1855, Andrew Jackson Sterrett Papers, Manuscript Division, Minnesota Historical Society, St. Paul.) In this same letter, Sterrett reported that entrants were taking up 20,000 to 25,000 acres per day in the Fort Dodge land district and that bankers and land agents were "innumerable."

[73] Nov. 3, 1855, "Letters of J. W. Denison," 102.

[74] The sluggish pace set by the land officers added to the crowds around the offices. During most of the winter of 1855–56 the officers at Council Bluffs, Fort Dodge, and other points arbitrarily decided to "call by ranges," that is, to allow entries only in a few designated ranges each day. The result was to hold down the daily entry rate. The Council Bluffs office reputedly averaged only eight to ten entries per day throughout January of 1856. Land agents complained that the officers were "stubborn" and "obstinate" and their actions "greatly interfere with ones' calculations" and are "an imposition on the people" (Casady & Test to James S. Easley, Dec. 6 and 21, 1855, Jan. 7, 15, 17, 23 and 30, 1856; Hoyt Sherman to James S. Easley, Dec. 22, 1855; James S. Easley Papers).

[75] Nov. 8 and 22, 1855, "Letters of J. W. Denison," 102, 111.

[76] New Hampshire investor Nathaniel Gordon received a request for funds from one of his Iowa land agents because, the agent noted, "without doubt I shall be obliged to pay Surveyors for assistance Something & possi-

From Council Bluffs the clergyman moved north to the Sioux City district, then east to the Fort Dodge district and finally back to Des Moines, where the real estate firm of Cook, Sargent & Cook was holding 16,360 acres of warrants for him. Here again he remarked on the "rush" in the land offices. "People seem bent," he observed, "on having some of this *cheap land* that a favoring Providence has given to the world." Later in the month Denison wrote from Council Bluffs that "the rush is still very great at the Offices. All land speculators and the 'rest of mankind' seem to be rushing into them, and the expectation is, that in the spring, all the rest of them will come, and make a general sweep of every thing in the shape of government land."[77]

By the spring of 1856, Denison had completed his locating task, entering approximately 23,000 acres. The clergyman secured most of the land at the minimum government price, having previously arranged compromises with all major competitors so none would force him to bid.[78] Of necessity, the selections were in western Iowa since land in the central counties was largely sold or claimed by the time his firm went into business. In the fall of the same year, 1856, the Providence Western agent began offering company land for sale with such inducements as long-term loans at low interest and five to ten acres of timber to go with each quarter section.[79] Seemingly, a successful land warrant operation, such as that of the Providence Western Land Company, was an admixture of eastern capital, "cooperative" land office officials, collusion among large buyers, and most of all, an agent with personal pluck and determination.

Two New Jersey partners, Robert Craig, a wealthy farmer, and Dr. John Honeyman, a New Germantown physician, similarly were able to acquire with ease two full sections of Iowa land

bly Something to clerks to let me in to a chance to locate" (N. Boardman to Gordon, Apr. 7, 1857, Nathaniel Gordon Papers).

[77] Dec. 12 and 22, 1855, "Letters of J. W. Denison," 120, 123. Denison was not the only observer to be amazed by the press for land. Andrew J. Sterrett as early as March of 1855 predicted that "Iowa will nearly fill up this year, judging from what I see & hear. All the good land will be taken" (A. J. Sterrett to David Brice Innis Sterrett, Mar. 18, 1855, Andrew Jackson Sterrett Papers). A Boston newspaperman also reported that the land offices were "overrun with business." At Iowa City, "land and land warrant dealers can be counted by the dozens" while at Des Moines he noted that "large numbers of land agents, landsharks, speculators, or land warrant dealers, as they are variously called, (according to taste and fancy . . .) swarm this town" (Boston *Transcript*, Sept. 13, Oct. 9, 1853, reprinted in Davenport *Gazette*, Sept. 29, Oct. 20, 1853).

[78] "There would have been bidding very high had I not compromised a few pieces with one or two gentlemen," Denison reported on Apr. 9, 1856 ("Letters of J. W. Denison," 292). One of the "gentlemen" was Thomas H. Benton, Jr., of the Council Bluffs real estate firm of Greene, Weare & Benton.

[79] Council Bluffs *Chronotype*, as cited in Iowa City *Daily Evening Reporter*, Nov. 1, 1856.

because they acquainted themselves with knowledgeable local men. Arriving by train at Dunleith (now East Dubuque), Illinois, on June 12, 1855, they ferried the Mississippi to Dubuque, Dunleith's sister city across the river. Proceeding directly to the land office located there, they were disappointed to find it overcrowded. They did, however, strike up a friendship with an investor, O. B. Ingalls, a trader and grain dealer from Belvidere, Illinois, who had previously explored much of the remaining vacant land in the district. Ingalls not only pointed out the choicest lands but directed the partners to D. A. McKinley, clerk in the banking and land agency of F. S. Jesup & Company, Dubuque. Here Craig and Honeyman effected a substantial saving by purchasing land warrants for cash at $192 per quarter section. More important, McKinley, a former clerk in the Dubuque land office, accompanied them to the office the next morning, ran interference past twenty applicants patiently waiting in line, and assisted in adapting their land warrants to the twelve tracts Ingalls had previously pointed out in Bremer and Delaware counties. Altogether they entered 1,290 acres. Shortly after noon the speculators were already en route home aboard the stage for Galena.[80]

VII

NOT ALL INVESTORS were as fortunate as Denison, Craig, and Honeyman in locating warrants on desirable land. Nathaniel Gordon of Exeter, New Hampshire, while on a western tour in May, 1856, left 3,040 acres of warrants with Cook & Sargent, Davenport land agents, to be located in the Fort Dodge and Sioux City land districts on "joint account" (i.e., the profits would be divided equally). No sooner had Gordon made his decision, however, than the land offices in Iowa closed for an indefinite period until the railroads could complete their selections.[81] Faced with the prospect of holding his warrants as a dead investment, Gordon sold some for cash to preemptors in Iowa and Minnesota. Then in January, 1857, his hopes revived upon learning that the President had ordered into market 25 townships in northcentral Iowa in the Osage Land District. S. M. Moore of Mendota, Illinois, one of Gordon's western agents, spoke highly of the area and urged Gordon to enter all of his warrants there. Moore noted that he had traversed the Osage district and knew the land to be good. "We have not sold one acre of land entered

---

[80] See entries of June 12 and 13, 1855, John Honeyman Journal, Rutgers University Library, New Brunswick, New Jersey.

[81] Cook & Sargent to Gordon, May 13, June 3, 10, 1856, Nathaniel Gordon Papers.

in those counties and those immediately south for less than five dollars per acre," he advised. "I entered several thousand acres & have only one qr. Sec. left. I consider the best of these 25 townships as soon as entered worth not less than five dolls. per acre." Cook & Sargent also advised that money invested in Osage lands "will yield a handsome return."[82]

Gordon planned to attend the Osage sales himself and invest upwards of 1,000 acres of warrants, but was urged to hire an agent for this "terrible job." This advice was well taken, for "swarms of speculators," one participant reported, were "so eager in their quest for land" that they stood in file before the doors of the land office through nights of such severity that some took the precaution to pour alcohol into their boots to prevent their feet from freezing.[83] Enduring punishment in the rush for the "remaining portion of Uncle Sam's land" was apparently an expected part of winter land sales in Iowa.[84] Gordon accepted the warning and hired a Mitchell County agent, Norman Boardman, to secure his entries. Boardman, however, anticipated that "the rush for land will be greater this spring than ever before," and he feared that he would not be able to enter all the warrants. His premonitions proved accurate, for, after spending two weeks at the public auction, he was unable to lay a single warrant on Iowa land. Gordon's disappointment was only assuaged by the information that another Osage land agent, John B. Wentworth, formerly of New Hampshire, had entered 2,000 acres of Gordon's warrants "on time" at 40 per cent per annum.[85] Gordon's nephew, a Nebraska speculator, also attempted to soothe his uncle's feelings by telling him that investments in Iowa land at that time were ill-advised, since "too much of the land is in the hands of speculators—whole Counties are owned by them,

---

[82] Moore to Gordon, Jan. 16, 1857; Cook & Sargent to Gordon, Feb. 3, 1857, *ibid.*

[83] S. S. Jones to Gordon, Mar. 23, 1857, *ibid.;* "Captain James E. Bennett," *Ia. Hist. Rec.,* XV (Jan., 1899), 389–90.

[84] See the Des Moines *Tri-Weekly Iowa State Journal,* Feb. 15, 1858. Andrew Sterrett laconically recorded in his diary what winter conditions at the land offices could be like. The following are excerpts from entries of the week of Jan. 7–13, 1856, written at Fort Dodge:

"*January 7:* Very cold. Land Office re-opened at 10 o'clock A.M. A rule was established by the Register that the first man at the counter could hold it all day if he wanted to with which there was much dissatisfaction. Ed. Lucas got in first & occupied all day. *January 8:* Mercury stood at 31° below 0 at 8 A.M. Ed. Lucas having stood at the door five hours got in first again. . . . *January 9:* Mercury 32° below 0 at daybreak. Sam Rees was first at the L. Office this morning, having got to the door at daybreak & stood there till 10 o'c. He occupied all day. . . . Mr. Cragg froze his feet badly." From "Diary, 1856," Andrew Jackson Sterrett Papers. See also A. J. Sterrett to David Brice Innis Sterrett, Jan. 27, 1856.

[85] Boardman to Gordon, Apr. 7, May 9, 1857; Gordon to Boardman, Apr. 16, 1857; Nathaniel Gordon Papers.

and settlers will not go there." Finally, in 1858 and 1859 Gordon
managed to locate his remaining warrants in northern and western Iowa.[86]

In marked contrast to Denison's success, Gordon's experience
illustrates the handicaps that uninitiated nonresident investors
faced as they tried to locate warrants in Iowa in the land rush of
the middle 1850's. As Judge Arden B. Holcomb of Boonesboro
aptly noted: "A man must have eye-teeth cut before it will do to
venture."[87]

---

[86] George C. Geaton to Gordon, Apr. 27, 1857; Cook, Sargent & Cook to
Gordon, Nov. 9, 1859; *ibid.*

[87] Brainard, "Opening an Iowa County," 261–62.

Chapter Seven

EASLEY & WILLINGHAM, SPECULATORS

B Y FAR the largest nonresident land operation in frontier Iowa, and indeed one of the most significant in the nation, was that of James Stone Easley and William W. Willingham of Halifax Court House, Virginia. Far outstripping all competitors, the firm in the 1850's loaned over $500,000 to credit-hungry westerners and entered more than 400,000 acres of land in the Midwest—80 per cent of it in Iowa (Table 7.1).[1]

Not only did these Virginians play an important part in frontier land history but their business papers and correspondence are the only complete records of early Iowa land speculation by nonresidents now known to be extant. Their operations, therefore, can serve to illustrate the varied aspects of a successful land venture of the mid-nineteenth century: the role of management and of land warrant and real estate brokers; the impact of congressional legislation and General Land Office policies, the effect of fluctuations in the business cycle; and the use of land warrants and the time-entry system.

1

JAMES S. EASLEY, the senior partner, was born in 1804 in Pittsylvania County, Virginia, the scion of a family whose forebears

---

[1] This chapter is based largely on the James S. Easley Papers, Alderman Library, University of Virginia, Charlottesville. Unless otherwise indicated, all manuscripts cited hereafter are from the James S. Easley Papers. Professor Paul W. Gates of Cornell University, heretofore the only scholar to use the collection, has briefly summarized his findings in "Southern Investments in Northern Lands before the Civil War," *J. So. Hist.*, V (May, 1939), 161–63; "Land Policy and Tenancy in the Prairie States," *J. Econ. Hist.*, I (May, 1941), 63–64; "The Homestead Law in Iowa," *Agr. Hist.*, XXXVIII (Apr., 1964), 69; *The Wisconsin Pine Lands of Cornell University: A Study in Land Policy and Absentee Ownership* (Ithaca, 1943), 83–84.

TABLE 7.1

ORIGINAL ENTRIES OF EASLEY & WILLINGHAM AND ASSOCIATES, 1852–58*

Year	Total acres in Midwest	Total acres in Iowa	Per cent in Iowa
1852	4,800	3,360	70.0
1853	40,850	38,850	95.1
1854	79,510	79,510	100.0
1855	91,824	91,824	100.0
1856	83,143	61,349	73.8
1857	73,443	29,593	40.3
1858	28,182	24,022	85.2
Totals	401,752	328,508	
Weighted average			81.8

*Tables 7.1–7.4 were compiled from data in the Easley Ledger 1853–57, Easley Journal 1854–81, and Easley Day Book 1853–81. The entries are dated from the time that Easley sent the warrants west for location. Yearly totals based on land office records might vary slightly but the overall total should be accurate.

emigrated from England in 1683. While yet in his teens, Easley launched his business career, hiring out to a local merchant for $25 a year plus room and board. The bright young man learned quickly and soon attracted the attention of a prominent Virginian, James Bruce of Halifax County. Bruce, purportedly the fourth millionaire in the United States and the first agricultural millionaire, was impressed with Easley's acumen and in 1830 accepted him as a junior partner in a new chain store venture. Under the firm name of Bruce & Easley, the partners established the first system of chain stores in the county where local farmers bartered their staple crop, tobacco, for produce and supplies. When Bruce died seven years later, Easley carried on the thriving business by himself.[2]

James Easley's financial resources increased rapidly and, as any sensible businessman, he sought safe yet profitable investments for his excess capital. Like many others in those years he turned to frontier real estate. At the time he was prepared to invest heavily, the national government lavishly threw into the market much of the remaining public domain in central and western Iowa and granted to veterans thousands of acres' worth

[2] For biographical data on Easley see American Historical Society, *History of Virginia*, VI (Chicago, 1924), 561. The author also benefited from correspondence with the Easley family, especially Mrs. Richard Coles Edmunds, Sr., of Halifax, Va. For data on James Bruce see "Bruce Family Geneology," *Va. Mag. Hist. and Biog.*, XI (Jan.–Apr., 1904), 328–32, 441–43. In 1850 the census marshal reported the value of Easley's Halifax County real estate at $17,000. His personal estate was not valued. In 1860, Easley reported local real estate valued at $36,100 and a personal estate of $55,000. None of his western land holdings are included in these figures. Although he lived until 1879, Easley's name did not appear in the 1870 census. See manuscript federal population censuses of 1850. 1860, 1870, for Halifax County, Va., National Archives, Washington, D.C.

Fig. 7.1. James S. Easley. (Courtesy of Mrs. Richard Coles Edmunds, Sr., Halifax, Va.)

of military bounty land warrants. A brief excursion to the "Northwest" (as Easley called the Midwest) in 1852 convinced the Virginian that the combination of Iowa land and military bounty warrants afforded a golden opportunity. Congress coincidentally gave additional encouragement by legalizing the transfer of the 1850 batch of land warrants to any who wished to buy them from veterans and by making Virginia military scrip eligible for entry purposes anywhere on the public domain.[3]

On returning home from his exploratory visit to western Illinois and eastern Iowa in early 1852, Easley decided to devote most of his time, energy, and financial resources to the "western land business," as he called it. He began by scouring the immediate locale for warrants and scrip. Through his countywide system of chain stores and many business and personal friends, he soon obtained most of the available land paper in the area.

[3] For details on land warrant legislation, see Chapter 6.

To finance the new operations, he drew on his own capital reserves and turned to friends and relatives. From several he merely borrowed at interest, but with most he made partnership agreements to invest funds on joint account without interest, dividing the profits equally.[4] Altogether, the initial capital investment of the firm was about $50,000. William W. Willingham, a clerk in Easley's home store at Halifax, joined the company as a junior partner in early 1853. Willingham thereafter was the firm's bookkeeper; he also traveled the eastern and gulf coasts from New York to Texas in search of warrants and spent at least two months annually in Iowa in company with Easley, viewing land and contacting agents. For his services he was to receive one-half of all profits on land entered on joint account after Easley had deducted all costs and 10 per cent interest on his invested capital. Willingham's role in the management of the business was always minor. Easley, with greater financial resources and more business experience, continued to hold the reins of control and make the important policy decisions.

James Easley liked to describe himself as "an old-fashioned businessman," prompt and meticulous in his affairs, and the record bears this out. He and his partner were competent and knowledgeable and kept fully abreast of the latest market developments. Subscribing to *Thompson's Bank Note Reporter*, the broker's manual, they followed the fluctuations in land warrant price quotations and money exchange rates from week to week as carefully as a modern investor reads the *Wall Street Journal* and watches the New York Stock Exchange ticker tape.

The Virginia speculators had firsthand knowledge of both the eastern and western land markets. In the East they knew where to buy warrants most advantageously and how to draw fine distinctions in price between the different-sized warrants. For instance, they bought as many warrants as possible from local residents or in the secondary markets like Richmond and Philadelphia in order to obtain the customary discount of one or two cents per acre below the two major markets of New York and Washington. In the West, Easley and Willingham dealt

---

[4] Between 1853 and 1858 Easley borrowed $8,508.94 at 6 per cent from the estates of William L. Owen and W. H. Easley and M. B. Easley. During the same period he borrowed $38,871.16 from Easley, Holt & Co. at 5 per cent compounded annually, and invested on joint account $25,135.96 for fellow Virginians George Carrington, John B. Carrington, Dr. C. J. Craddock, Nathaniel T. Green, Judge Thomas Leigh, Thomas E. Owen, and Evan J. Rugland. These figures were compiled from data in the Easley Ledger 1853–57, Easley Journal 1854–81, and Easley Day Book 1853–81. The investments on joint account proved profitable. Over a fifteen to twenty-year period, for example, Easley and Leigh divided profits of $7,822.34 or 262 per cent on invested capital, Easley and Owen divided profits of $22,419.23 or 224 per cent, and Easley and Rugland divided profits of $7,234.60 or 362 per cent.

TABLE 7.2

TIME-ENTRY AND PERSONAL-ENTRY ACRES AS A PERCENTAGE OF TOTAL ACRES
BY LAND DISTRICTS, 1852–58

Land district	Total acres	Time-entry acres	Per cent	Personal-entry acres	Per cent
Council Bluffs......	137,338	107,060	78.0	30,278	22.0
Decorah (Osage)....	640	......	....	640	100.0
Des Moines........	90,361	87,541	96.9	2,820	3.1
Dubuque (Marion)..	4,800	4,800	100.0	....	....
Fort Dodge........	6,074	2,240	36.9	3,834	63.1
Iowa City........	40,016	35,736	89.3	4,280	10.7
Sioux City........	49,279	43,585	88.4	5,694	11.6
Totals........	328,508	280,962		47,546	
Weighted averages.....			85.5		14.5

mainly with the largest and most reputable realtors and bankers, building strong personal ties through their annual visits and frequent correspondence.[5] Letters were often exchanged weekly and the partners required monthly statements of account. These they subjected to the closest scrutiny, often pointing out errors as small as a few pennies.

Under their combined energies, the business expanded rapidly. But warrants and scrip always seemed to be in short supply despite Willingham's best efforts. In order to meet the increasing western demand, Easley established permanent connections with prominent warrant brokers in New York, Washington, Philadelphia, and Richmond. The result was a smooth-functioning operation. Easley maintained a standing account with his brokers; when any western agent needed more land office paper on short notice, one of the brokers was ordered to buy at the prevailing market price for a commission of one-half per cent per acre and ship it directly to the man in need.

Once in the western agents' hands, over 85 per cent of the land paper (see Table 7.2) quickly passed into the hands of individuals who wished to take advantage of the 12-month credit advance—the so-called "time-entry" system. Easley in such cases entered the tract designated by the buyer but took title in his own or one of his partners' names, bonding himself to transfer title when the purchaser fulfilled the terms of the contract. Under the standard contract (see Figure 7.2) the buyer paid the

---

[5] The firm's major western agents were Ebenezer Cook and George B. Sargent of Davenport, the pioneer real estate firm in Iowa; Hugh D. Downey who headed the Iowa City branch of Cook & Sargent; William J. Barney of Cook, Sargent & Barney, Dubuque; Hoyt Sherman of Casady & Sherman, Des Moines, George Greene of Greene & Weare, Cedar Rapids; Jefferson P. Casady of Johnson & Casady, Council Bluffs; and George Weare of Weare & Allison, Sioux City. All of these men carved prominent niches for themselves in Iowa history. (See Chapter 5 for detailed information on Iowa land agents.)

Fig. 7.2. "Time-entry" instrument of Easley & Willingham.

BOND.

Printed for Messrs. CASADY, MYERS & MOORE, General Land Agents, Sioux City, Iowa.

I, M. Easley & Willingham of the County of Halifax and State of Virginia agree to sell and convey, by deed of Special Warranty, unto Paul Morton & Co. of Benner County, State of Iowa, the East Half of the North West 1/4 and the South West 1/4 of the North West 1/4 and the South East 1/4 of Section No Nine (9) all in Township No Ninety-five (95) North of Range No Thirty-five (35) West of the 5th P.M. containing 280 Acres more or less according to the Government survey

On Condition of said Paul Morton & Co. paying promptly—TIME being the Essence of the Contract—a certain promissory note, given May 25th 185 7, calling for Four Hundred & Ninety dollars, due May 25th 185 8. IF said note is not paid when due, I am privileged to enter upon and occupy said land, or to allow said Paul Morton & Co. to do so, at my option. It is understood by the parties hereto, that the said Paul Morton & Co. is to pay all taxes that may accrue on said land, and not to cut the timber, except for farming purposes; then this BOND to be carried into full effect; PROVIDED, no pre-emption right attach upon and vacate my present entry of said land.

SIOUX CITY, IOWA, May 25th 185 7

Easley & Willingham
By Casady & Coon
Agents

land office fee and taxes (if any) and agreed at the end of a year
to ante up $1.75 per acre—the customary price for the period
1852–57 when Easley contracted nearly all of his time entries.[6]
With warrant prices ranging between $1.00 and $1.20 per acre
during most of those years, Easley earned net returns on his funds
of 50 to 75 per cent, thus conforming to his initial objective of
investing "on time at good interest."[7]

At least a portion of Easley's time entries were for speculators and not settlers. Time entries required no cash outlay except
for the nominal land office fee on warrant entries, and the loans
were for one or two years—a relatively long time in a rapidly de-
veloping region. Speculators were therefore quick to realize that
with this form of almost riskless credit they could gain control
over large acreages and have time to sell it at a profit before the
loan fell due. This was a method of speculation earlier advocated
by such a prominent westerner as Missouri Senator Thomas Hart
Benton and later perfected by margin traders on the security ex-
changes.[8] Easley himself had no objection "to your selling to
[other] Speculators," he assured one agent, provided "you know
the locations to be good."[9] Margin buyers on the scene were obviously convinced that they could pay 40 per cent markup on the

---

[6] Most loans were for one year only although Easley had no objection to
two-year loans "if well secured & at good prices," (Easley & Willingham to
James B. Berryhill, June 14, 1853). Since Iowa law in the 1850's placed the
interest ceiling at 10 per cent—far below the market value of capital—Easley
did not include interest charges in his time-entry contracts but rather stated
an inflated sale price. Despite this precaution and the general disregard of
usury laws among westerners, Easley was threatened with a lawsuit at least
once for violating the usury law (J. P. Casady to Easley, Jan, 21, 1860).

[7] For monthly warrant prices in the 1850's, see Table 5.1. The firm's
earliest accounts illustrate the profitable nature of the business. Between
Aug. 20, 1852, and Jan. 12, 1853, Easley located 2,640 acres on time through
Greene & Weare of Cedar Rapids. The warrants cost him $2,273.67 (including
brokers' fees) and the net proceeds (less taxes and sale commissions), all paid
by Nov., 1855, were $4,115.06—leaving $1,841.39 as "profits," as Easley
called it. This was a return of over 80 per cent on his initial investment
within two years. Through Cook & Sargent of Davenport, the Virginian entered 840 acres on May 20, 1853, with warrants costing $750. In less than two
years, he had net returns in hand totaling $1,170.80, an increase of $420.80 or
56 per cent on his initial investment. First returns from central Iowa were
even more spectacular. On 58 warrants totaling 3,640 acres located on time
in the Iowa City district, Easley realized a net profit of 75 per cent within a
little over a year. Such returns were not unusual and continued until the depression of 1857. In 1856, for example, Easley located 5,140 acres on time in
the Des Moines district and within a little over a year earned a net return on
his investment of 58.5 per cent. (From data in the Easley Day Book 1853–81,
and Easley Ledger 1853–57.)

[8] See Malcolm J. Rohrbough, "The General Land Office, 1812–1826;
An Administrative Study" (Ph.D. dissertation, University of Wisconsin, 1963),
134.

[9] James S. Easley to Casady, Moore & Clark, Feb. 11, 1856. Easley's comments were in response to the request (Jan. 4, 1856) of this Sioux City real
estate firm to "locate time wts [warrants] for *Speculators* where we *know* the
selections to be good." See also Easley to S. Salisbury, Mar. 4, 1858.

raw land within a year and still make money.[10] Easley's own
agents also speculated in lands for themselves with his warrants
and some Iowa land agencies specifically appealed to speculators
to buy land under the time-entry system.[11] Apparently the technique was a popular and profitable one as long as the land market
was booming.

In addition to the time-entry business, but on a lesser scale,
Easley from time to time encouraged his agents to lay warrants
on choice tracts "for future speculation" on his own account,
provided of course that they met with an "extra good chance for
location," i.e., one that would appreciate in value at a *"much
better"* rate than the 50 to 75 per cent return customarily obtained on credit sales.[12] Given this seemingly prohibitive restriction,
it is surprising that the Halifax merchant entered any raw land
for himself and his associates. As Table 7.2 indicated, however,
he did locate in Iowa in the 1850's over 47,000 acres on his own
account.

Easley chose his speculation properties carefully. Proximity
to burgeoning towns and proposed railroad routes, he learned
from his initial investments near Iowa City and Cedar Rapids,
proved to be the most lucrative locations. In 1853, therefore,
when the Council Bluffs Land Office first opened, he was careful
to have an agent on hand with plenty of warrants to make judicious selections as near to that promising city as possible. The
same instructions went out when land offices opened later at Fort
Dodge, Decorah, Osage, and Sioux City.[13] In areas such as western Iowa where the natural timber supply was sometimes deficient, Easley occasionally advised his agents to obtain timbered
tracts if possible. Swamp- or wetlands there also proved to be a
strong attraction because of the likelihood that they skirted rivers
and streams and contained wood.[14]

---

[10] Hoyt Sherman, one of central Iowa's leading pioneer land agents, noted
that in the 1850's both settlers and speculators profitably entered land on
time at *"forty per cent. interest"* ("Early Banking in Iowa," *Annals of Iowa,
3rd Ser.,* V [Apr., 1901], 2).

[11] Easley's Sioux City agency entered on its own account several thousand
acres on time with his warrants (Easley to Casady, Moore & Clark, Oct. 7, 1856).
Another agency requested 25,000 acres of warrants, offering $3.00 per acre on
three years' time (Easley to J. N. Frazier, Sept. 11, 14, 1857). An advertisement
of Bruce & Son, Fort Dodge, in the Iowa City *Republican* (Mar. 10, 1858) read
in part: "We also pay particular attention to the loaning of land warrants to
non-residents."

[12] Easley & Willingham to Casady & Sherman, June 15, 1853; Easley to
same, Nov. 9, 1853.

[13] Easley to Hoyt Sherman, Sept. 20 and Aug. 1, 1855; to Johnson, Casady
& Test, Sept. 24, 1855; to Barney, Davis & Co., Nov. 5, 1855; to Greene &
Weare, Jan. 7, 1857. Easley & Willingham to Casady, Myers & Moore, Dec. 18,
1855.

[14] Easley's comments on timber are in letters to John Fitzgerald, June 26,
1855; to Ellwood B. James, May 16, 1855; to George Weare, Jan. 3, 1860; and

Selling his land holdings at attractive prices absorbed as much if not more of Easley's attention than selecting choice tracts. Initially in his pricing decisions, he relied on the experience gained in earlier ventures in western Illinois—an area roughly comparable to eastern Iowa.[15] But the Halifax merchant quickly supplemented this with a firsthand knowledge of frontier Iowa real estate, obtained in his annual western excursions across the state. In general, he never tried to hurry sales. Rather, as the oft-recurring phrase in his correspondence—"for future speculation"—indicates, he fully expected to carry his land until buyers met what he considered to be a "fair price." He had the capital resources to wait for values to increase and experience had shown that, in the long run, appreciation was inevitable. "Your fine soil and good crops must induce imigration [sic] to your country and consequently a demand for lands," he frequently opined.[16] In his pricing policy, the basic rule of thumb was that raw land was worth from $2.50 to $3.00 per acre at entry, $3.00 to $5.00 within two and three years, and $10.00 within five to ten years.[17] His terms of sale were quite standard for the period: one-fourth cash down, the balance in one, two, and three years with 10 per cent interest per year from the day of sale.

---

to Bosler & Hedges, Jan. 4, 1860. For queries about swamplands see his letters to E. B. Stiles, Nov. 20, 1854, and to Johnson & Casady, Feb. 19, 1855. Although Easley may have preferred timbered areas, an analysis of land that he entered for future speculation in a sample of eleven counties of central Iowa showed that he bought far more prairie than anything else. Of the 4,360 acres located there, 3,510 acres or 80.5 per cent comprised prairie soils, 410 acres or 9.4 per cent were soils that developed under woodlands, while the remaining 440 acres or 10.1 per cent were alluvial soils and likely timbered. Thus, about 20 per cent of Easley's speculation lands possibly contained timber—almost exactly the same proportion of timbered lands found throughout the eleven counties, where the total percentages were 80.5 prairie, 6.1 woodland, 12.9 alluvial, and 0.5 swamp/overflow. No matter what Easley sought, therefore, what he got was only a random selection of lands. (I am indebted to Conrad H. Hammar of the University of Minnesota for the soil classifications from which these statistics are derived.)

[15] In 1852, Easley had entered 1,400 acres in western Illinois at the Congress price and within two years had sold all at an average price of over $8.50 per acre. The Virginian reasoned, therefore, that his eastern Iowa land, entered three years earlier, "must advance considerably in a year or so," and would soon fetch $10.00 per acre. See Easley to Wm. J. Barney, Aug. 3, 1855; to Cook, Sargent & Downey, July 31, Oct. 8, 1855.

[16] Easley & Willingham to J. L. Frazier, Oct. 4, 1860.

[17] Easley & Willingham to Head & Russell, Aug. 23, 1867; Easley to Richardson & Likens, Dec. 2 and 9, 1856. For evidence that Easley's pricing policy was not out of line see John M. Brainard, "Opening an Iowa County," *Annals of Iowa*, 3rd Ser., II (Jan., 1896), 261–62; George B. Sargent, *Lecture on the "West," Delivered by Special Request, at the Tremont Temple, Boston, Mass., February 24, 1858, by Hon. George B. Sargent, Mayor of Davenport, Iowa* (Davenport, 1858), 12.

Fig. 7.3. Warranty deed of James Easley and wife

WARRANTY DEED.

Know all Men by these Presents, That we,

JAMES S. EASLEY AND ELIZABETH S. EASLEY, HIS WIFE,

of HALIFAX COUNTY, State of Virginia, in consideration of the sum of *One hundred and ninety-eight* Dollars, in hand paid by *Dempsey B. Mendenhall* of *Jasper* County, State of Iowa, do hereby sell and convey unto the said *Dempsey B. Mendenhall* the following described premises situated in the County of *Jasper* to wit: *The South-West*

ELIZABETH S. EASLEY hereby relinquishes her right of dower in and to the above described premises.

In Witness Whereof, We have hereunto set our hands and seals this *27th* day of *March*, A. D. 185*6*.

EXECUTED IN PRESENCE OF

William Medley

R B Moon

James S Easley [SEAL]

Elizabeth S Easley [SEAL]

STATE OF VIRGINIA,
Halifax County. }

I do hereby Certify, That before me, GEORGE C. HOLT, Commissioner of Deeds, &c., for the State of Iowa, in and for said State, personally appeared the above named JAMES S. EASLEY AND ELIZABETH S. EASLEY, who are personally known to me to be the identical persons whose names are affixed to the above conveyance as grantors and acknowledged the execution of the same to be their **Voluntary Act and Deed for the purposes therein mentioned.**

Given under my hand this 27th March 1856

Geo C Holt
Commr

II

EASLEY and his partner met immediate success in their early western land ventures. Frontier demands for land credit in the form of bounty warrants far outran supply, and by the winter of 1853–54, the Virginians were buying land paper and entering land by the thousands of acres and constantly urging their brokers to secure more paper. "I have received so many orders from the north west for warrants," the Halifax merchant reported happily in early 1854 to one of his New York City suppliers, "that I now wish you to take all that offers at Market rates until you hear from me again."[18]

But the ideal conditions were short lived. Other eastern investors shared Easley's success in the West and similarly escalated their demands for land paper. Pending legislation in Congress meanwhile also greatly affected the land warrant market during 1854 and 1855. Nearly four years had elapsed since the national legislators issued the last sizeable batch of new warrants in 1850. Land paper by early 1854 was thus becoming scarce and high priced. Easley was paying as much as $190 for 160-acre warrants, only $10 less than the land office value. Adding cost factors like brokerage fees and postage, the buying price in New York nearly equaled the land office price.[19] Only Congress could remedy the situation by awarding another land bonus to veterans in time for this negotiable paper to reach the market before the annual spring land rush. When the lawmakers failed to act, Easley temporarily despaired of success.[20] But finally, in March of 1855, Congress passed the long-awaited military bounty warrant act and by midsummer the first new warrants trickled into the brokerage houses and the firm could plan to resume normal operations.

With the months of frustration and uncertainty behind them, the partners invested more funds than ever in their land business. The last great spurt was on—from the Fall of 1855 until May of 1856, when most of Iowa's land offices were suddenly closed pending Congressional action on a railroad land grant bill. When investment capital sometimes ran short in this frenzied period, Easley solicited from friends and sold some of his slaves to secure additional funds for land entry. Because of the unusually heavy demand, the anticipated drop in warrant prices also failed to materialize. Prices remained above $1.10 per acre or

---

[18] Easley to Greenway Bro. & Co., Jan. 14, 1854.

[19] Easley to Wm. H. Brown & Co., Aug. 24, 1854. The risk involved should also be considered. Warrants sometimes were rejected at the land offices because of technicalities involving faulty assignment. To correct the defects often required much time and expense (see Easley to Isaac Medley, Nov. 9, 1854).

[20] Easley to Greene & Weare, Jan. 28, 1854; to P. M. Henry, May 16, 1854.

Fig. 7.4. Military bounty land warrant assigned to James Easley

THE UNITED STATES OF AMERICA,

TO ALL TO WHOM THESE PRESENTS SHALL COME, GREETING:

Whereas, in pursuance of the ACT OF CONGRESS, approved September 28th, 1850, entitled "AN ACT GRANTING BOUNTY LAND TO CERTAIN OFFICERS AND SOLDIERS WHO HAVE BEEN ENGAGED IN THE MILITARY SERVICE OF THE UNITED STATES," Warrant No. 98,347, for 40 ———— acres, issued in favor of *Elijah B. Smith, Private in Captain Ingersoll Company, New York Militia, War 1812,*

has been returned to the **GENERAL LAND OFFICE,** with evidence that the same has been duly located upon the *South West quarter of the North East quarter of Section thirty two, in Township seventy nine, North of Range seventeen West in the District of Lands subject to sale at Fort des Moines, Iowa, containing forty acres,*

according to the OFFICIAL PLAT of the Survey of the said LAND returned to the General Land Office by the SURVEYOR GENERAL, *which has been assigned to James S. Bailey.*

Now know ye, That there is therefore GRANTED by the UNITED STATES unto the said *James S. Bailey*

the Tract of **LAND** above described; To HAVE AND TO HOLD the said Tract of LAND, with the appurtenances thereof, unto the said *James S. Bailey,* ———— heirs and assigns forever.

In testimony whereof, I, *Franklin Pierce,* ———— PRESIDENT OF THE UNITED STATES OF AMERICA, have caused these Letters to be made Patent, and the Seal of the General Land Office to be hereunto affixed.

Given under my hand at the CITY OF WASHINGTON, the *first* ———— day of *March,* ———— in the Year of OUR LORD one thousand eight hundred and *fifty five* and of the Independence of the United States the seventy–*ninth*

BY THE PRESIDENT:

Franklin Pierce

By *Nathaniel Hall*, Secretary.

N. Branch, Recorder of the General Land Office.

RECORD OF MISC. &c., &c., MILITARY GRANTS, VOL. 27, Page 239.

very close to old rates; Easley commented more than once about this unexpected development.[21] Leaving no stone unturned to secure what warrants did reach the market, however, Easley placed standing orders with at least thirteen different brokerage houses along the eastern seaboard—four in Richmond, one in Philadelphia, six in New York, and two in the District of Columbia. That his efforts were not in vain is indicated by the fact that he and his associates entered over 150,000 acres of Iowa land in 1855 and 1856 (See Table 7.1).

With the passage of the Railroad Land Grant Bill in May, 1856, the General Land Office ordered the closing of most of Iowa's land offices to all but preemptors so that the roads could complete their selections.[22] Until the offices reopened in 1857 and 1858 the land business was relatively slack, although speculators like the firm of Easley & Willingham continued to sell 160-acre warrants on credit to preemptors. In such cases, unlike the typical time-entry contract, the claimant entered the land in his *own* name with the warrant, giving the moneylender his note, payable in twelve months, along with a signed deed to the land. If the debtor defaulted, the lender recorded the deed. If he paid promptly, the deed was destroyed.[23]

Although seemingly sound, this form of investment frequently involved greater risk. In the standard time-entry sale, the moneylender took title in his own name. When preemptors were involved, however, the warrants had to be assigned to the preemptor and the lands entered in his name. If such entries were later cancelled by the United States government for one reason or another (as many were which happened to fall within the limits of the numerous railroad grants in western Iowa) and if the preemptor subsequently moved without leaving a forwarding address (as some did), the moneylender lost both the warrant and the land entered with it unless he could find the preemptor and have the warrant reassigned back to him or get the duplicate certificate of entry.[24]

---

[21] Easley to H. W. Fry & Sons, June 11, 1855; to Hoyt Sherman, June 13, 1855. Easley & Willingham to Johnson, Casady & Test, July 2, 1855. The bottom finally did drop out of the market around mid-November when, with the Pension Office issuing 500–600 warrants daily, the market finally became flooded. See circular of J. H. Clarke & Co., Washington, D.C., Nov. 24, 1855, in the James S. Easley Papers.

[22] U.S. *Statutes at Large*, XI, 9: Iowa *House Journal*, 1856 (Extra Sess.), 3, 11. See also Roscoe F. Lokken, *Iowa Public Land Disposal* (Iowa City, 1942), 118, 126, 238–40.

[23] Easley to Cyrus Aldrich, Mar. 3, 1857; to Jas. S. Wilson, July 23, 1868.

[24] The General Land Office would issue duplicate warrants only if the duplicate certificate of entry was surrendered. If the lender could not locate the preemptor and obtain the needed certificate, he could either enter land in his own name for $2.50 per acre, thus in effect paying $3.75 for it, or he could petition the government to return the warrant. Easley eventually fol-

Besides extending credit to preemptors during the slack years, Easley and Willingham also loaned approximately $30,000 of their surplus cash funds in Des Moines and Council Bluffs on a short-term basis at standard frontier rates of 3 to 5 per cent per month secured by real estate mortgages. Since money in Iowa was in short supply, investors (including many local land speculators) eagerly seized the proffered cash. Altogether in the period 1856–59, the Virginians contracted 323 cash loans totaling in the aggregate over $195,000. Despite collecting over $20,000 in interest payments while earning an average net return on their funds of 32.7 per cent per year, the partners were dissatisfied.[25] Regular time-entry loans, after all, returned upwards of 50 per cent per annum. Moreover, nearly one-fifth of their loan capital eventually became tied up in land as borrowers defaulted, forcing the lenders, much to their chagrin, to foreclose and take over the landed security.

Because of their generally unsatisfactory experience with cash loans, the partners happily greeted President James Buchanan's announcement of May 4, 1857, reopening the land offices in northern Iowa at Osage, Fort Dodge, and Sioux City and proclaiming many new townships for sale as well. Easley and Willingham immediately called in some of their cash loans and began accumulating funds to invest at the public auctions. They hoped to secure fifteen to twenty thousand acres "to be held a few years"; but because of fierce competition were only able to enter a mere 6,383 acres.[26] Having already turned to Kansas, they also investigated the possibilities of buying public land in Florida, Texas, and Minnesota; but they located in Missouri and Wisconsin in-

---

lowed both courses successfully. Seven years elapsed, however, before the General Land Office issued any duplicate warrants to him. See Easley to Casady & Clark, Dec. 16, 1856; to George Weare, July 1 and Aug. 24, 1859. Easley & Willingham to Weare & Allison, Sept. 10, 1866; to S. V. Niles, Sept. 28, 1866. For a preemption case that Easley carried to the U.S. Supreme Court and lost, see *Easley v. Kellom et al.* in John W. Wallace (Reporter), *Cases Argued and Adjudged in the Supreme Court of the United States, December Term, 1871* (New York, 1906), 279–82.

[25] As recorded on the firm's books, the loans totaled $212,378.13 but cash discounts reduced the effective amount loaned to $195,056.52. The rate of return—calculated on the 239 loans (74 per cent) repaid prior to the Civil War—was determined by dividing the weighted average daily cash balance ($12,575.65) by the total interest earned ($20,060.71). The result (159.5 per cent) was then divided by the total number of years of the investment (4.88 years) to obtain the average annual return. On 21 loans (6.5 per cent), which remained outstanding until the immediate postwar years, the partners earned approximately 20 per cent per year. Sixty-three loans (19.5 per cent were defaulted in whole or in part and foreclosed. (Figures from accounts in the Easley Ledger 1853–57, Easley Journal 1854–81, and Easley Day Book 1853–81. Agent commissions were 5 per cent of the amount loaned, prorated if less than a year.)

[26] Easley to Hoyt Sherman & Co., Jan. 7 and 15, 1857; to Greene & Weare, Jan. 7, 1857.

stead. Meanwhile, all of the land offices in central and southern Iowa remained closed during 1857, so the Virginians continued to bide their time by loaning available funds there at "Iowa interest."[27]

The temporary closing of the land offices during the peak of the Iowa land boom was only the first of several major setbacks for Easley & Willingham. In September of 1857 they received the disheartening news of the financial distress on Wall Street, following the collapse of the highly respected Ohio Life Insurance Trust Company on August 29. Soon the entire country and particularly the West was in the throes of a serious depression which lasted until the Civil War. Remittances from the West grew increasingly infrequent in these years and Easley and his fellow investors faced a growing forfeiture rate. On the time sales of 1857, contracted immediately prior to the crash, the rate of forfeiture by 1858 surpassed 60 per cent and threatened to go even higher. Easley urged his agents to use every "gentle means" possible to collect the debts.

Until 1856, as Table 7.3 shows, the forfeiture rate on Easley & Willingham's time entries had actually remained very nominal. Then it began a steady ascent from 12.8 per cent on the entries of 1855 to 41.8 per cent on those of 1856, 60.5 per cent on those of 1857, and finally 66.0 per cent on the entries of 1858. These yearly rates are somewhat deceptive, however, and they hide the fact that the firm's western creditors were a fairly reliable group. Between 1853 and 1857, when the Virginians contracted nearly three-fourths of their total time entries, less than 7 per cent were forfeited. Fully one-half of the total acres that were defaulted, moreover, lay in the sparsely populated Sioux City and Fort Dodge land districts (Table 7.4). And here, judging at least from the agricultural census returns of 1860 which reported a mere 30,782 acres in farms (both improved and unimproved) in the entire twelve-county Sioux City Land District, it appears that speculative buyers with little money or time invested were the chief "sufferers," not bona fide squatters.[28] In any case, the Vir-

---

[27] Easley to J. A. Black, Feb. 11, 1857; to Cyrus Aldrich, Mar. 3, 1857. Easley & Willingham to Wm. T. Smithson, Jan. 28, 1857; to Casady & Clark, Aug. 11, 1857.

[28] See U.S. Bureau of the Census, Eighth Census of the United States, *Agriculture* (Washington, 1864), II, 46, 50. Easley's detailed correspondence concerning the forfeited tracts, it might be noted, at no time mentions homesteads or improvements of any kind. If buyers agreed to pay interest in advance, Easley would also have willingly extended the loans; by this time he preferred the money to the land. In any case he did not declare entries forfeited until at least three years had elapsed without any payments. And even then he frequently offered debtors a last chance. After declaring a contract forfeited, moreover, Easley allowed the former owner the right to repurchase at any time upon paying the principal and accumulated interest, provided no one else had bought the forfeited tract.

TABLE 7.3

FORFEITED TIME-ENTRY ACRES AS A PERCENTAGE OF TOTAL TIME-ENTRY ACRES
BY YEAR ENTERED, 1852–58

Year entered	Total time-entry acres	Forfeited time-entry acres	Per cent forfeited
1852....................	800	0	0.0
1853....................	35,810	720	2.0
1854....................	77,690	2,320	3.0
1855....................	88,424	11,288	12.8
1856....................	49,091	20,543	41.8
1857....................	18,705	11,320	60.5
1858....................	10,442	6,880	66.0
Totals...............	280,962	53,071	
Weighted average.......			18.9

ginia partners decided in late 1858 to contract no more time
entries until business conditions improved substantially, for the
growing forfeitures on which tax levies had to be met were es-
calating their taxes far beyond all expectations.

The third and most devastating blow to the western land
business of Easley & Willingham was the Civil War. Until the
very outbreak of hostilities, the partners hoped that open conflict might be avoided. As late as April 20, 1861, eight days after
the shelling of Fort Sumter and three days after Virginia's secession, they yet wished to make their annual spring visit to the
West. Writing to one of his agents, Easley asked: "Do you
think a Virginian who had been engaged in Western land speculations could pass through your country with safety and without
annoyance."[29] The letter was never answered.

III

DURING the war years Easley was forced to bide his time while
western agents hopefully attended to his affairs as they thought
best.[30] Surprisingly, he managed to smuggle a few letters through
the battle lines and even to collect drafts drawn on funds that
had accumulated in the hands of his agents.[31] Ironically, in April,
1863, one of the drafts (for $1,000) was honored by Hoyt Sherman
of Des Moines, brother of General William T. Sherman—who at

[29] Easley to S. Noble, Apr. 20, 1861.
[30] One agent explained immediately after the War that the best way to
handle Easley's property had been to ignore it entirely. With confiscation
"the order of the day" and public anger overflowing against " 'd———d rebels',
we were convinced that 'mum' was the word, & least said on the subject the
better for your interest, for the least agitation of the matter would cause you
to lose all" (Weare & Allison to Easley & Willingham, July 27, 1865).
[31] Easley to P. M. Henry & Co., Apr. 23, 1863.

Fig. 7.5. Judge Jefferson P. Casady, James Easley's Council Bluffs land agent.

that very moment was leading troops against the Confederates at Vicksburg. Of necessity, however, Easley was unable to give the required attention to his land affairs; taxes went unpaid for five years and tens of thousands of acres were sold at tax sales. County treasurers generally began issuing tax deeds in 1864 and 1865 as the three-year period allowed for redemptions expired. Thus, although legal proceedings to confiscate his land were begun only in Wisconsin, the tax sales threatened to be equally devastating.[32]

When the war ended, the company's affairs were in desperate

[32] In 1866 Easley journeyed to Wisconsin and secured the release of the suit (Willingham to Henry L. Brooke, Jan. 21, 1868). Easley may have saved some of his Iowa lands from tax sale by conveying them for the war's duration to his friend Judge Jefferson P. Casady of Council Bluffs, who paid the taxes. This at least is reported by Easley's grandson, James Easley Edmunds, Sr., in a letter to James E. Edmunds, 3rd, Jan. 31, 1940 (copy in possession of the author).

straits. Loans long overdue had to be collected, thousands of dollars in back taxes had to be paid, lands had to be redeemed from tax sales, and most difficult of all, compromises had to be reached with hundreds of tax-title holders.[33] Left destitute of funds by the war, the partners' only recourse was to turn their land assets into liquid capital, to sacrifice a part of their lands to redeem the rest. Barely a month after Appomattox the anxious Virginians penned gracious letters to all of their western agents and made plans for an immediate resumption of their annual trips. "We are truly happy to be able again to resume our former pleasant correspondence," the letters read, "and hope we may in future be able to make our usual annual pleasant visits to your beautiful country."[34] June and July were spent in the West and by August the first remittances from land sales began to trickle back to Halifax.[35]

While in the West Easley and his partner contacted many new agents, believing it best to deal with one in each county who would be thoroughly familiar with the local land market. To hasten sales, blank deeds were left with each man along with an authorization or power of attorney to sell and issue deeds immediately. Giving agents "positive" rather than "discretionary" powers was a complete reversal of prewar policy, but both Easley and Willingham realized that their current financial situation demanded it.[36] In the counties where they had no agents, the partners requested county treasurers or recorders to take charge of their lands since these officials usually doubled as land agents. All were allowed a 5 per cent commission and instructed to sell land at any price they felt was fair, all back taxes to be paid by the purchaser.[37]

Negotiating with tax-sale buyers who had received treasurers' deeds was another of the pressing problems. Easley and his

---

[33] Many of the tax buyers of Easley & Willingham's land during the War were northerners who had speculated largely in Congress land in Iowa in the 1850's, like Pitte Cook of Ohio, Austin Corbin of New York, John A. Roebling of Trenton, N.J., and Iowans LeGrand Byington, William J. Barney, and John W. Denison. Interestingly, several of Easley's own agents bought his land at tax sale. Barney, for instance, purchased 1,080 acres in northcentral Iowa. (See Easley to B. E. Morton, Oct. 3, 1865; to W. J. Barney, Aug. 23, 1867, July 21, 1868; to J. P. & J. N. Casady, Jan. 29, 1872. Easley & Willingham to Thos. Cox, Oct. 5, 1867; and "List of Easley and Willingham's Lands Sold by Weare and Allison, 1866." For correspondence dealing with Roebling's tax buying see John A. Roebling Papers, Rutgers University Library, New Brunswick, N.J.

[34] Easley & Willingham to Hoyt Sherman, May 12, 1865.

[35] Easley to A. T. Stewart & Co., Aug. 23, 1865; Easley & Willingham to J. P. Casady, Aug. 23, 1865; W. W. Willingham to Hoyt Sherman, Aug. 23, 1865.

[36] Weare & Allison declared it was an "imperitive [sic] necessity" that they have a power of attorney to be able to make warranty deeds without consulting the Virginians (see their letter to Easley & Willingham, July 27, 1865).

[37] Easley & Willingham to Treas. & Recorder, Boone Co., Aug. 30, 1865.

TABLE 7.4

FORFEITED TIME-ENTRY ACRES AS A PERCENTAGE OF TOTAL TIME-ENTRY ACRES
BY LAND DISTRICTS, 1852–58

Land districts	Total time-entry acres	Forfeited time-entry acres	Per cent forfeited
Council Bluffs..............	107,060	15,281	14.3
Des Moines.................	87,541	11,110	12.7
Dubuque (Marion).........	4,800	360	0.8
Fort Dodge.................	2,240	2,000	89.3
Iowa City.................	35,736	360	0.1
Sioux City.................	43,585	23,960	55.0
Totals................	280,962	53,071	
Weighted average........			18.9

partner preferred to compromise rather than test the tax title by
a suit in the United States district courts. Pleading that it had
been "impossible from the condition of the country" to pay their
taxes, they offered either to pay the amount of accrued taxes,
penalty, and interest to the tax-title holder in exchange for his
quitclaim deed, or else to sell him their original patent title for
half the present market value of the land.[38] With very few
exceptions the parties reached amicable settlements out of court—
but usually not without extensive correspondence—since tax titles
were not held in high esteem at the time.[39]

Through his own dismal experiences with tax titles, Easley
learned that rewards for the tax-title investor were high. As soon
as he had spare funds available in mid-1867, he decided that,
rather than enter the land mortgage field, he would bid at Iowa
tax sales "merely as an investment" for the 30 per cent penalty
and interest of 10 per cent per annum. "As we have lost so much
by letting ours be sold [for taxes] we would like to get some of
it back in this way," Easley reasoned.[40] Between 1867 and 1875,
he invested more than $37,000 at tax sales in nine counties of
western Iowa, buying 160,062 acres plus 438 town lots in Sioux
City and Council Bluffs.[41] He used county orders whenever possible and instructed his agents to buy good land that would likely

[38] Easley to B. E. Morton, Nov. 2, 1865.
[39] "From the information we get from the most of our correspondents in
Iowa," Easley wrote to one agent, "we find that tax titles are not held in very
high estimate" (Easley & Willingham to Alex. Ramsey, Feb. 23, 1867). See
also C. N. Overbaugh to Easley, Aug. 5, 1868.
[40] Easley & Willingham to Roseberry & Morehouse, July 31, 1867; to Durfee & White, Aug. 16, 1867. The penalty was reduced to 20 per cent in 1873.
Interest was charged against both tax and penalty (Iowa, *Revised Code*, 1860,
122–23; *ibid.*, 1873, 152). These tax-sale investments of James Easley are being
explored more fully as part of a larger study presently underway on the general subject of tax buying in Iowa.
[41] Figures from data in the Easley Day Book 1869–80, and Easley Journal
1859–75 (Land Book).

be redeemed.[42] Despite this precaution, however, some tracts inevitably were never reclaimed, and Easley's land inventory increased accordingly. At his death in 1879 he still held tax title to 9,159 acres of rural Iowa real estate, and 73 town lots.[43] In addition to tax buying, Easley increased his western land inventory in the 1870's by more than 10,000 acres when he purchased the holdings of his partner, Willingham, several associates, and his late brother Daniel B. Easley, who had also speculated widely in Iowa although independently of James.[44]

Once the tax problem was in hand, Easley concentrated on unloading his huge land inventory of 154,008 acres lying mainly in Iowa and Missouri.[45] Basically he followed the conservative policy of the ante bellum years in not pressing sales prematurely before the land had reached its "full value." "We feel confident," he frequently wrote, "that lands must advance in Iowa much more than interest and therefore had rather hold than take a low price."[46] Easley obviously believed Iowa land would annually advance in price by at least 10 per cent—which was then the maximum legal interest rate. Judging by the general prosperity returning to the state in the form of new railroads, increased immigration, new homes and farms, and more land under cultivation, such optimism was undoubtedly warranted. Once a brisk market developed in a given locale, Easley offered his land at a few dollars per acre above the prevailing market. He did not expect to sell immediately, but rather was prepared to wait for the right buyer to accept his price. As long as land continued to sell, he steadily raised his asking price. In this way he pushed the selling price on his raw land up to $6.25 to $7.50 per acre by 1870, and from $10.00 to $12.00 by the end of that decade.

At no time did Easley consider improving his raw land or

---

[42] Standard commissions were 5 per cent of the amount invested and 5 per cent for buying county orders or warrants to be used to pay the county part of the taxes. A few agents charged no fees for paying taxes, making their commission instead on the discounted county orders which they charged at par to Easley (Willingham to Durfee & McKillof, Nov. 17, 1868; Easley & Willingham to Durfee, McKillof & Dopf, Dec. 17, 1869).

[43] The 1879 totals are given in "Inventory and appraisement of the real and personal estate of James S. Easley decd.," Probate Records, Book 32, 140, Circuit Court, Halifax County, Va. (hereafter cited as Halifax Co. Probate Records).

[44] Easley to Henn, Williams & Co., Dec. 1, 1856; to Wm. T. Owen, Nov. 29, 1870; to Brockway & Elder, Aug. 5, 1873, July 17, 1874; to C. S. Carrington, Oct. 15 and Nov. 2, 1874; to W. W. Henry, July 29, 1874. James S. Easley, Jr., gradually took over the bookkeeping and correspondence from Willingham. Easley himself commented: "I am getting old and would like to close up all these partnership matters" (Easley to Polk & Hubbell, Feb. 15, 1875).

[45] The acreage, by state, compiled from data in Easley's tract book, "List of Western Lands, 1865," is as follows: Iowa, 92,531; Missouri, 37,934; Wisconsin, 17,090; Kansas, 3,413; Nebraska, 2,720; Illinois, 320.

[46] Easley & Willingham to H. C. Mathorn, Aug. 12, 1868; to D. Carr Early, Nov. 10, 1869.

Fig. 7.6. James Easley's Virginia home, "Magnolia Hill," constructed in 1855. (Courtesy of Mrs. Richard Coles Edmunds, Sr.)

renting it to farmers for a share of the crops. In fact, he insisted that his land remain unencumbered with any rental agreements which he felt might impede sales. For example, when a West Branch farmer in 1875 offered to fence a long-vacant tract in exchange for its use as a pasture, Easley replied that he did "not wish to do anything which might in any way interfere with the sale of the land *at anytime.*" Later in the year, however, he did allow two farmers in western Iowa to harvest the grass on his vacant lands adjoining theirs in exchange for the taxes, provided that the agreement in no way compromised his right to sell the land.[47]

The Halifax merchant was successful in gradually selling his lands in the postwar period. This is evident from a comparison of his holdings in 1865 with the inventory of his estate filed in pro-

[47] Easley to B. F. Yelter, Mar. 20, 1875; to Jeff Williams, July 16, 1875; to G. Mead, Aug. 21, 1875; Samuel W. Holt to Brockway & Elder, Apr. 20, 1881. Further proof that Easley dealt only in unimproved land is the designation "wild lands" (see Table 7.7) used by the appraisers of his estate when describing his western lands. The only real exception to Easley's nonleasing policy was his decision in the late 1860's to lease to several local miners a few tracts of lead lands in Christian and Ozark counties, Missouri (Easley to Thomas J. Gideon, Oct. 14, 1867, July 24 and Aug. 25, 1873; to H. B. Chandler, Apr. 2, 1875; to W. A. Love, Apr. 19, 1875). Although Easley's refusal to rent agricultural land may have been atypical, little evidence to the contrary exists regarding other nonresident investors in Iowa; nor did Iowa realtors in their frequent advertisements in the local press offer to manage rental property for nonresidents. But see Gates, "Homestead Law in Iowa," 68.

bate court in March, 1880. On taking stock, his executors found
that only 56,305 acres remained of the 154,008 acres listed in the
tract book in 1865.[48] His Iowa holdings had been reduced by almost two-thirds, Kansas and Missouri acreage had dwindled by
one-half, while Illinois, Nebraska, and Wisconsin lands were virtually all liquidated. Except for the brief period in 1865 and 1866
when the war had nearly bankrupted him, Easley did not press
for the premature sale of his lands. Near the close of his life he
specifically directed in his will that the executors of his estate
should "not be hurried in making sales." Otherwise his children
might not reap "the full benefit of my lands." Even on his death-
bed, Easley reiterated his conviction about land sales when he
instructed his wife: "Hold on to my western lands. They will be
worth something."[49]

IV

THE TEST of an investment ultimately lies in the income which it
brings and in its long-run value. By this measure, Easley was
also successful. Table 7.5 contains a summary of the annual
cash receipts and disbursements of Easley & Willingham and their
associates over the 27 years that Easley managed the business. For
purposes of presentation and explanation, the data has been
recast into four categories: (1) cash receipts from the sale of land
and land warrants; (2) cash paid for land and land warrants; (3)
miscellaneous expenditures (including commissions and fees, cost
of exchange and drafts, interest, taxes, and travel); and (4) annual
net cash income (total of cash receipts less disbursements).

The annual cash income of the joint venture varied widely.
In the first two years the firm had a net cash loss due to the
necessary time lag between the initial investments and the first
returns from the Northwest. But by 1855 and 1856, cash receipts
far outstripped disbursements and, except for the 1857 panic and
the Civil War, the firm had a cash income through 1870 ranging between $10,000 and $70,000 per year, an average earning

---

[48] See n. 45 for the 1865 totals. The 1880 figures, compiled from inventory data in the Halifax Co. Probate Records, Book 32, 139–40, are as follows:
Iowa, 34,367 (excluding 9,159 acres of tax-title land); Missouri, 19,698; Kansas,
1,600; Wisconsin, 640.

[49] "Last Will and Testament of James S. Easley," Art. V, Halifax Co. Probate Records, Book 32, 122; Mrs. Richard Coles Edmunds, Sr., to the author,
Apr. 6, 1967. Other large Iowa investors included similar stipulations in their
wills. John Baptiste Valle of St. Genevieve County, Mo., for example, declared: "In regard to my real estate for seeing that the same will probably be
increasing in value, my desire is that the same may remain unsold for the
term of twelve years" (copy filed with the clerk of the district court of Decatur County, Leon).

TABLE 7.5

Summary of Cash Receipts and Disbursements of Easley & Willingham and Associates, 1853–79 *

Year	Cash Receipts (sale of land and land warrants)	Cash Disbursements (for land and land warrants)	(for misc. expenses)	Net cash income [deficit]	Income as a per cent of cash receipts
1853	$ 572.91	$ 32,106.55	$ 526.78	$[32,060.42]	[5,596.1]
1854	37,408.80	37,884.96	2,408.26	[2,884.42]	[7.7]
1855	110,710.83	61,257.58	3,287.05	46,166.20	41.7
1856	157,835.51	84,363.69	3,733.69	69,738.13	44.2
1857	86,994.83	83,475.87	2,980.49	538.47	.5
1858	52,144.77	27,917.83	1,993.21	22,233.73	42.6
1859	23,172.55	4,144.58	3,871.66	15,156.31	65.4
1860–61	10,290.74	220.00	5,001.04	5,059.70	49.3
Civil War	.....	.....	.....	.....	.....
1865	27,231.59	.....	1,268.77	25,962.82	95.3
1866	21,881.53	100.00	8,836.44	12,945.09	59.2
1867	18,597.58	.....	8,329.25	10,268.33	55.2
1868	44,816.03	.....	9,747.86	35,068.17	78.2
1869	45,183.55	.....	2,910.83	42,272.72	93.6
1870	27,598.90	.....	2,023.88	25,575.02	92.7
1871	12,377.82	.....	5,120.14	7,257.68	58.6
1872	5,736.16	600.00	3,085.21	2,050.95	35.8
1873	5,542.47	11,323.40	2,135.02	[7,915.95]	[142.8]
1874	3,950.22	.....	3,356.04	594.18	15.0
1875	7,407.06	.....	5,299.24	2,107.82	28.4
1876	3,474.37	32,889.40	3,229.08	[32,644.11]	[939.6]
1877	3,337.20	.....	502.94	2,834.26	84.9
1878	1,758.23	.....	322.25	1,435.98	81.7
1879	2,791.51	.....	325.01	2,466.50	88.4
Totals	$710,815.16	$376,283.86	$80,294.14	$254,237.16	
Weighted average					35.8

*Tables 7.5 and 7.6 were compiled from data in the Easley Ledger 1853–57, and the Easley Journal 1854–81. The author is indebted to accountant James Burke, and professors Louis Baigioni and Richard W. Metcalf, of the University of Iowa, for advice in compiling and presenting the data in these tables.

for the period of 41.5 per cent on cash receipts. Thereafter, both sales and cash income dwindled because of a relatively inactive land market coupled with Easley's determined policy not to sell any tract unless it brought "full value."[50] In 1873 and 1876 the company failed to show a profit on a cash basis, because in those years Easley invested $45,000 to absorb the land inventory of his partner, Willingham, who gradually phased himself out of the business.

At Easley's death in 1879, the net cash income of the firm totaled over $254,000, or 35.8 per cent of all cash receipts. When total net income is considered as a percentage of total costs over the same period, the firm realized a rate of return of 55.7 per cent ($254,234.16 ÷ $456,578.00). To total net income, however, should be added the realizable value of the inventory in 1879: $15,000 due on notes of Easley's western land buyers (secured by real estate mortgages) and the 1879 market value of his 56,000 acres of western lands (exclusive of tax-title lands) conservatively estimated at $5.00 per acre or $280,000.[51] If these two items—easily convertible into cash—are added to the cash receipts of the firm, its total net cash income topped one-half million dollars, a net return on cash expended of more than 120 per cent.

By its nature, western land investments required large capital outlays in the early years but considerably less thereafter. The annual income under this type of operation is thus distorted when figured only on a cash basis. Therefore, the data in Table 7.5 has been recomputed in Table 7.6 using the accounting concept of accruals. By this method the total cost of the investment was allocated to each year's sales on a fixed ratio (0.37411 to 1), determined by dividing the total cash expended for land and land

---

[50] Easley's insistence on high prices definitely retarded the sale of his land. The executors of his estate, less demanding than he, were able in the first four years after his death to sell land worth $203,629.61, an amount equal to Easley's sales in the entire postwar period from 1865 to 1879 (compiled from the annual accounts of Easley's executors for the period, 1879–83, in Halifax Co. Probate Records, Books 32–33).

[51] The appraisers of Easley's estate (see *ibid.*, Book 32, 139–40) listed notes on hand totaling $14,195.77 with an additional undetermined number in the hands of western agents pending collection. The lands were listed with an appraised value of $136,244.08. This was based on a per acre valuation of $2.50 for Iowa and Kansas tracts and $1.50 and $1.25 for Missouri and Wisconsin lands, respectively. Iowa tax-title lands were listed at $1.50. That the current market value of at least the Iowa lands was two to three times as great as the appraised value is evident from an old office tract book of Cox and Kirkwood Realtors of Iowa City. The book lists all of Easley's Iowa land by county and quotes the fair market price in each for the years 1878–79. Prices ranged from $5.00 to $10.00 with the average being $6.53 per acre. (Willingham's 2,040 acres valued at $5.00 per acre are not included in the above figures.) See "Book No. 1, J. F. Richards, Office Tract Book for the Use of Cox and Kirkwood, Dealers in Real Estate," Special Collections Department, Library, University of Iowa, Iowa City.

warrants (Table 7.5, column 2) by the sum of the total cash
receipts (Table 7.5, column 1) plus notes receivable and the estimated value of the land inventory in 1879. For example, in 1856,
revenue from the sale of land and land warrants was $157,835.51.
To determine what part of the total amount paid for land and
land warrants should be allocated to that year's sales, the sum
was multiplied by the fixed percentage of 0.37411 to obtain the
cost of $59,047.84. By apportioning each year's cash disburse-
ments for land and land warrants in this way, of course, one is
left with a balance which is assignable to the inventory held at
Easley's death.

Using the accrual method of presentation (see Table 7.6) the
net income of the company by 1879 totaled an impressive
$365,000, a yearly average of $14,000. Net cash income as a
per cent of revenue—to borrow a familiar concept of modern-day
financial reports—was equally as sanguine. As column 5 shows,
the percentage varied widely but in general remained high, averaging 51.3 per cent over the span of time that Easley managed
the venture. When the total net income (column 4) is calculated
as a percentage of total cash expended over the same period (sum
of columns 2 and 3), the firm realized an annual rate of return
averaging 105.3 per cent, although in the booming 1850's annual
returns had soared above 150 per cent.[52] Earning such handsome
returns on a modest initial capital outlay of approximately
$50,000 was truly a remarkable achievement.

A final indication of the success of Easley's western land
ventures is the value of his estate, inventoried and appraised
shortly after his death. As Table 7.7 indicates, Easley's capital
worth in 1880, as judged by local court-appointed appraisers, was
$259,000. About two-thirds of the amount represented his western
land holdings and the remainder his notes, personal loans, and
securities. This was more than 15 times the sum of $17,000
reported to the local census marshal 30 years earlier, before he
began his western land business.[53] Easley's actual net worth,
however, was far greater than the appraisal figure given above.
His sizeable interests in a half dozen partnerships are not included in the appraisement and his western lands were valued at less
than one-half of their current market value. If these two items
are taken into consideration, the value of the Virginian's
estate was likely close to $800,000: the figure given by family

---

[52] Table 7.6, it will be noted, presented considerably higher earning ra-
tios because, on an accrual basis, the cost of the land inventory in 1879 was
carried forward in the amount of $110,360.80. In Table 7.5 on the other hand,
the full cost of the land inventory had been charged to the business before
1879 thus making it clear profit thereafter except for nominal management
and tax costs.

[53] See n. 2 above.

TABLE 7.6

SUMMARY OF ACCRUAL INCOME OF EASLEY & WILLINGHAM AND ASSOCIATES, 1853–79

Year	Revenue (sale of land and land warrants)	Operating Expenses (for land and land warrants)	(for misc. expenses)	Net income [deficit]	Income as a per cent of revenue
1853	$ 572.91	$ 214.33	$ 526.78	$ [168.20]	[29.4]
1854	37,408.80	13,995.01	2,408.26	21,005.53	56.2
1855	110,710.83	41,418.03	3,287.05	66,005.75	59.6
1856	157,835.51	59,047.84	3,733.69	95,053.98	60.2
1857	86,994.83	32,545.64	2,980.49	51,468.70	59.2
1858	52,144.77	19,507.88	1,993.21	30,643.68	58.8
1859	23,172.55	8,669.08	3,871.66	10,631.81	45.9
1860–61	10,290.74	3,849.87	5,001.04	1,439.83	14.0
Civil War					
1865	27,231.59	10,187.61	1,268.77	15,775.21	57.9
1866	21,881.53	8,186.10	8,836.44	4,858.99	22.2
1867	18,597.58	6,957.54	8,329.25	3,310.79	17.8
1868	44,816.03	16,766.12	9,747.86	18,302.05	40.8
1869	45,183.55	16,903.62	2,910.83	25,359.10	56.1
1870	27,598.90	10,325.02	2,023.88	15,250.00	55.3
1871	12,377.82	4,630.67	5,120.14	2,627.01	21.2
1872	5,736.16	2,145.95	3,085.21	505.00	8.8
1873	5,542.47	2,073.49	2,135.02	1,333.96	24.1
1874	3,950.22	1,477.82	3,356.04	[883.64]	[22.4]
1875	7,407.06	2,771.06	5,299.24	[663.24]	[9.0]
1876	3,474.37	1,299.80	3,229.08	[1,054.51]	[30.4]
1877	3,337.20	1,248.48	502.94	1,585.78	47.5
1878	1,758.23	657.77	322.25	778.21	44.3
1879	2,791.51	1,044.33	325.01	1,422.17	50.9
Totals	$710,815.16	$265,923.06	$80,294.14	$364,597.96	
Weighted average					51.3

TABLE 7.7
INVENTORY OF JAMES S. EASLEY'S ESTATE, 1880[a]

	Fixed interest securities	Stocks & real estate	Total
Notes and personal loans	$86,801,28[b]		$ 86,801.28
Securities			
Banks		$4,250.00	
Insurance		1,000.00	
Railroads		50.00	
		5,300.00	5,300.00
Real estate[c]			
Halifax Co., Va.		15,620.00	
Iowa "wild lands"		87,042.97	
Iowa "tax titles"		14,833.20	
Missouri "wild lands"		29,547.91	
Kansas "wild lands"		4,020.00	
Wisconsin "wild lands"		800.00	
		151,864,08	151,864.08
	86,801.28	157,164.08	243,965.36
Private estate		13,241.00	
Furniture, etc.		1,891.75	
			15,132.75
Grand Total			$259,098.11

[a]Compiled from "Inventory and appraisement of the real and personal estate of James S. Easley decd," dated Feb. 24, 1880. Probate Records, Book 32, 139–47, Circuit Court, Halifax County, Va.
[b]This includes a cash balance of $3,527.42.
[c]The western lands were appraised at less than 50 per cent of their actual market value.

sources.[54] Well-managed investments in frontier real estate must certainly be ranked with the very best capital opportunities of the nineteenth century. At least, so one would conclude from the business career of James Stone Easley.

V

THIS CHAPTER describes the frontier land market of the mid-nineteenth century and such related aspects of speculation as the time-entry system, moneylending, land warrants, tax-buying, foreclosure, real estate brokerage, and profitability. Between 1852 and the Civil War, Easley & Willingham entered 400,000 acres of land and lent impecunious westerners more than a half million dollars. But seven lean years followed the seven good ones as the economic distress of the late 1850's and then the disruptive civil conflict nearly bankrupted the southerners. The strife ended

[54] Mrs. Richard Coles Edmunds, Sr., to the author, Dec. 5, 1963.

just in time, however, to allow the Virginia speculators to redeem most of their tax-delinquent western lands before tax deeds were issued. Thereafter, until Easley's death in 1879, and continuing under his successors into the early years of this century, the firm gradually unloaded its huge land inventory.

Several significant facts emerged from this case study of the firm of Easley & Willingham. It might be noted in the first place that eastern capitalists likely played a much greater role as frontier moneylenders than as land speculators. Over 85 per cent of the entries that federal land officers struck off to Easley and his associates in Iowa were credit transactions under a bond for a deed arrangement: the typical form of frontier credit in the early years.[55] Also, contrary to much scholarly opinion, these time entrants proved to be a fairly reliable group in meeting their loan obligations. Except for the depression years, relatively few defaulted on their notes. And those who did found their eastern creditors most reluctant to foreclose, for the moneylenders were quick to realize that obtaining the money at interest, even belatedly, was more profitable than seizing the landed security.

Extensive operations like Easley's, needless to say, did not necessarily foster tenancy. With few exceptions, the Virginian refused to improve, rent, or lease his raw agricultural lands in the West, and he never allowed debtors in default to become tenants and work off their debt. Although frontier land agents have often been pilloried by Turnerians for continually defrauding unsuspecting nonresident investors, Easley's experience also indicates that easterners could, by exercising reasonable care, engage local realtors who were generally competent, dependable, and trustworthy.

Finally, as businessmen, Easley and his partner demonstrated a surprising mastery of the myriad facets, financial as well as political, of an interstate land business of a century ago. Keeping fully abreast of the fluid money and land warrant markets in the East and West, the fluctuating western real estate values and frequently changing governmental policy decisions, and at the same time maintaining accurate accounts with several dozen land agents and warrant brokers, was no small task. That the Virginians were eminently successful, despite an agonizing depression and war, is not only a tribute to themselves but an apt demonstration of the entrepreneurial talent that built America.

---

[55] An analysis of the transactions of the ten major Iowa real estate vendors whose total entries in nine central Iowa counties exceeded 25,000 acres also indicated that more than 70 per cent were entered for other buyers via the time-entry system. See Chapter 5.

Chapter Eight

THE RETURNS
ON IOWA LAND INVESTMENT

S HOW US a non-resident who has made money speculating in western land," wrote a western newspaper editor in 1850, "and we will show you a rare bird, more rare by far than a successful gold hunter."[1] Despite this warning and dozens like it, thousands of investors ventured surplus or borrowed funds on frontier land throughout the nineteenth century. Many, in fact, jumped from one frontier to the next, literally on the heels of government surveyors and land officers. Either these businessmen were gluttons for punishment or speculating in government land was far more rewarding than some contemporaries were willing to admit.

A growing number of twentieth century students of American economic development have turned their attention to this question of " 'Profits' and the Frontier Land Speculator," to use the title of the path-breaking article by Allan G. Bogue and Margaret B. Bogue.[2] In their perusal of the literature, the Bogues found that most researchers neither used adequate mathematical techniques to measure returns nor gave sufficient weight to the costs involved in land ownership. Few, indeed, even explained their methods of computation. Of those that did, most ignored such fixed costs as agents' commissions for buying and selling, land office fees, and taxes. More important, none attempted to calculate an annual rate of return per dollar invested. Nearly all of the analysts, the authors also reported, agreed that speculation in frontier lands was a losing proposition mitigated only by the occasional bonanza.[3]

After outlining the inadequacies of previous studies, the

---

[1] Madison (Wis.) *Argus,* cited in Benjamin H. Hibbard, *A History of the Public Land Policies* (New York, 1924), 221.
[2] *J. Econ. Hist.,* XVII (Mar., 1957), 1–24. This article contains a résumé of much of the literature on the subject.
[3] *Ibid.,* 2–7.

Bogues demonstrated their new concept—the annual rate of return per dollar invested—in an analysis of 77,500 acres of agricultural land in eastcentral Illinois and eastern Nebraska. Although their data suggested that profits may have been greater than previous students have allowed, they warned against any generalized conclusions on such scattered evidence as they and earlier scholars had amassed. Rather, they challenged the profession to make careful studies of returns from frontier land investments on an area basis.[4]

Prior to the age of the electronic computer, scholars understandably shunned the herculean task of undertaking area studies with sufficiently large samples and the requisite theoretical and mathematical precision.[5] With the increasing availability of data computation facilities, however, economic historians are now in a better position to attack this significant question. This chapter presents a theoretical framework for analyzing land speculation, a workable mathematical formula to calculate rates of return readily adaptable to computer use, and a summary of the results obtained when these techniques were applied to speculative activity in central Iowa. The chapter, it should be noted, deals with the large speculators as a group in a given delimited area rather than with specific individuals or land companies, as other studies have done.

I

INITIAL PROBLEMS concerned definition of terms and data collection. Some historians, as explained in Chapter 2, have followed Horace Greeley in considering a speculator to be anyone, nonresident or settler, who entered more land than he could develop. While accurate enough, this is a difficult yardstick to use since there is no way of knowing exactly how many acres any one person or family might utilize. Few would argue, however, that any-

---

[4] Ibid., 24.

[5] As Hibbard observed: "It would be an endless task to trace the land sales for any considerable area with a view to determine the extent of speculation" (History of the Public Lands Policies, 224). Two University of Mississippi graduate students devoted their masters' theses to the measurement of speculation in only one county (see Mattie Russell, "Land Speculation in Tippah County, 1836–1861" [M.A. thesis, 1940]; Edwin W. Chapman, "Land Speculation in Tate County, 1836–1861" [M.A. thesis, 1942]). Three University of Nebraska graduate students likewise devoted their theses to land disposal in single counties (John A. Caylor, "The Disposition of the Public Domain in Pierce County, Nebraska" [Ph.D. dissertation, 1951]; Evan E. Evans, "An Analytical Study of Land Transfer to Private Ownership in Johnson County, Nebraska" [M.A. thesis, 1950]; James A. Stone, "Disposition of the Public Domain in Wayne County, Nebraska, 1868–1893 [M.A. thesis, 1952]).

one needed as much as a thousand acres. For convenience in this analysis, therefore, speculators are defined as individuals who entered 1,000 acres or more of Congress land.[6] Using this definition, lists of large buyers were compiled from the books of original entry of 33 counties of central Iowa lying mainly within the confines of Royce Cession 262. The result was an enumeration of nearly 1,000 investors whose total entries topped 3,000,-000 acres.[7]

Having identified the largest speculators and the specific tracts that they entered, the initial resale information was abstracted from county deed registers. The mass of data required concentration on resales in the earliest years—from 1846 through 1860—in only nine counties indicated on Figure 8.1 by cross-hatching), chosen carefully in terms of geography and soil type as representative of the entire cession area.[8] For the ten largest entrants in each of the nine counties, however, the deed registers were searched for the initial resale of *all* original entry tracts—the final sale occurring in 1889.[9] Thus limited in geographic area

---

[6] Paul W. Gates ("Southern Investments in Northern Lands before the Civil War," *J. So. Hist.*, V [May, 1939], 178) also used the 1,000-acre figure in his investigation of land entry records in the Old Northwest and Middle West. Other researchers have arbitrarily selected other acreage figures as the minimum. Russell ("Land Speculation in Tippah County," p. iv) and Chapman ("Land Speculation in Tate County," p. ii) set the minimum at 2,000 acres, but this appears too large by Iowa land-use standards. The same figure was used by Mary E. Young, *Redskins, Ruffleshirts, and Rednecks: Indian Allotments in Alabama and Mississippi, 1830–1860* (Norman, Okla., 1961), 99. Paul G. Minneman ("Large Land Holdings and their Operation in Twelve Ohio Counties," [Ph.D. dissertation, Ohio State University, 1929]) used 500 acres, as did Harry N. Scheiber ("State Policy and the Public Domain: The Ohio Canal Lands," *J. Econ. Hist.*, XXV [Mar., 1965], Table 3, 95). Midwestern students have used both 1,000 and 640 acres (see Caylor, "Disposition of the Public Domain in Pierce County," 34–35; Stone, "Disposition of the Public Domain in Wayne County," 44–47).

[7] For the list of these large investors and their acreage totals, see Robert P. Swierenga, "Pioneers and Profits: Land Speculation on the Iowa Frontier" (Ph.D. dissertation, University of Iowa, 1965), Appendix IV.

[8] The nine counties were Appanoose, Benton, Boone, Carroll, Hardin, Madison, Marion, Poweshiek, and Wapello. When abstracting, all types of deeds (warranty, quitclaim, and indenture) were used except the following: those clearly pertaining to town lots; those containing metes and bounds descriptions or lot or block numbers that could not easily be translated into sectional descriptions; those reciting nominal considerations (twenty cents per acre or less); those that are illegible; those with obviously defective dates or descriptions; and those with sale dates prior to the date of original entry (such were usually quitclaims deeding only a color of title). When the deed contained two or more descriptions the total consideration was apportioned on the basis of the acreage for each description. When buyers defaulted and tracts were resold, the latter deed was used. Of the 984 entrants with a thousand acres or more in the 33-county area, 299 or about one-third, purchased land in the nine selected counties. I am indebted to several Iowa abstracting firms for granting free access to their tract indexes, which facilitated the tracing of resales in the county deed registers. Erling A. Erickson and Michael D. Green assisted in abstracting resale data.

[9] Breaks in title due to the failure to record deeds, common especially in the early years, made it impossible to chart about 3 per cent of the initial

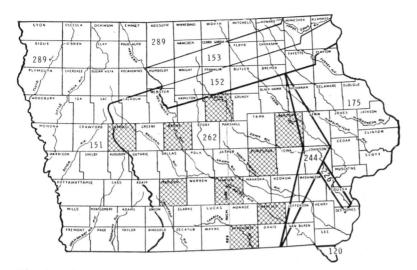

Fig. 8.1. Royce Cession 262, showing the nine counties in which land sales were analyzed.

and somewhat in time, the resale acreage to be analyzed amount-
ed to 460,119 acres—about 4 per cent of Royce Cession 262.[10]

The method of calculating returns on the investments of the
speculators was a refinement of the technique outlined in the
Bogues' seminal article. For each parcel of land sold, a data
card was punched recording among other things the acreage,
entry and sale price, month and year of entry and sale, the
standard fee charged by real estate agents and land officers for
locating and entering, and the realtor's commission for selling.[11]

---

resales. An additional 10 per cent were dropped because the deeds cited nominal considerations of less than twenty cents per acre.

[10] This smaller sample, it was expected, would be representative of the
larger group, but a comparison of the resales of the two groups in the period
1845–60 showed that the top ten entrants were not quite as successful in their
speculations as the other large-scale buyers. In the period after 1860, therefore, when the data rest on the activity of the smaller group only, the rates
are probably somewhat lower than if all resales of the large buyers had been
included. Had the situation been reversed it might have been expedient to
gather data for the entire large group, but in this case the results for the
later period will merely tend to the conservative side.

[11] All fractional acres were rounded to the nearest whole acre. The entry
and sale prices (recorded in dollars and cents) were those given in the books
of original entry and deed registers, respectively. The entry price was set at
$1.25 per acre if not given in the tract book. All dates were rounded to the
nearest whole month. Also included on the data card was a tract identification number corresponding to a tract in the book of original entry, a county
and buyer identification number, and a consecutive data card number. The
ten largest original entrants were distinguished from the other large entrymen. Warrant entries were distinguished from cash entries, and tracts sold
above $1.25 per acre were differentiated from those sold from twenty cents to
$1.25 per acre.

In time-entry transactions that were so common on the Iowa frontier, bor-

A tax series for each county based on the average yearly per acre tax on unimproved land for the period 1845 to 1889 was also transferred to data cards.[12] Other possible cost items necessarily had to be ignored—such as the owner's management time and expense and discounts on drafts and exchange—as well as any possible revenue prior to sale from rents and abortive sales.[13] For each tract of land the rate of interest was computed which, when

---

rowers paid land office fees and taxes; agent fees were deducted when loans were repaid. To distinguish credit entries from cash entries (when investors entered land on their own account and paid all fees and taxes themselves), the following rule of thumb was used: credit entries were classified as those in which the land was sold within two years after entry for less than $3.00 per acre or within one year for less than $2.00 per acre. Cash entries were all those in which land was sold 25 months or more after entry, or was sold within two years at a greater per acre price than $3.00 or within one year at a greater per acre price than $2.00. Two and three dollars were chosen as safe limits because, at the standard interest rate of 40 per cent on credit sales, approximately 50 cents per year was added to the usual land office price of $1.25 per acre.

Fees and commissions were quite standard for the period. On land warrant entries, agent fees were $5.00 for locating and entering 40-acre tracts, $7.00 for "eighties," $8.00 for "120's," and $10.00 for "160's." On cash entries, the fee was reduced by $1.00 for each 40 acres since the land office fee was abrogated. Beginning in 1856 when the flood of warrants issued under the liberal bounty act of 1855 (U.S. *Statutes at Large*, X, 701–2) hit the market, standard agent fees were reduced for warrant entries to $2.50 for 40 acres, $5.00 for "eighties," $7.50 for "120's," and $10.00 for "160's" with the corresponding reduction for cash entries. (See advertisements in Iowa City *Iowa Capitol Reporter*, Jan. 11, 1854; Iowa City *Daily Evening Reporter*, May 28, 1856; Fairfield *Iowa Sentinel*, Jan. 8, 1857; Fairfield *Ledger*, Apr. 30, 1857. See also LeGrand Byington, "Circular No. 4, Iowa General Land Agency, Iowa City," Iowa State Department of History and Archives, Des Moines.) Selling commissions varied between 2.5 and 5 per cent of the sale price, but the larger percentage seemed to be more common and was used here.

[12] The average yearly tax was based on a "visual mean average" of the annual tax assessments on unimproved land recorded in the county tax registers. Tax records in three counties had been destroyed; in these cases, the rates of the nearest sample county for which the data were available were substituted—Madison for Appanoose County, Hardin for Boone County, and Marion for Wapello County. Average yearly tax rates rose steadily from one cent per acre in the early years to approximately twenty cents per acre by the 1880's. For a tax series on one section of improved farm land in Muscatine County in eastern Iowa, see Allan G. Bogue, *From Prairie to Corn Belt: Farming on the Illinois and Iowa Prairies in the Nineteenth Century* (Chicago, 1963), 189.

[13] Additional costs might be postage, fees for notarizing deeds and paying taxes, revenue stamps on deeds (required after 1862), title abstract investigations, blank deeds and record books, redemption of tax-deeded land, defalcations of funds by agents, court litigation costs, and faulty assignments of warrants. The cost of investment capital might also be considered as a possible cost item, although scholars disagree sharply on this point. Offsetting factors were that much of the land was entered with warrants purchased at a discount and that some counties allowed payment of the county portion of the taxes with depreciated "county orders." Rental income, a much overemphasized aspect of speculation in Congress land in the Midwest, was not a factor in this analysis. Available evidence indicates that, at least in frontier Iowa, the large speculators primarily engaged in the "time-entry," not rental, business (see Chapter 7, Tables 7.1 and 7.2 and *passim*).

compounded[14] annually against the original investment plus selecting, locating, and entering fees and subsequent costs, gave a
total investment at the date of sale equal to the sale price minus
the sale commission.[15] This interest was called the net rate of
return on invested capital. This rate, of course, is not the equiva-

---

[14] Compound rather than simple interest was used because all contemporary evidence indicates that this was the customary practice, though computing with simple interest is the standard procedure in many present-day
financial arrangements. The simple interest method would result in a considerably *higher* rate of return than the rates here presented because interest
is not computed on the accrued interest of previous years. For example, $80
invested for 5 years at 5 per cent simple interest would yield $100, whereas
$80 invested for the same period at 4½ per cent compounded annually would
likewise yield $100. Use of constant dollars, often desired by purists in eco-
nomic studies, was not considered necessary here. Unsophisticated mid-nineteenth century investors seemingly were not aware of the subtleties of price
comparisons over time. Alternative investments, moreover, offered no escape,
since price changes affected all forms of investment, not only capital sunk in
land. Converting to constant dollars, in any case, would not have altered
significantly the overall average rates of return. In the first place, adding annual taxes and realtor sale commissions to the initial investment provides a
built-in hedge against the effect of price changes. During an inflationary
period, for example, converting taxes and sale commissions into constant dollars would result in smaller dollar amounts, thus increasing returns; at the
same time, converting revenue from land sales into constant dollars would,
of course, reduce rates of return. Secondly, general price indices during the
period of this study (1846–89) fluctuate over time and, therefore, inflationary
losses of one period might well be cancelled out by gains from subsequent
deflationary periods or vice versa. In the pre-Civil War period (1846–60), the
Snyder-Tucker general price index (Base: 1913=100) shows a general inflationary trend from a low of 66.5 in 1846 to a high of 79.6 in 1857—while in
the postwar years there is a marked deflation—from a high of 129 in 1864 to
a low of 76 in 1886 (see U.S. Bureau of the Census, *Historical Statistics of the
United States, 1789–1945; A Supplement to the Statistical Abstract of the
United States* [Washington, 1949], Series L1, 231–32).

[15] See Appendix XII for a more complete explanation of the computation
procedure. The polynomial equation used to determine rate of return r was
$Poly = PV (1 + r)^{nyear} (1 + r \times mons/12) + (1 + r \times mons/12) \Sigma T(I)$
$(1 + r)^{ntyr-1} \ldots n - SV = O$ when PV is the land office price (plus selecting
and entering fees), *nyear* is the number of whole years between the entry and
sale date, *mons* is the fractional months remaining, $T(I)$ is the annual tax,
ntyr is the number of whole tax years, and SV is the sale price (less the sale
commission). The first factor in the equation compounds interest annually
on the initial investment, while the second factor compounds interest annually
on taxes.

Taxes, computed only on noncredit entries, were determined by multiplying the tract acreage by the tax rate per acre for the respective years. Interest on these yearly tax investments was compounded annually (for a de-
creasing number of periods) from the date of the first tax payment, due under
Iowa law on the second January after entry (see Iowa *Revised Code*, 1860,
110, 117), until the last January before the sale date. Interest on this final tax
payment was computed at simple interest for the period from January first of
the year of sale until the sale date. The prorated tax amount levied against
the property during the calendar year of sale was subtracted from the sale
price, although speculators frequently passed this cost to the buyer. For a
column-by-column explanation of the information recorded on the 80-column
data cards and a complete listing of the PROFIT program in FORTRAN IV
language for use on an IBM 7040/7044 digital computer, see Swierenga,
"Pioneers and Profits," Appendices XV and XVI.

lent of profit. To obtain a figure which can be called profit, one must allocate an interest rate to the invested capital and subtract this from the rate of return. If the researcher hopes to be still more precise and specify net profit, he must subtract an allowance for the time spent by the investor in managing his real estate.[16]

Following the calculation of the annual rate of return for each tract, a new data card was automatically punched containing the original plus the newly computed data. With the use of a card-sorting machine and simple computer programs, the various rates of return per tract were then combined into weighted means.[17] These show the average rate of return per dollar invested for all tracts in the sample, or for those bought or sold in the same year or the same county, or by any of several other measures.

II

THE IOWA LANDS on which resale data were collected were confined to nine counties in the central and southcentral portion of the state, as indicated on Figure 8.1. Three of the counties—Wapello, Marion, and Boone—straddle the Des Moines River and represent the fertile river valley area. Appanoose County to the south adjoins the Missouri border, while Madison and especially Carroll represent the interior westcentral area where prairie predominated. Hardin County on the Iowa River typifies the northcentral mixed prairie-timber area. Benton and Poweshiek in the eastcentral region compare favorably with much of eastern Iowa in its combination of timber, prairie, and water resources.

Speculative activity was an important ingredient in the alienation of the public domain in all nine counties; but the amount of investment varied somewhat, depending apparently on

---

[16] Bogue and Bogue, " 'Profits' and the Frontier Land Speculator," 22.

[17] These means were obtained by multiplying the entry price of each tract by the rate of return which it earned and dividing the sum of the product by the sum of the entry prices. In addition to listing all of the input data, the computer print-out contained the following output data for each tract: the per acre sale price, the absolute percentage increase or decrease between the net entry and net sale price, the gross and net rates of return, and the total time held (in months). For any aggregate group of tracts (either all tracts within one county or all bought or sold in the same year, for example) totals were also printed, listing the total acres in the series, the total entry price, total fees, total sale price, total commissions, weighted average sale price per acre, weighted average gross and net rates of return, weighted average absolute percentage increase or decrease between the net entry and net sale prices, and the weighted average months per acre that all the tracts in the group were held between the entry and sale dates.

TABLE 8.1

ORIGINAL ENTRY ACREAGE OF CENTRAL IOWA LARGE ENTRYMEN (1,000 ACRES OR MORE) IN NINE SELECTED COUNTIES, 1845–64

County	Original entry acreage	Acreage of large entrymen	Per cent
Appanoose.................	264,712	64,108	24.2
Benton....................	411,933	108,712	26.4
Boone.....................	228,938	87,598	38.3
Carroll...................	192,958	87,956	45.6
Hardin....................	299,550	100,617	33.6
Madison...................	324,917	106,485	32.8
Marion....................	257,588	75,763	39.4
Poweshiek.................	341,389	135,337	39.6
Wapello...................	178,043	26,220	14.7
Totals...............	2,500,028	792,796	
Weighted average.....			31.7

the general business condition of the nation when the particular areas were first offered for sale. Wapello County on the Des Moines River in the southeastern sector was directly in the path of settlement when Cession 262 was first thrown open in 1843. Consequently, settlers quickly preempted much of it, and in 1846 and 1847 when the federal government first offered the area at public auction the large speculators had to be content with only 14.7 per cent of the original entry acreage in the county, as Table 8.1 shows. Competition from settlers was less intense in the other counties, however, and the large entrymen were able to absorb between one-fourth and one-half of all Congress land. On a percentage basis, the northwestern county of Carroll witnessed the greatest speculative activity, with the large investors acquiring 45.6 per cent of the original entry acreage. In terms of total acreage, on the other hand, the large entrymen together engrossed over 100,000 acres in each of four counties (Benton, Hardin, Madison, and Poweshiek) mainly in the years 1853 to 1856 as the business cycle climbed to its peak. Except for three townships in Boone and Carroll counties, buyers took up over 90 per cent of the original entry acreage in the nine counties within ten years (see Figure 8.2).[18] The average purchase price on all but land warrant entries was the Congress minimum of $1.25 per acre.

Occupationally, the nearly 1,000 large buyers on which this analysis is based (as explained earlier in Chapter 5) were engaged in the typical western pursuits: real estate and banking, merchandizing, farming and stock-raising, law, medicine, government service, and many of the trades. About one-third were from out

[18] For Figure 8.2 I am indebted to Raleigh Barlowe, Chairman, Department of Resource Development, Michigan State University, East Lansing.

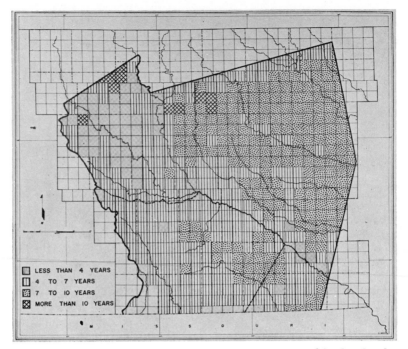

Fig. 8.2. Number of years from opening of township land sales in Royce Cession 262 until 90 per cent of the original entry acreage was taken.

of state while the remainder were Iowans. The Iowans were often not residents in the counties of their major speculative activities, so were as much nonresidents as the non-Iowans, at least from the standpoint of local residents. Realtors, bankers, and moneylenders accounted for the great bulk of the sample acreage. These professionals were engaged extensively in the time-entry system, earning the standard interest rate of 40 per cent per annum, which in part explains the high rates of return described in the following pages. The remaining acreage was entered by capitalists with surplus funds who sought long-term investments that would require little supervision but bring substantial rewards.

Land historian Benjamin Hibbard compiled statistics on the extent of large-scale speculation by 200 of the largest investors in early Iowa but did not find it feasible to follow the records of sales "minutely enough to determine what became of these big purchases or how well the purchasers fared." He suggested, however, that most speculators sold their land within a few years at about the same amount as the purchase price. Real estate values could not rise much, he believed, because of the abundance of Congress land offered at the minimum price and the free land available from 1862 until well into the Seventies in the north-western part of the state. "The result was that the big specula-tors . . . sold out long before land reached twenty or even ten dollars per acre"; thus few, Hibbard concluded, reaped "im-mense fortunes."[19]

It is true that most speculators unloaded the bulk of their lands within a few years: for the acreage here analyzed, the average investment period per acre was only 31.6 months, or slightly more than 2.5 years (see Table 8.2). It is also true that most speculators sold before land prices had increased tenfold: the average sale price of the land included in this analysis was only $3.10 per acre. Yet, to conclude from this that investments in frontier real estate were therefore unprofitable is erroneous. If land purchased for $1.25 per acre (or less if land warrants were used) was sold within a year for twice that amount and the money immediately reinvested to the same advantage, it is clear that such dealings could be "immensely profitable." Certainly one investor was satisfied with such returns. Norman Densmore of Emerald Grove, Wisconsin, entered Congress land in Iowa in 1854 at the minimum price and sold it a year later for $2.50 per acre. "If I can succeed in locating land where it will double the entrance money in one year I shall feel well satisfied," he con-cluded as he made plans for reinvesting.[20]

If Densmore doubled his money in a year, were other in-vestors as successful? At least one congressman thought so. "Are there not gentlemen within the sound of my voice," asked Rep-resentative Francis Johnson of Maryland, "who have purchased land of the Government, within the last twelve months, and have realized more than a hundred per cent upon it?"[21] That the law-maker knew the facts is evident from Table 8.2, which presents resale and rate of return data on 460,119 acres of unimproved central Iowa real estate entered by large speculators in the im-mediate pre-Civil War decades. The table is based on the land office price of each tract; or if entered with land warrants or scrip (or not given), the minimum price of $1.25 per acre was substituted.

While the average net rates of return varied widely between counties, from a low of 14.3 per cent per year in Wapello County to a high of 115.2 per cent in Poweshiek, the weighted average

[19] *History of the Public Land Policies*, 224–25. Cf. 221.

[20] Norman Densmore to Benjamin Densmore, Oct. 25, 1855 (Benjamin Densmore Letters, Wisconsin State Historical Society, Madison).

[21] U.S. Congress, *Congressional Globe*, 25th Cong., 2nd Sess., 1838, VI, Appendix 547.

TABLE 8.2

AVERAGE SALE PRICES AND ANNUAL RATES OF RETURN EARNED BY LARGE EN-
TRYMEN IN NINE SELECTED COUNTIES, 1845–89 *

County	Acres sold	Avg. price per acre	Avg. gross rate of return †	Avg. net rate of return	Avg. investment period per acre (months)
Appanoose	40,424	$2.82	23.4	16.8	30.5
Benton	59,739	3.09	40.6	31.8	37.3
Boone	51,904	2.70	44.2	35.8	45.1
Carroll	50,346	3.18	114.3	95.9	21.2
Hardin	60,056	2.65	62.9	51.7	26.7
Madison	56,781	2.59	47.2	39.3	23.5
Marion	44,029	2.51	24.6	17.7	29.3
Poweshiek	77,315	4.17	132.1	115.2	26.9
Wapello	19,525	4.55	20.7	14.3	69.1
Total	460,119				
Weighted average		$3.10	64.3	53.4	31.6

*Land warrant entries are valued here at $1.25 per acre.
†Does not include taxes, fees, and commissions in the investment. All average rates of return are weighted per dollar invested.

returns on the total investment of the large speculators was a stunning 53.4 per cent compounded annually.[22] Appanoose and Marion counties shared low rates with Wapello, averaging 16.8 and 17.7 per cent respectively while Carroll County speculators (at 95.9 per cent) made out nearly as well as those in Poweshiek. Returns in Benton, Boone, and Madison counties fell in the 30 per cent range while Hardin County averaged 51.7 per cent.

III

IT IS DIFFICULT to explain the reasons for the wide variance in annual rates of return between counties. Specific factors that must be considered are the date of entry, the time span of the

---

[22] Although not discussed here, the gross rate of return was also calculated for each tract by ignoring taxes, fees, and commissions. This raised returns by an average of approximately 10 per cent. Readers familiar with the Bogues' study and the generally lower rates of return earned on frontier land investments which they presented, will recall the major differences between that study and this which make comparison difficult. Their data reflected the experience of six specific investor groups, of which the three largest—accounting altogether for over 90 per cent of the acreage in the sample—were largely real estate developers who put tenants on their land. The entries of these investors, moreover, varied widely in time; three acquired their land in the 1830's, two in the 1840's and 1850's, and one in the 1870's. In addition, these investors purchased almost 75 per cent of their sample acreage in the post-Civil War period, 30 per cent of it from land grant railroads and state governments at prices from two to five times greater than the Congress minimum of $1.25 per acre. Finally, the Bogues lacked precise information on the market price quotations of land warrants.

investment, peculiarities in the action of individual speculators, general estimates of agricultural potential, and proximity to projected internal improvements and railroads. Speculators, for example, first reached Carroll County in 1854 and 1855, just as the business expansion of the 1850's was nearing its peak. Under the speculative boom, eager investors snapped up all of the Congress land in a matter of months, with nonresidents acquiring over 95 per cent of it. In the face of such tremendous demand, prices rose sharply and the original large entrymen unloaded quickly to other speculators. Only 21 months on an average separated the dates of entry and sale—the shortest average time among the counties studied. Consequently, yearly rates of return were nearly 100 per cent in Carroll County.

The experience in Wapello County, on the other hand, illustrated the time element in an adverse way. Although speculators there realized a higher average sale price ($4.55 per acre) than in any other county in the study, they earned the lowest average returns because they carried their investments, on an average, more than twice as long as speculators in other counties. This not only added to the tax burden but sharply reduced annual returns.

Circumstances surrounding the activities of several large buyers in Marion County indicate how composite analyses must be used with care. Speculators in that county seemingly earned an average net return of only 17.7 per cent compounded annually. However, about 800 Dutch immigrants chose Marion as their home in 1847 under the guidance of a leader who entered nearly 18,000 acres in his own name and that of a friend.[23] Much of this acreage, located largely with land warrants, was in turn deeded to the colonists at government price ($1.25 per acre) or only a slight advance above it. Some might argue, with good reason, that such entries were not speculative in intent and should not have been included in the sample; in any case, this acreage lowered the average rates in Marion by a considerable margin.

Poweshiek County is the best example of the influence of location, strategically situated as it was on the proposed line of the Rock Island and Pacific Railroad and midway between the temporary state capital at Iowa City and the proposed new site at Des Moines. Nonresident investors found themselves attracted as by a magnet. Altogether, the large entrymen entered 135,337 acres, or 39.6 per cent of all the public land in the county. On the 77,315 acres for which resale data were collected, average net returns were 115.2 per cent compounded annually.

Actual returns earned by the "average" speculators were

---

[23] Jacob Van Der Zee, *The Hollanders of Iowa* (Iowa City, 1912), 71.

even higher than the figures thus far presented. In nearly 60 per cent of their entries the large investors used land warrants, available in the middle 1850's at discounts of 5 to 15 per cent below the land office price.[24] In addition, 87,376 acres, or 20 per cent of the total acreage in the study, were sold at prices between twenty cents and $1.25 per acre—in other words, apparently at no profit. But it is very doubtful if many of these recorded prices were bona fide. Some involved partial financing in which the buyer provided part of the purchase price but the speculator entered the land in his own name to protect the loan. When such loans were repaid and the title transferred, the recorded consideration on the deed could range well below $1.25 per acre.[25] Similarly, when no down payment was involved, the credit arrangement might call for repayment of the original loan at the land office price plus an annual premium of fifty cents per acre per annum. In such cases the actual sale price would be fully 40 per cent higher than the price of $1.25 per acre shown on the deed.

Other sales at prices below the land office minimum covered transfer of land between members of the same family or, as in the case of the Marion County Dutch, from the immigrant leader to his individual colonists. Some deeds were only quitclaim deeds involving tax-clouded or contested land to which the seller had merely a color of title. Sheriff's sales for taxes or other liens and quitclaim deeds to replace earlier unrecorded deeds that had been lost or destroyed also accounted for a few sales below the government minimum price. At least some sales below $1.25 per acre were bona fide, however, especially in the early years from 1847 to 1852 when land warrants sold at discounts of 50 to 60 per cent. Speculators interested in short-run gains not infrequently entered land with them, resold quickly at prices equal to or slightly below the government minimum, and immediately reinvested. Such activity could be very rewarding even though sale prices were far below the actual value of the land.

That speculators would sell one-fifth of their land at a loss also seems illogical and does not conform to the assertion of one of the largest Iowa investors. In 1867 an Iowan charged that Virginia speculator James S. Easley had in the 1850's agreed through one of his western agents to sell an 80-acre tract in the Hawkeye State for $100 but had since refused to convey title.

---

[24] In six counties in the sample area, 173,064 acres out of 291,378 were entered with warrants. Boone, Hardin, and Madison county tracts were deleted from this part of the analysis because the records do not differentiate between cash and land warrant entries. In the state as a whole, warrants were used in lieu of cash in 52 per cent of all entries of Congress land.

[25] For example, if a settler provided three-fifths of the land office price but borrowed the remainder, the average consideration recorded at the time of sale might range below $1.00 per acre, even if the interest cost was included.

Easley replied in indignation that it was preposterous to think that he would have paid a commission to an agent to sell land at $1.25 per acre when it had cost him that amount; he continued, "We think this would have been rather an unprofitable [sale] & . . . it is the only case of the kind we ever heard of & at the time this land was entered for us, it was considered by all land dealers that lands at that time were as soon as they were entered worth from $2.50 to $3.00 pr acre. . . . This is the first [instance] in buying & selling several hundred thousand Acres through agents that we have ever known them to buy at $1.25 & sell at $1.25."[26]

In order to ascertain more realistic rates of return, the data were recalculated after deleting all tracts selling at the land office minimum or less. The result, as indicated in Table 8.3, was to raise the average rates more than 15 per cent—from 53.4 (see Table 8.2) to 67.8 per cent. However, in Appanoose, Marion, and Wapello—counties where investors seemingly earned the lowest returns—the average rates were doubled by the new calculation, illustrating that a greater than normal amount of non-bona fide sales had been recorded in the deed registers of these counties.

IV

NOT ONLY must the diligent researcher weigh the factor of non-bona fide sales, he must also consider the effect of the use of land warrants on profits, an element never measured precisely by previous scholars. In the six counties in the study where land records distinguished between cash and land warrant entries, the average per acre selling price of warrants on eastern markets during the month of entry (plus five cents per acre to approximate western rates) was substituted for the land office price on all warrant entries and the rate of return was recalculated.[27] Again, the upward trend was marked, as Table 8.4 shows, with the overall average climbing from 53.4 to 72.2 per cent. Limited only to sales above $1.25 per acre, as in Table 8.5, the average rate reached 82.2 per cent. Average annual returns in Poweshiek

[26] Easley & Willingham to Head & Russell, Aug. 23, 1867, James S. Easley Papers, Alderman Library, University of Virginia, Charlottesville.

[27] For the purpose of this study, the midpoint between the monthly high and low retail selling price quotations, based on 160-acre warrants on the New York and Washington markets (see Table 6.1), was designated as the "average per acre selling price" for each month. The data for the table were supplied by Miss Natalie Disbrow, St. Petersburg, Fla. Adding five cents per acre to approximate western rates was arbitrary. The spread between eastern and western retail prices varied somewhat over time, depending on factors of supply and demand (see Chapter 6).

TABLE 8.3

AVERAGE SALE PRICES AND ANNUAL RATES OF RETURN EARNED BY LARGE EN-
TRYMEN IN NINE SELECTED COUNTIES, 1845–89 *

County	Acres sold	Avg. price per acre	Avg. gross rate of return †	Avg. net rate of return	Avg. investment period per acre (months)
Appanoose..............	26,570	$3.72	40.9	33.7	38.9
Benton................	48,324	3.58	53.7	44.6	42.2
Boone.................	42,855	3.06	54.3	45.5	40.4
Carroll................	43,516	3.52	132.7	112.5	18.3
Hardin................	55,477	2.77	68.2	56.9	27.2
Madison...............	47,284	2.87	57.6	49.1	23.4
Marion................	27,608	3.29	41.7	34.3	42.6
Poweshiek.............	68,804	4.55	149.2	131.3	27.3
Wapello...............	13,305	6.17	33.1	27.1	86.7
Total.............	373,743				
Weighted average...		$3.56	80.7	67.8	33.2

* Land warrant entries valued at $1.25 per acre, and all cash sales at that price or less deleted.

† Does not include taxes, fees, and commissions in the investment. All average rates of return are weighted per dollar invested.

TABLE 8.4

AVERAGE SALE PRICES AND ANNUAL RATES OF RETURN EARNED BY LARGE
ENTRYMEN IN SIX SELECTED COUNTIES, 1845–84 *

County	Acres sold	Avg. price per acre	Avg. net rate of return	Avg. investment period per acre (months) †
Appanoose.......	40,424	$2.82	25.8	30
Benton..........	59,739	3.09	38.3	37
Carroll..........	50,346	3.18	135.1	21
Marion..........	44,029	2.51	30.9	29
Poweshiek.......	77,315	4.17	120.0	27
Wapello.........	19,525	4.55	34.6	69
Total........	291,378			
Weighted average.....		$3.37	72.2	32

* Land warrant entries valued at current market rates. Boone, Hardin, and Madison county books of original entry do not distinguish between cash and land warrant entries.

† Rounded to whole months.

TABLE 8.5

AVERAGE SALE PRICES AND ANNUAL RATES OF RETURN EARNED BY LARGE
ENTRYMEN IN SIX SELECTED COUNTIES, 1845–84 *

County	Acres sold	Avg. price per acre	Avg. net rate of return	Avg. investment period per acre (months) †
Appanoose........	32,161	$3.27	37.3	34
Benton...........	52,964	3.37	45.7	40
Carroll...........	47,230	3.34	144.0	17
Marion...........	39,673	2.66	35.9	31
Poweshiek........	71,795	4.42	130.5	27
Wapello..........	18.467	4.78	39.3	69
Total.......	262,290			
Weighted average.....		$3.63	82.2	32

* Land warrant entries valued at current market rates and all cash sales
at $1.25 per acre or less deleted. Boone, Hardin, and Madison county books
of original entry do not distinguish between cash and land warrant entries.
† Rounded to whole months.

and Carroll counties jumped to 130.5 and 144.0 per cent respectively.

Reckoned with estimated warrant prices, the results in
Wapello County also become more realistic, since the large investors used warrants for 90 per cent of their entries in that
county. The average net rate of return figure increased from
14.3 to 34.6 per cent when based on current warrant prices in
the West, and increased again to 39.3 per cent when the acreage
was restricted to sales above $1.25 per acre. Taking warrant en-
tries and seemingly non-bona fide sales into account, in short,
radically transforms the image of Wapello as a relatively poor
place to invest.

V

RETURNS from land investments, it is generally recognized, varied
over time as well as between different areas. The date of purchase and sale in relation to the business cycle and the rapidity
of settlement in the area of one's land holdings were factors that
could affect the profitability of investments. To test the time
variable, all of the tracts examined were arranged first by year
of sale, then by both the year of entry and the year of sale. The
figures for tracts sold in the same year are presented in Table 8.6.

The volume of sales and average returns fluctuated widely.
In the first years, 1846–48, the number of acres traded was not

TABLE 8.6
AVERAGE RETURNS ON IOWA LAND STUDIED, BY YEAR OF SALE, 1845–84*

Year	Acreage sold	Avg. price per acre	Avg. net rate of return	Avg. investment period per acre (months) †
1846.............	160	$ 2.50	70.2	13
1847.............	8,520	1.26	16.3	1
1848.............	232	1.25	2.7	3
1849.............	6,298	2.01	52.9	13
1850.............	5,896	1.75	58.2	10
1851.............	8,899	1.33	19.1	13
1852.............	16,390	1.67	27.1	14
1853.............	22,426	1.67	21.2	13
1854.............	46,904	3.54	156.6	9
1855.............	45,904	2.86	60.1	15
1856.............	29,720	2.90	72.5	19
1857.............	17,949	4.73	66.3	31
1858.............	14,051	4.73	73.2	36
1859.............	23,153	3.65	155.9	17
1860.............	13,319	3.77	45.0	53
1861.............	2,206	2.84	6.9	78
1862.............	3,195	3.81	32.2	92
1863.............	2,948	3.95	107.1	72
1864.............	3,214	3.94	31.4	97
1865.............	2,998	6.13	10.8	151
1866.............	5,805	3.55	4.1	120
1867.............	1,551	6.81	9.8	155
1868.............	4,143	8.60	12.1	163
1869.............	546	12.87	12.3	186
1870.............	490	7.90	8.3	185
1871.............	40	3.75	4.5	191
1872.............	125	7.36	6.3	214
1873.............	285	7.42	5.7	243
1874.............	760	20.38	10.1	292
1875.............	560	21.16	10.8	282
1876.............	502	8.36	−4.5	289
1877.............	349	8.60	5.9	308
1878.............	...	....	...	...
1879.............	240	7.50	6.4	256
1880.............	560	14.95	6.5	319
1881.............	480	16.48	6.9	336
1882.............	240	3.83	−.7	317
1883.............	...	....	...	...
1884.............	320	15.62	6.2	358

*Warrant entries valued at current market rates.
†Rounded to whole months.

sufficient to enable one to reach valid conclusions; in addition, they mainly involved the immigrant land distribution in Marion County. From 1849 through 1860, however, sales were frequent as speculators unloaded the great bulk of their holdings. Indeed, in the brief period from 1854 to 1856, the large investors sold almost one-half of all the acreage in the sample. Rates of return were as encouraging to speculators as the volume of sales, ranging as high as 156.6 per cent in 1854, and averaging 78.1 per cent for the period 1846–60.[28]

Until 1865, returns remained extremely high, with annual averages topping 100 per cent in both 1859 and 1863 as they had in 1854. Apart from 1861, when the unsettled conditions of the nation reduced profits to 6.9 per cent, the average annual rates of return remained above 30 per cent until 1865. In that year a decided break is noticeable as the average ownership time increased suddenly from six to a dozen or more years. Correspondingly, returns declined sharply to an average of approximately 8.5 per cent for the period from 1866 until 1871, when, with another slight break, they tended to level off at an average of about 5 per cent until the final sales in 1884. During the entire time span average returns dipped into the net loss column only twice, in 1876 and 1882—years when a mere 742 acres were involved. Of course, during every year some losses occurred, or at least so it appears from the considerations recorded in the deed registers.[29]

One can conclude from the data in Table 8.6 that land sold in the booming Fifties, as nine-tenths of it was, brought extremely high short-term profits. On the other hand, if the buyer retained title to his land until the postwar years, he could expect rather stable earnings averaging about 8 or 9 per cent per annum (compounded annually) until the early Seventies, and about 5 per cent thereafter. This steady earning rate, despite rising tax costs and the compounding of interest on interest, resulted because land prices in Iowa advanced steadily as the state gradually neared the stage of full agricultural development.

To determine the combinations of years which proved most profitable for buying and selling Iowa land, averages were calculated on all tracts entered in the same calendar year and sold in the same calendar year. For example, tracts entered in 1848 and sold the same year were averaged separately from those entered in 1848 and sold in 1849 or bought in 1848 and alienated in 1850. Table 8.7 lists only those combinations of years when average returns were above 50 per cent per annum. In the 1840's the highest returns came to those who bought in 1848 and sold the next year. In the next decade the most profitable earnings came in 1854, 1858, and 1859 on land bought and sold the same

---

[28] This is based on actual land warrant costs. If limited only to tracts sold above $1.25 per acre, the rate was 202 per cent.

[29] In the six counties in which original entry books distinguish land warrant from cash entries, investors suffered net losses on 34,937 acres, or 11.8 per cent of their acreage. However, on sales above $1.25 per acre only, the net loss figure dips to 5,094 acres, or 1.6 per cent, a remarkably small amount.

TABLE 8.7

MOST PROFITABLE COMBINATIONS OF BUYING AND SELLING YEARS IN IOWA*

Year of entry	Year of sale	Acres sold	Avg. net rate of return
1848	1849	552	196.2
1848	1850	1,325	60.3
1849	1849	2,634	66.1
1853	1855	6,842	98.7
1854	1854	35,774	188.4
1854	1855	46,145	54.4
1854	1856	14,736	53.9
1854	1857	7,368	50.0
1855	1856	46,172	57.4
1855	1857	8,467	64.7
1856	1856	13,247	110.6
1856	1857	20,717	80.7
1858	1858	4,767	262.2
1858	1859	3,128	188.0
1858	1860	1,520	56.7
1859	1859	14,776	200.6
1859	1860	3,000	162.6
1862	1862	160	481.2
1862	1863	440	116.2
1863	1863	920	316.2
1864	1864	640	151.5

*Warrant entries valued at current market rates.

year. The war years of 1862, 1863, and 1864 also appear extremely profitable for investors although too few acres were sold to make any safe generalizations.

These years of highest earnings conform, in general, to the business cycle of the period. The peak years were in the late 1840's and mid 1850's, with the troughs occurring in the early and late Fifties. The high earnings on sales during 1858 and 1859—normally considered depression years—are therefore difficult to explain. Yet as the figures in Table 8.6 also indicate, average rates of return seemingly were not affected by the recession, although the volume of sales steadily declined after 1857.

A somewhat similar picture is presented when the speculative tracts are grouped according to year of entry as in Table 8.8. The large buyers completed the bulk of their entries in the period from 1850 through 1856. Since the depression of 1857 did not strike until autumn, the dearth of entries in that year can only be explained by the government's closing of most of the land offices in 1856. They were not reopened until 1858 when investors had a final opportunity to buy the small amount of the public domain in central Iowa that remained unsold. That this was a profitable opportunity is evident by the high earnings on the entries of 1858 and 1859. Actually, annual average rates of return were encouraging during the entire 20-year period, except

TABLE 8.8
AVERAGE RATES OF RETURN BY YEAR OF ENTRY, 1845–64*

Year of entry	Acres entered	Avg. net rate of return	Avg. investment period per acre (months) †
1845	160	70.2	13
1846	560	7.2	113
1847	13,114	17.8	20
1848	6,269	47.5	70
1849	13,200	32.0	43
1850	27,306	20.0	48
1851	20,179	19.8	26
1852	22,649	23.6	19
1853	40,690	44.2	21
1854	136,078	79.9	34
1855	98,487	41.1	35
1856	45,960	73.8	23
1857	240	40.0	7
1858	12,295	152.4	45
1859	20,652	180.7	18
1860	40	−3.0	3
1861	80	−5.0	2
1862	600	128.3	8
1863	920	316.2	3
1864	640	151.5	1

*Warrant entries valued at current market rates.
†Rounded to whole months.

for 1846, 1860, and 1861; and in those years investors wisely bought virtually no land.

VI

FRONTIER LAND was only one of many avenues of investment in the nineteenth century. The researcher is impelled, therefore, to compare earnings returned on frontier land speculation in Iowa with average rates of interest and market yields of possible alternate investments. Prime market yields of long-term, high-grade bonds of the United States government, municipalities and states, and railroads provide valid indexes for comparison, as do common stock yields and savings bank deposit rates. Since many frontier real estate investments were short term in nature, interest rates on good commercial paper and call money—both ideal for short-term investments—can also be used in comparison.

In Table 8.9 ten-year averages of annual compound net rates of return on frontier land investments in Iowa for the period 1840–90 are listed beside ten-year average yield rates of federal government bonds, New England municipals, high-grade

TABLE 8.9

Average Ten-Year Rates of Return on Frontier Land Investments in Iowa as Compared With American Interest Rates, Short- and Long-Term, 1840–89*

Years	Frontier land investments in Iowa†	Per cent of land sold	U.S. govt. bonds "selected market yields"	New England municipal bond yields	High-grade railroad bond yields	Common stock yields	Commercial paper rates	Call money rates	Savings bank rate: regular deposits
1840–49	9.94 (4-yr. avg.)	5.2	5.41 (8-yr. avg.)	5.02	....	....	7.99	....	5.00
1850–59	71.66	83.9	4.33	5.06	6.50 (3-yr. avg.)	....	8.49	6.30 (3-yr. avg.)	5.00
1860–69	30.96	9.1	5.34	5.10	5.90	....	7.07	6.50	5.00
1870–79	5.97	1.3	3.75	4.98	5.67	5.94 (9-yr. avg.)	6.46	5.73	6.00
1880–89	3.88 (4-yr. avg.)	.5	2.71	3.60	4.00	4.80	5.14	3.98	4.00

*Common stock yields adapted from Series Y-a indexes, 372 et seq., in Alfred Cowles, 3rd, et al., Common Stock Indexes, 1871–1937 (Bloomington, 1938). Cowles' Series Y-1, 270 et seq., gives slightly lower yield rates. All other data is in Sidney Homer, History of Interest Rates (New Brunswick, 1963), 287–88, 318–20, a work which neatly summarizes data in Frederick R. Macaulay, Some Theoretical Problems Suggested by the Movement of Interest Rates, Bond Yields and Stock Prices in the United States Since 1856 (New York, 1938).

†Based on data in Table 8.6. Total land sales by decades were: 1846–49: 15,210 acres; 1850–59: 244,611 acres; 1860–69: 26,606 acres; 1870–79: 3,897 acres; 1880–84: 1,600 acres.

railroad bonds, common stocks, commercial paper and call money, and rates on savings deposits. Compared to these alternative investments, it is readily apparent, as pictured in Figure 8.3, that returns per dollar invested in frontier Iowa land, while fluctuating a great deal more from year to year, far outstripped the very best average bond and stock yields as well as the more speculative commercial paper and call money rates. This was

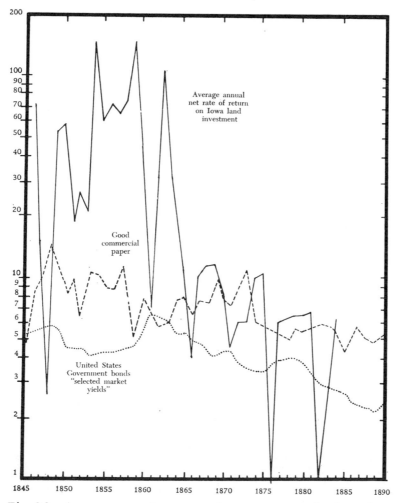

Fig. 8.3. Average annual net rate of return on frontier Iowa land investment as compared with long-term U.S. government bond selected market yields, and short-term good commercial paper interest rates, 1845–90.

particularly true in the decade 1850–59, when the speculators sold 83.9 per cent of the lands here analyzed.

Many eastern capitalists realized the bonus that could be earned on frontier land investments. A survey of the deed registers (see Chapter 3) indicated that a third of the nearly 1,000 large speculators in central Iowa were nonresidents. In addition, Iowa realtors entered countless thousands of acres under the time-entry system for eastern clients with a canny eye for high-yield, no-risk investments. Most of these easterners had likely shared James S. Easley's experience in the seaboard capital markets. The highest interest rates he could earn, Easley found, either by discounting good commercial paper, buying railroad bonds, or private lending, ranged no higher than 10 to 12 per cent.[30] Stock in manufacturing companies and public utilities seemed even less attractive, despite the blurbs of promoters who bombarded him with prospectuses and financial statements. Easley largely spurned all these alternatives and continued to invest in raw land or tax titles in the West. "We have never been able to make anything by trading [western land] for Stocks," the Virginian informed his Chicago agent in 1869 in reply to a proposal to swap a thousand acres of his tax-ridden Wisconsin lands for Illinois Gas Company stocks.[31] Alexander Koster of Gettysburg, Pennsylvania, agreed with Easley about eastern investment opportunities. In 1855 Koster decided to enter several thousand acres of land in Iowa "to make some money." His funds commanded only 6 per cent per annum at home, Koster declared irritably to his western realtor, and "this way of doing business I am getting tyred of."[32] Only a lack of knowledge of the western land market or a fear of its intricacies and complexities could have deterred all of the eastern capitalists from reacting in the same manner as Easley and Koster.

Since the average rates of return per dollar invested in frontier land in central Iowa in the mid-nineteenth century were superior to many other forms of investment, it is regrettable

[30] James S. Easley to J. D. Blair, Feb. 22, 1872; to E. S. Hedges, Apr. 17, 1872; to J. P. Casady, July 21, 1874; to G. W. Grance, May 18, 1875, James S. Easley Papers.

[31] Easley & Willingham to Josiah Bond, Jan. 12, 1869. This was the only such stock offer that Easley accepted, mainly because he could unload some of his unprofitable Wisconsin lands (Easley to Josiah Bond, Jan. 28 and Feb. 16, 1869). In the Sixties Easley invested 10,000 in Danville & Richmond Railroad bonds at 10 per cent and $1,300 in U.S. bonds. Earlier he had put $2,000 in Virginia coupon bonds. See Easley to A. Y. Stokes, Mar. 30, Apr. 8, and May 28, 1870; to Holmes & Macy, Sept. 29, 1868, Jan. 13, 1869; to J. D. Blair, Feb. 22, 1872. James S. Easley Papers.

[32] Koster to Hugh D. Downey, Dec. 29, 1855, Cook, Sargent & Downey Papers, State Historical Society of Iowa, Iowa City.

that most previous scholars have, after only cursory examination of the land records, created such a misleading picture. If the speculator who make money in frontier land dealings was truly a "rare bird," as has been asserted, then the American menagerie must have been well stocked with odd specimens. More likely, however, the investor who failed to show a profit was truly the rare bird.

Chapter Nine

THE SPECULATORS' ROLE
ON THE FRONTIER

UNTIL the stock offerings of modern corporations became the dominant attraction for surplus capital in the later decades of the nineteenth century, real estate—particularly western—was no doubt the principal form of American investment. Men from all walks of life, including future President Abraham Lincoln, turned to frontier Iowa for sound investments.[1] Beginning with the trade in claims in eastern Iowa in the 1830's and culminating in the land office rush of the Fifties, speculators, large and small, acquired an ever increasing quantity of raw land. Finally, at the outset of the Civil War, these land merchants probably owned more than one-half of the entire state.

I

IN THE FACE of such intense activity and what historians have written of it, the reader of contemporary literature expects to find a great deal of sustained criticism directed at speculators. Surprisingly, however, this is not the case. A careful survey of Iowa newspapers and periodicals reveals that speculators were excoriated only intermittently; usually in conjunction with the major depressions of the late 1830's and 1850's, with bitterly fought political campaigns, or with attempts to justify claim club activity.

During the depression years of 1838 and 1839, when President Martin Van Buren proclaimed for public sale dozens of

---

[1] In Iowa, Lincoln located two land warrants obtained for service in the Blackhawk War, 40 acres in Tama County in 1854, and 120 acres in Crawford County in 1860. Both tracts passed to his heirs at his death and were not sold until the end of the nineteenth century. See E. R. Harlan, "Lincoln's Iowa Lands," *Annals of Iowa, 3rd Ser.*, XV (Apr., 1927), 621–23.

townships in eastern Iowa, settlers immediately raised the traditional hue and cry for postponement. And almost as inevitably, they couched their appeal in the rhetoric of the poor settler who lacked funds to enter his land and was therefore in danger of falling into the clutches of "greedy" speculators "who grind the faces of the poor." Unless the sales were delayed, pleaded one group of petitioners in Des Moines County, "the people of Iowa [must] submit to the necessity of having the fairest portion of her Territory fall into the hands of these 'land sharks.' "[2] During the hard times of the late Fifties, nonresident speculators again came under fire from westerners searching vainly for simplistic explanations of the depression. "We might ask who have been the principal movers in the real estate speculations of the West?" queried a Keokuk editor. "Eastern men" he declared emphatically, answering his own question. "If Tom, Dick, and the Devil from New York, New England, and every place else towards sunrise, had not puffed and blowed at these bursted bubbles, the West would have been all right to-day." Several months later the distraught editor repeated the theme, only more briefly: "Much of our best land[s] . . . have passed into the hands of capitalists; and the growth of the country retarded in consequence."[3]

Although nonresidents bore the brunt of the criticism, local farmer-speculators did not entirely escape censure, at least not from agriculturalists such as B. F. Conkey, secretary of the State Agricultural Society. There was a lesson to be learned from the adversity, Conkey admonished: "The recent hard times have given a new impulse to agriculture, by teaching the people that speculating in lands is not the best use to which they can be put or the most sure to return large profits. . . ."[4]

Politicos also tried to capitalize on any ill will which might be engendered against speculators. One crafty Democrat pinned on his opponent the epithets "prince of speculators," "a 40 per cent man," and "a moneylender and shaver."[5] Conversely, early in 1841 when Congress discussed a preemption bill sponsored by the Democratic administration, a Whig editor, loath to have the

[2] Burlington *Iowa Patriot,* July 25 and Aug. 8, 1839; Burlington *Iowa Territorial Gazette and Burlington Advertiser,* Aug. 10 and 31, and Oct. 5, 1839.

[3] *The North-Western Rev.,* I (Dec., 1857), 59; I (Mar., 1858), 4.

[4] Iowa State Agricultural Society, *Report,* 1859, 235. A county secretary voiced similar sentiments: "The disposition to speculate in lands, rather than cultivate them, manifested here as well as elsewhere in the west, has injured the interests of agriculture in our county, but the late crisis has brought many farmers to their senses, and taught them that habits of industry and economy are more certain to procure the means of support for themselves and families, than the precarious chances of speculation." *Ibid.,* 1858, 243–44.

[5] Fort Dodge *Sentinel,* Sept. 10, 1859.

opposition gain any credit, denounced the proposed law as a mere gambit to get Western votes and charged that it would aid the "richest and most grasping speculator" instead of the poor settler.[6] A Republican mentor likewise castigated President James Buchanan in 1859 for his "needless and highly injurious act" of throwing into market most of the remaining public domain in the Hawkeye State. It simply offered "a large body of rich land for the speculators to monopolize and fatten upon," he concluded.[7]

Claim club advocates were probably the chief critics of nonresident speculators. Although the law allowed claimants to preempt no more than a quarter section of the public domain, early residents in Iowa invariably tried to monopolize two and three times this amount and force later arrivals to pay them a premium. A pioneer Des Moines resident, H. B. Turrill, recalled how in the spring of 1848, with the first land sales scheduled for the fall of the year, residents banded together to protect their illegal claims in the fertile Des Moines River Valley. The lands, Turrill asserted, "were worth from two to twelve dollars an acre, even at that time, and the holders of them, could they obtain a good title at reasonable rates, were to be esteemed fortunate." By "reasonable rates," he added, the claimants meant "no more than the lowest government price."[8] Understandably, these people were highly incensed at the prospect of nonresident speculators forcing them at the upcoming public auction to raise their bids and thereby lose a handsome profit. The claim club was the answer. Although these claims were illegal and often involved land other than settlers' homesteads, the club members customarily "resolved," as did the association in Des Moines, "that we will in all cases discountenance the speculator, or other person, who shall thus attempt any innovation upon the homes of the rightful settlers."[9] Thus, the nonresident speculator became the scapegoat—a role he has occupied ever since.

Derogatory comment concerning speculators can be matched with a fair amount of charitable utterances from those recognizing the social services of large investors to the frontier community. As moneylenders, they "assisted many a good man to secure

[6] Burlington *Hawkeye and Iowa Patriot,* Mar. 11, 1841; cf. *ibid.,* Oct. 5, 1839. For the opposing viewpoint, see the Democratic-controlled Burlington *Wisconsin Territorial Gazette and Burlington Advertiser,* Oct. 5, 1837.

[7] Fairfield *Weekly Ledger,* June 24, 1859.

[8] H. B. Turrill, *Historical Reminiscences of the City of Des Moines* (Des Moines, 1857), 25–26.

[9] For the resolutions and charter membership list of the Des Moines claim club, see *ibid.,* 27–29. Every subsequent county history which referred to claim clubs justified them on the same grounds. For a typical example, see James C. Dinwiddie, *History of Iowa County, Iowa and Its People* (2 vols.; Chicago, 1915), I, 73–74.

a home," declared an early county historian.[10] True, a western editor added, the settler "may be compelled to pay 50 and possibly 100 per cent for his loan for one year; but even at the latter sum his land will cost him but $2.50 an acre, which he probably deems worth $5 to $10."[11] Through their extensive advertising, observed another editor, speculators also "accomplish some good by being the means frequently of causing portions of our country thinly inhabited to become thickly populated." A fourth writer advised prospective settlers desiring better quality land to buy from speculators rather than the national government because the professionals knew how to select good land.[12] And a fifth boastfully reported the news that "several of our wealthiest Eastern capitalists passed through Chicago during the past month for Iowa, Minnesota, and Nebraska, with the intention of investment."[13] After the crash of 1857 the same editor valiantly tried to encourage nonresident investments. "While investments in Eastern securities have terminated in bankruptcy . . . our real estate has not diminished one dollar in its value or purchasable price," he asserted. "The productiveness of our soil has never been exaggerated. A ficticious value has never been placed upon it; and we venture the remark that the safest investments that have ever been made in the United States were made in Western lands."[14]

The variety of opinion expressed in the above paragraphs

---

[10] Lewis Publishing Co., *Biographical and Historical Record of Clarke County, Iowa* . . . (Chicago, 1886), 231. Other local historians shared this view. See the accounts of John Weare in American Biographical Publishing Co., *The United States Biographical Dictionary and Portrait Gallery of Eminent and Self-Made Men, Iowa Volume* (Chicago, 1878), 55–56, and Horatio W. Sanford in Western Historical Co., *History of Dubuque County, Iowa* . . . (Chicago, 1880), 875.

[11] Peoria (Illinois) *Register,* as cited in Burlington *Iowa Territorial Gazette and Burlington Advertiser,* Sept. 7, 1839. Adequate credit was actually available at the sales at from 25 to 50 per cent. See "Address of Edwin Manning, of Keosauqua," *Semi-Centennial of Iowa: A Record of the Commemoration of the Fiftieth Anniversary of the Settlement of Iowa, Held at Burlington, June 1, 1883* (Burlington, 1883), 53–54.

[12] Davenport *Gazette,* Oct. 24, 1844; Arthur Cunynghame, *A Glimpse at the Great Western Republic* (London, 1851), 100. Of John Weare, Cedar Rapids land agent, it was said that "he used to take immigrants up and down the Cedar Valley and out into the open prairie; select land and make entries for them and give them liberal time in which to make payments. . . . These settlers were almost invariably persons of very moderate means. . . ." (*U.S. Biographical Dictionary,* 55–56). Many buyers also preferred to pay a premium to speculators for choice lands rather than trek over unfamiliar country and make their own selections of unentered land. See L. F. Andrews, *Pioneers of Polk County, Iowa, and Reminiscences of Early Days* . . . (2 vols.; Des Moines, 1908), I, 396.

[13] *Real Estate News Letter* as cited in Des Moines *Iowa Weekly Citizen,* June 24, 1857. "We want more monied capitalists here," said the editor of *The North-Western Rev.* (I [July, 1957], 4).

[14] Des Moines *Iowa Weekly Citizen,* Oct. 14, 1857.

simply illustrates the fact that western communities split in
their attitude toward nonresident speculators. Bankers, lawyers,
and businessmen in general realized that local capital was inadequate to meet the needs of a burgeoning economy; eastern capital
must be courted. Settlers groups, on the other hand, contained
many who, rightly or wrongly, were critical. Apparently the
western attitude toward large investors was one of ambivalence.

II

UNLIKE the picture painted by claim club speculators and politi-
cians, the evidence suggests that in the Middle West as in the
eastern states earlier, nonresident investors and local residents
usually enjoyed rather cordial relations.[15] Common sense indeed
would indicate as much. As businessmen, capitalists were careful
to curry the good will of their prospective customers. Rare was
the moneylender who would rouse the ire of residents by bidding
on their claims at the public sales. At one of the first auctions in
the state, in Burlington in December of 1838, the local editor
reported that speculators "did not attempt to bid against the
settlers and the latter have thus been permitted to enter a half
section of the best land in the United States at $1.25 per acre."[16]
Similarly, as a speculator reported: "I have been here about two
weeks but have not been able to Secure a Single acre of . . . land
nor has any one Else obtained any except Settlers. . . . Big bidders" such as himself, he went on to explain, bid only on land
"not claimed by Settlers." Necessarily, therefore, competition was
fierce and few large investors obtained as much land as they
desired.[17]

At the sale of about 208,000 acres of the Delaware Trust
Lands at Fort Leavenworth, Kansas, the previous year, speculators likewise had deferred to the settlers. "Some four to five
thousand Squatter Sovereigns were in attendance besides a large
number of speculators," reported a nonresident investor on the

---

[15] This point is made about Colonial Connecticut in Charles S. Grant,
"Land Speculation and the Settlement of Kent, 1738–1760," *New Eng. Quart.,*
XXVIII (Mar., 1955), 52. Midwestern scholars who have argued similarly are
Paul W. Gates, *The Farmer's Age: Agriculture, 1815–1860* (New York, 1960),
72; and Mary E. Young, *Redskins, Ruffleshirts, and Rednecks: Indian Allotments in Alabama and Mississippi* (Norman, 1961), chap. viii, *passim.*
[16] Burlington *Iowa Territorial Gazette and Burlington Advertiser,* Dec. 1,
1838. Throughout the sales of 1838 and 1839 the editor continued to report
that there was no bidding against settlers (*ibid.,* Nov. 17 and 24, 1838, Oct. 26,
1839, Mar. 14 and Apr. 4, 1840). See also a clipping from the Peoria (Illinois)
Register in *ibid.,* Sept. 7, 1839.
[17] N. Boardman to N. Gordon, May 9, 1857, Nathaniel Gordon Papers,
Manuscript Division, Baker Library, Boston (italics mine).

scene. No preemption right was allowed on the lands and squatters received no legal recognition or protection. "But so far," the speculator continued, "their rights have been acknowledged and respected by speculators and they have without a single exception got their claims at the appraisement which on the lands yet sold was about $1.50 an acre. Up to the present time about 55,000 acres have been sold and of this about five-sixths were taken by actual settlers. The other sixth, which was vacant and open for bidding, sold at an average of about $3.50 per acre."[18] In many of the public auctions in Iowa, particularly in the early years, speculators seldom could have placed bids on claimed tracts even if they had desired to do so, for the public sales were often rigged in advance. A claim club officer left this description of the Dubuque sale of August 3, 1840:

> We had made all arrangements for the sale. The bidder and assistant bidder had furnished themselves with large plats of the two townships to be sold, with each claimant's name plainly written on the subdivision which he wished to purchase. When the time came for the sale to begin, the crier stepped out on the platform, and inviting the bidder and assistant to take places on the platform beside him, took hold of one side of the plat, and began at section No. 1, and called out each eighty-acre subdivision as rapidly as he could speak. When he came to a tract with a name written on it, he would strike his hammer down, and give the name to the clerk. . . . The two townships were offered in less than thirty minutes. During this time the claimants stood in a compact semicircle in front of the platform in breathless silence, not a sound being heard except the crier's voice. [19]

Settlers were equally as dependent on the willingness of businessmen to extend loans. Cyrus Sanders, assistant bidder of the claim association of Johnson County, recounted that many local settlers, although lacking funds, started for the Dubuque auction of 1840 "expectant of meeting capitalists at the sale, of whom they could borrow the money." John E. Stoner of Marengo in Iowa County was one such settler. As Stoner recounted in the third person some years later, he "went to Iowa City, when the land office was located there, to enter some land, without a cent

[18] Andrew J. Sterrett to David Brice Innis Sterrett, Nov. 25, 1856, Andrew Jackson Sterrett Papers, Manuscript Division, Minnesota Historical Society, St. Paul.

[19] Benjamin F. Shambaugh (ed.), *Constitution and Records of the Claim Association of Johnson County, Iowa* (Iowa City, 1894), xvii. At some public auctions the sheriff of the county served as the agent of the settlers, allowing no bids whatsoever on claims of settlers. See speech of Senator Henry Hubbard of New Hampshire in *Congressional Globe*, 26th Cong., 2nd Sess., IX, Appendix, 39.

of money, and asked in the office if there was a man there who
would enter forty acres of land for him and give him a bond for
a deed and one year in which to pay for it, when a Dr. Bower
said he would enter eighty acres and take his [Stoner's] note,
which was done. These gentlemen had never met before, and
never but once afterward."[20] Such acts of faith on the part of residents whose homesteads were likely at stake, presupposed a rather
solid working relationship between lender and debtor. As one
participant later declared: "It seemed opportune for both settler
and capitalist to meet and arrange terms so pleasantly. It demonstrated that capital and labor were friendly elements, and could
work together."[21]

That speculators eagerly foreclosed time-entry contracts
when debtors fell delinquent, as agrarians long maintained, is
likewise a myth.[22] Eastern moneylender James S. Easley, whose
extensive operations in Iowa have already been described, urged
his agents to use every "gentle means" possible to collect from
delinquent debtors during the depression of the late 1850's.
Under the circumstances, it was not in the interest of eastern
capitalists such as Easley to dispossess defaultors.[23] This would
force them not only to assume tax burdens at a time when money
was tight but to pay the realtors' location fees immediately—fees
ordinarily deducted from the proceeds when borrowers paid up
their loans. Understandably speculators preferred to keep the
people on the land, which would be constantly improved, and
extend the time of the loan. Usually, however, they insisted on
the payment in advance of another year's interest. Even if this
was not forthcoming, entries were normally not declared forfeited
until several years had elapsed and buyers were given a final
opportunity to redeem their land.

A final bit of evidence which indicates a lack of animosity
between land speculators and local residents is seen in the large
number of prominent Iowa speculators who won elective office in
local, state, or national government at some time during the ante
bellum period. Presumably, if Hawkeye citizens had felt a deep
antipathy to speculators they could easily have registered their

---

[20] Shambaugh, *Constitution and Records*, xvii; Union Historical Co.,
History of Iowa County, Iowa (Des Moines, 1881), 602. Richard F. Barrett of
Springfield, Ill., offered to supply as much long-term credit as buyers desired
at the Burlington land sale in November, 1838 (Burlington *Iowa Territorial
Gazette and Burlington Advertiser*, Sept. 15, 1838).

[21] "Address of Edwin Manning, of Keosauqua," *Semi-Centennial of Iowa*,
53.

[22] For examples of such accusations by Populist editors see Allan G.
Bogue, *Money at Interest: The Farm Mortgage on the Middle Border* (Ithaca,
1955), 264.

[23] Professor Bogue demonstrated this convincingly in *ibid.*, 26. A more
detailed discussion is in his "Farm Land Credit in Kansas and Nebraska, 1854–
1900" (Ph.D. dissertation, Cornell University, 1951), 77–79.

displeasure at the polls. For large land dealers and investors were perennial candidates for elective public office in frontier Iowa. A comparison of lists of large speculators with elected public officials, however, reveals a considerable overlapping. Of the 648 Iowans who entered over 1,000 acres of Congress land in Royce Cession 262 (see Chapter 5), 33 served in the Iowa senate from 1838 through 1860 (19 for two and three terms), while 38 secured seats in the lower house (15 for two to five terms). Two, James W. Grimes and Samuel J. Kirkwood, won the governorship and 10 held state-wide offices including treasurer, auditor, supreme court justice, superintendent of public instruction, and superintendent of the state penitentiary. On the national scene, James W. Grimes, George A. Jones, and Samuel J. Kirkwood represented the Hawkeye State in the U.S. Senate, and John P. Cook, Lincoln Clark, Henry Clay Dean, Bernhart Henn, and William Thompson won election to the House of Representatives. J. B. Grinnell began his stint in Congress in 1863.

Investigation at the local level was perforce more superficial, but the results are equally as instructive. Sixteen of the large speculators were elected mayors of major cities: Ira Cook, Barlow Granger, William H. Leas, and Robert L. Tidrick of Des Moines; George Gillaspy of Ottumwa; John A. Graham, William Patterson, and Hugh W. Sample of Keokuk; Jacob Record and Moses J. Morsman of Iowa City; John Hodgdon and David S. Wilson of Dubuque; George B. Sargent of Davenport; George D. Temple of Burlington; Lewis L. Estes of Webster City; and William Williams of Fort Dodge. Eleven were town councilmen, 30 served as county prosecutors, judges or township justices of the peace, and 38 held lesser offices such as county supervisor, surveyor, treasurer, recorder, district court clerk, school fund commissioner, and sheriff. At the barest minimum, therefore, over 125 large speculators, or nearly one in five, won elective public office in the ante bellum years, and a careful survey at the local level would likely double the figures. More significant, 62 of these speculator-officeholders were engaged professionally at the time as realtor-bankers, realtor-lawyers, and land agents, occupations supposedly most inimical to the public interest. Quite obviously Iowa's largest speculators experienced as little public hostility in the turbulent arena of frontier politics as they had at the government land auctions.

III

LEAVING ultimate moral judgments aside, it might be well to reassess the role of the frontier land speculator. The bill of indictment levied against him charges that he created "speculator's deserts" by forcing immigrants to look elsewhere for land they could afford; he "played hob with the finances of local governments by his refusal to pay taxes"; and, most important of all, he caused a rapid increase in the un-American institution of tenancy.[24] Speculators' deserts, it is argued, were the result of the deliberate policy of speculators to demand exorbitant prices for their land, or more simply to withhold it from market until population pressure in the vicinity brought the inevitable price rise. Settlers, unable to pay this "unearned increment" to the middlemen, looked farther afield for cheaper land they could afford, thus dispersing themselves over wider areas. The end result was to raise the cost of road construction and maintenance, necessitate the creation of many small and inefficient units of local government, and require extra facilities for schools, churches, libraries, grange halls, and other social institutions. The refusal of nonresident speculators to meet their tax obligations further increased the financial burden on local citizens, whose property was already all too easily assessed. Facing ruinous taxes and usurious interest rates on their mortgages, the farmers were virtually forced to deplete their soil, which led to erosion and lower land values. A year or two of bad crops and the independent yeoman slipped into the tenant class. Such are the major complaints against speculators, although the list is by no means exhausted.[25]

On closer scrutiny, most of these "social costs" cannot legitimately be assessed against speculators. The charge that speculators retarded settlement rests on the unproven assumption that they demanded excessive prices for their land or held it off the market for a number of years. Since most large investors and particularly the major operators in Iowa were professional

---

[24] These charges are conveniently summarized in Paul W. Gates, "Land Policy and Tenancy in the Prairie States," *J. Econ. Hist.*, I (May, 1941), 70; and *Farmer's Age*, 66, 84–87, 199. See also citations in Chapter 1, n. 1. Contemporaries made some of the same points. "Remarks of Suel Foster, of Muscatine," *Semi-Centennial of Iowa*, 41; Burlington *Iowa Territorial Gazette and Burlington Advertiser*, Aug. 8, 1839; Bloomington (later Muscatine) *Herald*, Oct. 23, 1846; *The North-Western Rev.*, I (Mar., 1858), 4; Des Moines *Iowa Weekly Citizen*, Jan. 12, 1859; Fort Dodge *Sentinel*, Apr. 14, 1860; Fairfield *Ledger*, Dec. 10, 1851 and Dec. 23, 1859; *Congressional Globe*, 24th Cong., 2nd Sess., IV, Appendix, 167–69, and 25th Cong., 1st Sess., VI, Appendix, 135–36.

[25] The frequent squabbles over the location of county seats, state capital sites, universities, and other social welfare institutions are often blamed on the machinations of speculators. Similarly, they are charged with raping Indians of their land, undermining the effectiveness of national land grants to the states, stunting the development of a democratic land system, and in general corrupting politics on every level of government. These charges are not considered here because they can neither be proved nor disproved, except by the most superficial sort of impressionistic evidence.

realtors, they could hardly have engaged in such practices and remained in business. Necessarily, they pressed sales at reasonable rates. Profits lay in increasing the volume of sales, thereby gaining a rapid turnover of their funds, not in withholding land from market. Senator John P. King of Georgia addressed himself specifically to this point in a congressional speech at the time. "It was a great mistake," King asserted, "to suppose that large land companies or speculators were in the habit of holding up their lands at exorbitant and forbidding prices. . . ." Operating frequently on borrowed capital and competing with low-priced government land, they generally offered their land at only a "moderate advance of the original cost." Nevertheless, he concluded, by "operating upon a large scale, a small advance affords a handsome profit. . . ."[26]

The statistics for central Iowa confirm King's observation. Of the nearly half-million acres of speculator-entered lands in the nine counties for which resales were analyzed in this book (see Chapter 8), the timespan between the dates of entry at the land offices and sale averaged only 31.6 months per acre. And the average price of the 259,821 of these acres sold in the period from 1844 through 1860 was only $3.00 per acre. By way of contrast, the average price of the 1,944,062 acres of nonspeculator-entered lands sold during these same years in the nine counties was $5.27 per acre. Deducting 20 per cent to allow for the value of possible improvements on this land, the average sale price figure is $4.21 per acre, or $1.21 higher than the average price received by speculators.[27] In short, the large speculators marketed their land at prices from 20 to 40 per cent *under* prevailing rates in the vicinity. In view of the risks involved, these prices were hardly exorbitant. For the speculator in making his land entries always had to consider the law of averages which restricted the advance of the frontier to a comparatively small area each year. If he chose unwisely and settlement temporarily bypassed the region of his holdings, he could not sell back to the government or hedge on his mistakes. The periodic panics of the nineteenth century, so unpredictable in their occurrences, also spelled disaster for any investor with inadequate resources.

---

[26] *Congressional Globe,* 24th Cong., 2nd Sess., IV, Appendix, 175.

[27] The 20 per cent figure is a generous approximation of the ratio between bare land values and farm land improvement values reported by the Census of 1900—the first to report this statistic. To be exact, improvements accounted for 16.1 per cent of Iowa's total farm real estate values in 1900. For the census data on Iowa and the application of this technique by recognized land appraisal experts, see Raleigh Barlowe and Conrad H. Hammar, "Valuation of Lands in Southcentral Iowa: 1839–1843, Royce Cession Area 262," presented before the Indian Claims Commission, Doc. 153, *Sac and Fox and Iowa Tribes v. The United States of America* (1965), 162–63.

Rather than retard settlement, speculators likely promoted it. As wholesale land buyers, they were, as one Iowa historian aptly stated, "the most potent of all agencies" in opening the West to settlement.[28] Their nationwide advertising and their reputation for offering land of better than average quality attracted many buyers to the Hawkeye State. Most important of all, they provided the credit that so many smaller investors and settlers needed to acquire real estate. Although interest rates of 3 to 5 per cent per month seem excessive by today's standards, they were not unreasonable by contemporary frontier norms. "Let it not be supposed," wrote a local editor in 1857, "that men are necessarily reckless or imprudent who engage to pay such an interest; the experience of the past five or six years has fully proved the contrary, beyond a doubt. The proof goes farther and shows that those men, as a general thing, who have paid such an interest, have made twice or three times as much as the lender." While grocers and drygoods merchants could not safely pay such rates, the editor continued, real estate men—"those who buy and sell city lots and other lands, and obtain an increase in value, from fifty to two hundred per cent"—had been doing this successfully in Iowa for more than a decade.[29] However, at least one moneylender confessed near the end of his life in 1890 (quite possibly under the impact of populist rhetoric) that "when I charged the current high rates I felt like a hog, and I guess that many who paid them thought I was one."[30]

Whether nonresident speculators carried their share of the tax burden is a question that must await a careful study of the voluminous local tax lists preserved in many Iowa courthouses.[31]

---

[28] George F. Parker, *Iowa Pioneer Foundations* (2 vols.; Iowa City, 1940), I, 123–24. An example is the advertisement of Ward Lamson in the Fairfield *Ledger,* Jan. 29, 1852, offering land in Davis County at a public auction to be held in Fairfield.

[29] *The North-Western Rev.,* I (June, 1857), 29–30. See also *ibid.* (July, 1857), 4. Although the interest rate was 25 per cent or more, claimed a county historian, "often within a single week, 50 to 100 per cent could be made by the purchase and sale of a town lot or quarter section of land." (Western Historical Co., *History of Appanoose County, Iowa* . . . [Chicago, 1878], 368). A Burlington preemptor, for example, in 1841 borrowed money at more than 5 per cent per month to enter his quarter section and within two months sold the land for $10.00 an acre. The new buyer, incidentally, earned enough from his first wheat crop to pay the entire cost of the land as well as its tillage, and pocket $4.44 per acre besides. See A. Coryell Edmunds (ed.), *The Western Life-Boat* (Des Moines, 1873), 93.

[30] The investor was Ward Lamson of Fairfield (Lake City Publishing Co., *Portrait and Biographical Album of Jefferson and Van Buren Counties, Iowa* . . . [Chicago, 1890], 655–57).

[31] Such records, which often date from the earliest years of settlement, must be analyzed soon, for the pressure of space is forcing one country after another to relegate all but its most recent lists to the local dump. At least through the 1860's, the records are conveniently arranged for historical inquiry since the assessed property of residents and nonresidents in each township is listed

A preliminary analysis of the records of one central Iowa county (Poweshiek) for the period 1853–58 indicates the plethora of available data on the subject and the direction in which future inquiry might lead. There are at least two facets to the question of speculators and taxes, that of assessment and delinquency. Were the lands of nonresidents, unimproved for the most part, assessed equitably in relation to the farms of residents, as federal law demanded,[32] or did frontiersmen abuse the tax power? And, secondly, did nonresidents enjoy a higher delinquency rate than local citizens?

Tables 9.1 and 9.2 present the results of the Poweshiek County study. Table 9.1 shows the total rural land assessed for taxes, the total valuation, and the average valuation per acre, computed separately for residents and nonresidents. Table 9.2 indicates the total tax assessment and the delinquency rate of the two groups. It is readily apparent from the first table that nonresidents' lands were, at least in the 1850's, assessed at substantially lower rates than residents'. In 1853, the average valuation on the 35,383 acres of resident lands stood at $3.52 per acre compared to $3.17 per acre, or 9.9 per cent less, on the 7,573 acres assessed to absentee owners. In succeeding years, the disparity increased as residents continued to improve their holdings. By 1858, the average valuation of the 109,611 acres owned by residents had climbed to $8.40 per acre compared to only $5.27 per acre on the 271,817 acres of nonresidents—a differential of 37.3 per cent. Farm improvements likely accounted for no more than 20 per cent of this difference.[33] At least in the 1850's, therefore, Poweshiek County residents likely bore more than an adequate share of the real estate tax load while absentee landowners found their assessments equitable to a fault.

This seeming charity toward speculators on the part of the local assessors and citizenry conflicts with a rather common belief that frontiersmen, federal law to the contrary, customarily overassessed the lands of easterners.[34] Perhaps the Poweshiek assessors were unaware of the disparity, or possibly they stood in a realtor-client relationship with the nonresidents, exchanging favors for commissions. The tax assessment data itself, however, suggest a

---

separately. In addition, a notation is appended to each entry indicating the date of payment.

[32] U.S. *Statutes at Large,* II, 226; Benjamin H. Hibbard, *A History of the Public Land Policies* (New York, 1924), 84–85.

[33] See n. 27.

[34] See, for example, Gates, *Farmer's Age,* 85–86, and *The Pine Lands of Cornell University; A Study in Land Policy and Absentee Ownership* (Ithaca, 1943), 143–44; Margaret Bogue, *Patterns from the Sod; Land Use and Tenure in the Grand Prairie, 1850–1900* ("Collections of the Illinois State Historical Library," Vol. XXXIV, Land Series, Vol. I [Springfield, 1959]), 41.

TABLE 9.1
LAND VALUATIONS OF RESIDENTS AND NONRESIDENTS, POWESHIEK COUNTY, 1853–58*

Year	Residents			Nonresidents			
	Total acres assessed†	Total valuation	Avg. valuation per acre	Total acres assessed†	Total valuation	Avg. valuation per acre	Per cent differential
1853	35,383	$ 124,438	$3.52	7,573	$ 24,042	$3.17	− 9.9
1854	61,381	251,908	4.10	112,931	345,839	3.06	−25.4
1855	90,752	447,543	4.93	233,126	768,709	3.30	−33.1
1858	109,611	920,313	8.40	271,817	1,433,359	5.27	−37.3
Totals......	297,127	$1,744,202		625,447	$2,571,949		
Weighted averages...			$5.87			$4.11	−30.0

*Tables 9.1 and 9.2 were compiled from township tax lists located in the office of the Poweshiek County Recorder, Montezuma, Iowa. No tax lists are extant for the years 1856–57.
†Excludes town lots.

TABLE 9.2
TAX DELINQUENCY RATES OF RESIDENTS AND NONRESIDENTS, POWESHIEK COUNTY, 1853–58

Year	Residents			Nonresidents		
	Taxes assessed*	Taxes delinquent	Per cent delinquent	Taxes assessed	Taxes delinquent	Per cent delinquent
1853	$ 2,225.71	$ 159.83	7.2	$ 226.45	$ 72.11	31.8
1854	3,294.28	465.67	14.1	2,312.68	888.64	38.4
1855	4,872.32	233.97	4.8	3,895.87	245.21	6.3
1858	13,892.35	2,588.69	18.6	12,070.08	1,008.53	8.4
Totals..........	$24,284.66	$3,448.16		$18,505.08	$2,214.49	
Weighted averages..			14.2			12.0

*Approximately one-fourth of total tax of residents is personalty assessment.

more plausible motive. As Table 9.2 shows, nonresidents in the 1850's carried a substantial part of the total tax bill in Poweshiek County. In 1858, in fact, they were assessed $12,070.08 of a total levy of $25,962.43 or 46 per cent. For all four years, the nonresidents' taxes totaled $18,505.08, or 43.2 per cent of the full amount. Limiting the figures to the levy on land alone, the speculators actually shouldered fully one-half of the total tax burden, for one-fourth of the residents' assessments consisted of personalty and poll taxes, obligations that nonresidents did not face except in their own home districts. Thus, absentee land-owners contributed heavily to the cost of operating the county government and schools of Poweshiek.

The low delinquency rate of the nonresidents also engen-dered harmony. Apart from the first two years, 1853–54, when the county treasurer marked a third of the nonresidents' taxes as delinquent (see Table 9.2), the absentee owners met their assessments regularly. In 1855, their delinquency rate dropped sharply to 6.3 per cent and likely remained nominal thereafter. By 1858, in fact, when the nation faced the crippling financial blows of the depression touched off the previous year in New York, Poweshiek residents had a delinquency rate of 18.6 per cent compared with only 8.4 per cent for nonresidents. Speculators, in short, saved the county from fiscal disaster in 1858. Overall, for the four years studied, residents had a delinquency rate of 14.2 per cent, nonresidents of 12.0 per cent. Absentee landowners in Poweshiek County cannot be charged with gross negligence in paying their taxes. This finding in Poweshiek, if confirmed in other counties, might indicate that the frequent complaint in the western press concerning the supposed refusal of speculators to pay their taxes was largely rhetorical.[35]

The few surviving business papers and correspondence of nonresident investors in Iowa confirm the Poweshiek findings. The financial records of James Easley and the incoming corre-spondence of Cook, Sargent & Downey of Iowa City both indicate that speculators generally met their tax obligations—particularly after the mid-1850's when county governments tightened their lax collection policies. As soon as he began extensive operations in 1853, Easley instructed his agents to be very careful to pay his

---

[35] Typical statements were these: "Men of small means, holding a home-stead or a small amount of property for their immediate use, have generally paid their taxes, city and county. The delinquency is on the part of heavy land holders, many of whom are reputed to be wealthy" (Des Moines *Iowa Weekly Citizen,* Jan. 12, 1859). "Non-residents and speculators within the limits of the State, have regarded with indifference the claims of the State upon them; suffering their property to remain delinquent year after year. . . ." (Fort Dodge *Sentinel,* Apr. 14, 1860). See also Fairfield *Ledger,* Dec. 10, 1851, and Dec. 23, 1859.

taxes.[36] When he nonetheless received delinquency notices in the next few years, he tightened his control by requiring agents to forward all tax receipts and posting his own books. Only during the Civil War period did Easley fail to meet his tax obligations in the West and this was of necessity, not choice. But local county treasurers did not allow war to thwart their tax collections. They simply relied on the ubiquitous tax sale and obtained the tax levies from other speculators who specialized in tax buying. Whether one speculator or another paid the taxes, therefore, the government obtained its revenue.[37]

The actual proportion of the total tax levy in Iowa contributed by speculators in any given year is impossible to ascertain. One can, however, reach a fair approximation by multiplying the average per acre tax rate by the estimated acreage in the state held by speculators. Some manipulation of aggregate data is required, especially to determine the tax rate, but the effort appears worthwhile for it allows the speculator to be seen in his important role as taxpayer. The estimated acreage held by speculators, as explained in detail in Chapter 2, is the sum of the total acreage assessed for taxes minus the total acreage in farms (both improved and unimproved). The average tax rate figure is obtained by: (1) dividing the total tax by the total valuation to determine the millage rate per dollar of valuation; (2) multiplying the millage rate by the total value of land to determine the total tax on land, exclusive of town lots and personalty; and (3) dividing the total tax on land by the total acreage assessed for taxes. The quotient is the average tax rate per acre.

Applying this technique to the data for the year 1862, a year in which sufficient information is available, we find that the estimated acreage in Iowa in the hands of speculators was 19.4 million (28.3 million acres assessed for taxes minus 8.9 million in farms). The total tax, $1.7 million (1861 figures), divided by the total valuation, $146.3 million (1861 figures), gives a millage rate of .1162 per thousand. This figure multiplied by the total

---

[36] Easley to Silas A. Noble, July 5, 1853; Easley & Willingham to Elias B. Stiles, Aug. 6, 1853, James S. Easley Papers, Alderman Library, University of Virginia, Charlottesville.

[37] The subject of tax buying is virtually unexplored by historians yet it has always been an important aspect of both land speculation and the tax system. As early as 1850, LeGrand Byington, an Iowa City realtor, was bargaining for tax titles at local treasurers' sales. William J. Barney, a Dubuque land agent, engaged in the same practice. So did eastern speculators John A. Roebling, Omer Tousey, and James Easley (after 1867). The few studies that include data on speculation in tax titles are: Theodore L. Carlson, *The Illinois Military Tract; A Study of Land Occupation, Utilization and Tenure* ("Illinois Studies in the Social Sciences," Vol. XXXII, No. 2 [Urbana, 1951]), 43–49; Allan Bogue, *Money at Interest*, 58; Margaret Bogue, *Patterns from the Sod*, 223–52, esp. 236–37; Gates, *Pine Lands of Cornell University*, 164–65.

value of land, $111.6 million, equals $1.3 million, the total
tax on land. Dividing this figure by the total acreage assessed for
taxes, $28.3 million, gives a tax rate per acre of 4.6 cents. The
tax rate of 4.6 cents, multiplied by the estimated 19.4 million
acres held by speculators, equals $0.9 million, or 52 per cent of
the total tax bill for all levels of government in the state.[38] This
figure also correlates with the Poweshiek County findings. In
brief, speculators as taxpayers contributed substantially to the
material progress of the Hawkeye State. They were more than
mere leeches fattening on the blood and sweat of honest agriculturalists.

Before speculators can be charged with fostering tenancy,
the extent to which they rented land or forced defaulted mortgagees into tenancy must be demonstrated. Again the experience
of James Easley, is illuminating. Over the 27 years of his career in the western land business, the Virginian rented but
a few quarter sections—mostly lead-bearing land in Missouri.
As mentioned in Chapter 7, Easley first considered renting his
raw land in Iowa in the mid-1870's, when two farmers requested
permission to harvest the grass in return for paying taxes. Because there were no strings attached, Easley agreed. But a third
farmer, who offered to fence one of Easley's vacant tracts in
exchange for its use as a pasture, met with an outright refusal,
despite the fact that the land had returned no revenue to offset
nearly twenty years of tax levies. In no way would he jeopardize
his freedom to sell at any time, Easley explained to the disappointed rancher.[39] The same rationale governed the Virginian's
mortgage policy and ruled out the possibility of tenancy when
his mortgagees defaulted on their notes. Rather than permit
farmer-owners to become his tenants, Easley granted extentions
of time and accepted token payments until the crises might pass.
Only after owners allowed three to five years to elapse without

---

[38] The figures on assessment and farm acreages are in Appendix IX; those
on valuation and taxes are in Iowa *House Journal*, 1862, 31–32, and *Report
of the Auditor of State*, 1863, 28. Iowa was not the only western state where
speculators bore the tax burden. Carlson, *Illinois Military Tract*, 43, notes
that the congressional appropriation of three million acres of land in western
Illinois for military bounties provided tax revenue to the state several years
earlier than if it had remained in the public domain. The taxes, borne largely
by nonresident speculators who had purchased the land from the veterans,
in fact provided over 90 per cent of the total state revenue from 1821 through
1832.

[39] Easley to B. P. Yelter, Mar. 20, 1875, James S. Easley Papers. See also
the citations in Chapter 7, n. 47. One agent advised Easley to send funds for
minor improvements (like "breaking" the prairie sod) on raw land that he
held for sale, for "a small piece of Breaking say ten acres is a great induce-
ment to a settler to buy" (Lafayette McCurdy to Easley & Willingham, Apr.
26, 1860. Easley ignored the suggestion. In any case, however, such improvements as these, financed by the speculators themselves, led to sales not tenancy.

payment did Easley foreclose, and then the property was resold to another buyer as soon as possible. Thus, owners did not become tenants, at least on Easley's land.

Although James Easley may have been atypical, there is little evidence that other large speculators in Congress land rented their property. No reference is found to tenants in any of their surviving business papers nor in the rather extensive incoming correspondence of Cook, Sargent & Downey of Iowa City.[40] This is not to assert, of course, that no large investors rented. By the 1870's and 1880's, one can find numerous instances of absentee landlords, particularly in the western counties along the Missouri slope.[41] These landlords, however, were not the large speculators of the ante bellum period who figured so prominently in the disposal of the public domain in Iowa.

The leading realtors throughout the state, when they advertised in the local press, similarly did not offer along with their other functions to manage rental property for nonresidents. The nearest approximation—one of only two examples found—was the proposal to "rent and lease Houses, Lots, and Farms," made in 1857 by the Iowa Central Real Estate Agency of Des Moines in the advertising section of the first published history of the capital city.[42] For a land agency to undertake the management of rental property, however, does not prove that nonresident speculators fostered tenancy on the Iowa frontier, or even that such individuals were the major leaseholders.[43] Retired

---

[40] Relevant collections surveyed, in addition to the Gordon and Sterrett papers cited above, are the John A. Roebling Papers, Rutgers University Library, New Brunswick; the Jesse Williams Papers, the Barlow Granger Papers, and the James Callanan "Letter Book, 1858–63," Iowa State Department of History and Archives, Des Moines; and the Cook, Sargent & Downey Papers, State Historical Society of Iowa, Iowa City.

[41] The best and most recent analysis is in Allan G. Bogue, *From Prairie to Corn Belt: Farming on the Illinois and Iowa Prairies in the Nineteenth Century* (Chicago, 1963), 56–66.

[42] The owners were John G. Weeks and Samuel G. Stacy. See Turrill, *Historical Reminiscences*, 127. The only other real estate advertisement mentioning the rental of property that came to my attention, was that of James D. Templin, Iowa City attorney and land agent, in the Iowa City *Iowa Capitol Reporter*, Jan. 11, 1854.

[43] If there is a link between land speculation and tenancy, it has yet to be demonstrated precisely. Methodologically, historians are ready for such a step. The data needed are tenancy rates and estimates of the extent of speculation for each Iowa county from 1850 to 1880. The incidence of speculation can be measured, as explained in Chapter 2, by comparing farm acreage with rural land assessed for taxes. The federal census records first included tenancy data in 1880, but the manuscript population and agricultural schedules of 1850, 1860, and 1870 can also yield such information if one is willing to follow the technique recently perfected by Allan Bogue and Seddie Cogswell, Jr. See Bogue, *Prairie to Corn Belt*, 63–65, and Cogswell, "Tenure and Nativity as Factors in Iowa Agriculture, 1850–1870" (M.A. thesis, University of Iowa, 1966), 2–9, and the same author's unpublished essay, "Tenure and Nativity as Factors in Iowa Agriculture, 1880," 10–11.

farmers and widows frequently preferred renting rather than selling their farms. Prosperous farmers sometimes leased their excess acreage to neighbors. Mechanics, craftsmen, and local professional and businessmen often owned farms which they rented. So did farmers who entered government employ. Charles Mason of Burlington, for example, leased his farm while serving as a judge on the Iowa supreme court.[44]

Within the framework of the social and economic assumptions of their time, nonresident investors served a useful and often beneficial function. By extending credit, paying taxes, hiring realtors to locate, enter, and sell land, buying advertising space in local newspapers, and employing residents to patrol timber tracts in their areas, speculators created many jobs and funneled large amounts of capital into frontier Iowa at a time when it was desperately needed. By increasing the rate of public land sales, especially of land not immediately optimum for farming, speculators widened the tax base of frontier communities and assisted the federal treasury to convert its vast land resources into much-needed revenue. Despite some criticism by contemporaries and almost universal disparagement in subsequent historical literature, these entrepreneurs were as essential to the economic development of the West as were their clients, the frontier farmers.

Earlier approaches to the tenancy problem, largely unsatisfactory, are Merle Curti, *The Making of an American Community* (Stanford, 1959), 59–60, and Blanche H. Clark, *The Tennessee Yeomen, 1840–1860* (Nashville, 1942), xvii–xxii. The only previous attempt utilizing census data to correlate land speculation and tenancy is that of Paul W. Gates in the 1930's. See his "Land Policy and Tenancy," 77–82. Gates extracted figures on tenancy and "large farms" (over 1,000 acres) from the published federal census reports of 1880, 1890, and 1900 in 16 counties of western Iowa and concluded that tenancy rates and the number of large-scale farms increased in a direct ratio. The method is faulty, however, because it rests in the unproven assumption that large farms were the result of speculation in government land. In addition, the figures presented do not correlate directly. The number of large farms in the selected counties, and indeed in the state as a whole, fluctuated widely in the 30-year period, whereas the tenancy rate increased steadily. Between 1880 and 1890 the number of large farms in western Iowa increased sharply from 80 to 131, but by 1900 the total had dropped nearly as much, to 91. The tenancy rate, on the other hand, increased from 26 to 36 to 42 per cent for the three census years. Factors other than land speculation or the quantity of large farms obviously influenced the development of tenancy.

[44] Charles Mason to Edwin Mason, July 12, 1843, in Charles Mason Remey (ed.), "Life and Letters of Charles Mason: Chief Justice of Iowa 1804–1882," (12 vols.; Washington, 1939), II, 99; typescript "Copy C" used here is owned by the State Historical Society of Iowa, Iowa City. See also Bogue, *Prairie to Corn Belt*, 59.

APPENDICES

I
YEARS WHEN TOWNSHIPS OF CESSION 262 WERE
FIRST OFFERED FOR SALE

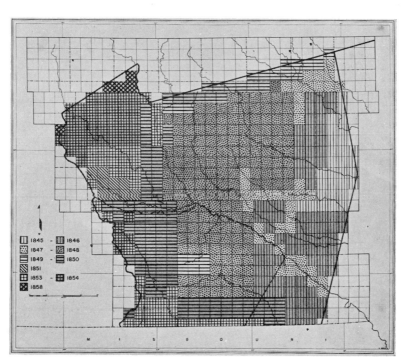

II
Dates of Establishment and of Organization
of Counties in Eastern and Central Iowa

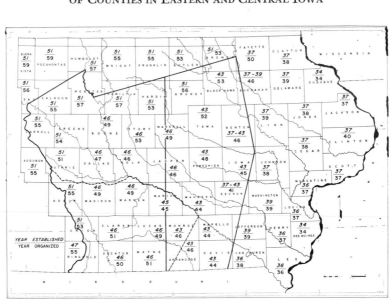

III
POPULATION TRENDS IN COUNTIES OF EASTERN AND
CENTRAL IOWA: 1846, 1847, 1850, 1854, 1860, 1870

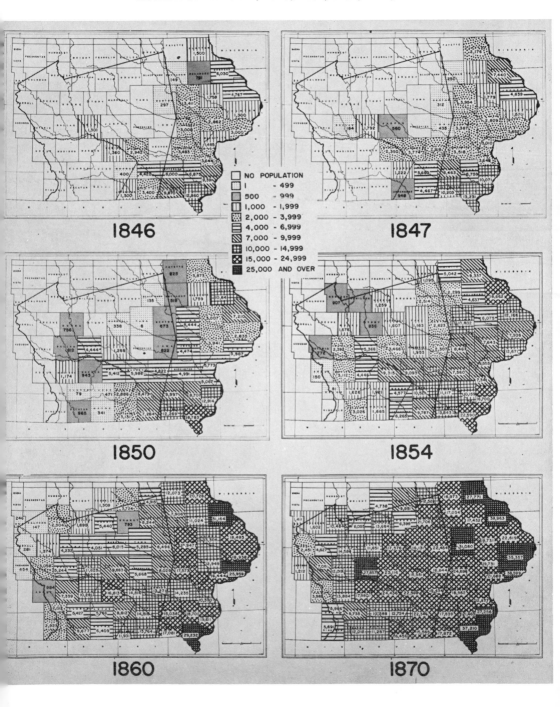

IV
Proportion of Original Entry Township Land Area
Sold in Eastern and Central Iowa, Biennially, 1846–60

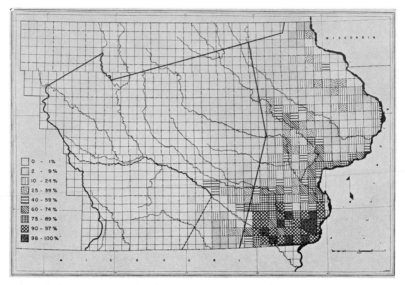

Fig. 1. Land area sold by 1846.

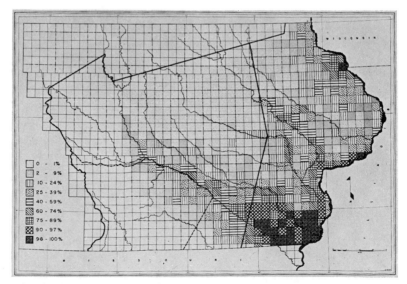

Fig. 2. Land area sold by 1848.

IV *(continued)*

PROPORTION OF ORIGINAL ENTRY TOWNSHIP LAND AREA SOLD IN EASTERN AND CENTRAL IOWA, BIENNIALLY, 1846–60

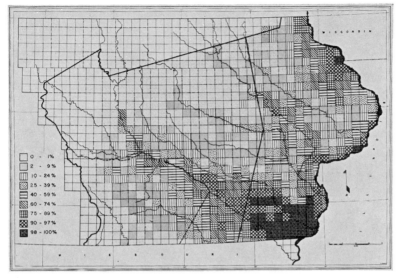

Fig. 3. Land area sold by 1850.

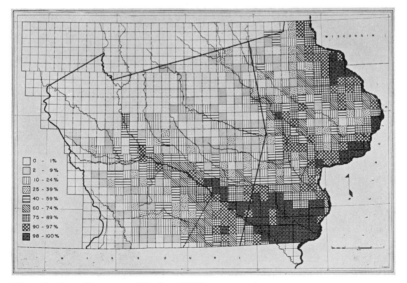

Fig. 4. Land area sold by 1852.

IV *(continued)*
Proportion of Original Entry Township Land Area
Sold in Eastern and Central Iowa, Biennially, 1846–60

Fig. 5. Land area sold by 1854.

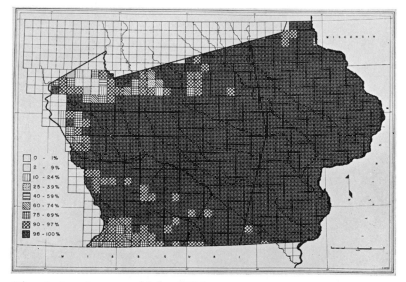

Fig. 6. Land area sold by 1856.

IV *(continued)*

PROPORTION OF ORIGINAL ENTRY TOWNSHIP LAND AREA
SOLD IN EASTERN AND CENTRAL IOWA, BIENNIALLY, 1846–60

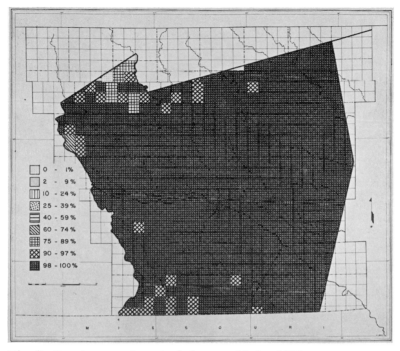

Fig. 7. Land area of central Iowa sold by 1858.

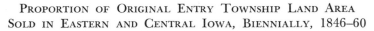

IV *(continued)*
PROPORTION OF ORIGINAL ENTRY TOWNSHIP LAND AREA
SOLD IN EASTERN AND CENTRAL IOWA, BIENNIALLY, 1846–60

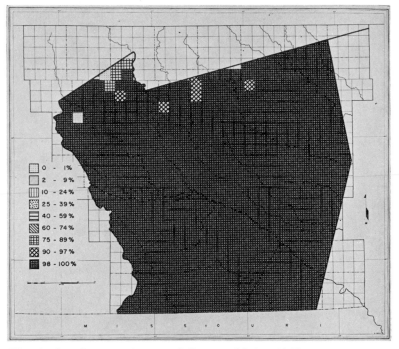

Fig. 8. Land area of central Iowa sold by 1860.

V
IOWA LAND AGENTS WHO WERE ORIGINAL ENTRANTS OF 1,000
ACRES OR MORE IN CENTRAL IOWA

Name	Business address	Original entry acres
Abell, Thomas B.	Marietta	3,715
Allen, Benjamin F.	Des Moines	35,308
Allen, William.	Davenport	1,760
Anderson, A. John	Chariton	1,970
Anson, Henry	Marietta	1,569
Arnold, Delos.	Marietta	3,237
Barclay, Henry	Mt. Pleasant	1,991
Barney, Wm. Joshua.	Dubuque	28,429
Bates, Curtis.	Iowa City	1,759
Berryhill, Charles H.	Iowa City	14,397
Bowen, Barzilla	Centerville	5,712
Braden, Joseph.	Chariton	1,681

V *(continued)*
Iowa Land Agents Who Were Original Entrants of 1,000 Acres or More in Central Iowa

Name	Business address	Original entry acres
Bruce, Cosmore G.	Fort Dodge	1,480
Byington, LeGrand	Iowa City	19,989
Carse, Henry	Fort Dodge	1,127
Casady, Phineas M.	Des Moines	6,381
Cassiday, John	Montezuma	1,125
Cochran, Addison	Council Bluffs	1,761
Connelly, Edward	Iowa City	5,541
Cook, Ira	Des Moines	37,359
Coolbaugh, William F.	Burlington	1,080
Cox, Thomas J.	Iowa City	3,130
Crookham, John A. L.	Oskaloosa	1,465
Culbertson, John C.	Iowa City	48,833
Davie, John C.	Davenport	1,760
Davis, Francis M.	Corning	1,712
Devin, John D.	Ottumwa	2,290
Devin, Thomas	Ottumwa	2,636
Dillon, John F.	Davenport	1,044
Downey, Hugh D.	Iowa City	50,576
Eckert, David E.	Fairfield	12,843
Edes, Samuel C.	Davenport	1,119
Ellis, John W.	Bloomfield	2,309
Fee, Oliver Perry S.	Centerville	2,575
Folsom, Gilman	Iowa City	1,471
French, George Henry	Burlington	1,439
Funk, Jacob M.	Webster City	1,211
Gatling, William J.	Des Moines	1,948
Gillaspy, George	Ottumwa	2,080
Gower, James H.	Iowa City	29,727
Graham, John A.	Keokuk	8,154
Granger, Barlow	Des Moines	1,633
Graves, Josiah G.	Marion	1,954
Grayson, Benjamin	Fort Dodge	1,067
Greene, George	Cedar Rapids	10,983
Grimes, James W.	Burlington	7,020
Hall, Reuben C.	Dubuque	4,358
Hamilton, William L.	Fairfield	5,715
Harsh, Samuel	Des Moines	3,214
Hedge, Jester	Des Moines	1,611
Henn, Bernhart	Fairfield	13,465
Higginson, John C.	Dubuque	4,073
Hirschl, Samuel	Davenport	1,120
Hodgdon, John M.	Dubuque	5,067
Hosford, Abram P.	Waterloo	2,440
Howe, George W.	Osceola	22,852
Huston, Samuel	Kostza	1,937
Hutchings, Joseph J.	Winterset	1,056
Jesup, Frederic S.	Dubuque	1,480
Judd, Hawkins	Leon	4,878
Kirkpatrick, David	Vinton	2,306
Kirkwood, Samuel J.	Iowa City	1,350
Lamson, Ward	Fairfield	34,085
Langworthy, James L.	Dubuque	3,062
Leas, William Henry	Des Moines	3,519
Leavitt, John H.	Waterloo	1,600

V (*continued*)

IOWA LAND AGENTS WHO WERE ORIGINAL ENTRANTS OF 1,000
ACRES OR MORE IN CENTRAL IOWA

Name	Business address	Original entry acres
Lehman, Henry	Cedar Rapids	3,538
McDaneld, John M.	Dubuque	1,661
McElhinny, Robert	Fairfield	3,311
McFarland, John A.	Boonesboro	3,987
McGaughey, David	Des Moines	1,040
Miller, Edmund	Waterloo	1,326
Morris, Jenkin W.	Des Moines	10,868
Newton, Eder B.	Guthrie Center	1,039
Ogg, Elias B.	Mt. Pleasant	4,099
Orr, John	Osceola	1,609
Parker, Samuel K.	Vinton	1,085
Phillips, William	Des Moines	1,078
Pusey, William H. M.	Council Bluffs	8,600
Rees, Samuel	Fort Dodge	3,392
Reno, Morgan	Iowa City	27,426
Reynolds, James	Knoxville	1,887
Rice, Byron	Des Moines	19,740
Richards, Benjamin B.	Dubuque	3,590
Richards, George	Fort Dodge	1,125
Richards, Seth	Bentonsport	10,698
Rider, Daniel	Fairfield	1,081
Ringland, Henry W.	Fort Dodge	1,720
Robertson, Thomas D.	Dubuque	1,895
Safford, William C.	Fort Dodge	1,098
Sanford, Horatio W.	Dubuque	19,251
Sargent, George B.	Davenport	5,502
Scholte, Henry P.	Pella	12,540
Scott, John	Nevada	2,283
Seevers, William H.	Oskaloosa	1,920
Sherman, Charles A.	Fort Do dge	1,519
Sherman, Hoyt	Des Moines	22,441
Skiff, Harvey J.	Newton	8,161
Smith, Samuel	Eldora	2,687
Stevens, Andrew J.	Des Moines	16,581
Stewart, Joseph B.	Des Moines	9,760
Temple, Edward A.	Chariton	60,841
Temple, George D.	Chariton	1,558
Tidrick, Robert L.	Des Moines	7,954
Tilford, John S.	Vinton	1,265
Trimble, Cary A.	Bloomfield	1,600
White, John	Oskaloosa	12,175
White, Lovell	Des Moines	4,222
White, Samuel	Eldora	2,520
White, William W.	Fort Dodge	12,128
Williams, Jesse	Fairfield	39,337
Williams, William	Fort Dodge	2,250
Wilson, David S.	Dubuque	2,960
Wilson, Robert K.	Fort Dodge	6,196
Wood, James	Vinton	1,082
Wood, Joseph P.	Iowa City	2,253
Wood, Thomas	Dubuque	3,264
Woods, William H.	Iowa City	1,245
Total acres		879,926
Number of realtors		118

VI

RESALE DATA FOR CENTRAL IOWA LARGE ENTRYMEN IN EASTERN IOWA, BY COUNTY, 1838–42*

County	Original entry acreage sold	Total price	Avg. per acre	Range in prices paid per acre
Cedar....................	520	$ 900	$1.73	$1.25–2.50
Clayton.................	320	444	1.39	1.14–1.64
Des Moines..............	80	100	1.25	1.25
Dubuque................	160	700	4.38	1.25–7.50
Henry...................	519	2,475	4.77	.62–9.43
Johnson.................	240	1,300	5.41	3.75–6.25
Jones...................	80	160	2.50	2.00
Lee †....................	1,460	3,714	2.54	1.25–12.50
Louisa..................	800	3,900	4.88	2.50–6.25
Muscatine...............	1,120	3,600	3.21	1.25–6.25
Scott....................	40	50	1.25	1.25
Van Buren.,...........	440	1,215	2.76	1.63–5.00
Totals..............	5,779	$18,558	$3.21	$0.62–12.50

*Compiled from the respective books of original entry and deed registers.
†Does not include acreage within the "Half-Breed Tract."

VII

RESALE DATA FOR CENTRAL IOWA LARGE ENTRYMEN IN EASTERN IOWA, BY YEAR OF SALE, 1838–42*

Year	Original entry acreage sold	Total price	Avg. per acre	Range in prices paid per acre
1838....................	320	$ 1,765	$5.52	$2.50–12.50
1839....................	439	2,450	5.58	1.25–9.43
1840....................	1,940	6,100	3.14	.62–5.47
1841....................	2,160	6,131	2.83	1.14–6.25
1842....................	920	2,112	2.30	1.25–5.00
Totals..............	5,779	$18,558	$3.21	$ .62–12.50

*Compiled from the respective books of original entry and deed registers.

VIII
Census of 1850—Instructions to Assistant Marshals*

"1. Under heading 1, entitled *Name of individual managing his farm or plantation,* insert the name of the person residing upon or having charge of the farm, whether as owner, agent, or tenant. When owned or managed by more than one person, the name of one only should be entered.

"2 & 3. Under general heading, *Acres of Land,* and under particular heading *Improved land,* insert the number of acres of improved land; by which is meant, cleared and used for grazing, grass, or tillage, or which is now fallow, connected with or belonging to the farm which the assistant marshal is reporting. It is not necessary that it should be contiguous; but it must be owned or managed by the person whose name is inserted in the column.

"Under the heading *Unimproved,* insert the number of acres of unimproved land connected with the farm. It is not necessary that it should be *contiguous* to the improved land; but may be a wood lot, or other land at some distance, but owned in connection with the farm, the timber or range of which is used for farm purposes."

* Source: *Senate Executive Documents,* 56th Cong., 1st Sess., XIV, Doc. 194, 235.

IX
Farm Acreage as a Percentage of Acreage Assessed for Taxes, Eastern Iowa (Cessions 175, 226, 244), Central Iowa (Cession 262), and Western and Northern Iowa (Cessions 151, 152, 153, 189) for 1850, 1856, 1859, and 1862.

	Assessed acreage	Farm acreage	Per cent
1850			
Eastern Iowa	3,396,922	1,971,953	58.1
Central Iowa	1,502,360	800,688	53.3
Western and Northern Iowa	83,934	13,283	15.8
Entire State	4,983,216	2,785,924	55.9
1856			
Eastern Iowa	6,500,655	3,596,596	55.3
Central Iowa	9,576,934	3,326,007	34.7
Western and Northern Iowa	7,178,883	1,636,834	22.8
Entire State	23,256,472	8,559,437	36.8
1859			
Eastern Iowa	6,455,104	3,572,754	55.3
Central Iowa	10,898,644	3,595,841	33.0
Western and Northern Iowa	9,596,123	3,276,498	34.1
Entire State	26,949,871	10,445,093	38.8
1862			
Eastern Iowa	6,563,768	3,792,951	57.8
Central Iowa	11,338,662	3,323,808	29.3
Western and Northern Iowa	10,433,915	1,803,740	17.3
Entire State	28,336,345	8,920,499	31.5

X
Approximate Acreage of Forest Land in 34 Counties of Central Iowa at Time of Survey *

County	Total county acreage	Total forest acreage	Per cent
Appanoose......................	328,320	133,760	40.7
Benton........................	455,680	64,204	14.1
Blackhawk......................	362,880	49,280	13.6
Boone.........................	364,160	62,080	17.0
Calhoun.......................	363,520	3,000	.8
Carroll........................	366,720	10,320	2.8
Clarke........................	273,920	55,560	20.3
Dallas.........................	376,960	64,640	17.2
Davis.........................	325,760	200,640	61.6
Decatur.......................	341,120	126,000	36.9
Greene........................	367,360	25,440	9.5
Grundy........................	320,640	640	.2
Guthrie.......................	380,800	44,032	11.6
Hamilton......................	364,800	19,520	5.4
Hardin........................	364,160	43,520	12.0
Iowa..........................	373,760	90,315	24.2
Jasper........................	467,200	68,800	14.7
Keokuk.......................	370,560	116,531	31.4
Lucas.........................	277,760	64,640	23.3
Madison.......................	360,320	72,800	20.2
Mahaska.......................	363,520	111,360	30.6
Marion........................	360,320	131,060	36.4
Marshall......................	366,080	32,320	8.8
Monroe.......................	276,480	86,400	31.3
Polk..........................	372,480	67,200	18.0
Poweshiek.....................	373,120	33,600	9.0
Ringgold......................	345,600	50,030	14.5
Story.........................	363,520	37,440	10.3
Tama.........................	460,800	79,680	17.3
Union.........................	273,280	28,800	10.5
Wapello.......................	273,920	145,280	53.1
Warren........................	364,800	82,640	22.7
Wayne........................	335,360	56,440	16.8
Webster.......................	456,960	46,080	10.1
Totals......................	12,192,640	2,304,052	
Weighted average.............			18.9

*County forest acreage information assembled by planimetric measurement of forest areas plotted on maps, based on the original land office surveys, 1832–59, and recorded in a typed manuscript at the Department of Forestry, Iowa State University, Ames, Iowa. See Robert R. Davidson, "Comparisons of the Iowa Forest Resource in 1832 and 1954," *Ia. St. J. Sci.*, XXXVI (Nov., 1961), 133–36.

XI

Total Acreages by Townships of Ten Largest Original Entrants in Nine Selected Counties of Central Iowa

Appanoose Twps.	Acres	Benton Twps.	Acres	Boone Twps.	Acres
T67N-R16W	880	T82N-R9W	1,000	T82N-R25W	2,040
T68N-R16W	4,800	T83N-R9W	760	T83N-R25W	1,440
T69N-R16W	6,040	T84N-R9W	2,560	T84N-R25W	1,880
T70N-R16W	2,000	T85N-R9W	1,920	T85N-R25W	2,520
T67N-R17W	760	T86N-R9W	2,880	T82N-R26W	240
T68N-R17W	1,400	T82N-R10W	600	T83N-R26W	40
T69N-R17W	3,320	T83N-R10W	4,000	T84N-R26W	2,120
T70N-R17W	2,320	T84N-R10W	3,280	T85N-R26W	4,280
T67N-R18W	120	T85N-R10W	3,400	T82N-R27W	1,160
T68N-R18W	1,840	T86N-R10W	1,720	T83N-R27W	480
T69N-R18W	2,320	T82N-R11W	840	T84N-R27W	480
T70N-R18W	2,920	T83N-R11W	3,480	T85N-R27W	2,160
T67N-R19W	1,720	T84N-R11W	1,440	T82N-R28W	3,520
T68N-R19W	960	T85N-R11W	2,080	T83N-R28W	2,560
T69N-R19W	3,600	T86N-R11W	1,680	T84N-R28W	3,400
T70N-R19W	1,560	T82N-R12W	1,320	T85N-R28W	480
		T83N-R12W	4,840		
		T84N-R12W	2,960		
		T85N-R12W	1,000		
		T86N-R12W	760		
Totals	36,560		42,480		28,800

Carroll Twps.	Acres	Hardin Twps.	Acres	Madison Twps.	Acres
T82N-R33W	4,080	T86N-R19W	1,240	T74N-R26W	760
T83N-R33W	4,960	T87N-R19W	1,680	T75N-R26W	1,640
T84N-R33W	400	T88N-R19W	2,320	T76N-R26W	2,840
T85N-R33W	560	T89N-R19W	1,600	T77N-R26W	560
T82N-R34W	280	T86N-R20W	1,280	T74N-R27W	3,040
T83N-R34W	280	T87N-R20W	1,840	T75N-R27W	5,040
T84N-R34W	0	T88N-R20W	2,040	T76N-R27W	3,960
T85N-R34W	0	T89N-R20W	680	T77N-R27W	2,080
T82N-R35W	7,520	T86N-R21W	3,000	T74N-R28W	1,640
T83N-R35W	2,120	T87N-R21W	960	T75N-R28W	1,240
T84N-R35W	2,160	T88N-R21W	1,960	T76N-R28W	2,120
T85N-R35W	0	T89N-R21W	2,560	T77N-R28W	600
T82N-R36W	10,440	T86N-R22W	1,440	T74N-R29W	1,080
T83N-R36W	3,960	T87N-R22W	6,520	T75N-R29W	2,400
T84N-R36W	2,480	T88N-R22W	680	T76N-R29W	1,000
T85N-R36W	0	T89N-R22W	2,560	T77N-R29W	1,200
Totals	39,240		32,360		31,200

Marion Twps.	Acres	Poweshiek Twps.	Acres	Wapello Twps.	Acres
T74N-R18W	1,440	T78N-R13W	2,800	T71N-R12W	80
T75N-R18W	240	T79N-R13W	3,400	T72N-R12W	200
T76N-R18W	5,480	T80N-R13W	1,360	T73N-R12W	2,680
T77N-R18W	9,360	T81N-R13W	2,080	T71N-R13W	200
T74N-R19W	5,280	T78N-R14W	3,480	T72N-R13W	800
T75N-R19W	1,760	T79N-R14W	6,160	T73N-R13W	1,880
T76N-R19W	1,160	T80N-R14W	240	T71N-R14W	1,600
T77N-R19W	1,840	T81N-R14W	880	T72N-R14W	920
T74N-R20W	4,440	T78N-R15W	2,480	T73N-R14W	1,120

XI *(Continued)*
TOTAL ACREAGE: BY TOWNSHIPS OF TEN LARGEST ORIGINAL ENTRANTS IN NINE
SELECTED COUNTIES OF CENTRAL IOWA

Marion Twps.	Acres	Poweshiek Twps.	Acres	Wapello Twps.	Acres
T75N-R20W	2,720	T79N-R15W	3,160	T71N-R15W	1,680
T76N-R20W	80	T80N-R15W	2,360	T72N-R15W	840
T77N-R20W	0	T81N-R15W	1,080	T73N-R15W	200
T74N-R21W	1,960	T78N-R16W	2,640		
T75N-R21W	440	T79N-R16W	2,520		
T76N-R21W	0	T80N-R16W	8,760		
T77N-R21W	160	T81N-R16W	2,080		
Totals	36,360		45,480		12,200

XII
COMPUTATION PROCEDURE (IN BRIEF) OF THE PROFIT PROGRAM

1. The total time period of the investment (in months) was determined by subtracting the year of entry from the year of sale, multiplying by 12, and adding the sum of the month of sale (expressed in arabic numerals) minus the month of entry. When the total investment period was zero (i.e., 15 days or less), .5 or one-half a month was substituted. The rationale is that in rounding the days of entry and of sale to the nearest whole month, one-half month is the midpoint random average investment period. If zero time is not converted, calculations are impossible as the answer lies in infinity. When the total time period was less than 12 months, it was set equal to 12 months. This was necessary to avoid gross distortion, although it reduced the rate of return considerably. For example, if an investment of one month's duration (which, incidentally, was quite common) yielded a return of 20 per cent, this, rather than 240 per cent (20 × 12), was considered the annual rate.

2. The total compounding period *(nyear)* was determined by dividing the total time in months that the tract was held by 12. For any fractional part of a year remaining *(mons)*, the rate of return was prorated $[(1 + r)^n(1 + r \times mons/12)]$. This is the standard procedure of banks when dealing with investments covering only a fractional part of a year. The rate of return can also be compounded annually to the full number of whole years plus the fractional part of the year remaining, if any, by the use of fractional exponents $[(1 + r) \ mons/12]$. For example, an investment held $1\frac{1}{2}$ years would be compounded as $(1 + r)^{1.5}$. Using the fractional exponent method of calculation on the 460,119 acres studied, it was found that the overall average rate of return was not even 1 per cent less per dollar invested than when simple interest was prorated for the remaining fractional part of a year.

3. The total number of tax years *(ntyr)* was determined by subtracting the month of entry (expressed in arabic numerals) from 25, subtracting this total from the total time in months, and dividing the result by 12. (If January was the month of entry, taxes were due and

payable on the first January after purchase, in which case the month of
entry was subtracted from 13 instead of 25.)

4. To solve the polynomial equation (n. 15, p. 191) it was first
necessary to test whether the sign was positive or negative by subtracting
the entry price and all subsequent costs from the sale price. If positive,
the computer was instructed to iterate by the interval-halving technique
between the limits of zero and 6,100 per cent. (The upper limit was
set deliberately large to obtain a safe margin.) If negative, the standard
logarithm routine was used. The log routine is necessary because, in
the interval-halving technique, any number of negative roots may solve
the equation and there is no easy way to determine which is correct.
There is only one positive root, however.

5. Upon the completion of the calculations for each individual
tract, weighted averages and totals were calculated for groups of tracts.
Weighted averages for the gross and net rates of return per dollar invested and the percentage difference between the net entry and net
sale prices were obtained by multiplying the entry price of each tract by
the gross and net rates of return and the percentage change which it
returned and dividing the sum of the products by the sum of the entry
prices. The weighted average time in months per acre was obtained by
multiplying the acreage of each tract by the number of months it was
held and dividing the sum of the products by the sum of the acreage.

A NOTE ON SOURCES

A STUDY of frontier land speculation must rely primarily on government land records, and this work is no exception. The basic sources were the books of original entry and early deed registers located in the county recorder's offices in Iowa. The original entry books are a record of the initial alienation by the national government of the public domain in each county. In conjunction with recent Indian Claims cases involving Iowa land, these books for 53 eastern and south-central counties—more than one-half of the entire state—were microfilmed, abstracted, and the data electronically tabulated. Printed listings of the tabulated data and Xerox reprints of each of the original entry books can be found in the Special Collections Department of the University of Iowa Library, Iowa City. The collection also includes tabulations of early deed registers and microfilm copies of the tract books showing the disposition of all of the national land grants to the state, except the swamp-land and railroad grants. The actual tract books of these special grants are in the Office of the Secretary of State, Des Moines.

Government manuscript material that proved most helpful, apart from the land records themselves, were township tax lists, probate records, and minute books of the boards of supervisors, all in the county courthouses; the Iowa "Governor's File, Incoming Correspondence: School Lands, Des Moines River Grant Lands, Swamp Lands, Saline Lands," in the Iowa State Department of History and Archives, Des Moines; and the "Records of the General Land Office, Miscellaneous Letters Sent, New Series," volumes 23–36, available on microfilm from the National Archives.

Although government land records served as the basic source for this study, manuscript collections are indispensable to an understanding of the actual workings of the land system and the speculation that inevitably surrounded it. Regrettably, important collections relating to Iowa are few in number and scattered about the country. By far the most significant collection is the James S. Easley Papers, housed at the Alderman Library, University of Virginia, Charlottesville. The papers span the years 1837 to 1904 and contain 115 bound volumes and several file folders of loose material. The part of the collection dealing with the western land business consists of 30 volumes of letterpress copy books, 18 bound volumes and one file drawer of incoming correspondence, 7 volumes of business records including ledgers, journals, and day books, and 2 volumes of map books of the western lands of the firm. For a brief inventory of the collection, see the University of Virginia, *Annual Reports of the Archivist* (1937–38) 28.

Although the Easley Papers are unmatched, several other collections of nonresident investors in frontier Iowa land are helpful. The Nathaniel Gordon Papers, Baker Library, Harvard University, Boston, consist of one box of approximately 100 letters describing Gordon's land and military bounty warrant dealings in Iowa and Minnesota in the 1850's. The Andrew Jackson Sterrett Papers, Manuscript Division, Minnesota Historical Society, St. Paul, comprise a four-volume diary and a series of letters that describe in detail a land-buying excursion to Iowa, Kansas, Minnesota, and Missouri in the 1850's. A similar account of a New Jersey speculator's visit to Iowa in the mid-Fifties is the John Honeyman Journal, 1798–1874, Rutgers University Library, New Brunswick. The John A. Roebling Papers, also at the Rutgers University Library, are very incomplete but shed some light on Roebling's Grundy County land entries and tax buying in the early 1860's. Several collections at the Wisconsin State Historical Society Library, Madison, pertain to Iowa land investments. The Joseph C. Kizer Papers contain a series of approximately 50 letters between Kizer, an Oregon, Wis., farmer and general merchant, and his land agent at Osceola, concerning real estate holdings in Clarke County in the years 1856–65. The letters are a classic illustration of the problems that can beset the careless investor. The Benjamin Densmore Papers, on the other hand, include several letters describing a successful land venture in northcentral Iowa in the ante bellum decade. The voluminous Cyrus Woodman Papers contain relatively little on Iowa but are nonetheless worth perusing for the detailed insights one can gain of the operation of a prominent and successful western land agent. The G. R. Clark Papers, Chicago Historical Society, include a few letters that illustrate the thinking of a small-time Iowa investor of the 1840's. The Wm. B. Ogden Papers at the same depository were disappointingly brief on

Iowa investments. The opposite is true of the Lucius Lyon Papers, William L. Clements Library, University of Michigan, Ann Arbor, and the David Davis Papers, Illinois State Historical Library, Springfield, which contain several dozen highly illuminating letters and a few significant legal documents relative to land ventures in the Hawkeye State.

Iowa depositories own surprisingly few manuscripts pertaining to frontier land speculation. Of the dozens of major pioneer land agencies that thrived in the early decades, the papers of only one firm—Cook, Sargent & Downey of Iowa City—are known to have survived, and these in very incomplete form. The collection, preserved at the Iowa State Historical Society at Iowa City, consists of several hundred incoming letters for a three-year period, 1855–57. Ledgers, account books, and letterpress copies of outgoing correspondence, all vitally important for reconstructing the firm's activities, apparently are not extant. The surviving letters, nevertheless, bear postmarks from many eastern cities and provide an invaluable glimpse into the aspirations and attitudes of nonresident investors. The frequent communiques from other Iowa land dealers also demonstrate the interrelationships of the frontier land business. The Cyrus Sanders Papers, Gilman Folsom Papers, and C. Z. Luce Papers, all at the same library, should not be overlooked. Sanders was a Johnson County claim club leader and small-time claim speculator, and Folsom a U.S. land office receiver at Iowa City and petty land speculator. Luce catered to real estate investors in his local law practice. A few scattered letters of Iowa land agents can also be found in the Jesse Williams Papers, William Williams Papers, and Barlow Granger Papers at the Iowa State Department of History and Archives, Des Moines, and the Henry Eno Papers in the Special Collections Department, University of Iowa Library, Iowa City.

Among published primary sources, local newspapers, county histories, contemporary periodicals, and government documents were most helpful. The ante bellum Iowa newspapers in the State Historical Society and the Department of History and Archives, some 60 in number, yielded a wealth of information on land investments in their news items, advertisements, and editorials. County histories, although notoriously untrustworthy, contained valuable biographical data. Contemporary periodicals consulted with profit were *The North-Western Review* (Keokuk, 1857–58) owned by the State Historical Society; *Hunt's Merchant Magazine and Commercial Review* (New York, 1850–60), and the *Proceedings of the Iowa Bankers' Association* (Des Moines, 1888–94, 1897) at the University of Iowa Library; and *The Home Missionary* (1839–45) at the Grinnell College Library, Grinnell.

Annual reports of state governmental officers, published as

appendices to the legislative journals until the mid-Fifties and thereafter bound separately, furnish a wealth of vital information. This is especially true of the reports of the state treasurer, auditor, public works commissioner, land office commissioner, superintendent of the census, and school superintendent. Annual reports to the U.S. Congress by the Secretary of the Interior, Commissioner of the General Land Office, and Commissioner of Pensions also contain essential data on land policy and military bounty warrants. A very useful summary of legislation, administrative directives, and court decisions regarding the public lands is th compilation of W. W. Lester, *Decisions of the Interior Department in Public Land Cases, and Land Laws Passed by the Congress of the United States: Together with the Regulations of the General Land Office* (Philadelphia, 1860).

For secondary sources, consult the general index.

INDEX

AN AUTHOR INDEX (including titles of anonymous works, manuscript collections, and serials) has been incorporated in this general index, to provide convenient reference to footnotes, in lieu of a formal bibliography. Since most references to notes are bibliographical only, the letter "*n*" following the page number ordinarily differentiates the bibliographical from the text references. The first and complete citation of each source in each chapter has been indexed. Abbreviated titles follow the author's name only when two or more items are involved. Newspapers are listed under place of origin. Journal titles in the index indicate use as a primary source, since articles in scholarly journals may be traced adequately from author entries.